"A typical omission in social histories is the consequences of reforms— did they solve the problems which led to their adoption? Lessons Learned? The History of Planning in Florida is not typical. From the perspective of active participants and scholars, Earl Starnes and Dick RuBino analyze the successes and shortfalls of the efforts to plan and act in a concerted way to achieve a proper balance between man and nature and to ensure that quantity will not destroy quality in our state. 'Lessons Learned' is a significant contribution to our understanding of the politics and economics of land and water use planning in Florida."

D. Robert (Bob) Graham, U.S. Senator from 1987 to 2005 and Governor of Florida from 1979 to 1987.

"Through careful research and personal experience, the authors have written a history of the relationship of planning to Florida's growth. It is a story of public and private planning endeavors toward long-term gains. Although there have been many positive results, the authors illustrate how the effectiveness of actions has been eroded by a historically prevailing attitude of growth at any cost."

Reuben O'D. Askew, Governor of Florida from 1972 to 1979.

"This book, by two growth management veterans, is an excellent commentary on the ups and downs of attempting to manage Florida's explosive growth. This comprehensive chronicle bears witness to the daunting challenges so many planners have labored to overcome."

Charles G. Pattison, FAICP, President and Executive Director, 1000 Friends of Florida.

"Lessons Learned? should be required reading for anyone who wants to understand the difference between the theory and practice underlying America's continuing challenge to balance growth and protection of the environment, and to pursue the public interest while protecting private property rights. The authors accomplish this feat by laying out the underlying history, explaining the legal framework of planning, and pointing out missed opportunities, such as funding needed infrastructure. The challenge for future leaders is can they learn from the failures and successes of Florida's long history of involvement in planning?"

James F. Murley, Director, Catanese Center for Urban & Environmental Solutions, Florida Atlantic Univeristy and former secretary of the Florida Department of Community Affairs.

Lessons Learned?

The History of Planning In Florida

By Richard G. RuBino and Earl M. Starnes

Designer and typesetter: Karen Towson Wells
Typeface: Times New Roman and Benguiat Book
Printer and binder: Durraprint

Library of Congress Number: 2008921864

ISBN 978-1-889574-31-8
(1-889574-31-7)

Sentry Press, Inc.
424 East Call Street
Tallahassee, FL 32301-7693
(850) 224-7423

This book is dedicated to the pioneers
of Florida's modern (post-1950)
wave of interest in planning:

John M. DeGrove,

Frederick H. Bair, Jr.

Ernest P. Bartley

Edward McClure,

and others.

TABLE OF CONTENTS

FOREWORD

The idea for writing this book came out of the blue during a lunchtime conversation between long-time friends at the Depot on the Dock, in Cedar Key, Florida. It was an idyllic setting, the restaurant had a true flavor of old Florida, and brown pelicans glided quietly in line by our window. We were leisurely enjoying a coastal meal with our wives and talking about our experiences in planning, when one of us leaned across the table and said, "We've got lots of experience behind us. Let's write a history of planning in Florida from our often-insider perspective." The other thought for a moment and then enthusiastically replied, "Let's do it!"

We thought it would go quickly, and that we knew what we were getting into. Little did we realize that we were committing ourselves to more than four years of being "unretired." Yet we had a story to tell, and once we started down the path, there was no turning back.

One of us is a native Floridian, the other moved in from the North; together we represent what Florida is today. Each of us have forty or more years of planning experience behind us. Most of our working years were spent in academia, but we did not consider ourselves just academicians. We had served on government-appointed statewide committees, we had been employed full or part-time with the executive or legislative branches of state government, and we kept involved in both local and regional matters. Prior to our university experiences, one of us formerly worked as an architect/planner and served as a county commissioner, and the other had worked with a major corporation and been engaged in state, regional, and local planning in other parts of the country and overseas. We consider ourselves relatively well-rounded people, and, certainly, we were—and still are—activists.

With one of us living in Tallahassee and the other in Cedar Key, much of our work was done electronically. Nevertheless, we found it necessary to get together a number of times a year, sometimes in Cedar Key, other times in Tallahassee, and on three occasions in Weaverville, North Carolina. Perhaps our most memorable meetings were in Steinhatchee, a quiet fishing village halfway between Cedar Key and Tallahassee. For a time, we even considered calling the book "The Steinhatchee Papers". But the book turned out to be more than just a set of papers.

We wanted to write a history of planning in Florida. After all, we had lived though most of its recent history. The book was to be more than just about the history of planning—or growth management, as many people now think of it. We wanted to go back further than the 1970s, back into the stage-setting years of the 1960s, the planning experiences of the early 20th century, and even back to the plans laid out by the Spaniards and the aboriginal Americans before them. Florida has a rich history of planning.

Little is done in isolation, so we also wanted to discuss the national environment within which planning events in Florida were taking place. Hence, our book evolved into both a history of planning in Florida and, in lesser detail, a history of planning in the United States.

We wanted the book to be more than a textbook. We wanted it to be of value to a wide audience of academicians (e.g., political scientists, geographers), students, professional planners, politicians, lawyers, architects, administrators, historians, and other people interested in learning how planning in Florida got to where it is today and why it is what it is now. We believed there were lessons to be learned from Florida's experience with planning—and there are.

We owe a depth of gratitude to our wives and a host of friends. The enduring patience and encouraging love and care of our wives, Janice Day RuBino and Dorothy Jean

Starnes provided us with the willingness and the fortitude to proceed. We are particularly pleased and thankful for Jan's persistent and most helpful editing of every chapter.

Our indebtedness is extended to the late James May, who caught a number of egregious errors, provided us with valuable references, and challenged our comfort zone with thought-provoking opinions. We are also beholden to the late Earnest Bartley, who reviewed our work and provided constructive criticism until he passed away, about the time the book was being completed. Our sincere appreciation goes to Tom Pelham, Charles Pattison, Jim Murley, Brian Teeple, and Robert Pennock for their review of certain chapters or parts of chapters. They helped to keep us in line and up-to-date. Thanks also go to former Governor Reuben O'D. Askew and former U.S. Senator Bob Graham. Among others who contributed through interviews and other means were Walker Banning, Charlie Justice, Hugh Macmillan, Jan Ollry, Howard Pardue, Helge Swanson, Fred Williams, and the late Homer Still. Helping to keep us on track were our publisher William Rogers and his aides-de-camp, Erica Clark and Karen Wells. Lastly, we apologize to the other people who we failed to name above, but who aided us in ways both large and small.

We tried to make this history of planning in Florida as complete as we could, yet far more waits to be done by other writers. We alone are responsible for errors we have made and important events we have overlooked, and we are accountable for our findings, assertions, and opinions. There are many lessons to be learned from this history. Perhaps the greatest lesson is that it is not just the process of planning that determines its success. The economic and political environment within which planning operates exerts an even greater influence.

CHAPTER I

INTRODUCTION: THEMES—AND REMNANTS OF THE PAST

> What experience and history teach is this—that
> people and governments never have learned any-
> thing from history, or acted on principles deduced
> from it (G.W.F. Hegel, 1832.)[1]

Commencing with the discovery of this lush and beautiful peninsula, the history of Florida has been rife with exploitation and land speculation. Spanish explorer Juan Ponce de Leon set sail late in the winter of 1513 from the Isle of San Juan de Puerto Rico in search of unseen resources. It had been only twenty years since Columbus landed at San Salvador, and little was known of Atlantic storms and ocean currents among the relatively unknown and uncharted islands of the Bahamas.[2] Ponce de Leon sought the rumored fountain of Bimini and elsewhere a river, "giving credence in this to the Indians of Cuba, who said that bathing one's self in it, or in the fountain, old men would be turned into youths."[3] Failing to find Bimini, Ponce de Leon sailed northwest until the second day of April, when the water became shallow at one league from land.[4] He anchored off what would later become St. Augustine and named the land *Pascua Florida*, for Spain's Feast of Flowers at Easter time.[5] He soon turned and sailed south and west around the peninsula, probably traveling as far north in the Gulf of Mexico as today's Sanibel Island. Eight years later, he was mortally wounded in a battle with the Calos Indians at Estero Bay[6] bringing an end to his second voyage and a small settlement. Historians disagree on whether this settlement was on Estero Island or further north near Charlotte Harbor.

From this meager beginning, Spain continued to establish imperial claim to Florida's land and to learn more about its natural resources from other adventurers such as Hernando de Soto and Panfilo de Narváez. For example, de Soto, in 1539, cast anchor in a port along the west coast that he named Espirita (sic) Santo, which is now known as Tampa Bay.[7] In his travels, de Soto discovered that Indian villages were all of the same general plan: "The central feature of the village was a mound, two or three pikes high."[8] This seemed an accommodation to the potential for flooding and easier protection from animals and enemies. On the mesa thus created, there were usually ten to twenty huts. The foundation of the mesa was a battered earthen wall, with "access provided by a great stairway built of logs."[9] The arrangement of the buildings may have indicated some ritual ranking based on social or ethnic order.[10] The records of native villages and artifacts are testimony to the earliest history of planning in Florida. Recording of typical layouts of Indian villages by de Soto and his conquistadors, though vague, supports early environmental accommodation by societal and cultural norms and development guidelines.

The first evidence of European-style planning in Florida fell to Pedro Menendez de Avilés who sailed in 1565 from Cadiz, Spain, and "after calling in Caribbean ports for supplies arrived at what is now the site of our earliest city on St. Augustine's day, August 28."[11] Unlike earlier Spanish adventurers who sought magic waters or gold, Menendez had with him the Spanish Crown's edict for colonial development in the Americas[12] and his mission was the establishment of a colony. The Ordinance of 1563, better known as the *Laws of the Indies*, set the physical form of Spanish settlements in the New World. As John Reps observed in his seminal work, *The Making of Urban America*, the ordinance "represented … practices that had become fairly standardized some years earlier."[13] The ordinance provided procedures for selecting a new settlement site and provided both guidelines and standards for the town plan.

As pointed out by Reps, "The plan of the place, with its squares, streets and building lots is to be outlined by measuring by cord and ruler, beginning with the main square from which streets are to run to the gates and principal roads and leaving sufficient open space so that even if the town grows it can always spread in a symmetrical manner."[14] The instructions defined the square as being two by three in proportion and that its four corners should be oriented to the cardinal points of the compass. The detailed instructions described all aspects of a town's layout, the provision of open spaces and the location of important gateways and other structures, particularly the church and public buildings. With these guidelines, Menendez began building this permanent European colony in North America in 1565. As reported by Reps, "St. Augustine combined three distinct functions in one community. The city was, first of all, a military post with its fort and military garrison. Secondly, it was designed as a civil settlement for trade, farming, and handicraft industry. And, finally, it was intended as a center from which religious orders would begin the work of converting the Indians to Christianity."[15] Thus, in 1573 Florida's—and North America's—first European planned city was established. Franciscans followed and succeeded in building missions throughout today's north Florida and south Georgia. "By the middle of the next century they could count thirty-one missions in the peninsula..."[16]

Florida's Development Paradigm

The early Florida adventurers and colonizers clearly foretold of discovery, land speculation, development, and spurts of private and public planning that would take place over the coming centuries. Time and a myriad of speculative pipe dreams and seductive public policies, often responding to market demands or political whims, had a lasting influence on the history of Florida. While the impacts of development were incremental, they also were cumulative, thus permanently impacting Florida's natural environment, settlement patterns, and urban and rural character.

Expanding Kevin Lynch's concept that "cities are unique historical processes,"[17] we submit that tracing planning and development in a larger geographic range, such as the state of Florida, is also worthwhile. We see it as an *unfolding process* that can reveal major development management policies as interactions of social, cultural and political systems and the larger environment in which they are embedded.[18] Such "special historical studies are useful when one is considering local action in a particular place, where one is dealing with immediate decisions, concrete patterns, and modification of ongoing forces."[19] We attempt to portray planning—whether an ordered institutionalized process, or a process of disjointed, incremental choices—as a decision system that has influenced or passively allowed the direction of development in Florida.

It may be useful to visualize a model of political life that was advanced in David Easton's treatise, *A Systems View of Political Life.*[20] He describes his model "as a system of behavior imbedded in an environment to the influences of which the political system itself is exposed and in turn reacts."[21] Adapting this model to a planning and development management context such as we find in Florida's planning history, we begin to see the interaction among value systems of Florida's unique geography and its environmental, economic, social, and political history. This may be explained as a communication process that is an integral part of its environment, thus the entire process of filtering demands and nurturing support cannot be interpreted as existing in a void.[22] Nor does planning exist in a void.

There are noteworthy and deep-rooted principles and themes in Florida which have driven state and local political systems as they have processed demands, political support, and choices regarding development. Foremost among these is the principle that speculation in land development is a fundamental source of capital, profit, economic and political power. Most of the planning history of Florida is directly related to land development. Let there be no mistake, it is a positive principle—unless it is misguided or allowed to override public decision-making to the end that a balance with the general welfare is lost. When misuse or over-dominance occurs, as it has throughout much of Florida's history, then other fundamental values are neglected or aborted. For example, up until the past decade municipal and county taxes have been used to pay for the infrastructure needed to support new development based solely on the pretext that development paid for itself. Quality affordable housing and other basic urban services were relegated to extremely low priority, and irreplaceable natural resources (e.g., great interior wetlands, water recharge areas, sand dunes, central Florida scrub, and coastal mangroves) were over-developed or destroyed in many parts of the state.

Themes

In developing a framework for this planning history, we sought to lace the unfolding process with three themes permitting them to flow along with the narrative. The themes we have selected are land speculation, geographic localism and citizen participation.

Land Speculation

Land speculation in Florida began with imperial land grants for the settlements of St. Augustine, Pensacola, and other coastal places; then, much later for inland locations. Thus land speculation was seen as the primary economic motive for European settlements in the New World. Historian Walter A. McDougall observed that, "...the colonists had to display enough overall progress to lure still more investors and settlers and drive up the value of property."[23] Later, this policy of value appreciation was made more promising when Congressman Thomas Jefferson, of Virginia, offered the Land Ordinance of 1785 to the Continental Congress of the United States.[24] The bill, which was enacted into law, divided land into townships, ranges, and sections thus simplifying the description of land. This facilitated the transfer of real property because it laid a future grid across most of the continental United States with adjustments here and there to accommodate the curvature of the earth. The original thirteen states were *not* included in this system of land boundary definition. Aided by simplified descriptions of land, speculation became a driving force for westward expansion toward and beyond the Ohio and Mississippi rivers. As the United States annexed new territories, the government's land agents auctioned much of the land to eager buyers at very little cost, and in many cases made outright grants.[25] Territorial Florida, coming late into the Union (1845), was surveyed and mapped in ranges east and west and in townships north and south from the meridian marker located in Tallahassee. Though colonial agriculturist Morris Birkbeck had never been to Florida, his 1818 observation fits land speculation in the Sunshine State exceedingly well: "GAIN! Gain! Gain! Is the beginning, the middle and the end, the *alpha and omega* of the founders of American towns...."[26]

Developing whole towns from private sources was common practice during 19th century Florida. Towns such as Winter Haven were built on the promise of profits as lots were sold and often resold many times before being physically developed. The original platted land on which Winter Haven is located was owned and surveyed by the Florida Land and Colonization Company Limited of London, England, which incorporated the settlement pursuant to the Companies Acts of 1860 to 1862.[27] In 1881, farther south from Winter Haven, "Jonathon Skipper received a land patent west of Sebring encompassing present day Highlands Hammock. Additional patents were received for settlements in the vicinity of Avon Park, De Soto City, and Venus..."[28] As railroad construction proceeded throughout the 19th century, the State of Florida and the federal government granted alternating sections of land on either side of proposed railroad corridors.[29] This practice of railroad land grants set out thousands of acres of land for eventual development. Railroad companies frequently developed towns to meet their own needs; like the Florida Railroad Company, which in 1859 platted the Town of Cedar Key.[30] It served as a rail-to-ship transfer point for transport of lumber and other commercial products. With access provided by the railroads, land grants covered much of the landscape in Florida as the last half of the 19th century unfolded. Speculation in land has had a major influence upon Florida's growth and development, driven by a constant stream of new Floridians, and continues into the 21st century in every region of the state.

By simply recording the plats in a county record, lots could be sold to speculators looking for short-term returns. Such properties, more often than not, remained vacant many years until population growth and local housing markets created a demand for development. Many decades-old undeveloped subdivisions lie empty even today throughout Florida; there is a history of undeveloped ghost towns and streets to nowhere in the state.[31] These are artifacts of the boom times in the early 1920s and the land sales explosion of post-World War II. One reason for these failed ventures is that developers often fell into bankruptcy in attempting to provide public services until such time a town could be incorporated and take over public expenses. Coral Gables, located just outside Miami, provides an example of this situation. It was a well-planned, visionary new town created by George E. Merrick, south Florida's leading boom time real estate developer. As the development unfolded, it became burdened with debts. Perceiving bankruptcy to be imminent, community leaders organized and incorporated the City of Coral Gables.[32] The new government then assumed the development debts and proceeded to build out the city based on the original plan, zoning regulations, and architectural standards. In other cases, developers and land speculators abandoned their projects once sufficient profit was in hand, leaving homeowners to fend for themselves.

A modern day story of land speculation can be found in the "Great Northwest of Florida," which is the coined term the St. Joe Company prefers to use for the narrow extension of the state from Tallahassee to Pensacola instead of its historic, but less glamorous name, the Florida Panhandle. The company, which evolved from the former St. Joe Paper Company, owns at least one million acres of land, most of it in former slash pine plantations. It is currently in the process of planning or developing several complete communities. This all began when Alfred I. duPont, in the 1920s, acquired about 900,000 acres in eleven of the Panhandle counties, plus other large properties around the state. In the summer of 1929, Edward Ball, DuPont's brother-in-law and top business trouble-shooter, was given power of attorney over DuPont's Nemours Securities. Following DuPont's death in 1935, Edward Ball parlayed the estate's holdings into a vast timber, paper, railroad and banking empire.[33] In the late 1980s, the production of Kraft paper and other paper products became unprofitable, which left vast acreage across north Florida ripe for other uses. Thereafter, land development, community building, and home construction became the mission of the empire. In association with its residential development arm, the Arvida Corporation, the St. Joe Company has become northwest Florida's major real estate developer.

Localism

The riding-partner of land speculation is localism, especially as it relates to land development. Localism is a fundamental American value, but it can be exercised excessively. There was a time when most municipalities were self-contained; they were able to sustain themselves because almost all of their citizens worked, played, studied and lived within the municipality. The rural residents in the surrounding hinterland depended upon the city for markets, education, social, spiritual and economic support. Today, these organic communities exist in only a few of north Florida's rural counties. Most Floridians now work, live and play in an opportunistic, unplanned and uncoordinated patchwork of local governments. In urbanized counties such as Miami-Dade, Pinellas, and Broward, this patchwork of local governments has led to balkanization, often with cities bounded on all sides by neighboring cities; and some, seeking exclusion, have walls. Despite the many positive virtues of this venerable democratic principle, we must recognize that excessive localism often drives short-term, disjointed, and unplanned development. Such development can have unintended consequences that have ruinous impacts upon the natural environment, investment capital, and surrounding economic and public services. Urban populations have merged into communities of municipalities, communities of counties, and a community of the state. Planning thus has the promise to work best as an intergovernmental system of data gathering, comprehensive analysis and shared decision-making.

Localism and land speculation have driven a large part of economic and political decision making in Florida since the days of the first Spanish, French, and English settlements. They are forces of significance in both the market place, and in local and state legislative settings. Profiteers in land development and the state government have often tended to ignore environmental impacts and, on occasion, intentionally hamper effective citizen participation in the governmental decision-making process. However, in recent years, state and development interests have become more conscious of environmental and political impacts of development schemes. The influence and consequences of land speculation and localism have varied widely over time as popular concern for the natural environment has varied. The behavior of Floridians with regard to the natural environment has ranged from centuries of unrestrained and sometimes unscrupulous exploitation of land to a finding in a 1972 survey that three out of five voters listed "harm to the natural environment" as the most important issue in Florida.[34] Localism has also varied over time from a passive and permissive role of the state in planning and development policies to what may be described currently as a State-imposed process on all matters of planning and development management. As was said by a former secretary of the Florida Department of Community Affairs, "We have so much process because we cannot agree on substance."[35] It is not our purpose to be overly critical of these economic and political norms, but to try to understand how they have influenced public planning and private investment with regard to the management of development.

Not until the early 1970s did the State of Florida move to assess and reconsider its planning and zoning laws and the state's role in managing development. Its outmoded permissive zoning law, patterned after the U.S. Department of Commerce models of the 1920s, had been in place since 1939. The Florida Planning and Zoning Association observed, "As one might expect, this act (of 1939) was very general, with no specific guidelines."[36] Since special acts of the Florida legislature were needed for cities and counties to engage in zoning, few counties and municipalities attempted to regulate land use and development. Even today, local prerogative is an entrenched political value. The interposition of state mandates remains politically unpopular in many locales. However, some local governments have found interposition provides political encouragement when difficulty looms in resolving conflicting public interests in plan making.

Planning, if it is anything, is the conscious thought for the future and the capacity to move toward that future with a quiver of strategies best suited to meet economic, environmental, and social needs. Planning also provides the table for resolving conflicts when local citizens view the community's future. As we progress through the pages to come, we will note instances where the will to plan and to see beyond the next election cycle has resulted in innovative planning initiatives at local, regional, and state levels of government. In the alternative, we will also note the consequences of a lack of political willpower to sustain progressive and comprehensive development management policies and strategies. Are these lessons to be learned?

Citizen Participation

Finally, citizen participation has not always been considered a necessity in the arena of public planning. Citizen participation, though an informal part of democratic decision making since the birth of the nation, enjoyed a strengthened and institutionalized role in planning during the administration of President Lyndon B. Johnson, the era of the Great Society. One Great Society program was the Demonstration Cities and Metropolitan Development Act of 1966. The act required maximum participation of citizens in planning. "In the Model Cities program, residents of subdistricts [sic] designated as Model City districts created their own quasi-political organization, decided their problems and priorities, and proposed their own means of arriving at solutions."[37] Thus, the Model Cities program may be seen as ratifying and perhaps foretelling the need for citizen participation in planning. Paul Davidoff, in reviewing his experiences later, noted that, "The prospect for future planning is that of a practice which openly invites political and social values to be examined and debated."[38]

This mid-twentieth century experience helped to raise the level of citizen involvement and heightened sensitivity of politicians toward the planning process. This suggests that it is an imperative function of citizenry to learn, discuss, and work together so that they become more attuned to decisions, which may improve the future of their community and thus their own personal future. The value of citizen participation was later affirmed by Saul Alinsky in his book, *Rules for Radicals,* when he said, "No politician can sit on a hot issue if you make it hot enough."[39] Today, citizen participation is an embedded part of Florida's intergovernmental planning process. It is an essential and well-established component of planning law in Florida, if not in actual practice.

We have also taken note of some "movers and shakers" who, along the way, surfaced as visionary leaders: governors, legislators and citizens who met the criteria set out by Coleman Ransome in describing governance as being "concerned with long range plans and programs for the development of a state's human and natural resources."[40] Too often leaders, buffeted by tumultuous events and pressures, simply hold onto the *status quo* to protect prevalent perceptions of economic and political realities. Such perceptions seem to lead to unplanned and piecemeal change or no change at all. "If it ain't broke, don't fix it" is very often a political leader's maxim protecting the *status quo,* thus avoiding the need for creativity or the risk of adverse political consequences.

We engaged this brief discussion of values to provide a thematic framework on which to mold the experiences of planning. Often, the history of success and failure is incremental, disjointed, and erratic. It will be our intent here to weave into our narrative vestiges of these values at work in the history of Florida planning.

Our Approach to This Book

This book is in large part the result of the life experiences of the authors and of research gleaned from many official and archival resources, personal interviews and the authors' memories and notes reflecting the history of planning in Florida. It is our hope it will advance understanding just how planning and development management intertwine with complex processes of public policy-making; processes which are ruled by the controlling maxims of land speculation, localism, minimal governance, and negligible interference with private property rights. However, the book provides a base for understanding the Florida of today is the product of its past and how knowledge of its past can provide lessons for the future.

Our journey begins by establishing that an ever-emerging form of city planning was practiced in Florida over 400 years ago. Initial efforts at planning trace back to early Spanish settlements and even the specialized village layouts of the indigenous peoples before them. Hence, counter to popular knowledge, planning is not just a recent activity in Florida. Planning is a certainty in the development of human habitations and communities. Having established the ancestry of planning in Florida, we turn to the larger mosaic of the history of planning in the United States. What happens in Florida, after all, is inextricably related to what happens in the rest of the nation. Though Florida can boast of its own innovative actions, its planning and policy systems have been decidedly influenced by events affecting the nation as a whole.

In Chapter II, we cover the early history of Florida, from the mid-1500s to about 1900. The intent of this chapter is to help the reader understand the economic and political motivations that contributed to Florida's historically intense devotion to growth. We track colonial, provincial, state, regional, and local planning and policy making within Florida. We attempt to uncover relationships between public and private planning strategies, such as government-capitalized railroad building and unregulated private development of settlements and towns. These policies led to certain physical land development patterns and significant alterations to the natural environment. Our emphasis is on planning and management of development as an unbalanced amalgamation of economic, environmental, social, and political interests. The linkages may not always be explicit, but the reader should be able to visualize ties between public policy choices and the intended consequences of the accepted course of action—or inaction.

In Chapter III, we discuss planning activity nationally and in Florida during much of the first half of the 20th century. Special attention is paid to planning in Florida during its boom and bust years of the 1920s and early 1930s. These were years of rowdy and boisterous land speculation driven by tourism, the mystique of the Sunshine State, and expanding interest in agriculture. It was a time when land in Florida was selling so fast that often a binder on a parcel was sold multiple times before the first payment was due.[41] Numerous settlements were laid out using survey maps, simple block and street plans prepared by land surveyors employed by developers. However, some new towns engaged nationally known private planners, architects and landscape architects to prepare their plans. The heritage of these early planners is still seen throughout the state. For example, John Nolen, one of the fathers of city planning in the U.S., prepared plans for several communities in Florida, including Venice, Sarasota, and Kelsey City, all during the 1920s. In a rather measured observation he said, "Florida has been spoken of as the last frontier of the country and unusual interest has accompanied its development."[42] The state was promoted as a "land of dreams."

This unusual interest not only reached people in cities such as New York, Cleveland, and Chicago, but also spread to residents of small rural hamlets. Taking advantage of the national publicity and the crowds attending the Scopes "monkey trial" in 1925, a truck drove up and down the main street of Dayton, Tennessee, carrying a large sign that in big, bold letters read, "ASK US ABOUT TAMPA, FLORIDA."[43] "If you did not ask, then you were lucky, for within a year or two the real estate market in Florida went bust. As we venture through this history, this is but one example of Florida boosterism. As John DeGrove remarked, "... we need to remember Florida began as a pioneer state whose leaders were convinced that it was unlikely that anyone would voluntarily come to Florida to live."[44] But come they did.

During the 1930s, President Franklin D. Roosevelt initiated far-reaching national planning programs. One such initiative was the creation of a national planning office, with its requirement that states establish a state planning function if they wanted to become eligible for funding under Title II of the National Industrial Recovery Act.[45] This pioneering program and others contributed to rebuilding the national economy following the stock market crash in 1929. The Roosevelt administration also set up federal programs for economic development, housing, health, and even ventured into early efforts at regional planning. With financial assistance from the federal government, many communities for the first time engaged in promulgating general plans for community development. Chapter III extends into the early 1940s, the time of U.S. involvement in World War II, a time when interest in planning waned and the whole nation focused on the immediate demands of the production of goods and armaments for the war effort and the universal marshaling of the population to the common purpose.

We begin Chapter IV with the years following World War II, a phase in planning history that we describe as the doldrums of state and local planning, a period in which interest in planning was submerged under a quest for normalcy and an overpowering surge of interest in economic development. Within a few years, however, the federal government once again offered grants for planning. The prime impetus was to develop local programs for adequate housing, particularly for low and moderate-income families. The Housing Act of 1949 and its principal vehicle, urban renewal, provided "the first political action justifying direct federal aid to local planning,"[46] but it was Section 701 of the Housing Act of 1954 that allowed planning to blossom. Initially the grants were restricted to small local governments, but in following years, the scope of the urban planning and renewal program gradually expanded to include municipalities of all sizes, counties, regions and metropolitan areas, and eventually state governments. The 701 program fostered a renewed interest in planning—and gradually, though reluctantly, a system of intergovernmental planning coordination.[47]

For the third time in four decades, the federal government had initiated a planning movement. Without the federal incentive, most local governments had chosen to ignore the utility of planning as a municipal or development management tool. Florida was among the more hesitant of the states to rekindle an interest in planning, and it was especially disinterested in things regional. Eventually, the temptation of the federal dollar overcame this hesitancy, and public planning was born again in Florida, though only at the local government level. Only a handful of state governments had carried on with some form of the state planning work they had started in the 1930s. Florida was not among them.

In Chapter V, we cover the principal planning-related events occurring from the early 1960s to the early 1970s. The nation experienced significant unrest and tumultuous change during the 1960s. Most cities were incapable of contending with this change on their own, and states, for the most part, were still underplaying the needs of urban jurisdictions and environmentally endangered areas. State governments were still in the hands of malapportioned legislative bodies dominated by rural legislators unsympathetic to urban problems. However, by the middle of the decade, states like Florida, helped along by the U.S. Supreme Court decision in *Baker v. Carr*,[48] began to respond to urban demands and needs by updating their constitutions, strengthening the management capabilities of the governors, and responding to urban needs by creating departments of urban or community affairs. With aid from the federal 701 planning assistance program, more local governments were becoming involved in planning, and the easing of 701 participation requirements fostered a growth in planning at regional, metropolitan, and state levels. In Florida, the number of local governments engaged in planning gradually increased, some regional planning efforts began to appear, and interest in planning again emerged at the state level.

All of this planning activity still followed the guidelines of the municipal planning model set out in the 1920s. However, state planning was about to set off on a parallel course, a more politicized course of policy planning. The leaders of this new effort saw an opportunity to instill planning into the policy process as a tool to better manage functions of the executive branch of state government. State leaders in Florida also recognized this opportunity, and similarly moved to strengthen the executive office, but the various levels of planning activity in the state were not acting in harmony.

Chapter VI focuses on planning events in the early 1970s, especially The Quiet Revolution[49] and its effect on planning and managing growth in various states such as Hawaii, Oregon, and Vermont. Regional bodies like Portland Metro, the Twin Cities Metropolitan Council, the Tahoe Regional Planning Agency, and the Hackensack Meadowlands Development Commission were just a few of the nascent regional institutions that arose during this period. We also cover "A Model Land Development Code" prepared by the American Law Institute (ALI) and its influence in reshaping the context of planning in a number of states, especially Florida.[50]

Highlighted by an astute mass media, an accumulation of unscrupulous land developments, escalating environmental degradation, and public infrastructure backlogs and shortfalls contributed to a growing concern on the part of citizens of Florida. Developments of significantly more than local impact and developments of statewide concern were extant across the southern and central regions of the state. Local governments were overwhelmed by huge housing developments, with little attention paid to impacts on adequacy of roadways, sewer, water distribution, and schools. Consequently, a cadre of political leaders intent on directly meeting and coping with Florida's growth problems stepped forward.

In the early 1970s, initial steps were taken toward establishing a statewide intergovernmental system of planning. The new cadre of leaders decided that Florida could no longer depend solely on *voluntary* local management of growth: the response to rapid, uncontrolled growth must be an intergovernmental effort involving the state, sub-state regions, and all local governments. In this chapter, we describe the intergovernmental strategy Florida leaders designed to address rapid and uncontrolled growth. Basically, the strategy reflected a need for all levels of Florida government to become involved "…in an effective meshing of state, regional, and local government activities…creating an intergovernmental system of consistency, coordination, and compactness, all with…a sharply limited supervisory and monitoring role."[51] Among successful legislative actions in 1972 were the enactment of the Environmental Land and Water Management Act and related new laws and programs such as the State Planning Act, the Water Management Act, and the Environmentally Endangered Lands Act. The most significant among the ignored or delayed pieces of the proposed system were regional planning and local government comprehensive planning; the first continued to be ignored, whereas action on the second was delayed until 1975.

In Chapter VII, we discuss implementation of the new state planning laws and promulgation of a new local government comprehensive planning act. An Environmental Land Management Study Committee (ELMS), created by the above-mentioned Environmental Land and Water Management Act, was a citizen committee responsible for developing recommendations for implementing the new laws, and working with State and local officials in preparing a local government comprehensive planning bill. Administrative responsibilities were assigned to a new Division of State Planning (DSP) that had the task of preparing a state plan, and putting together the areas of critical state concern and developments of regional impact programs, the two major sections of the Environmental Land and Water Management Act. The DSP also focused on the organization of sub-state planning agencies to administer regional responsibilities in the developments of regional impact program.

The legislature adopted a Local Government Comprehensive Planning Act in 1975. Despite the mandate carried by the new act, most local governments continued to underutilize planning as a tool for managing growth. Most local plans, though reviewed by the state land planning agency (at the time the DSP), simply gathered dust. Thus, it became necessary for a new set of executive and legislative leaders to come together to strengthen local planning, regional planning, and the State's role in the intergovernmental development management planning process.

Steps were taken in the early to mid-1980s to strengthen the intended intergovernmental development management system we discussed in Chapter VIII. By the mid-1980s, determined political leadership succeeded in bringing changes leading to a greater role for the state government in planning and growth management. The first actions improved planning at the state and regional levels. These resulted in a new state plan, state agency functional plans, and somewhat strengthened regional planning. Local planning needed considerable attention—and it received it in the form of an omnibus Local Government Comprehensive Planning and Land Development Regulation Act,[52] complete with strong state government oversight and sanctions. The pieces of the intergovernmental development management system envisioned a decade earlier finally were being put together, and a new era of growth management had begun.

In Chapter IX, we cover the late 1980s to early 1990s, with special emphasis on the *implementation* of the state, regional, and local planning initiatives passed in the mid-1980s. Attention is directed to planning at all three levels because Florida had finally put in place a more complete intergovernmental development management system. However, the segment of that system which receives the greatest attention is the local planning and land development regulation act. This act requires all local governments to prepare a comprehensive plan following the substantive and procedural guidelines mandated by the state. Local (and regional) plans are also required to be consistent with the state plan. Local plans are reviewed for compliance by state and regional planning agencies. The local government is also required to adopt land development regulations, which in turn must be consistent with the local comprehensive plan. Thus, the plan is legally enforceable. Citizen participation is a required procedure giving local citizens the opportunity to play a greater role in local plan making.

We review nationwide state and regional activity in the early to late 1990s in Chapter X. Planning initiatives such as smart growth, new urbanism, and sustainability are also covered. Then, we turn our focus on Florida, and follow the partial dismantling of the state's policy of oversight. Some of the changes that occurred merely tweaked the system using the experience gained by implementing the laws. However, some of the tweaking began to conflict with principal components of the system. For example, the state comprehensive plan[53] slipped away from its intended central role in driving the growth policies of the state and fell into obscurity. Among the most troublesome of these "tweaks" was enactment of the Bert J. Harris, Jr. Private Property Rights Protection Act of 1995.[54] In the short term, this act further dampened the political will of local government officials in vigorous implementation of local planning responsibilities. In addition, there have been legislative attempts to narrow the opportunity for citizens to challenge local planning decisions, but the administrative judges and courts have generally blunted the effect of these efforts.[55]

Using the same approach of addressing national activity first, in Chapter XI we quickly leave that scene and move into a discussion of the myriad of planning-related activities that occurred in Florida from the late 1990s to 2007. It was a time of subtle dismantling of the intergovernmental development system, especially in regard to State oversight of local comprehensive planning. A shift in political ideology had occurred, and representatives of growth machines were walking the halls of the state capitol with impudence and getting most things their way. Though frontal attacks on the planning system were usually blunted, behind the scenes, planning was being put on a downward slope. Continued rapid growth, urban sprawl, rural land development programs, and rural transportation corridor initiatives were overwhelming the effectiveness of the planning system. However, just as all of this was peaking, a new administration stepped into the scene.

We bring our venture through the history of planning in Florida to a close in Chapter XII. In this final chapter, we draw conclusions from history and identify lessons that appear to have been learned from Florida's three and a half decades of experience with intergovernmental planning and management of development. We go on to discuss lessons only partially learned, as well as lessons not learned. Going beyond lessons learned or not learned, we proffer some "givens" regarding whether development will continue in the manner and at the rate it has in recent decades.

We have made numerous excursions to specific settlements, towns, cities, and counties along the way to provide markers in time as the urbanization of the state has proliferated and sprawled. Throughout much of its history, planning in Florida has more often than not been nonexistent, far less than comprehensive, sporadic, and, at best, an afterthought. Public and private development management choices reflect uneven and often devastating consequences, but it is the experience of history we are interested in revealing. Furthermore, lessons learned from Florida's experience may be useful to other states, regions, and localities as they face ever-increasing problems of sprawling development and inadequately managed growth. Yet, the title of this book, *Lessons Learned?* comes with a question mark, suggesting that some lessons have yet to be learned.

NOTES FOR CHAPTER I

1   Hegel, G.W.F., *The Philosophy of History*, 1832, in Bartlett, John, *Bartlett's Famous Quotations*, Emily Morrison Beck, et al., eds., fifteenth edition published in 1980, Canada: Little, Brown, & Company, p. 422.

2   Columbus called them "Baja Mar," obtained from The Islands of the Shallow Sea, History of the Bahamas, accessed from www.bahamas.com, June 19, 2004.

3   Lawson, Edward W., "The Discovering of Florida and Its Discoverer Juan Ponce de Leon," *The Hispanic American History Review* 27: 3, 1947, p. 11.

4   Ibid, p. 15.

5   Tebeau, Charlton W., *A History of Florida*, Coral Gables, FL: University of Miami Press, 1971 (revised 1980), p. 21. It is also recorded that John and Sebastian Cabot "viewed" Florida near today's Biscayne Bay in 1498 or 1499. The Florida Memory Project: Timeline, State Archives of Florida, and the *Florida Handbook*, compiled by Joan and Allen Morris. Obtained from www.floridamemory.com/timeline, accessed on May 25, 2005. We have emphasized the Spanish discovery because from a planning standpoint, it was their discovery that led to the state's early development.

6   Lawson, ibid, p. 55.

7   Ibid.

8   Ibid, p. 32.

9   The remains of mesas or mounds can be seen at the Crystal River State Historic Site, and the Indian Mounds State Park in Tallahassee.

10 Van Doren, Mark, ed., *Travels of William Bartram*, New York, NY: Dover Publications, Inc., 1955. In 1773, many years after de Soto's transit through Florida, William Bartram discovered aboriginal villages with similar mounds.

11 Reps, John W., *The Making of Urban America*, Princeton, NJ: Princeton University Press, 1965, p. 33.

12 Tebeau, ibid, pp. 32-38.

13 Reps, ibid, p. 28.

14 Ibid, p. 29.

15 Ibid, p. 33.

16 Gannon, Michael, *Florida: A Short History*, Gainesville, FL: University Press of Florida, 1993, pp. 10-11.

17 Lynch, Kevin, *A Theory of Good Urban Form*, Cambridge, MA: MIT Press, 1981, pp. 327-328.

18 The term "development management" as used by the authors is defined here: "Development" means any manmade alteration to real property, be it in a natural or developed state, in terms of its physical appearance, use, size, capacity or any other characteristic. "Management" means the manipulation or utilization of means to accomplish some end related to the alteration of real property. We use the term "management" only in the context of public planning and policy.

19 Lynch, ibid.

20 Easton, David, *A Systems View of Political Life*, New York, NY: John Wiley & Sons, Inc., 1965, p. 32.

21 Ibid, p.18.

22 Ibid.

23 McDougall, Walter A., *Freedom Just Around the Corner, A New American History, 1585-1828*, New York, NY: Harper Collins Publishers, 2004, p. 41.

24 Reps, ibid, p. 216.

25 Ibid.

26 Reps, ibid, p. 349.

27 Burr, Josephine G., *History of Winter Haven Florida*, Winter Haven, FL: The Larry Burr Printing Company, 1974, p. 1.

28 Olausen, Stephan A., *Sebring, A City on a Circle*, St. Augustine, FL: Southern Heritage Press, 1993, p. 3.

29 Holbrook, Stewart H., *The Story of American Railroads*, New York, NY: American Legacy Press, 1981, p. 158.

30 This information was provided by Peggy Rix, director of the Cedar Key Historic Society and Museum, June 2004.

31 For reviews of this experience, see Frank Schnidman, "Resolving Platted Lands Problems: The Florida Experience," *Land Development and Assembly* 1, 1987, pp. 27-44; and Herbert B. Stroud and William M. Spikowski, "Planning in the Wake of Florida Land Scams," *Journal of Planning Education and Research* 19: 1, 1999, pp. 27-29.

32 "Between October 1923 and March of 1924, seven million dollars of property was sold. During that time, more than six hundred homes were constructed, sixty-five miles of roadway of crushed local limestone (and later asphalt) were built, and over eighty miles of sidewalks were added. Fifty thousand trees, shrubs, and flowering plants were planted and a system of lighting was installed which covered twenty-eight miles of the city. The city of Coral Gables was incorporated in 1925." Quotation obtained from Dona Lubin, Director of Historical Resources, Coral Gables, in an email message to Earl Starnes, on August 11, 2003.

33 Burnett, Gene M., *Florida's Past: People & Events That Shaped the State,* Vol. 1, Sarasota, FL: Pineapple Press, 1986, pp. 38-39.

34 "Environment and Florida Voters," Cambridge Survey Research, 1972, in Work Paper No. 7, Urban and Regional Development Center, University of Florida, June 1974.

35 Attributed to Linda Shelley, former Secretary of the Florida Department of Community Affairs, from notes taken by Starnes, 18 February 2005, at a meeting of former secretaries of the Florida Department of Community Affairs, Shands Hospital Conference Room, University of Florida, Gainesville, FL.

36 "The History of Florida Planning & Zoning Association, Inc.," the Florida Planning and Zoning Association, Orlando, FL, undated.

37 Gerkins, Laurence Conway, "Historical Development of American City Planning," in Frank S. So and Judith Getzels, eds., *The Practice of Local Planning,* 2nd edition, Washington, DC: International City Management Association, 1988, p. 48.

38 Davidoff, Paul, "Advocacy and Pluralism in Planning," in Andreas Faludi, ed., *A Reader in Planning Theory*, New York, NY: Pergamon Press, 1973, p. 277.

39 Alinsky, Saul, *Rules for Radicals*, Vintage Books, New York, NY: Random House, Inc., 1972, p. xxiv.

40 Ransome, Coleman D., *The Office of the Governor in the South*, Bureau of Public Administration, University of Alabama, Tuscaloosa, AL, 1951, p. 27.

41 Burnett, ibid, p. 283.

42 Nolen, John, "Report on Comprehensive City Plan for Sarasota, Florida," Harvard Square, Cambridge, MA, 1925.

43 de Camp, L. Sprague, *The Great Monkey Trial*, Garden City, NY: Doubleday & Company, Inc., 1968, p. 139.

44 DeGrove, John, "Florida's Growth Management Legislation: 1969 to 2000," a paper presented at the Richard E. Nelson Symposium of Florida's Growth Management Legislation, Gainesville, FL, October 13, 2000.

45 New Deal legislation creating the Federal Emergency Relief Administration and the National Recovery Administration. Later these agencies together became the Works Progress Administration. The projects across Florida, particularly municipal buildings, armories, schools, etc., all had an impact on urban development.

46 Feiss, Carl, "The Foundations of Federal Planning Assistance: A Personal Account of the 701 Program," *Journal of the American Planning Association* 51: 2, Spring 1985, p 178.

47 Ibid. For an excellent discussion of this history regarding the pro-
    mulgation of the 701 program, see pp. 175-184.
48 *Baker v. Carr*, 369 US 186, 1962.
49 The term "The Quiet Revolution" refers to the influential report en-
    titled *The Quiet Revolution in Land Use Control*, which was pre-
    pared by Fred Bosselman and David Callies, Washington, DC, for
    the Council on Environmental Quality in 1971. As used herein, "The
    Quiet Revolution" is extended to include state and regional actions
    that occurred in the 1980s and early 1990s, far later than the publish-
    ing date of the book.
50 American Law Institute, *A Model Land Development Code*, Phila-
    delphia: The American Law Institute, 1971.
51 DeGrove, John M., *Land Growth & Politics*, Chicago, IL: The Ameri-
    can Planning Association, 1984, p. 161.
52 Chapter 163, Part II, *Florida Statutes.*
53 Chapter 186, *Florida Statutes.*
54 § 70.001, *Florida Statutes.*
55 Earl Starnes interview with Terrell Arline, who has been instrumental
    in cases in which the Florida court and administrative judges have
    protected citizens' rights to redress in land use cases, May 19, 2004.

CHAPTER II

THE EARLY YEARS

From 1564 to the Early 1900s

Fellow citizens, we cannot escape history.[1]
(Abraham Lincoln, 1862.)

In this chapter, we look at the years of Spanish, French, and English colonization of Florida, as well as the territorial period and the early years of statehood. We highlight the political, economic, and social influences as settlements were located, planned and materialized. In addition, we will trace the impacts federal economic development initiatives had on the location of settlements in Florida. Those were years well before the ubiquitous automobile had such a major bearing on both settlement location and patterns.

The First Spanish Years (mid-1500s-1763)

In 1564, the Frenchman Jean Rebaut landed on the banks of the River May (today the St. Johns River), about five miles upstream at St. Johns Bluff, and built a triangular fortification known as Fort Caroline."[2] Satouriona, an Indian chief of the lower River May, and eighty men helped the French build the fort. The incipient success of this French colony must have been grave news to the Spanish Crown because King Philip soon dispatched Pedro Menendez de Aviles to renew attempts to settle Florida.[3] A fleet of thirty-four ships sailed from Cadiz, Spain to Puerto Rico, carrying 2500 soldiers and civilians. However, many of the ships were delayed by storms, and only four arrived in Puerto Rico.[4]

Without waiting for the remainder of his fleet, Menendez hastened toward Florida, knowing the French were on the River May, and were waiting for reinforcements from

France. During August of 1565, Menendez sighted Florida "…on the day of St. Augustine, and a few days later cast anchor off the shallow harbor and inlet where there was an Indian village called Seloy."[5] Menendez named the place St. Augustine. In selecting the site for the settlement, he must have been guided by the instructions of King Ferdinand the Catholic to early Spanish colonists: "One of the most important things to observe is that ... the places chosen for settlement ... be healthy and not swampy, good for unloading goods; if inland, on a river if possible ... good water and air ... close to arable land."[6] These imperial instructions of 1501 later evolved into the ordinance of 1563, better known as the *Laws of the Indies*. The 1563 laws required the town "to be laid out surrounding a central plaza, the *plaza mayor*, around which were the four main streets. Other streets were to be established in a grid pattern."[7]

"Someday, all this will be infrastructure."

Warren Miller, cartoonist; permission granted by Meredith Miller of the Cartoon Bank.

Kathleen Deagan, of the University of Florida, has found that the old section of St. Augustine "today still exhibits many of these planning criteria."[8] Though archeological digs have revealed no plaza constructed by Menendez or his successors, later developments adhered to the 1563 ordinances. Incremental change certainly seems reasonable in view of the slow population growth through the 16th and 17th centuries. Thus it appears any violations to that early Florida planning law resulted from incomplete works or omissions, not commissions. Florida's first European town was a planned community developed in the Spanish colonial tradition. Other early settlements such as the original Pensacola (Florida), Santa Fe (New Mexico), and towns across the Spanish Caribbean were also laid out following the provisions of the *Laws of the Indies*. Today, a visit to the old town center of St. Augustine quickly reveals the manifestations of this early planning law.

Family members and heirs of Menendez ruled St. Augustine for nearly one hundred years.[9] These were not peaceful times because the Spanish had agitated the Indians with their efforts toward Christianization and Europeanization. Nor were they prosperous times for the Spanish as they struggled to cope with this new climate and problems of food production. In addition, the Englishman Sir Francis Drake burned the city of St. Augustine in 1586. Moreover, the French, located to the north along the River May, were a constant threat to the tranquility of the Spanish colonists. However, by 1646, "St. Augustine had increased to three hundred householders, a quaint, crowded little town, reproducing the architecture and customs of ancient Spain."[10]

At the beginning of the second century of Spanish Florida, the Spanish were beginning to lose their grasp on so great a territory as the Florida of 1597. At that time, Florida included the entire known southeastern part of the North American continent and west to today's Texas. Upper Florida was being annexed by the English and part of the east coast north of Cape Fear was renamed Virginia by Sir Walter Raleigh. An English settlement was established at Cape Fear in 1663. Charles II of England granted to several noblemen that part of Florida between the 31st and 36th parallels (from somewhat north of the present-day boundary between Florida and Georgia northward to the Delmarva Peninsula). He based his claim on the alleged discoveries of Cabot as far south as the 28th parallel[11] (this extended the claim southward to around present-day Fort Lauderdale). However, in those times, a few degrees here or there may not have been of much concern to an English king so far away. The 31st parallel is some miles north of the St. Mary's River and Cumberland Island (Georgia), but probably at the time it was believed to be the latitude of the St. Mary's River. Thus, Charles II appears to have established the historic northern boundary of Florida with a new colony called the Carolinas.

East Florida, that part of Florida east of the Suwannee River, was under competition from the north. Buccaneers, such as Captain John Davis, sacked St. Augustine in 1665. In 1675, Juan Hita de Salazor became the governor of Florida. He checked the advancing English and even attacked Charleston, "but the Carolinians entrenched themselves and made a stubborn defense, so that the effort of the [Spanish] Floridians came to nothing."[12]

Spanish Franciscan priests established missions up and down the Florida peninsula and well up into today's Georgia. They succeeded in building an effective and humanitarian mission system. According to historian Michael Gannon, "The missionaries appear to have had no other purpose than to elevate the minds and spirits of the Indians among whom they dwelled."[13] However, while the Christianization of the native inhabitants seemed to be a remarkable accomplishment, it left only a veneer of Christianity and European culture.[14] Gannon relates that during the early years of the 18th century, the missions were destroyed by James Moore, English governor of the Colony of South Carolina. Some of the Christian Indian survivors were enslaved by the Yamassee,[15] a tribe allied with the English, and some of the surviving Franciscan priests were sent to Cuba; others moved on west toward Mobile.[16]

Figure II-1
The Missions of La Florida, 1674-1675.

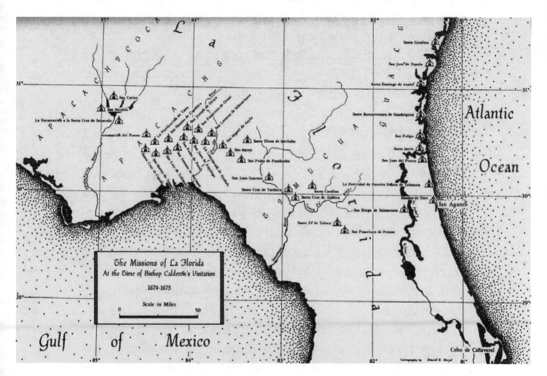

Map by David E. Boyd, used with permission, from Michael Gannon, Florida: A Short History *(Gainesville, FL: University Presses of Florida, 2003.)*

Later, in the 1690s, a permanent Spanish settlement was established at Pensacola, in West Florida, on the site of Fort Barancas, which is located today on the Pensacola Naval Air Station.[17] Pensacola fell into French hands, but was restored to the Spanish in 1723. In 1752, a great hurricane swept away the town, and the survivors moved across the bay to the mainland to a site protected from the Gulf of

Mexico by Santa Rosa Island, rebuilding the settlement at the location of present-day Pensacola.[18] Pensacola was platted under British control in 1764 when surveyor Elias Dunford was authorized to prepare "a plan for the city, dividing the town into building and garden lots."[19]

The French sought to settle East Florida by spreading south from Fort Caroline, but were discouraged by the presence of the Spanish. Battles between the French and Spanish ensued, with the French suffering the greatest losses. During negotiations for settlement agreements, in a move of deception, the Spanish executed many of the Frenchmen on Anastasia Island. Discouraged, the French gave up and moved west into the Mississippi River country.

The English Years (1763-1783)

As part of the Treaty of Paris in 1763, Spain ceded Florida to the British. The English plan for governance of Florida established St. Augustine as capital of East Florida and Pensacola as capital of West Florida. Renowned historian Rowland Rerick noted that, "the governor [of each province] was assisted in the enactment of laws by a council, and an elective general assembly was authorized, but the calling of this legislative body into being was left to the discretion of the governor."[20]

The English set out to exercise land reform by surveying the land grants from the English Crown. The governors of East Florida and West Florida established guidelines for these land grants, which included 5000 acres to field officers, 3000 acres to captains, and lesser acreage to others down the chain of command.[21] Though settlers were slow to come, towns in East Florida were established upstream along the St. Johns River at Palatka and Green Cove Springs. New Smyrna also was started, as well as several plantations such as the Bulow Plantation in present day Flagler County. The towns were connected by land along the King's Highway to

St. Mary's in Georgia, and parts of that road corridor remain today along the east coast of Florida. The towns established simple grid layouts for streets in order to facilitate access to private property and to ease description and fee simple sales. Private property rights, real estate transfers, land speculation, and ad valorem assessments were important to the English colonists.

Political unrest resulted from the reluctance of British governors to organize legislative branches. Unrest was exacerbated in 1774 when the governors sent troops from Florida to Massachusetts to help quiet the pending revolution in the North. However, "The Florida colonists, mainly recent beneficiaries of the generous land grants of England, generally remained loyal to the King."[22] Though some Floridians deserted the prevailing political culture and joined the colonies' cause against England, Loyalists in St. Augustine burned John Adams and John Hancock in effigy.[23] Many Floridians failed to seize the opportunity to join the American Revolution.

After the British evacuated Savannah in 1782, "peace began to return to the [Georgia-Florida] border."[24] This period represents Florida's first great land rush: British Loyalists fled the former colonies and settled into St. Augustine and along the St. Johns River.[25] However, peace was short-lived, and Spain once again moved to reclaim West Florida. In 1783, by treaty with Great Britain, West Florida was ceded *back* to Spain in exchange for Cuba, which the British had captured during the Seven Years' War. The ceded lands reached westward from the boundary with East Florida to the Mississippi River, but excluded the lands in the then-colony, but soon to become state of Georgia.

During the tumultuous last half of the 18th century, His Majesty's botanist for East and West Florida, John Bartram, a Pennsylvanian, traveled through the provinces in 1763. His son, William, followed him in 1768. These travels for the first time recorded information regarding Florida's biological bounty and diversity.[26] The data and information gathered by the Bartrams is cited by environmentalists, analysts, and historians. The data provide baseline information, though fragmental, that is unique and portrays Florida before Europeans and Americans had a pervasive impact upon its ecosystems, its natural landscape, and its pre-history settlements. Subsequent years of development have caused monumental changes in every stream, estuary, lake, sand hill community, wetland, coast, ocean reef, and sea floor.

The Second Spanish Years (1783-1821)

With sovereignty returning to the Spanish in the mid-1780s, they made special efforts to induce general immigration. Thomas Jefferson, with an eye always to the extension of the United States across the continent, wrote to President Washington: "I wish a hundred thousand of our inhabitants would accept the [Spanish] invitation. It would be the means of delivering to us peaceably what must otherwise cost us a war. In the meantime we may complain of this seduction of our inhabitants, just enough to make the Spanish believe it is a very wise policy for them."[27] Speculation seemed to be the theme of Spain's second term of Florida dominion. Spanish land policy was also more generous than that of the English, for the Spanish made very large land grants. Even today, some of these old grants have lingering impacts on local land boundary descriptions. They show up on section maps as being geometrically unique to the usual grid. Only a few, if any, remain intact, but the names often appear in abstracts of title, names of settlements, subdivisions and commercial enterprises.

Florida, East and West, emerged as the spoils of a long period of competition between Spain and England, with the United States negotiating—and threatening—at strategic points to wrest title from the Europeans. For a brief period in this milieu of political and military turmoil, the flag of the

Republic of Florida flew over Fernandina on the St. Mary's River in East Florida, a settlement established by a small renegade army of patriots who moved even further south into the colony.[28] "The patriots, commanded by [Captain John] Mathews, established a United States station at Pecolata,"[29] but when the Spanish protested, U.S. Secretary of State James Monroe admonished Mathews that his measure of annexation was unauthorized. The political and military pressure from the United States did not cease. By 1819, General Andrew Jackson quelled the threat of British and Indian military actions against Georgia. He subsequently captured Pensacola, an action, among others, which forced the Spanish to cede East and West Florida to the United States. Land grants made by the Spanish crown prior to January 24, 1818 were allowed to stand. However, U.S. Secretary of State John Quincy Adams did not know that, prior to that date, the Spanish King had granted *all the unoccupied land* of Florida to three of his favorite aides.[30] Adams demanded a revocation of these very expansive grants of land. The Spanish Crown yielded and a treaty was ratified in 1821. So, the lands of Florida have always been prized, and over several centuries have been subject to ever-growing and often aggressive public and private land speculation. Colonial land policies were not always driven by a concern for the public good. Thus, the early development of the state's land and natural resources has been random, unplanned and, more often than not, destructive of natural systems.

The Territorial Years (1821-1845)

Territorial Florida was first governed by the same Andrew Jackson whose "mailed fist"[31] had forced secession from Spain. His first ordinance divided the territory into two counties, Escambia to the west and St. Johns to the east. Jackson established the town of Pensacola (in Escambia County) as the territorial capital, but he remained in Florida only until

November 13, 1821, before leaving to pursue higher ambitions. A year later, Congress conferred legislative powers "upon the [territorial] governor and 13 of the most fit and discreet persons of the Territory."[32] Judicial powers were vested in two superior judges. By 1826, the voters of Florida were permitted by Congress to elect their first legislature. Troubles with Indians soon followed, for they had been provided no rights to land or slaves by the treaty with Spain. This omission was to plague the conscience of Floridians and the nation well into the 20th century. Legal, social, and military squabbles ensued as Indian claims and colonists' claims continued to conflict.

In 1826, the Seminole population was estimated to be about 5,000, living in 37 villages, with the villages averaging 140 Indians each.[33] The inevitable conflicts between early white settlers and Indians would lead to serious land use conflicts. While Jackson was still governor, he advocated the removal of "all the Indians in Florida up into the Creek nation," assuming that they had no rights in the land. "Why should we hesitate to order them up at once," he wrote to Washington.[34] In East Florida particularly, "there were Seminoles who had long been residents of the forests, and from that quarter the chiefs sent an eloquent memorial to Washington regarding the neglect of any guarantee of their rights in the treaty of cession from Spain."[35]

In East Florida, there was much plundering of Indian cattle, and rumors threatening the safety of the Indians persuaded some of the Indian farmers to abandon their crops and sell many of their slaves at nominal prices. Burdened by these conflicts of property interests between Indian and whites, territorial governor William Pope Duval[36] arranged for a council to be held at St. Marks on November 20, 1821, the outcome of which was to demand that the Indians surrender such Negro slaves as belonged to whites in the neighboring states. Seven years later Duval wrote that, "the issue of slave property, has imposed more labor and difficulty on me than any other superintendent has encountered in the discharge of all of his duties."[37]

Had Duval embraced a broader vision and commitment to resolving the problem of land for the Indians, the shape of Florida might have been quite different today. Rerick gives an account of the next few years, but no specific information is revealed as to how the Indian issues were resolved. It was the general feeling that Florida Indians were not aboriginal and had little rights in the land they occupied. At least in part due to these political views, the Second Seminole War began in 1835 and it was not until the twentieth century, during the administration of President of Harry S. Truman, that a lasting resolution was found regarding the Seminoles.

Meetings of the territorial legislative council were alternately held in Pensacola and St. Augustine. The long voyages were often hazardous on the Gulf of Mexico and the Atlantic Ocean. Seeking a midpoint between East and West Florida, the legislative council enacted a provision in 1823 to establish a site for a capital near St. Marks, a village located near the Gulf of Mexico, along the St. Marks River. St. Marks is about equally distant from St. Augustine and Pensacola.[38] The selection of an appropriate site for the capital was assigned to William H. Simmons of St. Augustine and John Lee Williams of Pensacola. They chose a site agreed to by the local Indians. As recorded by Rerick, "Congress donated a quarter section of land for the seat of government, and three quarters of a section adjoining, to be sold to provide a fund for public buildings and a survey of twenty townships round about was ordered so that they might be open to settlement in the territory. This was the first land surveyed [in Florida] and consequently the principal meridian and base line for the State intersected at Tallahassee."[39] Thus, the state capital was located on land today known as Tallahassee, a name derived from an Indian term meaning "old town."[40] It was here that the model of dividing land into sections, ranges, and townships was established pursuant to the provisions of the U.S. Northwest Territory Ordinance of 1787.

As the capital was being located, Isaiah D. Hart (the founder of Jacksonville) convinced landowners of Cowford,[41] on the St. Johns River, to donate streets, and thus the town of Jacksonville was surveyed. The new town was named for General Andrew Jackson who had played a major role in the cession of Florida from Spain.[42] Jacksonville utilized the most popular system of street layout in early America, the simple grid. These platted lands were located on the north bank of the river. The new town was then served by a river ferry connecting the older settlement of Cowford on the south bank of the river to Jacksonville.

Far to the south of Jacksonville, a settlement at the confluence of the Miami River and Biscayne Bay had a meager beginning. Hanson Brock, a Miami writer, remarked that, "In 1827 James Egan, whose father John had bought the land from Spain some years before, presented to the United States Commissioners at St. Augustine a claim for 640 acres of land on the north side of the Miami River. This [his claim] was confirmed by an Act of Congress, but soon after he sold the land to R.R. Fitzpatrick."[43] Fitzpatrick owned many slaves and had the tropical jungle just west of today's central Miami cleared. Today none of the tropical fruit trees then planted exist, but the park is set aside as an historic site known as Fort Dallas Park. Fitzpatrick finally abandoned the place to prevent the Indians from inducing his slaves to join them in their fight against the white settlers. The land was later rented to the U.S. government for the establishment of a military post. Brock found that, "There is very little record of this first occupation, and it is not known how many of these [occupants] there were, or, how long they stayed, but we know the [military] company was commanded by Lt. L.M. Powell, all in the summer of 1856, and it was likely that the Lt. Powell named the tiny stockade, Fort Dallas."[44]

Other settlements such as Tampa and Cedar Key also began to appear. Cedar Key was an important Gulf of Mexico port. However, inland settlements throughout the central and north areas of the peninsula were under constant threat from Indian attack and settlers were "crowded in confined parts for safety."[45] Immigration to Florida was impeded by the on-going Second Seminole War. It was a long, bloody, and costly war that did not come to a close until 1843.[46] A number of places, towns, and cities throughout Florida carry the names of U.S. Army leaders from this war, such as Dade County, and the location of many forts later became towns and cities; e.g., Fort Lauderdale, Fort Meade, Fort Myers, and others.

During these times, besides the Indian wars, financial difficulties, weather disasters, and political forces were at work. The territory suffered from financial concerns, partly a consequence of the Second Seminole War. A period of hurricanes started in 1841 and Apalachicola had snow in February of 1842. Cedar Key and other emerging Gulf coast towns were inundated by storms in November of 1842, "sweeping away all of the government property."[47] On May 25, 1843, Tallahassee was ablaze and later in the same year another great storm visited St. Marks and Port Leon on Apalachee Bay. Apalachicola and Key West both suffered great damage from storms, and shipping between Key West and Havana was destroyed.

Considering all these adverse circumstances, many people of the territory opposed the assumption of statehood and the loss of federal support of the territorial government and judiciary. In 1843, the legislative council advised their delegate in Congress to oppose admission to statehood on the ground that a constitution written for the state was not acceptable to a large part of the people.[48] Conventions at Palatka and Fort King were held in July 1844. The delegates from the few established counties east of the Suwannee River were inclined to support a division of the proposed state into East and West Florida, divided along the Suwannee River. The Territorial Legislative Council supported two Floridas and it "… memorialized Congress to divide Florida in two territories, separated by the Suwannee River."[49] The political motivation for the division of Florida into two states was designed to preserve the balance of power between slave holding states and non-slave holding states. It was this vexing problem that finally decided the admission of Florida as a single state, and "on February 13, 1845, the clause providing for future division was stricken out by a vote of 123 to 77 … and the house adopted the enactment."[50] Florida and Iowa were thus admitted to the Union in February of 1845—one as slave, one as non-slave.

Florida was ill prepared for statehood. It had little urban development, no manufacturing, and proceeded to squander its major natural resources to support the state government by selling lands granted to the new state by the federal government. Embracing the opportunity to use public land as a means of economic development, U.S. Senator David Yulee Levy incorporated the first cross-state railroad company in 1853. The railroad was authorized in 1855 and began to operate in 1861. The state policy of giving private entities title to public lands was a dominant state strategy for economic development until the beginning of the 20th century. This policy permitted grants of sections of land alternating along each side of the proposed railroad right-of-way.[51] It set in place the location of future towns and settlements, and tens of thousands of acres of land ripe for land speculation adjacent to the railroad.

The Early State Years

On March 3, 1845, President John Tyler signed an act of Congress admitting Florida to statehood. A constitution for the new state had been drafted at Port St. Joseph in 1839. It was adopted in 1845 as the state's organic code, providing for election of the executive and members of the general assembly. "In providing for revenues for the State," the first General Assembly "fixed a poll tax on white males at 50 cents, slaves 50 cents,[52] every free man of color between the ages of twenty-one and sixty, $3; [and taxed the capital value of] money at interest, bank stock, stock in trade, carriages, town lots, wharves, saw mills, incomes of doctors and lawyers, etc. [at the tax rate of] 20 cents on $100 of value, while rural land was taxed but three-eights of a cent to one cent an acre, according to quality."[53] This policy encouraged agricultural development to the detriment of urban development.

The poll tax, which more often than not could not be paid by slaves or "people of color", also perpetuated the slave and racist policies of Florida and the other Southern states. Taxing of real property and improvements developed in urbanizing places at rates much higher than rural lands and improvements clearly memorialized and facilitated the plantation society and an agrarian economy. Such policies discouraged urbanization and set in place state development policies that continued into the 20th century. Thomas Jefferson would have been pleased with this agrarian view of Florida's future.

Congress, by means of its supplemental acts, provided Florida with two townships east of the Suwannee River and one west of the Suwannee River for the establishment of seminaries. The acts also provided that five percent of funds from sales of public land be set aside for education. In addition, to support public education within each township, statewide the sixteenth section was set aside for public schools. The state was also granted 500,000 acres for an internal improvement fund. These earliest statewide policies of taxation and selling of public lands and resources, not to mention the outright grants of public lands, had a lasting consequence on land development patterns well into the future. It was not until 1900 that the wisdom of such policies was revisited and altered.

With the gradual lessening of a federal military presence in Florida and the wanderings of settlers into the areas of south Florida set aside for Indians, conflicts were inevitable. The legislature attempted to solve the problems in 1852-1853 by decreeing that it was unlawful for Indians to remain in the state and established a militia designed to capture and evict the Indians. While intended to protect white settlements, these policies were not effective to that end. Rerick describes the Florida of 1850: "...of the estimated area of Florida—37,931,520 acres—22,315,000 had been surveyed, and only a million acres had been sold. There were *temporarily* [emphasis added] reserved for the Indians 3,600,000 acres, and the United States reservations included 163,889 acres of live oak for the navy, various keys and islands on the coast, sites of forts and lighthouses, certain lots in Pensacola and St. Augustine ...."[54] Rerick continues, "The sale of the land was slow—not enough to pay the expenses of the land agencies. It was time for the general law [U.S.] of 1850, donating to the states the lands within their borders."[55] Thus, land commonly known as swamp became the state's land, which it could sell or grant for development purposes.

With the state government literally living off the land by selling or mortgaging public lands, certain internal improvements were envisioned. Among these were a railroad from Jacksonville to Pensacola Bay, with branches to St. Marks, Crooked River, Apalachicola Bay, and St. Andrew Bay; a railroad from Amelia Island to Tampa Bay, with a branch to Cedar Key (soon provided by David Yulee Levy); and a canal connecting the St. Johns and Indian rivers. The state continued to donate thousands of acres of land to the railroad companies to implement this policy of economic development. An air of optimism permeated the state, which encouraged Governor James E. Broome (1853-1857) to say in a message to the legislature that he was, "Hoping for better things in the future" (i.e., being freed of the United States government in anticipation of secession). Expanding his roseate view, he went on to say, "The tendency is to annexation; and if we look down the stream of time we may in imagination see a period when Cuba and other West Indian islands, with the states of Mexico and Central and South America, may be added to this confederacy."[56] This flight of gubernatorial fancy reflected the drift toward secession. But in 1856-1857, the optimism faded as a state of war with the Indians erupted.[57] It would not be many years before the state was embroiled in a far greater conflict.

By early 1857, railroads were under construction or operating between Jacksonville and Tallahassee and between Fernandina (Amelia Island) and Cedar Key. Villages were springing up along the rights-of-way as if by magic.[58] Towns were established at places where the most significant roads and trails intersected the new railroads. The depot, often simply rail cars with wheeled trucks removed and set upon temporary supports, became the gravitational center of such new villages. The depot was recognized as the "middle" of town.

By January 1861, Florida entered a tragic phase of its history, with serious consequences on the development of its resources and land. The optimistic, though meager, advancements of the 1850s ill-prepared Florida for its role in the new Confederate States of America. It had no cities, no factory system, few railroads, a sparse population (probably 140,500), and less than 1,000 skilled laborers "within the length and breath of the state."[59] However, on April 18, 1861, the General Assembly ratified the Constitution of the Confederate States of America.[60] This political disposition was not unanimous, for in Key West citizens formed a volunteer company for the Yankee Army.[61] By 1862, the policy of selling the land continued: "The public domain, claimed by virtue of secession, was opened for sale at one to two dollars an acre."[62]

However, the monetary system collapsed. Though Tallahassee was never captured, many other places in the state were occupied by the U.S. Army. By 1865, Florida had become a place of destitution, a place whose economic and social structure had been shattered.[63] It was to remain in the mire of rural poverty into the twentieth century.[64]

The Reconstruction Years

Reconstruction began with the appointment of William Marvin as provisional governor (1865-1866). Marvin was a federal judge from Key West. Lands confiscated by Florida as a Confederate state were restored to the original owners, and planters were cautioned regarding the new status of ex-slaves. Black citizens were admonished to recognize new social responsibilities, and an election was called to select delegates to a constitutional convention.[65] A new constitution was adopted, and followed quickly by legislation creating double standards for black and white citizens. Unrest followed, exacerbated by Florida's rejection of the 14th amendment to the U.S. Constitution. Unrest led to violence resulting in the Congressional enactment of the "Military Bill",[66] which established five military districts, with Florida, Alabama, and Georgia comprising the third district. Historians Cox and Dovell note, "Under military law, the southern states were to write new constitutions, grant universal suffrage to all males over twenty-one years of age, and ratify the fourteenth amendment."[67]

Pursuant to the Military Bill, President Ulysses S. Grant appointed General John Pope to command the Third District, with headquarters in Montgomery, Alabama. He immediately appointed incumbent civil officers and developed a plan to broaden the base of the electorate.[68] In spite of charges of gerrymandering districts (probably designed to delay military reconstruction), the electoral base was broadened, and a referendum calling for a constitutional convention was scheduled for January of 1868. The fear of many Floridians was that radical Republicans and carpetbaggers would dominate the convention. In January, "As radical delegates arrived [in Tallahassee] they were met at the railroad stations and hauled to the hospitable free boarding house" rented by the "schemers".[69]

The first lobbying effort of many to come manifested itself in a foretelling style. Radicals took over the convention, due it is said, to inclement weather that delayed the arrival of moderates. It is not clear why the weather affected the moderates more than the radicals. During the tumultuous convention, moderates repaired to Monticello just thirty miles east and reconvened. This move left the radicals without a quorum. A few days later the moderates returned at night, found the radicals absent from the hall, elected their own leaders, and prevailed by adopting the 1868 constitution.[70] The new Florida Constitution provided universal male suffrage, a three-tiered court system, a strong executive, free public education, Indian representation, and in every way conformed to the federal imperatives. Moderate Republicans had prevailed, resulting in the State's readmission to the Union. During the ensuing years, the leaders of the Republican Reconstruction period managed to enact plans for the school and penal systems of the state.

The south Florida of the twentieth century was yet of little consequence. The population of northern Florida grew to over 187,000 by 1870. Farm crops were annually generating $9,000,000, livestock $5,000,000 and 736,000 acres of land were improved for agriculture. The pre-war skilled labor force of 1,000 had increased to 2,750 and 23 newspapers were being published.[71] By 1876, places like DeLand and Sanford, upstream 130 miles from the Atlantic Ocean on the St. Johns River, were established by northerners who "were delighted with the country, in which several young and enterprising men had settled."[72] Major investments in developing new settlements appeared throughout East Florida. Orlando was organized as a town on June 23, 1875.[73] Six years later, it was described by George M. Barbour, writing in his *Florida for Tourists, Invalids, and Settlers*, thusly, "Orlando, the [Orange] county seat, is ... a genuine native community of the kind that the traveler finds in all sections of the state, almost always located in a beautiful region where nature has done everything to aid and please ... and the surrounding country studded with little lakes, is remarkably pleasing. A courthouse and a jail are among the most conspicuous features of the place."[74] We suspect Walt Disney must have read this early commercial extolling the virtues of Orange County and the region. The engaged state policy of promoting development and migration was very early represented in local promotional literature.

Living Off the Land

T. Frederick Davis, noted that the Congressional Grant of 1841 "was supplemented in 1850 by another granting to Florida of all the swamp and overflowed land then unsold (not including lands submerged under navigable waterways), with the provision that the proceeds received from the sale or appropriation of the land be applied exclusively to the purposes of reclaiming them by means of levees and drains. The number of acres thus accredited to Florida was estimated to be about fifteen million."[75] In 1854, the legislature created the Internal Improvement Fund.[76] It is this trust fund that holds title today to all of the state lands and is administered by the Governor and Cabinet, which are authorized to sell, buy, lease, or otherwise manage state real property. A very important part of Florida history concerning land grants and development created a problem described by Cox and Dovell: "... the predicament [of the] the Internal Improvement Trust Fund [resulted in] ... the pledging of lands for railroad and canal construction and payment of railroad construction bonds ... [the]

issued bonds ...were endorsed by the trustees of the fund."[77] During reconstruction, the railroads defaulted on bond payments and the state was required to accept the debts and eventually had to sell the lands to satisfy the state's indebtedness.[78]

Cox and Dovell continue with a discussion including the several means the Trustees of the Internal Improvement Fund sought to relieve the indebtedness. A number of offers were forthcoming, but the most important offer regarding the future of land use and development management came from Hamilton Disston. This Pennsylvania industrialist and his associates offered to drain lands in the vicinity of Lake Okeechobee, and in January 1881 an agreement was made between the trustees of the fund and Disston. He agreed to "reclaim by draining all overflowed lands in the state of Florida practicable and laying south of Township 23 (afterwards amended to read Township 24) and east of Peace Creek."[79]

These lands belonged to the State of Florida, and at the time were subject to overflow by Lake Okeechobee, the Kissimmee River and its tributaries, and lakes contiguous to the river. "In return, Disston would receive half of the area reclaimed. By 1882, [the] Okeechobee Land Company, formed by Disston, was operating dredges near Lake Okeechobee. Hamilton Disston was cited as 'a large scale investor who could play fairy godfather to the tune of $1,000,000'."[80] He paid approximately twenty-five cents an acre for the right to reclaim and possess the state lands. This desperate state policy of land reclamation has since been one of Florida's environmental legacies of wetland degradation. The entire process of land reclamation was driven by the objective of making wetlands suitable for agriculture and other development.

How could Florida not accept such an arrangement? It relieved the state of indebtedness and forwarded its policy of extreme generosity with public lands. The changes to the south Florida landscape were significant as a result of the Disston deal. The state affirmed its policy of literally living off the land and making tens of thousands of acres freely available to developers of railroads and other economic interests in land reclamation and speculation. We must accept that the policy did provide for economic development, but at a long-range cost to the environment. State planners, if there were any, and decision makers could not have understood the consequences of such policies at the time. We now know the environmental damage was catastrophic and the eventual public cost monumental. Governor William D. Bloxham accepted the Disston deal in June of 1881.

The Bourbon Years

Governor Bloxham and Governor George F. Drew, who had been elected in 1876, were the first of the Bourbon Democrats. Many Florida historians refer to the Bourbons as landed gentry of the state. The tone of the Bourbons was set by Drew in his executive message to the Florida legislature: "That government will be most highly esteemed that gives the greatest protection to individual and industrial enterprise at the least possible expense to the taxpayer. Theories may be formulated and suggestions accumulated, but the simple truths which have been the basis of nearly all personal success in business, can be equally applied to state finances."[81] During his administration, the legislature failed to reduce the ad valorem tax millage rate from 12.5, so by executive order Governor Drew reduced the rate to 9 mills. In addition, he reduced state spending by 37 percent between 1877 and 1878.[82] In 1881, after being succeeded by Governor Bloxham, Drew stressed "immigration, transportation and education" as the systems designed to lead to prosperity.[83]

The state policy of giving or selling the public domain "was marked by rapid population growth, accelerated economic development and a great upsurge in railroad construction."[84] These policies resulted in reducing taxes from 9 to 4 mils and by the end of Bloxham's term, the state had wiped out its indebtedness and showed a balance of $5,000.[85] Railroads were built, "but critics answered that they [the state] paid an extremely high price in public land and other subsidies."[86] The railroads objected because they too were taxed after expecting exemptions under the provision of the Internal Improvement Fund. The U.S. Supreme Court disagreed and Bloxham's programs worked. The 1870s and 1880s were marked by immigration, transportation, and *urbanization*. Florida's population grew from 140,500 in 1860 to almost 188,000 by 1870, an increase of 34 percent.

The state was beginning to experience annual growth rates of four percent in population that continued throughout the 20th century until the late 1990s. In only a few years during World Wars I and II did the rate drop below four percent per year. Many Florida promoters published tour guides extolling the virtue of moving to this or that place in Florida. Regularly scheduled steamboat service on Florida's major rivers preceded the rapid development of railroads during the 1880s and 1890s. Jacksonville had a considerable increase in population. It soon emerged as the major maritime shipping and passenger port and the railroad hub of Florida. The state was beginning a boom, but with minimal local planning except for surveyed, platted, and recorded subdivisions and towns.

As Cox and Dovell found, "In the last report of the Commissioner of Lands and Immigration, Dennis Eagan, was the statement that all of the copies of the first edition of the *Florida Settler* [an immigrants' guide] had been distributed and that five thousand copies of a second edition had been printed. Eagan reported that in the last half of 1876 some '2,500 letters from all parts of the Union, and many portions of Europe, have been received at this office, all asking for information with regard to the climate, soil, and general resources of the state.'"[87]

The greatest drawback to settlement in Florida was its rudimentary road system. The state and investors first turned to natural waterways to meet transportation needs of settlers in both the interior and coastal regions. Where rivers were not naturally connected, water transport was combined with railroads. A fanciful example is reported by Cox and Dovell: "the arrival of the railroad opening to the lower east coast followed the Halifax-Indian River lagoons from Daytona, New Smyrna, and Titusville by boat to Jupiter Inlet where in 1888 an eight-mile railroad connected the towns of Jupiter and Juno on to Lake Worth."[88] It would become known as the "Celestial Railroad," given that its four stops were Jupiter, Mars, Venus, and Juno. From Lake Worth, a stage line connected to Fort Lauderdale, Lemon City (Miami), and Biscayne Bay.

In addition to such intermodal practices, growth of railroads themselves boomed. The redemption of the Internal Improvement Fund by Disston literally paved the way for Florida's era of railroad building, spurred on by large-scale land bonuses. More than 9 million acres of state lands and over 2.2 million acres of federal lands were conveyed to land grant railroads. More than 11 million acres amounting to approximately thirty percent of the land and water area of the entire state constituted this land giveaway. When Bloxham became governor there existed 550 miles of operating railroads. In 1891, ten years after the Disston sale, over 2,500 miles of railroad were in operation in Florida. By 1905, there were 3,500 miles of railroad in Florida.[89]

Early railroad entrepreneurs soon became major land developers. Properties they acquired through land grants for railroad building are today some of the most valuable lands within the urban centers of south and central Florida. Hotels built by these pioneers appeared in Ormond Beach, West Palm Beach, Miami, St. Augustine, Tampa and other cities. Many of these buildings exist today, and have been architecturally preserved and converted to other uses. Another example of the legacy of railroad lands and corridors is the Tri-Rail system in southeast Florida, which uses the abandoned Florida East Coast Railroad right-of-way to serve Palm Beach, Broward, and Miami-Dade counties with intra-regional transit. In addition, the "Eastward Ho" plan proposal (see Chapter X) and strategy in these counties has recommended redevelopment along this same rail corridor, and Miami-Dade's Metro-Rail, connecting south Miami-Dade and the urban center of Miami, is located along the corridor.

In 1885, a new Florida Constitution was adopted. It provided for a unique cabinet system of executive government, what David R. Colburn and Lance deHaven-Smith refer to as a *collegial* form of executive governance.[90] The Governor and Cabinet were constituted as the head of several state agencies. Members of the state Supreme Court became elective and the governor was limited to one four-year term. In these changes are found a weakened executive branch, which even today is unique to Florida. The capacity of the state to deal progressively with statewide planning and statewide issues was severely limited by the 1885 Bourbon constitution until its major revision in 1968. It may not have been amended even then without the interposition of the U.S. Supreme Court's interpretation of the principle of "one man-one vote."[91] In that year, a new Florida constitution was adopted which provided for the complete reorganization of state government, but elements of the old Bourbon cabinet system emerged intact.

By 1897, the Florida Farmer's Alliance and the more general populist politics had brought together the independents and farmers. A general agrarian platform emerged from the populist coalition, a plank of which included the regulation of railroads and businesses. The Alliance flirted for one election with the Populist party but returned to the Democratic ranks in 1896. This influence and political power brought to an end the Bourbon rule in Florida. In Cox and Dovell, the times are summed up this way: "The heyday of unbridled business enterprise was definitely over; municipally owned public utilities began to replace private corporations. Public education turned the corner toward greater activity than ever before while railroads received the regulation they had richly deserved for years."[92]

The Populist Years

The beginning of the twentieth century brought with it two governors dedicated to changing state policy by directing public concern toward state and public land and toward efforts to conserve natural resources. Cox and Dovell reflect: "Millions of acres had passed to the railroads and in lieu of further lands to grant, the Trustees had issued land certificates to be granted when additional land was patented to the state under the Federal Swamp and Overflowed Land Grant Act of 1850. The only appreciable amounts of swamp and overflowed lands left in the hands of the [Internal] Improvement Fund when [William Sherman] Jennings became a trustee were those in the Everglades and even there the State's title was uncertain."[93]

Jennings was elected governor in 1900, on a "railroad regulating and corporation busting platform" that derived its political policies from the Populist platforms. In an effort to resolve title to lands south of Lake Okeechobee, the Trustees of the Internal Improvement Fund employed attorneys who rendered a collective opinion that the state did hold title. This resulted in a dispute resolved in 1907 by the Federal District Court in Pensacola. The court upheld the Jennings position and authorized the Trustees to sell or dispose of the lands for the original purpose of drainage and reclamation. A revisionist view of Florida history will certainly credit Jennings with inaugurating the first plans for developing the *wasteland* [emphasis added] at the southern end of the state. He collected data on the possibilities of drainage and cleared the state's title to the land. The Jennings plans were merged in subsequent programs for drainage and economic development of south Florida.

Jennings was succeeded by Napoleon Bonaparte Broward, a native Floridian and descendant of the original French Huguenots who settled on the St. Johns River. Broward wrote in 1903, "I decided to become a candidate and give the people an opportunity to elect a governor who has never allowed himself to be put under obligation to the land grant corporations of this state, and who will not be hampered in voting against giving away state lands."[94] After Broward's election, his message to the legislature included plans to expand business license laws, equalize assessments by means of a state board of equalization, raise salaries for teachers, codify school laws and create a uniform textbook program, and he requested that "laws be enacted to protect the wildlife and forests of the state" and its marine resources.[95] An executive had been elected who seemed to fulfill Terry Sanford's later admonition that governors must be planners if states are to deal effectively with the future (see Chapter V).[96] Virtually all of his recommendations, though form and technical changes have been made, remain in Florida's constitution and statutes today. W. T. Cash said Broward "saw with far more than the usual clearness what the state needed and he stated his position in language that was unmistakable."[97]

As evidenced by Broward's clarity of thought and advanced ideas, factors which enhanced his leadership qualities were his personal honesty and sincerity. It is observed by historians Cox and Dovell that his "sincerity made him one of the most convincing speakers ever to appear upon a platform and one of the best-loved public men."[98] Broward's enlightenment and integrity brought to the state the capacity to visualize and plan for the state's future, throwing off the mantle of public indulgence to the whims and wishes of corporate interests concerning the public's resources. It represented the emergence of state planning and policies chosen to preserve natural resources and exercise a modicum of stewardship. He did, on the other hand, proceed with plans to build a canal from Okeechobee to the St. Lucie River in order to lower the lake level by four feet. This would drain the surrounding wetlands to provide arable land on which to grow sugar cane and truck crops. Agricultural expansion followed as thousands of acres were cultivated. This was the beginning of Florida's winter "vegetable basket" in western Palm Beach County and areas surrounding Lake Okeechobee.

Though seemingly visionary at the time, the state and federal governments have spent hundreds of millions of dollars in the past fifty years repairing the damage to the south Florida ecosystem that was a direct result of sixty years of exploitive state initiatives. The Everglades Restoration plan today will cost many more billions of dollars and, in the end, the project will only restore about a third of the Everglades area. Even the completion date has been set forward to 2015 from the original date of 2010. One can argue that there was little understanding of the interaction and connectivity of nature's system, but Floridians seemingly did not try to learn. The details of the drainage and reclamation programs in south Florida during the 1930s, 40s, and 50s are well beyond the pale of this chapter, but many volumes have been filled with descriptions and consequences of those projects.

The years following Broward found the state building upon his initiatives. In 1912, Park Trammell of Lakeland was elected governor. His most significant program was the creation of the State Road Board. By 1920, automobile licenses and gasoline taxes provided state and county revenues for road planning and building. Responding to matching federal funds and federal imperatives, an incipient state road system did grow. Generally, the roads followed section, township, and range lines because these lines were set aside by statute. This often resulted in sharp 90° turns, which many years later were smoothed into sweeping curves as automobiles evolved to higher speeds. In the decennial census of 1910, the population in Florida was over 752,000, a 42 percent rate of growth during the first decade of the 20th century.

During the 19th century, citrus growing had emerged along the St. Johns River upstream from Jacksonville. It gradually spread into Putnam, Alachua, and Marion counties. During the freezes of 1895 and 1896, the trees were destroyed, resulting in a 20th century southward retreat of the citrus industry. Polk, Orange, and Lake counties became the new region for citrus production. Thousands of acres of upland scrub lands were cleared. It is difficult to appraise the environmental cost today of the loss of these upland scrub forests prized for citrus cultivation. In retrospect, it may have been as devastating as the loss of so many natural wetlands. Today, because of subsequent freezes in the 1980s, many of these uplands have been abandoned and citrus has moved further south into Hendry, Collier, and neighboring counties. The lands in Lake, Orange, and Polk counties have ultimately been converted to housing developments, shopping centers, and medical facilities along the U.S. Highway 27 corridor. It is simply another regional example of Florida's history of land development, converting wetlands, uplands, and farmlands to urban development.

Adding to this land conversion was the discovery of phosphate in the Peace River Valley. Rock phosphate had been mined in north and central Florida, but the discovery of the "soft" phosphate ore permitted hydraulic mining, a much less expensive means of extracting phosphate from the bearing rock. The land thus strip-mined had a major impact on land development, water conservation, and the unfolding of the history of Florida's land development already buffeted by economic opportunities, climatological events, and historically permissive state planning policies.

Summary

The Spanish, the English, Thomas Jefferson, and successive Floridians by public and private means have publicized the advantages of immigration to Florida. The rationale was not always forthright, but the effect was the same. By the 1920s, Florida was in a real estate and population boom. Railroads served every place in the state, even Key West. Many new towns had emerged along the rail lines, and a traveler could visit every town by using regularly scheduled train service. A rudimentary but disconnected system of roads existed. The quality of state and county roads varied widely from simple ruts in the sand or mud to corduroy roads[99] to a few rock or shell and asphalt-surfaced roads. Most urban places in Florida were served by electricity and private or public water systems, but far less frequently by sewer systems. Septic tanks and cesspools were pervasive across the state. It was common to find land subdivided along or near the railroads for lot sales with no local planning, zoning, or subdivision regulations.

Land speculation had its origins with the Spanish and British, followed by American expansionism, and then by entrepreneurs within a state eager to use—and even abuse—its land in order to entice growth. This provided a sanguine setting for Florida as it moved into the next century. The cartoon shown in the beginning of this chapter portraying a Spanish explorer envisioning future "infrastructure" is especially apropos to what began occurring in Florida during the 20th century—and is still happening today.

NOTES FOR CHAPTER II

1   Lincoln, Abraham, "Second Annual Message to Congress," December 1, 1862. John Bartlett: Justin Kaplan, general editor, *Bartlett's Familiar Quotations,* fourteenth edition, New York: Little, Brown & Company, 2002.

2   Rerick, Rowland R., *Memoirs of Florida*, Atlanta, GA: The Southern Historical Association, 1902, p. 40.

3   Rerick, ibid, p. 42.

4   Ibid.

5   Ibid. There is evidence that Pensacola, not St. Augustine, almost became the nation's oldest city when Tristan de Luna set up a colony on the shore of Pensacola Bay in 1528, but it was abandoned after only two years. See Gene M. Burnett, "Almost the State's First Town," in *Florida's Past*, Volume III, Sarasota, FL: Pineapple Press, 1986, pp. 159-162.

6   Reps, John W., *The Making of Urban America*, Princeton, NJ: Princeton University Press, 1965, p. 28.

7   Ibid.

8   Deagan, Kathleen, "St. Augustine, First Urban Enclave in the United States," *North American Archeologist*, Volume 3, Farmmingdale, NY: Baywood Press, 1982, p. 195.

9   Rerick, ibid, p. 53.

10 Ibid, p. 60.

11 Ibid, p. 62.

12 Ibid.

13 Gannon, Michael, *A Short History of Florida*, Gainesville, FL: University Press of Florida, 1993, p.10.

14 Ibid, p. 11.

15 Ibid, p.14.

16 Rerick, ibid, p. 63.

17 A model of this village can be viewed at the Pensacola Museum of History, in Pensacola, FL.

18 Alexander, John F. and Earl M. Starnes, "Water Front Development and Change: Pensacola, Florida" Urban Waterfronts Lands, National Research Council, National Academy of Sciences, Washington, DC, 1980, p. 40.

19 Accessed from www.geocities.com/Heartland?Prairies/3226/Pensacola/index.html on November 15, 2007.

20 Rerick, ibid, p. 85.

21 Rerick, ibid.

22 Rerick, ibid, p. 90.

23 Ibid, p. 91.

24 Ibid, p. 94.

25 Mormino, Gary R., *Land of Sunshine, State of Dreams: A Social History of Modern Florida*, Gainesville, FL: University Press of Florida, 2005, p. 45.

26 See Mark Van Doren, ed., *Travels of William Bartram*, New York, NY: Dover Publications, Inc., 1955, pp. 97-98.

27 Rerick, ibid, p. 101.

28 The Republic of Florida referred to here is a predecessor to the more organized, though equally short-lived Republic of West Florida in 1810.

29 Rerick, ibid, p. 16. Pecolata is located on the east bank of the St. Johns River, about halfway between Jacksonville and East Palatka.

30 Ibid, pp. 139-140.

31 Ibid, p. 138.

32 Ibid, p. 147.

33 Ibid.

34 Ibid.

35 Ibid.

36 Duval served as territorial governor for twelve years.

37 Rerick, ibid., pp. 150-151.

38 In the early 1800s, the peninsular part of Florida, south of Gainesville, was not perceived to be important, a view that pervaded politics, economics, and development management for at least the next 100 years.

39 Rerick, ibid. The Spanish and French had used rudimentary surveying earlier, but this was the first "official" surveying done during the Territorial Years.

40 Morris, Allen, *Florida Place Names*, Coral Gables, FL: University of Miami Press, 1974, p. 141.

41 Alexander and Starnes, ibid., p. 79. (Cowford or Cow Ford was the name of one of the fords that Spanish settlers used to get their cows across from one side of the St. Johns River to the other.)

42 Ibid, p. 122.

43 Brock, Hanson, "Primrose Paradise," Miami, FL: Strange Printing Company, 1921, p. 25.

44 Brock, ibid, p. 27.

45 Rerick, ibid, p. 206.

46 For an excellent documentation of the Second Seminole War, see John K. Mahon, *The History of the Second Seminole War 1835-1842*, revised edition, Gainesville, FL: University Press of Florida, 1992.

47 Rerick, ibid, p. 210.

48 Ibid, p. 211.

49 Ibid.

50 Ibid.

51 Holbrook, Stewart H., *The Story of American Railroads*, New York, NY: American Legacy Press, 1981, p. 157, not a "poll tax" per se.

52 This was probably a head tax on slaves.

53 Rerick, ibid, p. 215.

54 Ibid, p. 219.

55 Ibid.

56 Ibid, p. 232.

57 Ibid, p. 228.

58 Ibid, p. 232.

59 Cox, Merlin G., and J. E. Dovell, *Florida from Secession to the Space Age*, St. Petersburg, FL: Great Outdoor Publishing Co., 1974, p. 1.

60 Ibid.

61 Rerick, ibid. p. 245.

62 Cox and Dovell, ibid, p. 12.

63 Ibid, p. 29.

64 Colburn, David R. and Lance deHaven-Smith, *Government in the Sunshine State: Florida Since Statehood*, Gainesville, FL: University Press of Florida, 1999, p. 9.

65 Cox and Dovell, ibid, p. 34.

66 Ibid, p. 37.

67 Ibid.

68 Ibid, p. 58.

69 Ibid, p. 45.

70 Ibid, p. 1.

71 Rerick, ibid, p. 325.

72 Ibid, p. 335.

73 From A.G. Breakfast, "Romantic History of Orlando, Florida," Orlando, FL, 1946, p. 23. The original source was George M. Barbour, *Florida for Tourists, Invalids, and Settlers*, publisher unknown, c. 1884; see Library of Congress catalogue.

74 Ibid, p. 25.

75 Davis, T. Frederick, "The Disston Land Purchase," *Florida Historical Quarterly* XVII, Gainesville, FL, 1939, pp. 203 and 210.

76 Chapter 253, *Florida Statutes*.

77 Cox and Dovell, ibid, pp. 77-79.

78 Ibid.

79 Ibid.

80 Ibid.

81 Ibid, p. 73.

82 Ibid, p. 74.

83   Ibid, p. 75.

84   Ibid, p. 76.

85   Ibid.

86   Ibid.

87   Ibid, pp. 80-81. The *Florida Settler*, a 160-page immigrants' guide, was prepared by Dennis Eagan in 1873.

88   Ibid, pp. 84-85.

89   Ibid, pp. 85-86.

90   Colburn and deHaven-Smith, ibid., p. 5.

91   Baker v. Carr, 369 US 186 (1962).

92   Cox and Dovell, ibid., p. 110.

93   Ibid, pp. 124-128.

94   Ibid.

95   Cox and Dovell, ibid, p. 130.

96   Sanford, Terry, *Storm Over the States*, New York, NY: McGraw-Hill Book Co., 1967, pp. 192-194.

97   Cox and Dovell, ibid.

98   Cox and Dovell, ibid., p. 133.

99   Corduroy roads were the result of permanently laying logs across the pathway of the automobile, particularly in sloughs, creeks and wet areas. The many logs laying together formed a surface simulating corduroy fabric and making for a lively ride, but more or less dry.

CHAPTER III

EMERGENCE, EXPANSION, AND WANING OF INTEREST IN PLANNING

From About 1900 to the Early 1940s

> In the same manner that economic and social groups are bound to each other, the various units of government are also tied in interdependence. In solving our municipal problems we must take cognizance of the affect of the solution on the County, the State, the region and the nation, thus a program for the general good of all is developed.[1]
> (Florida State Planning Board, 1939.)

The 1900s opened to scenes of change: change spawned largely by advances in technology, shifts in population from rural areas to urban areas, governmental reform, and unforeseen national emergencies. These changes created pressure for increased governmental responsibility, services, and reform in the management and regulation of development. It was a time that saw the concept of planning emerge in Florida and across the nation. Florida was nothing like it is today; it was, at that time, one of the last *frontiers* of the United States. However, signs of change were appearing, especially in speculation in land development, railroad development, the lumber industry, agriculture, mining, and tourism. The state had a population of under a million people in 1920. It was still a rural state. Just one city, Jacksonville, ranked in the nation's 100 largest urban places. The Sunshine State had a lot of growing ahead of it.

In this chapter, we will review some of the movements and direction-setting activities that influenced public planning in its formative years. We will touch upon the major planning related events during the first four decades of the century, but our attention will focus on early privately sponsored planning in Florida during the land boom of the early 1920s and the emergence of federally sponsored intergovernmental planning in the decade that followed. The land boom peaked in 1925, and it began to go bust that same year, as Florida preceded the rest of the nation into a severe economic depression. The severity of the national depression resulted in major initiatives at the federal level, some of which directly affected the practice of planning. At the behest of President Franklin D. Roosevelt, the national government stepped onto the planning stage in a major way: public planning became part of the nation's path to economic recovery. This action subsequently stimulated planning activity at the state, regional, and local levels of government. We place special attention on the effect these national activities had on planning in Florida. However, as the national economy grew stronger with the advent of World War II, interest in public planning waned rapidly. There are lessons to learn regarding the absence of planning during this period, some of which are still waiting to be learned half a century later.

Direction-Setting Happenings

Planning in the United States has many historical precedents. Prominent among early city plans were the St. Augustine, Florida, plan in 1565; William Penn's Philadelphia plan of 1628; the Charleston, South Carolina, plan of 1704; James Oglethorpe's 1733 plan for Savannah, Georgia; and the plan sponsored by Senator James McMillan in 1902, which updated and brought to fruition Pierre L'Enfant's 1790s plan for Washington, DC.[2] However, Frederick Law Olmsted, Sr., the founder of American landscape architecture, noted that most of these cities quickly outgrew any plans they had at the start and "it was seldom indeed that any effective effort was made to face the problems of extension and growth in the town planning spirit."[3] Local planning still struggles with the persistent dilemma of extension and growth; today it is called sprawl.

Despite sporadic initiatives such as those named above, the nation was slow to accept planning. There was—and still is—concern that planning might restrict private development and inhibit profits to be gained through land speculation. For example, L'Enfant's plan for Washington, DC, and early plans for New York City and Detroit (1790-1810) were, as planning historian Lawrence Gerckens put it, "rejected, changed, ignored, in keeping with the concept of minimal government responsibility, rampant land speculation, and minimal interference with private property."[4] These concerns prevail to current times, especially in Florida. Thus, we will return often to Gerckens' points in the following chapters.

Land speculation itself is not a wicked activity; it is when it is *rampant* that it becomes a problem, especially when buttressed with the concepts of the application of minimal government responsibility and minimal interference with private property. This statement might appear to imply we champion big government, but we do not. However, we do champion government that acts in the interests of both individuals *and* the general welfare in meeting its short- and long-range constitutional and statutory responsibilities. Concern about centralization of power, especially in the executive offices of governments, is understandable; however, as the country grew so did the need to protect the health, safety, and welfare of all Americans, not just those capable of wielding financial and political power and influence.

A plethora of movements arose in the late 1800s and early 1900s. Initially each focused on its own issue, but some of them converged. Planning historian Donald A. Krueckeberg identifies three converging ideas of planning which impinged upon the landscape of individualism and unbridled industrial enterprise: one of "scientific efficiency" (e.g., centralizing water and sewer systems), a second of civic beauty, and a third of social equity.[5] We bring attention to Krueckeberg's work not just to emphasize ideas of the time, but also to illustrate that seldom does any single event or idea fully represent a shift from one paradigm to another; the initiation of a movement is usually a convergence of two or more ideas. Despite this maxim, the City Beautiful movement, exemplifying the civic beauty idea, is often, though debatably, referred to as the "beginning" of planning.[6] The movement began between 1897 and 1902 as separate interests in municipal art, civic improvement, and outdoor art. According to Jon A. Peterson, another planning historian, each interest "played a vital, if now forgotten, role in launching the movement; each had distinct historical roots predating the Chicago World's Fair, and each began with different constituencies."[7] The fair, which opened in 1893, featured a life-scale model showing how public buildings and public space should relate to one another; it immediately attracted attention. Gerckens believes this idea of planning for public places and spaces might have carried across America had it not been for a national economic recession which "effectively halted the creation of other such 'model' communities in America for decades."[8] Nevertheless, the seed of public planning had been sown, and the planning idea began to emerge in different ways.

Spurred by the government reform movement, Wisconsin, in 1909, was the first state to grant a clear right for its municipalities to engage in city planning, and four years later Massachusetts went to the extent of making planning mandatory for cities and towns with populations over 10,000.[9] According to Florida historian Gene M. Burnett, in 1908, St. Petersburg became the first modern city in Florida to initiate a plan.[10] The notion of minimal government responsibility was showing the first signs of weakening under the pressure of unmanaged urban growth, and interest in planning was gradually spreading.

Plans prepared during the City Beautiful movement were beginning to gather dust by 1915. Part of the reason was that a new breed of planners was taking a more comprehensive approach, one not solely dependent on physical ideals.[11] A number of other reform movements had arisen since the late 1800s and room had to be made for planners who saw a need for a broader, more process-oriented solution to municipal problems. Planning had begun to widen its scope.

Interest in zoning and other development regulations often preceded interest in planning, however. The presumed ability of zoning to protect residential property values was one of its most popular selling points according to Richard F. Babcock, a renowned land use attorney.[12] The popularity of zoning increased even more when the U.S. Department of Commerce distributed its first edition of a model state zoning enabling act in 1924 (a revised edition was issued in 1926); many states used the model as a guide to enact their own zoning enabling acts. Interest in zoning solidified when in 1926 the U.S. Supreme Court upheld its constitutionality in *Euclid vs. Ambler Realty*.[13] This decision deterred any further question about the legitimacy of zoning as a proper exercise of the police power.

Many communities used their zoning map as their master plan—to them, zoning *was* planning. However, advocates of planning argued that zoning based on a plan is more comprehensive and long-range than a zoning map. The logic behind this argument brought the U.S. Department of Commerce to publish a model Standard City Planning Enabling Act in 1928. The hope was that the model act would clarify the situation, but, despite many progressive features, it only added to the confusion.[14] A major fault, according to Gerckens, was that, "The act recommended separate adoption of pieces of the plan, denying its essential quality as an integrated statement of public policies."[15] The model act thus failed to integrate planning and zoning. Babcock and Siemons derisively summed up the result by calling planning "a stepchild of land use regulations."[16] In many states, failure to integrate planning and zoning remains a problem to this day.

The concept of planning regionally was another of the progressive movements of the late 19th and early 20th centuries. In 1890, a Boston journalist wrote a series of articles proposing a greater Boston area federation; shortly after this, Boston developed a regional park system (between 1893 and 1899) and followed this with the Boston Metropolitan Improvement Commission in 1902.[17] The idea of regionalism later jumped to other metropolitan areas and several counties. Business interests, such as the Commercial Club of Chicago,[18] initiated many of these regional planning efforts. Business people tend to look at urban regions from a market perspective, thus they were quick to grasp the economic advantages of regionalism. Parochial perspectives, on the other hand, hamstring regional planning.

"The noblest of the era's comprehensive plans," according to Warren H. Wilson, "was the great Regional Plan of New York and Its Environs."[19] This privately sponsored plan, completed in stages during the 1920s by the Regional Plan Association,[20] was touted a success because many of its proposed highways, rail routes, parkways, and an air terminal were actually constructed. Despite its pioneering approach and scope, some people did not look upon it as noble. Architectural critic and philosopher, Lewis Mumford, for example, criticized the plan as being a vehicle to continue the dominance of New York City over its surrounding region. To him, it was "mere camouflage for continuing centralization" and it failed "to supply a vision of a more just, equitable future for the region as a whole."[21] Fear of dominance by a central city has continued to constrain regional planning. For example, representation on regional planning councils is usually by unit of participating government not by ratio of population, thus, few regional councils are truly democratic, that is, representative of all the people they serve.

Interest in planning reached the state government level, as well. New York State, in 1925, is credited with creating the first state planning program.[22] It prepared a plan the following year that has since been called more of an analysis than a plan. Albert Lepawsky described it "as an inventory of the State's resources with a description of its land-use trends."[23] The pattern was set: inventories and analyses were to become the modus operandi of state planning in the 1930s. Regardless, the New York State report is still the earliest example of a state government moving toward comprehensive planning. Other states quickly followed the lead of New York. Jacob Crane, in a paper presented at the 1932 National Conference on City Planning, identified ten states involved in statewide planning projects of some kind: California, Illinois, Massachusetts, Michigan, North Carolina, New Jersey, New York, Texas, Virginia, and Wisconsin.[24] Though state planning was in its infancy, what was to come next could hardly have been anticipated: untold horizons were about to open for planning and planners.

Florida: Boom and Bust

Florida's population rose to almost 1.5 million people by 1930, and its urban population (51.7 percent) had overtaken the population in rural areas (48.3 percent), reflecting the development of new towns in the 1920s. By 1940, the state's population had climbed to 1.9 million, and it had become 55 percent urban. Florida was becoming an urban state, yet its image and politics remained in control of a legislature dominated by rural interests.

In the early part of the 20th century, communities spawned by railroad development began to appear in peninsular Florida. Some were planned communities, some just materialized. One of the planned communities, Sebring, was designed around a circle park that served as the settlement's town square, surrounded by commercial buildings and a radial pattern of development.[25] Additional designed communities would soon follow.

In the decade of the 1920s, the theretofore sleepy, relatively undeveloped state of Florida went into the first of a long series of development-related ordeals. The Butler Act of 1921[26] initiated things by permitting development on filled tidal lands. This generated an immediate focus on sales of reclaimed land, which became a great source of revenue for the state.[27] It also permitted residential and agricultural expansion into the Everglades.[28] Additionally, the act cleared the way for residential infill of tidal lands along Biscayne Bay, and islands appeared where only sea water and bay bottom formerly existed. Before long, residential development crept northward from Miami into Broward County and beyond. Dredge and fill became the vanguard of developers—and the *locus classicus* for future environmental disasters. Florida developers became notorious for selling wetlands, which later prompted comedian Milton Berle to remark, "I just got wonderful news from my real estate agent in Florida. They found land on my property."[29] In reality, this was no joking matter.

The "Roaring Twenties" was a time of rampant land speculation in Florida, where land was sometimes sold and resold before the initial sale was filed and recorded. Former newspaperman and legislator Walter P. Fuller called the land boom "the story of one of the periodic epidemics of gambling that have swept this country three or four times each century; a something-for-nothing fever with more color and substance than most; a disease born of the intoxicating tonic of Florida sunshine and sand."[30] Real estate development in Florida even outpaced development in California, enough so that noted author Daniel J. Boorstin referred to Florida as "a twentieth-century Fountain of Wealth," a play on words referring to the fabled sixteenth-century Fountain of Youth.[31] Florida historian and newspaperman Gene M. Burnett, said somewhat more caustically, "The seeds of the great Florida land boom of the 1920s—that classic study in mass delusion—were probably planted earlier in the World War I era when Prest-o-lite millionaire Carl Fisher dredged up his golden sand-bar, Miami Beach."[32] Fisher had turned a spotlight on the Gold Coast of Florida. Burnett found that, "… real estate expansion, which up to 1921 was lively but unfrenzied, began to take on feverish intensity as more visitors poured into the Gold Coast, especially Miami, the epidemic's center."[33] Speculators, by the thousands, flocked to Florida.[34] The snowball—in this case a beach ball—of development was rolling.

Salesmen line up to greet prospective customers in Winter Haven: State Library and Archives of Florida.

Determined to open more land to development, the State committed itself to public works projects on a grand scale. During the 1920s, according to Cox and Dovell, two thousand miles of highways were constructed.[35] The most significant of the highway projects crossed the Everglades from Miami to Naples and then turned north to Tampa, a stretch of highway now known as the Tamiami Trail (U.S. 41). In 1924, construction of the Gandy Bridge connected St. Petersburg to Tampa, thus accelerating residential and commercial development in Pinellas County.[36] Projects like these opened tens of thousands of acres for development. The rush to develop was in full swing—and urban sprawl, Florida style, began in earnest.

Riding in Land Developer's Tour Bus: State Library and Archives of Florida.

John Nolen, an early planner of national repute, noted that Florida's geographic location and climate attracted people for health, recreation, and business reasons; many of them came for a short first visit, followed by prolonged return visits, and eventually permanent residence.[37] This routine, repeated uncountable times over the following decades, still occurs. Nolen's earliest involvement in Florida was in 1908, when he was hired by St. Petersburg (then part of Hillsborough County) to develop a bold plan for the downtown and bay front area.[38] The visionary W. L. Straub, publisher-editor of the *St. Petersburg Weekly Times* (later to become the *St. Petersburg Times*) had been relentless in pressuring the city council to hire Nolen. Thus, St. Petersburg, through Straub's foresight, earned the distinction of being Florida's entrée in the City Beautiful movement.

Florida's land development boom in the early 1920s brought John Nolen back to Florida, along with other nationally known architects, landscape architects, and planners. Nolen, and Frederick Law Olmstead, Jr. and John Charles Olmsted (sons of Frederick Law Olmstead) were employed by Harry S. Kelsey to plan Kelsey City, Florida's first "model city" of the development boom.[39] Kelsey was president of Waldorf Systems, a national restaurant chain. The 70,000-acre tract was incorporated in 1923, and its charter included what was one of the first zoning codes in Florida history. Kelsey City, later renamed Lake Park, was a manifestation of the utopian ideal espoused by Henry Ford and other industrialists of the time: that industry, agriculture, and homes should be located so as to be self-supportive, convenient, and in open, natural surroundings; in today's jargon, this would be called sustainable development. However, at that time it was a Jeffersonian concept reborn in the early 20th century. Kelsey City was a community meant to sustain itself, but the age of the automobile would prove otherwise: it is now a small suburb north of West Palm Beach. Another embodiment of the Jeffersonian concept was Penney Farms, a development begun by retail magnate J.C. Penney in the 1920s. It is today a town of a few hundred people located in Clay County, west of St. Augustine.

Coral Gables, located along the shore of Biscayne Bay, was planned by former Dade County commissioner and real estate developer George E. Merrick in 1921. The land had been his father's citrus grove. He described Coral Gables as a "great work of building a distinctive Spanish suburb which would be a worthy expression of the finer sense of the city, a reflection of the architectural splendor of Old Spain in a setting of tropical luxuriance."[40] Donna Lubin, director of historical resources for Coral Gables, reports that seven million dollars of property was sold in six months; in addition, "more than six hundred homes were constructed; sixty-five miles of sidewalks were added; fifty thousand trees, shrubs, and flowering plants were planted; and a system of lighting was installed which covered over twenty-eight miles."[41] The Coral Gables of today still reflects its original concept: it is the outcome of Merrick's vision and the dogged determination of several generations of city council members, city staff, and a supporting constituency of both citizens and practicing architects who thoroughly embraced the vision. Just as importantly, the people of Coral Gables, through the years, have supported the implementation of the plan through tightly drawn land use regulations. Furthermore, the city has continually employed architectural design standards administered by a review committee of architects. Coral Gables has attracted nationwide attention both because of the extraordinary scope of the improvements and of the consummate artistry of the work. It is today a suburb of distinction, but this took strict adherence to the original plan, which is a rare occurrence in Florida.

Sarasota found itself in need of planning, and turned to John Nolen for assistance. Nolen noted that Sarasota's rapid growth "crowded the hotels, congested the streets, [and] caused a shortage in business, residential, and recreational facilities."[42] The spirit of expansionism was everywhere, and with it, the consequence of increasing demand—and costs—for public improvements. Nolen's plan for Sarasota was adopted in 1925. Nolen, a national leader in the early organizational efforts of professional planners (e.g., he helped organize the American City Planning Institute), was also involved in planning a number of other Florida communities during the 1920s.

Palm Beach, home of the ultra-rich, the Palm Beach suit, and the sport shirt,[43] was another of the cities participating in the early venture into local planning. It had put a zoning ordinance and map in place, but the Garden Club of Palm Beach commissioned Bennett, Parson & Frost, consulting architects from Chicago, to propose a more comprehensive plan.[44] This plan was adopted by the city in December 1929. The architects found numerous advantages to the area, including exotic vegetation, the ocean with its excellent beaches, and a warm climate tempered by the Gulf Stream. These advantages have continued to lure northerners to Palm Beach decade after decade.

Architect Addison Mizner, who retired to Palm Beach, kept himself occupied by revamping the community of wealthy residents with lavish "designer" mansions.[45] Mizner, at the height of popularity with billionaire clientele, was afflicted with land-boom fever, "the most fateful disease of the day."[46] His ambition soared in neighboring Boca Raton, where he set out a master plan designed to create a Mediterranean-style Venice and Riviera in Florida. The plan called for oceanfront estates encompassed within parks and gardens, with its centerpiece, the medieval-styled Cloister (later a hotel), approached by a *twenty-lane highway* with a Grand Canal down the middle. Although $11 million in lots sold in one day, the boom soon became a paper nightmare and its demise was foretold when T. Coleman du Pont withdrew his financial backing and caused a panic.[47] Though the elitism of Boca Raton survived, Mizner's dream was unfulfilled; for example, the huge highway and the canal never materialized. The dream became a victim of the land development bust that brought many speculators to the ground. Among them, Burnett wrote, were George Merrick (Coral Gables), who in the last years of his life struggled to operate a fish camp in the Florida Keys;

Carl Fisher (Miami Beach), who died broke and alcoholic; and Addison Mizner (Boca Raton), who lived hand-to-mouth and died on a paper pyre of litigation.[48]

Interest in planning was not limited to cities backed by wealthy entrepreneurs. A small number of cities throughout Florida received special state legislative approval to create planning boards in the 1920s; among them were Lake Worth, Leesburg, Palatka, Tampa, and West Palm Beach. Some cities, like the latter three, melded their planning and zoning boards or required that amendments to the zoning ordinance be submitted to the planning board for approval. Though master planning was not high on the list of needs for the majority of municipalities in Florida, there was enough interest in the 1920s for George Simons, Jr. and J. Clifford R. Foster to form the Florida Planning Association, the first planning organization in the state.[49] Simons was a planning consultant from Jacksonville and Foster was Florida's adjutant general. Though the association was active in sponsoring legislative bills for local planning, zoning, and subdivision regulation, the group soon disbanded. Nonetheless, this group of Florida planning pioneers helped pave the way for later initiatives.

A greater number of communities engaged in zoning than in planning. Among the first cities to participate in zoning were Bradenton, Jacksonville, Maitland, Miami Beach, Orlando, St. Petersburg, Sanford, and Tampa, all in 1923.[50] Many other cities soon followed their lead. The late Ernest Bartley, professor of urban and regional planning at the University of Florida, along with William W. Bayer, observed that cities during the 1920s needed to have authorization for zoning approved by *special acts* of the State legislature.[51] It was not until 1939 that the legislature finally approved a *general enabling act* for municipal zoning. This was thirteen years after the U.S. Supreme Court, in its *Euclid v. Ambler Realty* decision,[52] legitimized the constitutionality of zoning.

When the housing market collapsed, local government services were reduced and support for planning and zoning was cut or eliminated altogether.[53] Damaging hurricanes in 1926 and 1928[54] added to the woe by wreaking havoc in south Florida. The severe national economic depression then dragged Florida's economy further into the muck. Nonetheless, development remained foremost in the minds of Florida entrepreneurs and politicians; for example, in 1929, incoming Governor Doyle E. Carlton ironically called for reclaiming the Everglades, in "a wise engineering and sound economic manner."[55] Most political leaders were paralyzed by the depression, but Carlton was bold enough to attempt to counter political ineptitude by pushing for an increase in taxes to reduce a state deficit and assist counties in reducing their bonds.[56] Carlton also sought a gasoline tax to pay for roads and schools, but he encountered overwhelming opposition.[57] Thus, as David R. Colburn and Lance deHaven-Smith, note, the Sunshine State looked to the federal government to provide "the lifeline that kept Florida afloat during the 1930s."[58]

Across the nation, interest in planning began to wane as the Great Depression took hold. In 1931, 716 local planning commissions and 97 regional planning councils (including county planning commissions) existed across the United States, but the bottom dropped out in 1932.[59] Most cities and regions dismissed their planning efforts and few new ventures occurred; this was as much the case in Florida as it was elsewhere in the nation. For Florida, the 1920s had gone from boom to bust, and as the 1930s began, it was time for someone to step forward and lead the states and the cities out of the depths of the Great Depression.

Advent of Planning as an Intergovernmental Activity

The national economic depression made it difficult for local governments and regional organizations to find financial support to sustain an interest in planning. Thus, planning activity began to wane until President Franklin D. Roosevelt stepped in and used planning as a management tool to help recover from the depression. The nation was in the throes of an emergency and radical steps had to be taken. One of these steps was the enactment of the National Industrial Recovery Act of 1933.[60] Title I, Industrial Recovery—the section of the act that drew most attention, and criticism—was designed to establish codes to support prices and wages, which were considered important to encouraging economic revival. However, critics of the act rejoiced two years later when the U.S. Supreme Court declared Title I of the act unconstitutional because it illegally gave legislative powers to the executive branch, infringed on the authority of the states, and over-extended the commerce clause.[61] What was left to carry on the president's agenda was Title II of the act, which authorized public works and construction projects to be undertaken by the Public Works Administration.

Harold L. Ickes, Secretary of Interior, established the National Planning Board (NPB) in 1933 to assist in the preparation of the comprehensive public works program required by Title II.[62] The board was renamed the National Resources Board (NRB) when it was moved into the president's office by executive order a year later.[63] Caught in a vortex of name changes (see Figure III-1), it became the National Resources Committee (NRC) in 1935, the third change of title in three years. The final name change occurred in 1939 when Congress authorized the National Resources Planning Board

Figure III-1
Sequence of Name Changes for the National Planning Office
1933-1943

1933-1934	1934-1935	1935-1939	1939-1943
National Planning Board →	National Resources Board →	National Resources Committee →	National Resources Planning Board

(NRPB) as one of six principal divisions in the Executive Office of the President. To avoid confusion over these multiple titles, we will hereafter use the generic terms national planning office or planning office to blanket these four bewildering name changes.

Elevating the national planning office to the Executive Office in 1934 was a move to help the president achieve his primary objective of revitalizing the nation's economy. However, the planning office faced a number of significant hurdles. Among these was reluctance by the cabinet to strengthen the management hand of the chief executive at their expense. Ickes, as a member of the cabinet, was concerned about his public works projects being coordinated by a planning office run by three special presidential appointees, so he led a revolt by the cabinet.[64] Roosevelt compromised by restructuring the board to include the six cabinet officers. He had strengthened his policy management hand somewhat, but not as much as he had wanted. As Herman Miles Somers, U.S. Senator from South Carolina at the time, observed, "For most of our history the President had no staff services ... He was a man with a secretary who was presumed to be able to call on the departments for all the help he wanted."[65] Nonetheless, a national emergency was at hand, and if the president was to lead the nation out of its economic depression, he needed a staff to help him set and coordinate the policies of recovery.

The task of coordinating all government public works affecting natural resources was handed to the national planning office.[66] However, intra-governmental coordination within the federal bureaucracy was a hurdle too difficult to surmount. Most federal agencies were reluctant to allow the centralized planning function to exert influence over their domains.[67] (Florida would experience similar difficulty decades later.) Thus, the task of coordinating the varied activities of the executive branch was underachieved. What planning accomplished was on "a fragmented departmental basis," and thus, David E. Wilson states, the planning office succeeded in entrenching only "partial planning in American public policy."[68] As will be seen in later chapters, executive control of executive branch activities was to be an issue for some time to come—for both the federal government and many state governments.

The national planning office also wanted to achieve consistency in economic recovery policies through coordinated interstate, state, and local planning. The federal government blanketed the nation with interstate planning commissions; these bodies, in turn, coordinated the work of state planning commissions. The New England and the Pacific Northwest commissions were created first, but it took seven years for the remaining interstate commissions to be named. For example, the Southeastern Regional Planning Commission (which included representation from Florida) was not established until 1940.[69] However, initiating public planning at state and county levels of government was another matter. Not surprisingly, the key was financial assistance.

The concept of state planning was unexplored territory for most state governments, but the federal government wanted the states to participate in Title II of the National Industrial Recovery Act. Despite a general lack of appreciation for how planning might be useful, governors were quick to take advantage of the available federal funding. As a result, governors created state planning agencies by executive order in state after state between 1933 and 1935. In most states, however, statutory authority was not conferred until a few years later, if at all. One of the reasons for the lag in legislative action may have been the absence of model legislation. Alfred Bettman of the Harvard School of City Planning, resolved this aspect of the problem in 1935 by developing a model state planning act that was circulated by the national planning office.[70]

A more persuasive reason for the lag in legislative backing was, as at the federal level, ambivalence about placing a planning function in the executive branch where a governor might use it to strengthen his policy-making power. Though authorization eventually came, it came reluctantly. Congressional recognition of the national planning office did not occur until 1939, however. By this time, all states but Delaware had state planning boards,[71] and, in five states, governors had established non-statutory planning boards.[72] Most of these fosterling state planning boards received only minimal budgetary backing from their state legislatures. Lepawsky provides us with a revealing statistic: "The degree of dependence upon the Federal Government is shown by the fact that at the end of 1937, 82 percent of the employees of the state planning boards were furnished by the Works Progress Administration."[73] This was a less than positive indicator of the commitment of state governments to state planning. Part of the reluctance to embrace state planning also may have been that it was seen as a threat to the status quo. State legislators, like their counterparts in Congress, considered it a threat to the policy-making responsibilities of the legislative branch.

A related complication may have been that few governors had a personal interest in planning, but to be eligible for federal Title II financial aid, state planning boards were expected to be placed at a high enough level—at least theoretically—to coordinate the planning activities of other state agencies. This was a threat to semi-autonomous state line agencies. According to John T. Howard, a professor at the Massachusetts Institute of Technology, "the strength and jealousy of existing state agencies was principally responsible" for limiting the coordinative authority of the state planning boards.[74] One way of neutralizing this assumed threat was to ensure that state planning would be no more than an advisory function. Bettman's model act, based largely on the municipal model, did this. It emphasized an *advisory* state master plan,[75] thereby reducing the potential threat of centralized policy-making. This concept was readily accepted, particularly since most planners believed state planning should follow the municipal model, the prevailing planning model of the time and for long afterwards. Fifty years later Florida would find its own state comprehensive plan cast in advisory language, and thus rendered mostly ineffective, its legal effect seldom invoked in regional or local planning issues.

The national planning office pointed out that coordinating the plans of other state agencies provided a unique opportunity for state planning boards because "no other agency in the State government is charged with taking an overall, long-range view of the activities of the State government."[76] This viewpoint was echoed by Howard, who contended that the most successful planning boards would be those "which have achieved acceptance as integral, working parts of an organic government system."[77] Howard, however, knew this was not likely to happen. He had undertaken a survey of ten northeastern and midwestern states in 1936, and came to the conclusion that, "the very fact that many of the state planning boards have failed to achieve statutory permanence is proof that, in the minds at least of the policy-forming branch of government, they are not essential to good state government."[78] This illustrates the dilemma of the state planning boards: how could they coordinate the planning activities of other state agencies from weak, unaccepted, non-integrative positions? This issue would also revisit Florida in later years.

The focus of state planning was another issue. Despite espousing a long-term, comprehensive perspective, the national planning office took the position that, "… for the immediate future, the major emphasis of state planning will tend to be on those types of state activity which affect the physical environment."[79] The emphasis was to be on physical planning, especially relating to land, water, and public works.

Despite considerable debate, planning for social issues (for example, health and housing) was not to be a major consideration. The national planning office encountered another problem: should they concentrate on long-range or short-range planning? They wrote, "To be effective State planning must be long-term, comprehensive planning."[80] Yet, they went on to caution, "This inherent factor in planning creates a difficulty since the planning agency, especially in its formative stages, needs an atmosphere of accomplishment in which to operate." The relevancy of planning was tied to both long-range and short-range objectives, but short-range planning was to have priority. Given the advisory nature of planning, the need to show short-range accomplishments in a highly political environment dominated. This remains a matter of discussion among planners and clients of planners to this day.

Since they were restricted from intruding on the functions of other state agencies, most state planning boards were left searching for unclaimed territory. Thus, the great bulk of planning work focused on undertaking surveys."[81] Lepawsky, in writing *State Planning and Economic Development in the South*, agreed when he noted that, "planning boards came to be regarded as the 'research boys' in the state house."[82] This restriction in activity resulted in negative comments from scholars both then and later. Among the early planning scholars, Howard's impression was that many, if not most, of the boards failed to accomplish anything that would justify the continuance of state planning as such.[83] Twelve years later, Lepawsky was a touch more prudent when he reported that the accomplishments of state planning were generally not tangible.[84] The bottom line was the same, however: state planning in the 1930s did not accomplish all it was intended to achieve.

Though regional planning got its start around the turn of the century and was spurred on by the formation of the Regional Planning Association of America in the 1920s,[85] public regional planning (other than in a few areas like Boston) did not come of age until the 1930s. It was the federal government, through the New Deal, that stimulated this endeavor. State and local governments were overwhelmingly disinterested in anything regional—until monies were made available through federal grants. Over three hundred multi-county and county planning agencies came into being by 1937.[86] Some of Florida's counties were among them.

In the late 1930s, the nation began to swing from a depressed economy to preparation for war. President Roosevelt, by executive order in September 1939, charged the national planning office to "act as a clearing house and means of coordination for planning activities, linking together various levels and fields of planning."[87] However, it was too late for the national planning office to do much coordinating and linking, since it had been isolated from policy-making. It was not capable of real coordination, certainly not the kind of coordination that might be interpreted as an intrusion (for the good of the whole) on the activities of other federal agencies. The state planning boards were even less capable of playing such a role. Planning agencies at the national and state levels were desperate to be relevant, and the opening of the 1940s appeared to provide the opportunity. Or did it?

Planning is Relegated to the Back Bench and Beyond

In 1940, the year before the United States officially entered World War II, the national planning office was directed to study *post*-defense planning.[88] This must have appeared to be an opportunity to frame policies for the future, a planning oriented task. Once again, the national planning office saw a role for state planning boards. As it subsequently reported, studies by state planning boards provided "a useful basis for planning in the war emergency—for locating war plants and military establishments, supplying and transporting labor and raw materials, and guiding wartime programs so that they will be as beneficial as possible to the post-war development of the State."[89] The die had been cast, from this point on state planning boards began to direct the greater portion of their efforts toward finding locations for industrial plants. *Comprehensive* state planning was submerged under a wave of interest in a vital but more narrowly focused need: industrial plant location and related economic development. Before the end of the war most of the state planning boards had been swept into newly created industrial/economic development agencies, though a few survived in name by assuming a strong economic development role.[90]

President Roosevelt's interest in the national planning office lessened as the economy improved, and Congress abolished the office in 1943. As someone pointed out, "All technical staff in Washington and in the eleven field offices of the board ceased active work at the end of the fiscal year 1943."[91] This was the same year an Office of War Mobilization and Reconversion (OWMR) was created in the president's office. Somers, in his case study of the OWMR, considered this congressional action as "the broadest grant of power ever legislated by Congress, creating for the first time by statute a superdepartmental director over the whole range of home-front executive activities for war and reconversion."[92] Somers felt it gave the president a strong staff arm for executive policy and program coordination, something the national planning office had never been in a position to do as an advisory agency. Given the powers of the OWMR, why should the president have continued to use the national planning office, an agency torn in a multitude of directions, never fully trusted by Congress, and not welcomed by other executive branch agencies? It was an agency without significant popular, political, and administrative support for promoting comprehensive planning at all levels of government.[93]

The national planning office foretold as early as 1938 that if national planning was eliminated then many of the state planning boards would likely disappear, whereas "in others they would remain, but their work would probably suffer from the absence of national leadership and technical advice."[94] Its prediction came true, and within ten years, almost all trace of state planning work was eliminated, except in a small number of states. Among the factors Lepawsky listed as contributing to the demise of national planning were:

- The failure to show direct benefits from planning.

- The failure to formulate in concrete terms the positive results of planning.

- The distrust of comprehensive surveys as 're-search for research's sake.'

- The misgivings about planning on the part of some conservative interests including a fear that it might operate to the detriment of the laissez-faire philosophy.

- Fear on the part of Congress that its policy-making functions were being impaired by this executive planning body.

- Conflict between the National Resources Planning Board and other departments or agencies of government, such as the War Department Corps of Engineers over the function of water planning.[95]

These factors—some which were used against state planning as well—hindered the objective of the national planning office to relate all governmental functions to a harmonious whole. Each of these arguments contains a lesson for future efforts of public planning *at any level of government.*

Impacts of Wartime Growth on Local Governments

Meanwhile, planning at the local level was facing its own issues, principally the lack of housing and inadequate public facilities. City historian Carl Abbott, in addressing changes to Sunbelt cities during the war, noted that, "the flush times that came with rearmament and full mobilization brought a common set of problems," and the response to these problems was "painfully inadequate in most southern and western cities."[96] He went on to observe that, "the essential problem of the boomtowns was to stretch limited resources to serve an exploding population with almost no lead time for preparation."[97] First on everyone's list was the need to meet a rapidly expanding housing supply, and close behind, Abbott went on, was "the need to provide trolley and bus service to connect housing projects to war plants, bases, and downtown stores and theaters and worries about the interrelated problems of recreation, prostitution, and crime."[98] Mobile home parks sprang up in many places, but they were only a temporary answer to the housing problems of civilian workers employed at military installations or in shipyards and other war-related industries.

Cities were hesitant to plan for permanent housing and infrastructure because they were not sure the strong economy would continue after the war. Public officials "worried about overbuilding public facilities for a temporary population and the possible impact of a postwar housing glut on local taxes."[99] Elected officials, unwilling to believe the good times would last, must have been even more reluctant than usual to raise taxes to support the need for new infrastructure. At the same time, Congress and most state governments rejected thoughts about providing financial aid to cities. This left local government infrastructures with deficits that continued to worsen until the federal government attempted to fill this need through categorical grant programs in the 1950s. For the most part, Florida and other states continued to be silent in responding to the needs of their urban places.

Intergovernmental Planning in Florida

By 1933, President Roosevelt's emergency economic recovery programs made it imperative for Florida to initiate state-level planning. Governor David Sholtz (1933-1937) created the Florida Advisory and Planning Board, the state's first planning board, in December of that year (see Figure III-2). He did this by executive order, placing the board within the Governor's Advisory Council on Unemployment Relief. The new board did not receive legislative authority until June 1935 when the legislature created a successor agency, the Florida State Planning Board (SPB).[100] A small number of people worked in the Tallahassee office with the executive secretary, but most of the staff was located in Jacksonville, where they worked closely with a field office of the national planning office in undertaking surveys of public improvements.

Figure III-2
Organization Chart—Florida State Planning Board
1936

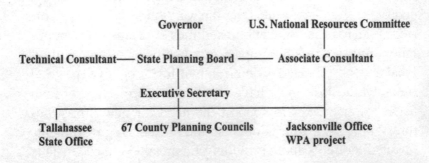

Source: Loose page from a 1936 planning report by the Florida State Planning Board, found in the Florida State Library.

The new planning legislation—Florida's first *intergovernmental* planning law—prescribed the preparation and adoption of a state master plan and permitted the formation of county planning councils.[101] This was a major accomplishment, but it would never have occurred if many programs with considerable federal largesse were not at stake. The sixty-seven county planning councils created by the act funneled the survey data and information to the SPB. In turn, this became part of the nationwide agenda to prepare six-year inventories of proposed public works construction for each state.[102]

The Florida SPB raised the level of planning consciousness in a state historically driven by a quest for quick profits through land speculation and development. Among its tasks was to help create county planning councils. The membership of the county planning councils—Florida's first *regional* planning councils—was made up of both local and gubernatorial appointees. Each county planning council consisted of one member appointed by the board of county commissioners, one member of the board of public instruction, an ex-officio member of each municipal planning board within the county, and "a number of at least three greater than the ex-officio members" appointed by the governor.[103] The authority for the creation of county planning councils was not mandatory, but it provided counties with a chance to participate in the state's public works inventory and the preparation of a statewide master plan:

> ... planning is not one broad program designed by a central agency and inflicted on all the various communities. It is rather the beginning of a program, or a pattern, to which the pieces must be fitted in much the same manner that a jig-saw puzzle is put together, with community plans constituting the process.[104]

The county physical master plans were to be submitted to the SPB for review and approval, and to ensure coordination with the anticipated state master plan (this is another concept revisited by Florida decades later). The county plans were expected to provide the local detail, whereas the state plan was to restrict itself to elements that were of statewide concern by reason of their function, size, extent, location, legal status, or other rationale.[105] This seemed simple and reasonable, but simple it was not. Distinctions between statewide and local interests did not become a major issue in the 1930s, partly because neither the state nor the counties completed their plans. Most of what was accomplished during this brief period of state and county planning activity was inventorying and research-related work. The concern of what is of statewide interest and what is strictly of local interest would arise again in the future.

Florida provides an example of the broad range of activities in which state planning boards across the country were involved. Among the tangible achievements of the SPB noted in a 1936 report by the national planning office were:

- The board originated the idea of a state citrus commission and suggested various measures that were passed by the 1935 legislature affecting the citrus industry.

- The board was influential in recommending legislation which created a state park service.

- The work of the board resulted in the formation of a number of new municipal planning boards, and stimulated several of the county planning councils to engage in long-range planning.[106]

A list of accomplishments published by the SPB, itself, includes a number of other far-reaching activities:

- Public works: the board engaged in a public works inventory in anticipation of preparing a six-year public works building program, particularly in association with the county planning councils.

- Highways: it sponsored a highway planning survey staffed by the state road department.

- Water: it provided services to a drainage basin study covering all of Florida.

- Schools: the board was involved in studies relating to the administration, finance, and physical plants of schools in preparation of a long-range public works program.

- Government structure: the board studied the administrative and financial structures of the political subdivisions in the state to point the way toward more efficient and economical local government.

- Special requests from the governor or legislature: the board participated in a study to show the variation in assessment taxes in the state; updated the records of the tax-delinquent lands of the state; compiled maps showing school districts and the road and bridge districts in each county; and provided information leading to the compilation of a composite map showing overlapping debt structure in Florida.[107]

Both of the lists refer to some policy-oriented activities, but the majority of work was survey-related or what might be called "early-stage" planning. The SPB apparently was trying its best to be relevant, but the focus of that relevancy was directed mostly to the national planning office. The SPB was never given the time to mature, it did not stay in existence long enough to move into more advanced stages of planning. The commitment of the state and its counties to planning went only as far as the continuance of federal funding—and that was soon to disappear.

By 1940, the Florida SPB had been divided into two sections: a State Planning Program and a Defense Program. Activities placed under the State Planning Program were typical of the research studies the board had been involved in since its inception, but the Defense Program category was soon shifted to the Florida Advisory Committee for National Defense. This turned out to be the first step in the devolution of the state planning function to defense and later to industrial development. The planning board's major tasks under the defense program were an industrial survey of the state and research on statewide population characteristics.[108] However, within a year the industrial survey component was transferred to the Florida Economic Advancement Council.[109] After having its most important wartime functions taken away and being left with population studies and assorted other research tasks, the relevance of the Florida SPB steadily declined.

In 1945, the legislature moved the SPB and the Economic Advancement Council into a newly created Florida State Improvement Commission.[110] Though statutory authority was carried over to prepare plans for future development, only the state public works program was kept operational. Servicemen and women were returning from the war, and homes and jobs needed to be made available to them, thus the state and its local governments began to focus solely on economic development, a concern that had dominated the thinking of politicians for decades.[111] As the SPB said in *Florida Communities: Their Problems, Their Future*, "Most important … is the question of employment for our citizens returning from the armed forces, for the newer citizens attracted to our town by a war plant or an Army camp, and for the people who left the community to obtain war work, but will return."[112] Interest in public planning was set aside, and planning in Florida entered a period of dormancy.

Summary

Florida was an almost overlooked state when the twentieth century began. The most populated part of the state was the northern tier, stretching from Jacksonville to Pensacola. The peninsula was sparsely settled, though railroads had already pushed their way south to open the east coast and across to Cedar Key and Tampa Bay.[113] However, enough development was beginning to occur for St. Petersburg to initiate a plan during the City Beautiful movement that swept across the United States at the turn of the century. Florida was changing, but this was only a whisper of the changes that were to come during the 1920s and 1930s. Transportation improvements were then, as always, the catalyst to development.[114] The railroads had carried thousands of people to the subtropical resorts, but the dawning of the automobile age and the so-called "tin cans" (automobiles, often with trailers) brought additional thousands of people to Florida. These transportation improvements opened the gates to massive change.

Beginning in 1920, the Sunshine State experienced the greatest real estate boom the nation had yet seen. Hundreds of thousands of lots were sold. Plans for lavish settlements and new towns were backed by wealthy entrepreneurs. Land speculation reached unforeseen heights. By the middle of the decade, the economics of land development had been overplayed, and the development boom came crashing down, bringing with it scores of bank closures and leaving communities in heavily bonded debt.[115] Hurricanes added to the woe, and the national depression, which began in 1928, solidified the collapse. The age of Florida's lavish design plans collapsed, too.

President Roosevelt, in attempting to lead the nation out of the depression, instituted his New Deal policies, among which was the attempt to institutionalize public planning at the national, interstate, state, and local levels of government. This was not the lavish local urban design planning of the 1920s. Instead, it was an attempt by governments—under the leadership of the national planning office—to set their own houses in order through the vehicle of public planning, a long-range component of public management; in a more limited sense, a specialized reincarnation of the good government movement that occurred at the turn of the century. Sponsored by the New Deal, participation in state and county-level public planning in Florida and across the nation rose sharply—and disappeared just as quickly when federal funding dried up. Left behind by this short-term experience were multiple lessons—from both successes and failures—that might have proved valuable to later generations.

Among the questions that the lessons generated was how can public planning be an effective tool for public management within the constraints of minimal government responsibility, rampant land speculation, and minimal interference with private property? And how can executive planning be helpful without the mandate of coordination among agencies which may have conflicting agendas? However, most of the questions and the possible lessons to be learned from them became lost as the nation—and Florida—focused a Cyclops eye on a different priority: industrial development and the jobs it could create.

NOTES FOR CHAPTER III

1   Florida State Planning Board, *County Planning: Florida: A Handbook of Local Planning Procedure,* Tallahassee, 1939, p. 4.

2   For a general account of early planning in America see Olmstead, Frederick L., Jr., "The Town-Planning Movement in America," *Housing and Town Planning, The Annals* 51: 1914, pp. 172-181. His famous father was the co-designer of Central Park in New York City, and among his many other projects were the U.S. Capitol grounds in Washington, DC, the Biltmore Estate in Asheville, NC, and the chapel at Duke University. Frederick Law Olmstead, Jr., went on to become a celebrated planner in his own right. One of his achievements was serving as the first president of the American City Planning Institute in 1917.

3   Ibid, p. 173.

4   Gerckens, Laurence Conway, "Historical development of American city planning," in Frank S. So, et al., *The Practice of Local Government Planning*, Washington, DC: The International City Management Association, 1979, p. 24.

5   Kreuckeberg, Donald A. ed., *Introduction to Planning History in the United States*, New Brunswick, NJ: The Center for Urban Policy Research, Rutgers University, 1983, p. 6. His words have been shortened for convenience; the quotation in full is "...one of sanitation and scientific efficiency, a second of civic beauty and the building arts, and a third of social equity and charity."

6   Starnes, Earl, "The Relationship of Architecture and Planning," in Joseph Wilkes, ed., *The Encyclopedia of Architecture*, Vol. 1, New York: John Wiley, 1988, p. 348. See also Jon A. Peterson, *The Birth of City Planning in the United States, 1840-1917*, Baltimore: The Johns Hopkins University Press, 2003, p. 131.

7   Peterson, Jon A., "The City Beautiful Movement: Forgotten Origins and Lost Meanings," in Krueckeberg, ibid, p. 53.

8   Gerckens, ibid, pp. 24 and 31.

9   Robinson, Charles Mulford, in John Nolen, ed., *City Planning: A Series of Papers Presenting the Essential Elements of a City Plan*, New York: D. Appleton and Company, 1917, p. 407; see also, Gerckens, ibid, pp. 34-35.

10 Burnett, Gene M., "St. Pete's Visionary Town Planner," *Florida's Past: People & Events that Shaped the State*, Vol. 3, Sarasota, FL: Pineapple Press, 1991, pp. 19-21.

11 Wilson, William H., "The Plan of Chicago," in Kreuckeberg, ibid, p. 88.

12 Babcock, Richard F., *The Zoning Game*, Madison, WI: University of Wisconsin Press, 1966, p. 3.

13 272 U.S. 365, 1926.

14 Gerckens, ibid, 40. See also Mel Scott, *American City Planning Since 1890*, Berkeley, CA: University of California Press, 1969, p. 243; see also Starnes, ibid, p. 349.

15 Gerckens, ibid, p. 40.

16 Babcock, Richard F. and Charles L. Siemon, *The Zoning Game Revisited*, Cambridge, MA: Lincoln Institute of Land Policy, p. 261.

17 Merino, James A., "Cooperative Schemes for Greater Boston: 1890-1920, *The New England Quarterly* 45: 2, 1972, pp. 196-226.

18 American Planning Association, "The Evolution of City Planning," in Roger L. Kemp, ed., *Forms of Local Government: A Handbook on City, County and Regional Options*, Jefferson, N.C.: McFarland, 1999, p. 160.

19 Wilson, ibid, p. 96.

20 The Regional Plan Association still exists.

21 Lewis Mumford as referenced in Wilson, "Plan of Chicago," p. 101.

22 U.S. National Resources Committee, *Regional Factors in National Planning*, Washington, DC: USGPO, 1935, p. 18.

23 Lepawsky, Albert, *State Planning and Economic Development in the South*, National Planning Association Committee of the South Report No. 4, Kingsport, TN: Kingsport Press, 1949, pp. 8-9.

24 Crane, Jacob, "Whither State Planning," paper delivered at the National Conference on City Planning, Pittsburgh, PA, November 16, 1932, in Harold F. Wise, *History of State Planning—An Interpretive Commentary*, Washington, DC: Council of State Planning Agencies, an affiliate of the National Governors' Association, 1977, p. 10. Also see Aelred J. Gray, chairman, "The States Begin to Plan," from proceedings of the American Institute of Planners annual conference, 1963, and Raymond J. Burby and Peter J. May, *Making Governments Plan*, Baltimore: Johns Hopkins University Press, 1997, Table 1.1, p. 4. Though not state level planning, it should be noted that California mandated city and county master plans as early as 1937.

25 Olausen, Stephan A., *Sebring, City on a Circle*, St. Augustine, FL: Southern Heritage Press, 1993, p. 32.

26 Ch. 8537, *1921 Florida Laws 332*; the Butler Act clarified the Riparian Rights Act of 1856, Ch. 791, *Laws of Florida*, 1856.

27 See especially Wulbern, Allan E., "Improvements Under Florida's Butler Act: Can We Have a Definition Please?" *Journal of Land Use & Environmental Law* 14: 2, 1999, pp. 249-274.

28 The land attack on the Everglades had begun in the early 1900s when its wetlands were peddled to buyers in the northern states; see Burnett, ibid, pp. 199-201.

29   As reported in Mormino, Gary R., *Land of Sunshine, State of Dreams: A Social History of Modern Florida*, Gainesville, FL: University Press of Florida, 2005, p. 44.

30   Fuller, Walter P., *This Was Florida's Boom*, St. Petersburg, FL: Times Publishing Co., 1954, p. 1.

31   Boorstin, Daniel J., *The Americans: The Democratic Experience*, New York, NY: Vintage Books, 1973, p. 278.

32   Burnett, Gene M., ibid, Vol. 1, Sarasota, FL: Pineapple Press, 1986, p. 232.

33   Ibid.

34   Florida Department of Public Instruction, *The WPA Guide to Florida: The Federal Writers' Project Guide to 1930s Florida*, New York: Pantheon Books, 1939, p. 61.

35   Cox, Merlin G. and J.E. Dovell, *Florida from Secession to the Space Age*, St. Petersburg, FL: Great Outdoor Publishing Company, 1974, p. 166.

36   Burnett, ibid, pp. 5-8.

37   Nolen, John, "Report on Comprehensive City Plan for Sarasota, Florida," Harvard Square, Cambridge, MA, 1925, p. 5.

38   Burnett, ibid, Vol. 3, p. 21.

39   "Kelsey City Preservation," West Palm Beach, FL, June 4, 1981.

40   Merrick, George E., "Coral Gables," Coral Gables, FL: Parker Art Printing Association, 1924.

41   Facsimile and email from Donna Lubin, Director of Historical Resources, Coral Gables, FL, on August 11, 2003.

42   Nolen, ibid.

43   Jahoda, Gloria, *Florida: A History*, New York, NY: W.W. Norton & Company, 1986, p. 47.

44   Bennett, Parsons & Frost, Consulting Architects, Chicago, *The Plan of Palm Beach*, Chicago: Bennett, 1930.

45   Burnett, ibid, Vol. 2, 1988, p. 33.

46   Ibid, p. 36.

47   Ibid, p. 37.

48   Burnett, ibid, in reference to Merrick in Vol. 3, p. 168; to Fisher in Vol. 1, p. 206; and to Mizner in Vol. 2, p. 37.

49   Florida Planning & Zoning Association, 2003, "The History of Florida Planning & Zoning Association," obtained from http://www.fpza.org/fpza/history.html, on October 23, 2003.

50   U.S. National Resources Planning Board, "State Legislation on Planning, Zoning and Platting," September 10, 1939, pp. 9-13.

51   Bartley, Ernest and William W. Bayer, Jr., "Municipal Zoning: Florida Law and Practice," Gainesville, FL: Public Administration Clearing House, 1950, p. 15.

52 *Village of Euclid* (Ohio) *v. Ambler Realty Company*, 272 U.S. 365, 1926.

53 Bartley and Bayer, Jr., ibid, p. 15.

54 The hurricane of 1928 killed 1,836 people in southeast Florida; it was the second-deadliest hurricane in U.S. history. Source: National Oceanic and Atmospheric Administration via www.infoplease.com/ipa/A0778120.html.

55 From the inaugural speech by Governor Doyle E. Carlton, as it appeared in the Jacksonville *Florida Times Union* on January 9, 1929, and used in Patricia Lasche Clements, *Legacy of Leadership: Florida Governors and Their Inaugural Speeches*, Tallahassee, FL: Sentry Press, 2004, p. 205. Governor Napoleon B. Broward had made a similar statement in his inaugural speech of January 4, 1905; see Patricia Lasche Clements, ibid, p. 113.

56 Colburn, David R. and Lance deHaven-Smith, *Government in the Sunshine State: Florida Since Statehood,* Gainesville, FL: University Press of Florida, 1999, p. 29.

57 Ibid.

58 Ibid, p. 30.

59 Black, Russell Van Nest, *Planning and the Planning Profession: The Past Fifty Years 1917-1967*, Washington, DC: American Institute of Planners, 1967, p. 7.

60 73rd Congress, Session 1, ch. 90.

61 *A.L.A. Schechter Poultry Corp. v. U.S.*, 295 U.S. 495.

62 Beckman, Norman, "Federal Long-Range Planning: The Heritage of the National Resources Planning Board," *Journal of the American Institute of Planners* XXVI: 2, 1960, p. 90; see also Lepawsky, ibid, p. 13.

63 For a comprehensive review and bibliography of national planning efforts in the United States see David E. Wilson, *The National Planning Idea in U.S. Public Policy: Five Alternative Approaches* and its companion *National Planning in the United States: An Annotated Bibliography*, both published in Boulder, CO, by Westview Press, 1980.

64 Otis L. Graham, Jr., *Toward a Planned Society: From Roosevelt to Nixon*, New York, NY: Oxford University Press, 1976, pp. 52-53. President Roosevelt had intended to set up a three-member board made up of his uncle, Frederick Delano, economist Wesley Mitchell, and Charles Merriam, a political scientist, without cabinet involvement.

65 Somers, Herman Miles, *Presidential Agency: The Office of War Mobilization and Reconversion,* Cambridge, MA: Harvard University Press, 1950, p. 205.

66 Graham, ibid, pp. 52-56.

67 Lepawsky, ibid, p. 26.

68 Wilson, David E., ibid, p. 36.

69 Lepawsky, ibid, p. 124.

70 Ibid, p. 11.

71 So, Frank S., Irving Hand, and Bruce D. McDowell, eds., *The Practice of State and Regional Planning*, Chicago: American Planning Association and the International City Management Association, 1985, p. 54.

72 U.S. National Resources Planning Board, ibid, p. 1.

73 Lepawsky, ibid, pp. 14-15.

74 Howard, John T., "Summary Report on Survey of State Planning," Massachusetts Institute of Technology, unpublished paper, 1937, p. 3.

75 Curry, Tilden, *The State Comprehensive Plan: An Evaluation of Its Relevance to Public Decision-Making and State Planning Methodology*, doctorial dissertation, Department of Urban and Regional Planning, Florida State University, 1978, p. 81.

76 Ibid, p. 14.

77 Howard, ibid, p. 8.

78 Ibid.

79 U.S. National Resources Committee, *The Future of State Planning*, Washington, D.C.: USGPO, 1938, p. 12.

80 U.S. National Resources Committee, ibid, p. 10.

81 U.S. National Resources Committee, ibid, p.1.

82 Lepawsky, ibid, p. 115.

83 Howard, ibid, p. 8; see also, Beckman, ibid, p. 93.

84 Lepawsky, ibid, p. 17.

85 The RPAA was led by noted thinkers like Benton MacKaye, Lewis Mumford, and Clarence Stein. For more on the RPAA see various volumes of the *Journal of Planning History*.

86 U.S. Advisory Commission on Intergovernmental Relations, *Regional Decision Making*, Washington, DC: USGPO, 1973, pp. 53-55. Countywide planning agencies were considered to be regional bodies at that time.

87 U.S. National Resources Planning Board, *National Resources Development Report for 1943*, Washington, DC: Superintendent of Documents, 1943, p. 58.

88 U.S. National Resources Planning Board, "Post-War Planning," Washington, DC: Superintendent of Documents, c. 1942, p. 1.

89 U.S. National Resources Planning Board, *National Resources Development Report for 1943*, ibid, p. 82.

90 Curry, ibid, p. 86.
91 Beckman, p. 90.
92 Somers, ibid, p. 1.
93 Beckman, p. 97.
94 U.S. National Resources Committee, *State Planning*, Washington, DC: USGPO, 1936, p. 18.
95 Lepawsky, ibid, p. 28.
96 Abbott, Carl, *The New Urban America*, Chapel Hill, NC: The University of North Carolina Press. 1981, p. 101.
97 Ibid.
98 Ibid.
99 Ibid, p. 105.
100 Curry, ibid, (see footnote 2, p. 148) *Laws of Florida*, Acts of 1933, vol. 1, Chapter 17275. The State Planning Board in 1936 consisted of five members: A.B. Dooley, chairman, a citizen member; C.B. Treadway, ex officio member; Walter S. Hammons, member at large; Mrs. M. M. Ebert, member at large; and Fred C. Elliot, a state employee of the Trustees of the Internal Improvement Fund. M. L. Montgomery served as executive secretary and W. T. Wallis was an associate consultant; these names are listed in U.S. National Resources Committee, State Planning: Programs and Accomplishments, Washington, DC: USGPO, 1937, p. 11.
101 Ch. 17275, §§ 8 and 9, *Laws of Florida*, Acts of 1935, "Authority for the creation of County Planning Boards. City planning boards could participate, but they needed to obtain authorization to plan through special acts of their legislature.
102 Cornwell, Robert, ed., *Planning Digest* 1: 1, Florida State Planning Board, September 1936-April 1937.
103 Ch. 17275, §§ 8 and 9, ibid. See especially, Florida State Planning Board, "County Planning in Florida: A Handbook of Local Planning Procedure," Tallahassee, 1939, pp. 19-20.
104 Florida State Planning Board, ibid, p. 4.
105 Ch. 17275, §§ 8 and 9, ibid.
106 U.S. National Resources Committee, *State Planning* ..., ibid, pp. 11-12; pages 102-103 of this report contain a bibliography of twenty-five Florida State Planning Board reports.
107 Cornwell, Planning *Digest*, 1: 4, ibid, p. 4.
108 U.S. National Resources Planning Board, "Current Programs of Work: State Planning Boards," Washington, DC, mimeographed, pp. 35-38.
109 Curry, ibid, p. 149.
110 Ibid.
111 Colburn and deHaven-Smith, ibid, p. 13.

112 Florida State Planning Board, "Florida Communities: Their Problems, Their Future," Postwar Planning Bulletin No. 2, Tallahassee, January 1944, p. 1.

113 See Seth Bramson, "Railroads, by Henry!" in *Yesterday in Florida*, number 19, Fall 2004, pp. 23-26, for coverage of how "the Three Henrys" (Henry Sanford, Henry Plant, and Henry Flagler) opened Florida to railroad development.

114 See, for example, Rembert W. Patrick, *Florida Under Five Flags*, Gainesville, FL: University of Florida Press, pp. 63-71.

115 See Walter P. Fuller, ibid; see pp. 54-57, for a discussion of bank foreclosures in Pinellas County.

CHAPTER IV

A PERIOD OF QUIESENCE

Mid 1940s to Late 1950s

> Planning is the continuous application of knowl-
> edge, foresight and common sense in the pursuit
> of clearly defined and properly related objectives.
> It is a process which treats the problems of the
> community as a related whole. It defines attain-
> able long range objectives and furnishes guidance
> for day to day decisions. ... It makes it possible to
> foresee impending needs and to deal with them
> before they become crises.[1] (Frederick H. Bair, Jr.,
> 1951.)

Following World War II the national economy rode an upsurge fueled by the wartime economy. Men were working,
women were working, and military personnel were returning
to their civilian jobs or continuing their education. The mood
of the nation was on the upswing of a pendulum of industrial
development. It was a time of change from a wartime economy
to a rising and promising peacetime economy: change from
dependence on rail for transport of materials and goods to the
more flexible advantages of truck transportation, and change
from high-density, center-city industrial development to
sprawling plants in the countryside. In the years following
the war, cities and states competed for new industries—often
pirating industries from one part of the country to another
(e.g., the flight of the textile industries from New England to
the Piedmont of the Carolinas). With the assistance of the
Federal Housing Administration and the housing assistance
program of the Veterans Administration, new subdivisions
laid out in non-urban places (e.g., Levittown, New York) added
to the expansion of urban areas. A new and virulent form of

sprawl had begun, and the positive—and negative—features of rapid growth and population mobility spread with it.

As interest in peacetime industrial development accelerated, interest in public planning decelerated. Planning was entering a period of quiescence. State planning boards found themselves being slipped into newly created state industrial improvement commissions, regional planning almost disappeared, and it seemed that only the largest or most progressive of cities retained an interest in planning. In his 1947 book titled *State Planning and Economic Development in the South*, Albert Lepawsky noted that by the end of the war the development urge overshadowed the planning approach.[2] It was clear to him that when the functions are combined, interest in economic development dominates and generally dampens or suppresses planning.[3] Economic development has greater potential for satisfying immediate wants and needs (e.g., job creation and opportunities for making money on land development) and thus generates greater interest.

Given this scenario, we move to a discussion of the spread of urbanization, a fitting—though partial—background for why the federal government initiated a broad range of categorical grant-in-aid programs for local governments. Among these grant-in-aid programs were the urban renewal program, the 701 planning assistance grant program,[4] and a cornucopia of other grants providing financial assistance for local infrastructure and other services. Our attention will be on the 701 planning assistance program and its expansion beyond its initial intent. This was the federal program that fostered a resurgence of involvement in planning—albeit unenthusiastically on the part of many state and local governments. Thereafter, we turn our attention to the impact of this program on Florida, and the generally reluctant but gradual rejuvenation of planning in the state.

Suburbanization

Urban sprawl was not a new phenomenon: for decades if not centuries,[5] some variant of sprawl occurred with the advent of each new advance in transportation technology. In his book on the appearance of residential suburbs on the outskirts of Boston, Henry C. Binford provides examples of suburbanization from 1815-1860.[6] Kenneth Jackson, writing about the history of suburban America, found similar development tendencies across the United States.[7] But in the period immediately following World War II, urban sprawl took hold like it never had before.

Before the war, most of the nation's factories were located in high-density industrial areas near the center of cities. These industrial buildings depended on local waterpower, rail transport, and dense residential neighborhoods to house the workers. All this was about to change. During the early years of the war some industries dispersed into more scattered locations for defensive reasons, thus creating industrial job opportunities in places apart from large urban industrial centers. Industrial decentralization left older industrial sections near the center of cities to sit idle and decay. This decay spread to central city businesses and lower-income residential neighborhoods whose workers had been dependent on jobs in close-by factories and shopping at central city retail stores. While economic growth was good for suburban America, it was just the opposite for the central areas of older cities.

Improved highways, increased reliance on truck transport, affordable automobiles, and federal backing for home mortgage insurance were among the significant new ingredients to the recipe of sprawl. Trolley car, passenger rail, and even bus ridership plummeted. To Alan A. Altshuler, "the mass conversion to auto travel seemed to be relentless."[8] Elaborating on this point and using Minneapolis and St. Paul as examples, he noted, "Auto registrations in the Twin Cities area increased by 58 percent in the years 1947-1950 alone (twenty times the rate of increase during the previous two decades)."[9] The picture was much the same throughout America. The conversion to road traffic would get a further boost from the Federal Aid Highway Act of 1956 (also called the National System of Interstate and Defense Highways),[10] which featured the creation of a limited access interstate highway system. This road system had an immense impact on the use of land in America, leading to theretofore unfathomable spread of population and economic activity—and unforeseen pressures upon agriculture, forestry, and the natural environment.

The Federal Aid Highway Act had greater impact on the physical development of the nation than any previous development policy since the federal land grants giving railroad companies alternating sections along railroad rights-of-way. As biographer Stephen Ambrose stated in President Dwight Eisenhower's memoir, *Mandate for Change: 1953-1956*:

> More than any single action by governments since the end of the war [World War II], this one would change the face of America ... Its impact on the American Economy—the jobs it would produce in manufacturing and construction, the rural areas it will open up—was beyond calculation.[11]

Eisenhower enthusiastically supported the authorization to fund the Interstate Highway System. After all, he had been highly impressed by what he had seen of the German Autobahn, begun by Adolph Hitler in the early 1930s.[12] In 1955, Eisenhower observed, "Together, the united forces of our communication and transportation systems are dynamic elements in the very name we bear—United States. Without them, we would be a mere alliance of many separate parts."[13]

The interstate system, indeed, has brought the parts closer together.

The impact was significant in Florida. Broad bands of transportation corridors ripped through central cities like Miami and Tampa; the displacement of housing, churches, neighborhood groceries, and historic social and economic networks caused concern over destruction of the existing urban structure. On the other hand, elected officials in then-rural counties (e.g., Pasco County) adjacent to urban counties saw the development of interchange service areas as a boost to local economies. In a way they were, but in time, the character of these counties changed from rural to suburban and public costs rose. Riding sidecar to this change were problems of mismanaged or under-managed growth: traffic jams, billboard jungles, inadequate public facilities and services, crowded schools, inadequate housing for low-income families, and severe degradation of the natural environment.

This rural-to-urban metamorphosis occurred in counties adjacent to Atlanta, Boston, Denver, Milwaukee, St. Louis, Seattle, and other large cities throughout the nation. The problem was not that these counties began to grow, but rather in the haphazard, public revenue-demanding way in which they grew. The Federal Aid Highway Act of 1956 was changing the face of the nation. Developers were eager to focus on interchanges to locate motels, restaurants, service stations, and other highway related commercial developments. Orjan Wetterqvist, former professor of planning at the University of Florida, used the phrase, "A new highway culture has emerged with the Interstate Highway system."[14] It also fueled a frenzy of land speculation and subsequent sprawl that is yet to ebb.

Stimulated by the convenience of the interstate system and assisted by the residential mortgage insurance program provided through the U.S. Housing Act of 1934[15] and the home loan program of the Servicemen's Readjustment

Act of 1944 (the G.I. Bill),[16] urban sprawl spread its tentacles in a land-grabbing way never before experienced. Almost without realizing it, communities that once were relatively independent, self-sustaining units became subservient pieces of a larger urban whole. The majority of American people found themselves living in an interdependent web of metropolitan communities. They resided in one community, worked in another, and socialized in others. Peoples' livelihoods and lifestyles were being woven into a regional mesh.

Urban redevelopment/renewal

The 1940 U.S. census made it obvious that blight and decay had become commonplace in many of the older center cities, but it was beyond the political and fiscal capabilities of most urban municipalities and urbanized counties to adequately address the problem. While the new suburban communities saw themselves as economically opportunistic, the inner cities found themselves economically landlocked. Restrictive annexation laws and permissive incorporation laws left them no room to grow geographically. The tax base was going up for one and down for the other. Middle and upper income residents were fleeing the central cities for suburbia. To retain these greater spenders and higher property taxpayers and reverse the spread of blight and slums, advocates of center city dominance called for redevelopment.[17] Between 1941 and 1948, legislatures in twenty-five states responded by passing some form of urban redevelopment act, but only two states went so far as to provide financing for slum clearance.[18]

During the same period, a debate raged in the national capital over whether redevelopment should simply address the clearing of slums for economic development or whether it should include provision of public housing, as well. During World War II, Congress had cut off funds for the public housing program authorized under the U.S. Housing Act of

1937.[19] The funds were diverted to defense purposes rather than low-income housing. In addition, the war created a slump in the private home building industry. As Harvard professor Alexander von Hoffman noted, "The long drought in residential building had created a housing shortage that would only become worse when the soldiers returned from the war."[20] The private home market would resuscitate itself with the help of the home mortgage insurance program and the G.I. Bill, but conflicts would continue to rage over the need for public housing.

It was not until 1949 that things began to come together for the supporters of public housing as part of urban redevelopment. In the 1948 presidential campaign, President Harry S. Truman, who was running against Governor Thomas E. Dewey of New York, made public housing the centerpiece of his campaign. To the surprise of voting analysts, Truman won the election. With the assistance of housing organizations, social welfare groups, trade unions, and the U.S. Conference of Mayors, this provided the momentum that resulted in the enactment of the U.S. Housing Act of 1949.[21] However, it was, as von Hoffman put it, "a shotgun wedding between enemy lobbying groups."[22] In other words, an accord was reached, but differing opinions had yet to meld.

The Housing Act of 1949 authorized federal assistance for redevelopment, reinstalled the public housing program of 1937, and reorganized and expanded the loan program under the U.S. Farm Tenant Act of 1937.[23] The "headline" of the act promoted the goal of a decent home and suitable living environment for every American family, a goal often still referred to, but as history shows us, a goal difficult to attain. Given the long battle over whether redevelopment (e.g., slum clearance) should include public housing, it is not surprising that the law took only a small step toward that goal.[24] The goals of the newer housing act seemed promising, but a number of factors, especially the outbreak of the Korean War and real estate industry opposition to its implementation, contributed to a delay in starting the program. Thus, only a few municipalities were able to take their redevelopment projects past the planning stage.[25]

The urban redevelopment section of the housing act required that a project area be either 55 percent residential at the time of the application *or* 55 percent residential when redeveloped.[26] The ambiguity (or purposeful flexibility?) created by the use of the word "or" resulted in some of the projects being completed with little if any housing, particularly low-income housing. Many of the projects ended up as primarily industrial or commercial land uses or higher-income residential uses. One of the key changes in the Housing Act provided for slum prevention as well as slum clearance, which made it possible to include areas that were not run-down, by claiming they could potentially become slums. G. William Domhoff believes that this provision, "freed local growth machines to move ahead with their plans."[27] Whether this was an example of Molotch's growth machine theory (sometimes called "growth coalition theory") at work is arguable, but in his study of urban renewal in Atlanta, Clarence Stone arrived at a position similar to that of Domhoff. Stone concluded that land exploitation is the key issue in local politics, and urban renewal is "part of a general struggle over the control of land."[28] In separate works, Clarence Gelfand, John H. Mollenkopf, and Jon A. Peterson also reported on the eagerness of downtown realty and business interests for commercial redevelopment.[29] It does seem that Molotch's growth machine was at work.[30]

The federal urban redevelopment program may have had the support of downtown real estate developers and local elected officials, but the program faced the wrath of both sides of the political spectrum. From the political Right, Martin Anderson objected to the principle that government could take someone's private property and give it to another (e.g., a developer) for personal profit.[31] Among those contributing from the Left were Jane Jacobs and Herbert Gans who argued against the trend of tearing down low-income neighborhoods to create luxury housing and non-residential uses.[32] They defended the need for better housing for low-income people, but without destroying existing neighborhoods in the process. Urban redevelopment has remained a controversial issue to this day.

The redevelopment aspect of the 1949 law often required participating local governments to use the power of eminent domain to secure properties from reluctant sellers within the project area. Eminent domain is a power granted to local governments by state governments to allow them to take property for a public purpose. How far the power could go was in question, especially concerning the interpretation of the words *public purpose*. For example, according to renowned planner Fred Bair, the State of Florida at this time, "did not have a valid act for slum clearance and urban renewal ... despite several attempts to pass such legislation."[33] The reason for this, he said, was that, "Back in 1952, in the case of *Adams vs. The Housing Authority of Daytona Beach*, the urban renewal situation in Florida got all fouled up."[34] The Daytona Housing Authority had proposed clearing six and a half acres of residential slums and then selling the property for non-residential development. The Florida Supreme Court sided with the plaintiff in deciding that the proposal would be for private, not public, gain and profit. But, as Bair exclaimed, the court "went on and threw the baby out with the bathwater."[35] It declared the whole act unconstitutional, thus, the statute could not be used, even for low-cost housing. Urban renewal programs in Daytona Beach, Jacksonville, Lakeland, Orlando, Panama City, and Tampa had to stop where they were. There were various attempts over the next five years to revive the act, but to no avail until the legislature passed a special enabling act for Tampa in 1957. The act was challenged, but in 1959 the Florida Supreme Court found the Tampa law constitutional, thus reopening the door for urban renewal projects throughout the state.[36]

Many of the problems of the U.S. Housing Act of 1949 were thought to be resolved by the amendments included in the Housing Act of 1954.[37] One of the principal amendments stipulated that federal aid for urban renewal would be available only to projects that were a part of a "workable program". A basic premise of the new housing act was, "that there is no justification for Federal assistance except to cities which will face up to the whole problem of urban decay and undertake long-range programs to eliminate present blight and prevent the formation of future slums."[38] Facing up to the *whole problem* meant addressing the community as a whole, not just the area proposed for redevelopment. Preparing a comprehensive plan was one of the requirements of a workable program. The need for a plan had been alluded to in the Housing Act of 1949 but never fully implemented.[39] The 1954 act provided a new starting point for urban planning.

Section 701 Planning Assistance

Like Title II of the National Industrial Recovery Act of 1933, Section 701 of the Housing Act of 1954 stimulated interest in planning, but for a different purpose. The section read in part:

> To facilitate urban planning for *smaller communities* lacking adequate planning resources, the Administrator is authorized to make planning grants to *State Planning agencies* for the provision of planning assistance (including surveys, land use studies, urban renewal plans, technical services and other planning work, but excluding plans for specific public works) to cities and other municipalities that have a population of less than

25,000 according to the latest decennial census. The administrator is further authorized to make planning grants for similar planning work in *metropolitan and regional areas* to official State, metropolitan or regional planning agencies empowered under State laws to perform such planning.[40] (Italics added for emphasis.)

Initially, Section 701 made planning assistance funds available only to municipalities under 25,000 population on the assumption that larger municipalities were capable of generating their own funds for planning. Carl Feiss, who helped write Section 701, reported that many of the larger cities had adequate planning staffs and commissions, but the status of planning in smaller cities was appalling.[41] However, over the ensuing years, the scope of the 701 program gradually expanded to include all cities; counties; metropolitan, regional and interstate planning commissions; Indian reservations; and, in 1959, state governments.

Once again, the federal government had taken the lead in calling for planning. It saw planning as a means for ensuring that legal governments managed federal grants for infrastructure and other improvements as efficiently and effectively as possible. It was understandably reluctant to hand out financial aid without some assurance the funds would be used with more foresight than local and state governments might otherwise exercise. The National Municipal League agreed when it wrote, "Foresight is an essential ingredient of good government as it is of good business."[42] From the federal perspective, planning was a vehicle for a foresightful, yet fiscally conservative approach to handing out financial assistance.

In order for local governments to be eligible to receive 701 planning assistance, it was necessary for each state to designate a state planning agency to administer the program. The responsible state agency was to be the middleman in three-party contracts: the first contract was between the federal government and the administering state agency, the second between the state agency and the local government seeking a grant, and the third between the state and the consultant selected by the local government to do the planning for the local body.[43] "Administering" meant administrative oversight of the contracts from start to finish. To qualify as a state planning agency the agency had to have in place the statutory authority to participate in planning-related activities and to have a competent professional staff to administer the program. However, in the mid-1950s only a handful of the old 1930s state planning commissions were still in existence to be designated to administer the 701 funds.[44] In other states, such as Vermont, legal searches by state attorneys general often found a legally usable planning clause somewhere in state law that had not been stricken when the planning statutes were converted into state economic development statutes. Some states lacked the authority to participate in planning-related activities at the state level or were deficient in the number of professional planners needed to administer the program competently. Such states had to first satisfy these requirements before their local governments could take advantage of the federal planning assistance monies. Eventually, every state authorized a state planning agency to be the intermediary in 701 three-party contracts. Metropolitan or regional planning agencies could receive the assistance directly, as long as they were legally empowered to plan.

Most small local governments were not enthusiastic about preparing a comprehensive plan, but they did so because it was often a prerequisite for other federal aid grants. The prevailing attitude of many local government officials was that the 701 planning program was merely an administrative hurdle to overcome. They saw little value in planning beyond opening the door to other federal grants; to them, planning was not an essential component of management. Getting financing for infrastructure and development projects was more immediate to their needs—especially their political survival. Jon A. Peterson noted that "comprehensive planning ... survived more as a program requirement than as the framework for actions."[45] Once the federal planning requirement was completed, the plans were usually shelved with hardly a later reference made to them. They became infamous for gathering dust.

The 701 planning process did have subtle, lasting effects, however. One of its greatest benefits was its educational value: citizens were tuning-in to planning. A requirement that citizens have opportunities to be involved in the process made planning a participatory process. As a result, interested citizens came to understand the value of foresight in local decision-making. Some of these interested citizens also came to realize that their local government was not an island unto itself, but merely one facet in a larger, interconnected whole. Several of these early citizen planners eventually became advocates for the growth management movement that began in the 1970s. Feiss saw the '701' program as helping to "establish the planning function at all levels of government and give it public standing as an essential element in promoting the general welfare."[46] Thus, the program set in motion an incrementally escalating educational process that today is one of the most beneficial features of planning.

State Planning

Interest in planning for state government itself began to resurface across a number of fronts in the 1950s. Among its partisans was Coleman Ransome who, in addressing responsibilities of governors in 1951, suggested that a governor "is or should be concerned with long range plans and programs for the development of a state's human and natural resources."[47] Interest expanded further in 1953 when the American Institute of Planners (now known as the American

Planning Association) supported the use of planning as a tool of management science.[48] The word "management" had greater meaning to chief executives. The Council of State Governments added its influence in 1955 when it issued a report recommending that "each state establish an Office of Planning Services in the executive branch of the state government, either in the office of the governor or coequal with the budget office in an integrated Department of Administration or Finance."[49] The barometer of support rose even higher in 1958 when the American Institute of Planners produced a report called, "State Planning: Its Function and Organization."[50] The list of advocates for state-level planning was growing gradually.

The growing support for a rebirth of state planning culminated in a 1959 amendment to Section 701 of the Housing Act of 1954 that authorized resumption of federal support for state planning. The first grant was given to Alaska, but it was Hawaii—under its own initiative—that was the first state to complete a comprehensive plan: The General Plan for the State of Hawaii, prepared in 1960.[51] The principal objective of the plan was to save the state's agricultural industry from urban development pressures. It was a land use plan that supported state government-imposed zoning districts, a giant step toward managing growth, an extent to which no other states were willing to go. However, it was not long before other states initiated 701 supported state planning projects, even though these efforts were far less pervasive and controlling than Hawaii's plan.

The concept of planning as a management tool, as espoused by the Council of State Governments and others, was different from planning under the 701 program, which was loosely based on the physical land use-oriented local planning model of the 1920s. Thus, as the 1950s ended and the 1960s began two different strains of state planning were emerging: one based on the physical land use model and the other more oriented to policy management. The availability of federal 701 planning assistance would lead to considerable state-level planning activity in the 1960s, with some states going with the 701 model, others with a more management-oriented focus, and still others attempting to combine the two approaches. Florida was to try all three approaches.

Recognizing that many states would need to reintroduce or rewrite their planning statutes following the enactment of Section 701 of the Housing Act of 1954, the National Municipal League prepared model state and regional planning legislation for state legislatures to consider. Even though the principal focus of this organization was municipal, they also recognized that state government and regional—as well as local—entities needed to be involved in the planning mix:

> The more governments do, the more complex their programs become and the more points at which they tie in with each other and with private organizations and enterprises, the greater is the need for analyzing and improving their methods, of avoiding conflicts and work at cross purposes, of foreseeing problems, of devising ways and means of dealing effectively with them, of fitting together the many departmental and functional activities into consistent, harmonious programs. In short, the greater is the need for planning.[52]

This advice from a national municipal organization was written in 1955; it would take some states twenty or more years to begin to some kind of proper intergovernmental planning mix, though some states continue to ignore this advice.

Stimulating Florida's Interest in Planning

In an economic sense, World War II was kind to Florida in that it brought military bases with their support services, both military and civilian. Florida found that defense contracts would be limited, but its climate made her a valuable resource for military training grounds.[53] The war became a catalyst for Florida's postwar growth: the state's population more than doubled in the two decades between 1940 and 1960. In the 1930s, the Sunshine State's population had grown 29.2 percent, whereas the rate of growth spurted to 46.1 percent during the 1940s, and skyrocketed by 78.7 percent in the decade from 1950-1960 (see Figure IV-1). This equates to an increase of 118 persons per day in the 1930s, 239 per day in the 1940s, and 597 per day in the 1950s, five times that of the 1930s. Florida was riding the initial swell of a tsunami of rapid growth. This was the beginning of what one author called "Florida's Big Bang".[54]

Figure IV-1
Florida's Rate of Population Increase: 1930-1960
By Decade

Category	1940	1950	1960
Percent population increase over prior decade	29.2	46.1	78.7
Numerical population increase *per day* during prior decade (e.g., 1930s)	118	239	597
Total population at the end of the decade	1,897,414	2,771,305	4,951,560

The population explosion that occurred following World War II was the consequence of a number of factors; foremost were the lasting impacts of the wartime economy, a more affluent society, returning veterans who had enjoyed Florida while stationed there, retirees, air conditioning, increased mobility, and the changes to transport and industrialization discussed earlier in this chapter. These factors, combined with the absence of a state income tax and a homestead exemption on residential property assessments (approved by a 1934 constitutional amendment), all contributed to the rapid in-migration of people to the Sunshine State.

Before the war, there were eight military bases in Florida, but the number of military installations increased to 172 by 1943.[55] Military bases and support facilities were established throughout the state: for example, Camp Blanding, near Starke, became one of the largest training bases in the Southeast; liberty ships were built in Tampa; there was a submarine chaser training center in Miami; Jimmy Doolittle's bomber pilots trained for their raid on Japan at Eglin Field, near Pensacola; and the all-black, 99th Fighter Squadron trained at Dale Mabry Field in Tallahassee. French and Chinese cadets also trained in Florida. Amphibious training was held at Camp Gordon Johnston, near Carrabelle, and Key West was a major naval base and air station. There were large shipyards in Tampa, Panama City, Pensacola, and Jacksonville. The Farm Machinery Corporation produced amphibious vehicles in Dunedin and Auburndale. About 70,000 hotel rooms in Miami Beach were taken over by the Army Air Force.[56] Twenty-two prison camps were spread throughout the state. Earl Starnes grew up across the railroad track from a German POW camp in Winter Haven. The prisoners were used in all aspects of citrus production, harvesting, packing, and shipping. He remembers German prisoners practicing pole vaulting—that is, until the day one of the prisoners vaulted over the fence and escaped. The influence of wartime-related activities did not end with the war: in 1946 the Atlantic Missile Range, which eventually became the John F. Kennedy Space Center, was established at Cape Canaveral.

In the 1950s, the time it took to get to Florida decreased immensely, especially after the construction of the interstate highway system. Commercial air travel in and out of Florida increased significantly, using airfields abandoned by the military. The hundreds of thousands, and then millions, of tourists who visited the state every year found the sunshine bright, the beaches grand, and when it got too hot they could always retreat into an air-conditioned building. People, who decades earlier had scrimped and saved just to exist, found they now had the time, the money, and the means to vacation in Florida. What they saw they liked, and many of these visitors later retired there. The land sales industry quickly took advantage of the opportunity and welcomed them into its fold. America's great rediscovery of Florida had begun. Growth was coming whether the state was adequately prepared for it or not. It was not.

One of the reasons the Sunshine State was unprepared is that it was a political paradox, said Luther J. Carter, an author of an early book on growth management in Florida.[57] He observed that the composition of its population and economy was different from most southern states, but it was locked in the political tradition of the one-party South. Carter believed the root cause of backwardness of state government in Florida was due to reluctance of the rurally dominated legislature to reapportion in keeping with the growth of urban population.[58] The control of rural politicians known as the "Pork Chop Gang"[59] meant that the needs of the under-represented urban areas were customarily disregarded. Rural control was so dominant that in the mid-1950s only eighteen percent of the population controlled both houses of the legislature.[60] The rural-area-first attitude was even found in the executive branch: a former Florida state budget director was reported to have said, "What happens to the cities of Florida is not a proper concern of state government."[61] The strength of the Florida Crackers "did not expire suddenly," as Gloria Jahoda accurately wrote, "Its death was prolonged and painful."[62] Florida's political paradox was to remain in place until the early 1970s.

Some of Florida's local governments had an earnest interest in planning; for example, in 1959, Sanibel Island convinced the state legislature to pass a special act enabling it to create a planning and zoning authority and providing for taxation for planning purposes.[63] Fifteen years later, with the Florida legislature's approval to hold a referendum,[64] the citizens of Sanibel voted overwhelmingly to incorporate the community. They took this measure to get out from under the jurisdiction of county commissioners who tended to be lax on growth controls.[65] The islanders had been voicing a demand for a policy limiting growth on the island, but the county commission had continually turned a deaf ear to their requests.

Most of Florida's local government officials were like the Lee county commissioners: focused on accommodating all the growth they could attract. An all too common assumption was that growth brought only positive attributes, such as jobs, infrastructure improvements, and wealth to private enterprise. It did bring those things, but there was an opposite side to the shiny coin of growth. Most Floridians failed to realize that negative features accompanied the positive aspects of growth, especially if the process of growth was ill managed by its recipients—the recipients being state government, counties, municipalities, and all Floridians. Florida was beginning to grow rapidly and all three levels of government—and the people—shared a responsibility for exercising good management practices. However, Florida had four major flaws to overcome before it could place itself in a position to begin to effectively, as well as efficiently, manage its growth: (1) state planning had been relegated to a secondary—if not tertiary—role, (2) regional comprehensive planning was virtually non-existent, (3) a local government had to have a special act passed if it wanted to engage in planning, and (4) though some local governments prepared master plans, most were more interested in just zoning (or in neither planning or zoning). It would take almost twenty years before Florida finally attempted to address the matter of managing rapid growth adequately. By then, it would be mostly a matter of too little, too late.

The Florida State Improvement Commission (FSIC) retained a small degree of statutory authority for planning when it replaced both the Florida State Planning Board and the Economic Advancement Council in 1945, but planning became a low-priority concern. The comprehensive state planning function was eliminated, and most of the commission's attention was directed to what it called "more urgent specialized fields," such as planning for hospitals, aviation, and public works.[66] The FSIC claimed it did not have the personnel or funds to engage in general state planning because the personnel in its planning and industrial development division worked almost full-time with the operating divisions in these specialized fields. Federal assistance was available for a specialized task, such as preparing a plan for hospitals throughout the state,[67] but not for *comprehensive* planning.

Nor was the FSIC in a position to administer federal Section 701 planning assistance funds when they became available in the mid-1950s. Municipalities in Florida were ineligible to receive grants for local planning under the U.S. Housing Act of 1954 because the FSIC did not qualify as an *official* state planning agency. Its planning responsibilities were largely under-attended. The attitude within the FSIC appeared to be that it was not responsible for matters of local planning; it assumed that local governments, especially municipalities, were capable of doing whatever needed to be done without interference from the state. Concerning planning, the

1951-1952 biennial report of the commission went so far as to say, "There is a serious question as to whether a state agency should make a wholesale invasion of a field of private enterprise."[68] This possibly was another way of saying that it was all right for local governments to initiate planning (if they had the special statutory authority to do so), but state government itself should not instigate local planning or zoning. At that time, many people considered zoning a threat that would constrain actions of private enterprise.

Despite the FSIC's overall disinterest in planning, some of the personnel in the commission's Planning and Industrial Development Division did provide planning and zoning assistance to local governments whenever time was available. For example, during 1951 and 1952, the planning and industrial development division provided planning-related assistance to Manatee County and the municipalities of Delray Beach, Miami, and Penney Farms.[69] It also provided support on planning and zoning matters to the communities of Crestview, Daytona Beach, Ft. Myers, Gainesville, Homestead, Keystone Heights, Kissimmee, St. Augustine, and Stuart. Providing advice to communities regarding zoning was another responsibility of the division. Among the municipalities it aided strictly on zoning assistance in the early 1950s were Daytona Beach, Dade City, Groveland, Melbourne, North Miami Beach, North Miami Springs, Punta Gorda, South Miami, Surfside, Wauchula, and Terra Ceia. On another regulatory front, the division helped Ocala in preparing a sign ordinance.

Less direct, yet significant, was the role Frederick H. Bair, Jr., the head of the planning and industrial development division, played in the formation of the Florida Planning and Zoning Association (FPZA). He and local government planning advocates such as Earnest Bartley of Gainesville and Howard Rybold of Orange County organized the FPZA in April 1951.[70] The organization started with 15 members, but by December of that same year its membership had climbed to 76 individual and 17 organizational members.[71] Bair, credited by the American Planning Association with stirring up planning interest in Florida, also served as secretary of the FPZA.[72] He began his planning career in the late 1940s as a planning circuit rider for the State of New York, then moved West and prepared a long-range plan for Jasper, Wyoming, before joining the industrial commission. He formed his own consulting firm (Bair, Abernathy, and Associates) in 1953. Without the continuing agitation for planning from Bair and a handful of other planners, local government planning in Florida might have almost disappeared. Zoning was a different matter.

Bair was an advocate of both planning and zoning, but he believed planning should occur *before* zoning. In Florida, as well as throughout the U.S., local government interest in zoning far outweighed interest in planning. In December 1951, at the first annual conference of the FPZA, Bair caustically warned that planning boards seemed to have become preoccupied with zoning, and there are "many cases where zoning takes on certain Amazonian characteristics in the planning-zoning marital relationship, and planning becomes the henpecked spouse."[73] Despite this admonition of zoning, Bair became a national expert in the field; his fame as a planner spread nationally with his books, *The Text of a Model Zoning Ordinance, Zoning Board Manual*, and, with Richard Hedman, *And On the Eighth Day*.[74] His national reputation was further expanded through his preparation of a number of Planning Advisory Service reports for the American Institute of Planners (later the American Planning Association), and his service as reporter and editorial board member of the *Zoning Digest* (renamed *Land Use Law and Zoning Digest*).

Even local planning received a barb from Bair. While elaborating on successful efforts in local planning in Florida, he noted, "At the other extreme there are cities where planning is a process carried on in a sort of dreamy fourth dimension, a wishful and pleasant weaving of visions unrelated and unrelatable [sic] to the realities of city development."[75] What he was probably referring to was the kind of planning that reaches for idealistic values but ignores the pragmatism of implementation. A thought to remember.

Despite the efforts of Bair and other planners, only a small number of Florida's local governments were involved in planning in the early 1950s. Even the FSIC admitted, "There is no other state in the union in which there is so much growth and so little long-range planning for it, and there is no other state in which planning would pay off more than in Florida."[76] Long-range planning was needed to contend with the rapid rate of growth being experienced by Florida; however, the higher echelon of FSIC leadership seemed to believe this was strictly a local, not state-shared, responsibility. What local planning existed in Florida in the early 1950s was accomplished principally through the efforts of a relatively small number of foresightful thinkers.

Seeking changes, Governor LeRoy Collins got legislative support in 1955 to merge the Florida State Improvement Commission and the Florida State Advertising Commission into a Florida Development Commission (FDC).[77] Though the principal purpose of the new commission was economic development, it was also authorized to establish a planning and research division. This appeared to be the step needed to become eligible to administer the federal 701 planning assistance program—but the step was not completed.

State-level authority for participating in the 701 planning assistance program was in place, but there was too little money and an insufficient number of qualified staff for the new planning and research division to administer the program. "Qualified staff" meant properly trained and experienced professional planners.[78] As far as planning was concerned, things were not much different than they had been with the FSIC. Because of these state-level deficiencies, Florida communities remained ineligible to receive federal funds from the U.S. Housing Act of 1954. The *authority* for planning existed, but there were inadequate staff resources to implement that authority. Fred Bair reflected that at the end of its first year of operation the FDC had "made no real start on most of the things the law setting it up said that it should do and golden oratory promised that it would do."[79] The agency had become not much more than an advertising commission: over ninety percent of its budget was appropriated for advertising and promotion.[80] It was not until some time later that the Florida legislature provided a sufficient amount of financial support and professional staff positions to become eligible to administer the 701 program. However, general enabling legislation for planning would not be enacted by the Florida legislature until 1969.

Despite the awkwardness of having to obtain special legislative approval to plan, the number of communities engaged in planning gradually increased during the late 1950s and early 1960s. Among the local governments receiving assistance in this period were the cities of Belle Glade, Bristol, Ft. Myers, Graceville, Kissimmee, Milton, Panama City, St. Petersburg Beach, Stuart, Tallahassee, and Williston. Dade County, having adopted a home rule charter which, among other things, created a mandatory provision for a countywide planning advisory board and provided for a countywide planning agency, took advantage of the 701 program as an entitlement community. It also set zoning standards that applied to unincorporated areas and municipalities alike,[81] but no enforcement authority. Directly or indirectly, federal aid for planning was once again in place, and interest in planning gradually increased throughout Florida.

Summary

Following WW II, the nation turned its attention to economic development, and planning became a neglected stepchild. Planning experienced a renewal of interest only after Section 701 of the U.S. Housing Act of 1954 made local comprehensive planning a requirement for local governments to receive grants for urban renewal and other federal aid programs. Eventually, agitation for planning assistance at other levels of government brought about a series of expansions of the 701 program. At the state level, a number of national organizations were trying to interest state governments in policy management planning at about the same time they were becoming eligible for 701 planning assistance. However, the 701 requirements took state planning in a different direction than policy management; therefore, most state planning programs used the older municipality-based model of planning. Nevertheless, the policy model would resurface later in the 1960s.

The period after the war brought escalating population to Florida, and accompanying negative as well as positive aspects of growth. As its cities grew, the need for urban services increased, as did the need to improve public management practices. Planning was a tool that could provide foresight to local decision-making, but the rurally dominated state legislature was not interested in planning nor the plight of urban areas. Consequently, during the mid 1940s through the early 1960s, Florida was far behind much of the rest of the nation regarding participation in planning. Too many obstructions had been placed in its way.

Among these obstructions was the Pork Chop Gang, a group of rurally oriented state legislators who had relatively little interest in urban issues. Furthermore, Florida's plural executive system made effective management of the executive branch virtually impossible. Under such restraints, there certainly was not a great deal of interest in planning at the state level. Another hurdle was, given the legislature's severe tilt away from urban interests, no general enabling law for planning had been enacted; local governments had to have special acts passed authorizing them to engage in planning. This put a significant burden in the path of communities. The problem was complicated further by a relative lack of concern by the state agency responsible for helping local governments interested in planning. It had other priorities. The final hurdle was that most local governments were more interested in growing as rapidly as they could rather than showing any concern that growth might carry negative, as well as positive, features. Though progress was being made, the number of Florida communities interested in planning grew excruciatingly slow. But things were about to change.

NOTES FOR CHAPTER IV

1   Bair, Frederick H., Jr., Planning & Industrial Development Division, Florida State Improvement Commission, "What is Planning All About?" in *Proceedings of the Florida Planning and Zoning Association: First Annual Conference*, St. Petersburg, 1951, p. 3.

2   Lepawsky, Albert, *State Planning and Economic Development in the South,* National Planning Association Committee of the South, report no. 4, Kingsport, TN: Kingsport Press, 1949, p. 19. See also Carl Abbott, *The New Urban America*, Chapel Hill, NC: The University of North Carolina Press, 1981, p. 98.

3   Lepawsky, ibid.

4   U.S. Public Law 83-560, § 701 of the Housing Act of 1954.

5   Fagan, Brian, *The Long Summer: How Climate Changed Civilization*, New York: Basic Books, Perseus Books Group, 2004, p. 5. As early as 4800 B.C., Urak, near the Euphrates River in what is now Iraq, experienced suburbanization. In the same vein, BBC News reported on August 15, 2007 that a team of researchers believes it has found evidence that medieval Angkor City (in present-day Cambodia) covered over 1,150 square miles, about the size of the Los Angeles metropolitan area. What is new today is the rapidity of sprawl that began after WWII and has continued to increase ever since; also, central city boundaries failed to follow this growth because the new suburban communities preferred to remain politically separate from the central cities. On this last point, see Jon C. Teaford, *City and Suburb: The Political Fragmentation of Metropolitan America, 1850-1970*, Baltimore, MD: Johns Hopkins University Press, 1979.

6   Binford, Henry C., *The First Suburbs: Residential Communities on the Boston Periphery 1815-1860*, Chicago, IL: University of Chicago Press, 1985.

7   Jackson, Kenneth, *Crabgrass Frontier: The Suburbanization of the United States*, New York, NY: Oxford University Press, 1985.

8   Altshuler, Alan A., "The Intercity Freeway," in Donald A. Krueckeberg, ed., *Introduction to Planning History in the United States*, New Brunswick, NJ: Center for Urban Policy Research, Rutgers University, 1983, p. 193.

9   Ibid.

10 U.S. Public Law 84-627.

11 Weingroff, Richard F., "Creating the Interstate System," *Public Roads* 60:1, 1966, p. 12.

12   Mohl, Raymond A., "Ike and the Interstates: Creeping toward Comprehensive Planning, *Journal of Planning History* 2: 3, p. 243.

13   Ibid.

14   From the notes of Earl Starnes.

15   U.S. 48 Statutes 1246.

16   U.S. Public Law 346 (Ch. 268).

17   von Hoffman, Alexander, "A Study in Contradictions: The Origins and Legacy of the Housing Act of 1949," *Housing Policy Debate* 1: 2, Fannie Mae Foundation, 2000, p. 303.

18   Ibid, p. 304.

19   Ibid. p. 303.

20   Ibid, p. 305.

21   Ibid, p. 308. The House Act was codified under Title V of Public Law 81-171.

22   Ibid, p. 299.

23   7 U.S.C. 1001-1006.

24   von Hoffman, ibid, p. 309. See also, *Congressional Quarterly,* "Housing a Nation," Washington, DC: Congressional Quarterly Service, 1966.

25   "Urban Renewal and the Growth Machine," via www.worldfreeinternet.net/news/urban.htm, July 23, 2005.

26   Ibid, footnote 44.

27   Domhoff, G. William, *Who Rules America Now?* Englewood Cliffs, NJ: Prentice-Hall, Inc., 1983, pp. 173-184; obtained from "Urban Renewal and the Growth Machine," via www.worldfreeinternet.net/news/urban.htm, on July 23, 2005.

28   Stone, Clarence N., *Economic Growth and Neighborhood Discontent: System Bias in the Urban Renewal Program of Atlanta*, Chapel Hill, NC: University of North Carolina Press, 1976.

29   Gelfand, Mark I. *A Nation of Cities: The Federal Government and Urban America*, New York, NY: Oxford University Press, 1975, pp. 72-173; John H. Mollenkopf, , *The Contested City*, Princeton, NJ: Princeton University Press, 1983, pp. 113-114; Jon A. Peterson, *The Birth of City Planning in the United States, 1840-1917,* Baltimore, MD: The Johns Hopkins University Press, 2003.

30   See Andrew E.G. Jonas and David Wilson, eds., *The Urban Growth Machine: Critical Perspectives Two Decades Later*, Albany: State University of New York Press, 1999, for a comprehensive analysis of two decades of research on Molotch's growth machine thesis.

31   Anderson, Martin, *The Federal Bulldozer: A Critical Analysis of Urban Renewal 1949-62*, Cambridge, MA: The MIT Press, 1964.

32 Gans, Herbert, *The Urban Villagers*, Glencoe, NY: Free Press, 1962; Jacobs, Jane, *The Death and Life of Great American Cities*, New York, NY: Random House, 1961; see also von Hoffman, ibid.

33 Bair, Fred, Jr., ed., "State Aid to Community Planning in Florida," *Newsletter of Florida Planning and Zoning* 10: 6, June 1959, p. 1.

34 Bair, Fred, Jr., ed., "Urban Renewal in Florida—1959 Status and What Led Up to It," *Newsletter of Florida Planning and Zoning* 10: 12, December 1959, p. 4; see also Fred Bair, Jr., ed., "Florida Now Eligible for Benefits of Housing Act of 1954?" *Newsletter of Florida Planning and Zoning* 6: 7, July 1955, p. 2. The case is listed as Florida 60 So. 2d 663.

35 Ibid, p. 4.

36 Ibid.

37 U.S. *Public Law* 83-560.

38 Carroll, Margaret, "The Workable Program—What is It?" *Newsletter of Florida Planning and Zoning Association* 9: 5, May 1958, p. 1.

39 Feiss, Carl, "The Foundations of Federal Planning Assistance: A Personal Account of the 701 Program," *Journal of the American Planning Association* 51: 2, 1985, p. 178.

40 U.S. Housing Act of 1954 (68 *Statutes* 590), Section 701.

41 Feiss, ibid, p. 179.

42 National Municipal League, *Model State and Regional Planning Law*, New York, NY, 1955, p. v.

43 Use of consultants was not required, but relatively few communities or regional entities were adequately staffed to do the task themselves.

44 Hartley, David K., "Organizational Arrangement for State Planning," a report to the Office of Regional Economic Development, Washington, DC: American Institute of Planners, 1967, p. 5.

45 Peterson, ibid.

46 Feiss, ibid, p. 175.

47 Ransome, Coleman B., *The Office of the Governor in the South*, Tuscaloosa, AL: Bureau of Public Administration, 1951, p. 67.

48 National Governors' Conference, Committee on State Planning, "A Strategy for Planning," Chapel Hill, NC: Institute on State Programming for the 70s, 1967, p. 5.

49 Hartley, ibid, p. 6.

50 American Institute of Planners, "State Planning: Its Function and Organization," Washington, DC, 1958.

51 Ch. 205, HRS, Land Use Commission (Hawaii State Land Use Law).

52 National Municipal League, ibid, p. 3.

53 Revels, Tracy Jean, "World War II-Era Florida: Change in the 1940s," ch. 11 in Mark I. Greenberg, William Warren Rogers, and Canter

Brown, Jr., eds., *Florida's Heritage of Diversity*, Tallahassee, FL: Sentry Press, 1997, p. 139.

54 Mormino, Gary R., *Land of Sunshine State of Dreams: A Social History of Modern Florida*, Gainesville, FL: University Press of Florida, 2005, p. 2

55 Coles, David J., "Keep the Home Fires Burning: Florida's World War II Experience, Florida Department of Veterans' Affairs, from www.floridawwii.com/history.asp, January 26, 2004.

56 Colburn, David R. and Lance deHaven-Smith, *Government in the Sunshine State: Florida Since Statehood*, Gainesville, FL: University Press of Florida, 1999, pp. 33-34.

57 Carter, Luther J., *The Florida Experience: Land and Water Policy Experience in a Growth State*, Baltimore, MD: published for Resources for the Future, Inc. by The Johns Hopkins University Press, 1974, p. 41.

58 Ibid, p. 42.

59 The Pork Chop Gang was made up primarily of rural northern county legislators who catered to agricultural and resource extraction industries. Though not a legislator, Ed Ball of the DuPont conglomerate (banks, railroads, the St. Joe Paper Company) was a power among them, oftentimes influencing state political decision making from behind the scenes. The Pork Choppers also worked to preserve Florida's white supremacy policies by resisting reapportionment, even going to the extreme of drafting proposals calling for massive resistance against the 1954 U.S. Supreme Court ordered *Brown v. Board of Education* decision. For discussions about the Pork Chop Gang see Gloria Jahoda, *Florida: A History*, New York: W.W. Norton & Company, 1984, pp. 129-143; Gene M. Burnett, *Florida's Past*, Vol. 1, Sarasota, FL: Pineapple Press, 1998, pp. 106-108; and Coburn and deHaven-Smith, ibid, pp. 38-39.

60 Dáte, S.V., *Quiet Passion: A Biography of Senator Bob Graham*, New York, NY: Tarcher/Penquin, 2004, p. 65.

61 As recorded in Bair, Fred, Jr., ed., "The Development Commission— What Happened?" *Newsletter of Florida Planning and Zoning* 7: 6, June 1956, p. 4.

62 Jahoda, ibid, p. 140; see especially Chapter 11, "High Times in the Pork Chop Latitudes, pp. 128-143.

63 Florida Planning & Zoning Association, "Planning and Development" 10: 6, 1959, p. 1.

64 House Bill 4001, 1974 session.

65 Patric, William, "Ten Years of Sanibel City Government," prepared for the Sanibel City Council, November 1985; this information was provided via email by Roy Gibson on December 19, 2007.

66 Florida State Improvement Commission, "Developing Florida: The Biennial Report, 1949-1950," Tallahassee, 1951, p. A-10.

67 Ibid, p. S-13. Planning for hospitals throughout the state was supported by the Federal Hospital Survey and Construction Act of 1946 (Public Law 725).

68 Florida State Improvement Commission, "Biennial Report: 1951-1952," Tallahassee, 1953, p. 10.

69 Ibid, pp. 11-13.

70 Obtained from an interview with Earnest Bartley, in Gainesville, FL, on 13 September 05.

71 Ibid.

72 American Planning Association, "In Memoriam / Fred Bair Jr.," obtained from www.planning.org/ memoriam/bair.htm on 24 February 2005. According to "The History of Florida Planning & Zoning Association, Inc." (obtained from www.fpza.org/fpza/history.html), during a national meeting of the American Planning and Civic Association, in Miami, Frank F. Stearns, director of planning for the City of Miami, organized a meeting of people interested in setting up a planning organization in Florida; the FPZA was formed during this meeting.

73 Bair, "What is Planning All About?" ibid, p.6.

74 See Fred Bair, Jr., *The Text of a Model Zoning Ordinance*, Chicago: American Society of Zoning Officials, 1966; *The Zoning Board Manual*, Chicago: American Planning Association, 1984; and, with Richard Hedman, *And On the Eighth Day,* Chicago: American Society of Planning Officials, 1961.

75 Bair, "What is Planning All About?" ibid, p. 3.

76 Florida State Improvement Commission, "Biennial Report: 1951-1952," ibid, p. 9.

77 Bair, Fred, Jr., ed., "Florida Now Eligible for Benefits of Housing Act of 1954?" *Newsletter of Florida Planning and Zoning* 6: 7, July 1955, p. 1.

78 Bair, Fred, Jr. ed., "The Development Commission – What Happened?" ibid, p. 3.

79 Ibid, p. 1.

80 Ibid, p. 2.

81 DeGrove, John M. and Nancy E. Stroud, "New Developments and Future Trends in Local Government Comprehensive Planning," *Stetson Law Review* XVII: 3, 1988, p. 599.

CHAPTER V

RE-EMERGING INTEREST IN PLANNING

Early 1960s to About 1970

> Powerful and effective state governments did not
> emerge overnight. A series of reforms in the struc-
> ture and process of government—some carefully
> planned, others accidental—have occurred over
> the last three decades. The cumulative effects of
> these independent reforms have been stronger,
> more capable state governmental institutions and
> a desire on the part of state government officials
> to expand the scope of their responsibility even
> further.[1] (Carl E. Van Horn, "The Quiet Revolution,"
> 1989.)

The 1960s were years of transition for state and local governments. There was a sense of renewal focused by President
John F. Kennedy in his inaugural address: "… the torch has
been passed to a new generation of Americans, born in this
century, tempered by war, disciplined by a hard and bitter
peace."[2] As the decade dawned, the United States was still in
the process of shifting a large portion of its economic weight
from the industrialized states of the Northeast and the Midwest to the more climatically attractive states of the West Coast
and the South. Improvements in highway transportation, the
rapid expansion of commercial airline service, and other technologies accelerated this movement. For example, the proliferation of air conditioning systems made Florida and other
southern states more attractive to residents of northern climes.
The nation was awash with housing starts, job opportunities,
and other indicators of economic growth. However, these indicators did not account for the other side of the growth coin:
the downside of rapid, unmanaged growth. Signs of stress

were appearing, transportation congestion; environmental degradation, such as air and water pollution; and urban unrest culminating in riots in New York City, Los Angeles, Detroit, Miami, and other cities. These issues were not new to the nation, but the degree of stress they were exerting was mounting, and something needed to be done.

Population growth, especially in areas outside of established urban centers, was being experienced by most states, particularly Florida. By 1960, the population of the Sunshine State had climbed to almost five million people; the state had added almost 2.2 million people in the decade of the 1950s. This was more growth during that decade than North Carolina, South Carolina, Georgia, Alabama, Mississippi, and Louisiana *combined*. The 78.7 percent increase was, and still is, the greatest increase for Florida in any modern decade. The rate of growth slowed somewhat in the 1960s, but the state still added over 1.8 million people, an increase of 504 people per day. The prolonged high growth rate during the 1950s and 1960s presented the state and its local governments with challenges beyond comprehension.

Most of the growth was in south Florida, where urban development insistently pushed back the Everglades and other wetlands and bracketed the U.S. Route 1 corridor along the southeast Florida coast. In partnership with this sprawl, developers filled in bay and estuary bottoms for new construction sites. But the land boom was also becoming significant in the central part of the state, especially in the Orlando area where Disney World was breaking ground.[3] In the minds of people who wanted to move to Florida, there was no ice or snow, the sun always shined, the beaches beckoned, the golf courses were always green, you could fish in salt water or fresh water, cool air was just inside the next doorway, and natural and man-made attractions were nearby. Florida was a magnet to millions of people from the North. To other immigrants, like scores of thousands who fled Cuba for south

Florida following Castro's takeover, it meant freedom. Along with Disney World, the 1960s brought other major private and public development projects, including canalizing the Kissimmee River, planning for an Everglades (Miami) Jet-port, and renewed construction of the Cross-Florida Barge Canal. Though the last two projects were not completed, the face of Florida was changing.

Another wave of land development was under way; land barons were changing the Florida landscape at a far greater pace than in the 1920s. Among them, as Gary R. Mormino of the University of South Florida noted, were national giants like Arthur Vining Davis, John D. MacArthur, Sam J. Keller, and the Mackle family.[4] Davis, founder and chair of Alcoa, also founded the Arvida Corporation and pursued development of the Sarasota area, especially Lido and Longboat keys. MacArthur, "who laid claim to title of Florida's largest private landholder," launched developments in Sarasota, the Orlando area, and forty-one square miles of Palm Beach County.[5] As for the Mackle family, they merely developed Key Biscayne, and from there went on to sell other Florida lands "at ten dollars down", eventually combining with a Canadian firm to create General Development Corporation, which developed portions of Charlotte, St. Lucie, and Volusia counties and other locations in Florida.[6]

Ineptitude of State and Local Governments

In Florida and across the nation, changes were also occurring in the intergovernmental arena. Due principally to long-term neglect of urban areas, state governments realized they had allowed their role in the federal system to be compromised. Most of them for so long ignored the needs of their urban communities that the federal government had to step in with financial assistance to provide urban infrastructure and other services. In some cases, a direct link between the federal government and local governments was being established to the exclusion of the states—and in some cases, even to the exclusion of local elected officials themselves. Frank Grad, in *The States and the Urban Crisis*, warned, "An impotent state government can no more deal with urban problems than it can with any other, and since the problems of the cities are the foremost problems of government today, the general inadequacy of state constitutions—and of state government— is particularly disabling in this (urban venue) area."[7] Concern about inept state and local governments was beginning to grow.

The ineptitude of state and local governments in contending with urban change brought the U.S. Advisory Commission on Intergovernmental Relations to report that,

> … there was too little action, and by the mid-six-
> ties, Washington was stepping into the void left
> by reluctant communities and recalcitrant states,
> and was attempting to rationalize, at least its own,
> growing investment in urban affairs through mini-
> mal measures for policy coordination.[8]

Thus, it was the federal government—not the states—that took the initiative in addressing the pressures mentioned above. The president and Congress, elected on the principle of one-man, one-vote, were more responsive than the states to the needs of where most of the people lived: the urban areas.

In this chapter, we look back on the tumultuous activities that affected planning in the 1960s, principally because of what occurred—or did not occur—at the state level of governance. We begin with a review of the status of planning in the early part of the decade, particularly as it was influenced by federal programs designed to improve public management and coordinate the multitude of federal grant programs. Next, we delve into the movement to reform state governments, with emphasis on the emerging role of planning as a tool for policy management. Lastly, we discuss how these national events combined with changes internal to Florida to set the stage for its quantum leap in planning in the early 1970s.

Planning as a Federal Requirement for Categorical Grants-in-Aid

The 1950s and 1960s set high-water marks in the number of federal categorical grant-in-aid programs made available to local governments. In its desire to respond to the needs of cities the federal government inundated local government officials with somewhere between 170 and 200 grant-in-aid programs with varying sets of planning requirements.[9] There were grants for economic development, urban renewal, water and sewer facilities, highway systems, airport facilities, parks and outdoor recreation, health facilities, law enforcement, civil defense, rural areas, and sundry other purposes. A grant from one federal agency sometimes duplicated a grant from another agency (water facility grants could be obtained from at least three different federal sources). This led to competition among federal agencies and confusion on the part of many local governments. Ralph Widner, former executive director of the Appalachian Regional Commission told a story that illustrated this confusion: "Last year, I watched an audience of several hundred local officials stare in disbelief as federal spokesmen from five different agencies explained how they could help a community build a sewage treatment plant."[10] There was confusion among federal programs for model cities, public housing, urban renewal, water, sewer, and recreation grants in rapidly growing metropolitan areas such as Tampa Bay, as well as in smaller cities like Gainesville. It was evident that something had to be done about this uncoordinated proliferation of federal grant requirements.

Through a series of amendments, the federal 701 planning assistance program gradually became a broad vehicle for attempting to coordinate the proliferation of grants and grant requirements. A 1959 amendment to the program had extended eligibility for 701 planning assistance for statewide planning, and a number of states quickly rekindled their interest and submitted applications. By 1962, 701 grants for state planning had been given to sixteen states and one territory.[11] In addition, some of the functionally specific federal grant-in-aid programs were required to ensure that their projects were in harmony with the more *comprehensive* regional/metropolitan and state 701 assisted plans. This was only a partial step toward coordinating federal grant-in-aid programs; broader steps were to follow.

Perhaps the broadest initiative to improve coordination of federal grants was the U.S. Intergovernmental Coordination Act of 1968. The stated intent of this act was:

> ... to promote more harmonious intergovernmental relations and to encourage sound planning, zoning, and land use practices by prescribing uniform policies and procedures whereby the Administrator shall acquire, use, and dispose of land in urban areas in order that urban land transactions entered into ... shall, *to the greatest extent practicable* [italics added], be consistent with zoning and land-use practices and shall be made to the greatest extent practicable in accordance with planning and development objectives of the local governments and local planning agencies concerned.[12]

The act was designed to improve the efficiency of federal programs through coordination of planning between levels of governance. It heightened awareness of a need for intergovernmental coordination in general, but parochial objectives often superseded the desire for consistency—perhaps taking advantage of the caveat "to the greatest extent practicable" in the statement of intent.

It was Bureau of the Budget Circular A-95, however, that put the Intergovernmental Coordination Act into practice, particularly in combining Title IV of the act and Section 204 of the U.S. Demonstration Cities and Metropolitan Development Act of 1966.[13] Title IV required rules and regulations governing the formulation, evaluation, and review of federal programs and projects having a significant impact on area and community development. Section 204 implemented this requirement by mandating that applications for federal assistance for a wide variety of public facility projects in metropolitan areas include comments of an areawide (i.e., metropolitan or regional) comprehensive planning agency concerning the relationship of the proposed project to the planned development of the area. An applicant for federal financial assistance was required to notify both the responsible state-level clearinghouse and regional or metropolitan clearinghouse of the intent to submit an application. This project notification and review system was considered an early warning system to encourage coordination of state, regional, and local planning and development.[14]

The Myth of Superabundance

As the 1960s drew to a close, an emerging environmental and resource protection consciousness began to have an effect on policy and planning choices being taken by some local and state political leaders. A precursor of concerns to come occurred as early as 1947 when Marjory Stoneman Douglas, writing in *The Everglades: River of Grass*, identified the critical environmental conditions of the Florida Everglades.[15] She warned of environmental degradation caused by fifty years of state and federal land reclamation policies and flood management in south Florida. Douglas focused the attention of Floridians on environmental concerns, which were later debated by politicians and planners at state, regional, and local levels from one end of the state to the other.

However, the idealism and beginning of the environmental movement in the United States is mostly associated with the 1962 publication of Rachel Carson's *Silent Spring*,[16] followed a year later by Stewart Udall's *The Quiet Crisis*.[17] In these books, the authors raised issues of environmental degradation, land speculation, minimization of interference with private property rights, and addressed vital concerns associated with these long-term public and private policies. Carson warned that, "The most alarming of all man's assaults upon the environment is the contamination of air, earth, rivers, and sea with dangerous and lethal materials." To this warning, Udall added,

> It was the intoxicating profusion of the American continent which induced a state of mind that made waste and plunder inevitable. A temperate continent, rich in soils and minerals and forests and wildlife, enticed men to think in terms of infinity rather than facts, and produced an overriding fallacy that was nearly our undoing—the Myth of Superabundance. According to the myth, our resources were inexhaustible. It was an assumption that made wise management of the land and provident husbandry superfluous.[19]

These observations and assertions in the early 1960s were supported by ecological and environmental research in academic and governmental institutions across the globe, the nation, and in Florida. Until these warnings, environmental issues were simply not part of the guidelines for decision-making among policy makers and planners.

Persuasive guidelines in the environmental arena soon became reality. Most notable among these was enactment of the National Environmental Policy Act in 1969.[20] The act established a Council on Environmental Quality (CEQ) in the president's office to report annually on the quality of the nation's natural environment. All federal agencies were required to file with the CEQ "an impact statement for all major actions, including proposed legislation, regulations and procedures, policy determinations, and proposed projects which might significantly affect the quality of the environment."[21] This introduced the term "environmental impact statement" into the lexicon of planners and grant administrators at all levels of government seeking federal financial assistance.

Urban Mass Transit Returns to the Fold

Other significant federal actions included the Urban Mass Transportation Act (UMTA) of 1964[22] and the consolidation of transportation-related agencies into the U.S. Department of Transportation in 1966. The UMTA provided matching funds for public transportation projects ranging from bus to urban-wide light and heavy rail transit systems. This program provided funds to initiate mass transit planning in major cities across the country, including a technical study leading to the Metrorail project in Miami-Dade County, Florida.[23] As always, transportation improvements would leave their mark on the landscape.

The Practice of Minimal Government Responsibility Catches Up With the States

In order to retain a county-based, rather than population-based, distribution of voting power, most state legislatures ceased to reapportion themselves voluntarily in the late 1800s. Cities, like Chicago, were beginning to amass large concentrations of population, and legislators from rural areas feared the cities would take control of state legislatures and diminish the political power of rural representatives. Using a false assumption that cities were capable of taking care of themselves, rurally dominated state governments lost touch with the needs of their urbanized areas, the areas that housed the majority of their people. This set in place a role of minimal responsibility for state governments across the nation.

Florida was one of the worst offenders. As late as 1960, Miami-Dade County, Florida, with a population of over 900,000 people, had only three seats in the state house, whereas rural counties such as Glades, Lafayette, and Liberty, each with a population of about 3,000, had one seat each. Their combined 9,000 constituents had the same voting power as the 900,000 people in Miami-Dade. It is no wonder that municipalities like Miami, Tampa, St. Petersburg, Orlando, and Jacksonville suffered from neglect.

In his aptly titled book, *Storm Over the States*, Terry Sanford, former governor of North Carolina, felt that unless state governments revitalized themselves, they were in danger of becoming mere pawns in a disintegrating federal system of government.[24] Centralization of power at the national level was more than threatening: it was fast becoming reality. States had been sitting on the sideline idly watching the evolution of a direct connection between federal and local governments. Sanford, a leader among this new breed of governors, believed, "The first step in improving the federal-state-local system is the internal improvement of state government," and the best place to start was to strengthen the hand of a state's chief executive, the governor.[25] Harold F. Wise and Bertram Wakeley later commented, "From the mid-1960s well into the 1970s the predominant theme in governors' offices throughout the country was good government and improved public administration and management."[26] What Sanford and others were building upon was similar to what the National Municipal League and other national organizations had proposed ten years earlier.[27] Thus began what James K. Conant, of New York University, named the fourth wave of comprehensive state executive branch reorganization.[28]

As with other beginnings, rejuvenating the role of state governments in the federal system was the product of a variety of initiatives. In this instance, one of the most significant efforts came from the governors themselves, through the vehicle of the National Governors' Conference (later called the National Governors' Association). They seized upon earlier contributions by the Council of State Governments, the National Conference of State Legislators, the National Municipal League, the American Institute of Planners (later the American Planning Association), and other key organizations that had contributed to the movement.

Another step identified by Sanford, one closely related to the first, was for states to recognize their responsibilities to cities. He pointed out that the problems of cities are the problems of states.[29] "The state is at fault if the interaction between authorities, special purpose districts, cities, towns, townships, boroughs, and counties does not add up," echoed Harold F. Wise, a consultant who worked closely with the governors of a number of states.[30] Sanford felt a significant step toward working with local governments would be for each state to "develop a forceful and competent department or agency for urban affairs."[31] He was not alone in this opinion.

Building on earlier recommendations,[32] state and local leaders, such as Paul Ylvisaker of New Jersey,[33] initiated a movement to create departments of community or urban affairs in almost every state. There was a significant difference in the responsibilities of these agencies, however. Referring back to Sanford's advice, though each department might have been *competent* in light of its assigned responsibilities, very few were authorized to be *forceful* regarding urban matters. When it came to oversight of local government comprehensive planning, for example, the initial Florida Department of Community Affairs had no authority to be forceful; it carried no "stick"—this was to come later.

These two initiatives, strengthening the management hand of the governor and the creation of state departments of urban or community affairs, caught on quickly. Within a few years most states had created state planning offices in either the governor's office or in an administrative agency and had taken other steps to improve a governor's authority to manage the executive branch. In addition, virtually every state created an agency to focus on the needs of local governments; Florida established its department of community affairs in 1969, under the leadership of its first secretary, James G. Richardson.[34]

Sanford, who later became president of Duke University, did not let his recommendations rest within the pages of his book; he took steps to implement them. The first of the steps was setting up the Institute on State Programming for the 70s, at the University of North Carolina at Chapel Hill.[35] The Institute served, in part, as a staff arm of the State Planning Committee of the National Governors' Conference.[36] Former New Mexico governor Jack Campbell, who headed the Institute, and Governor John A. Love of Colorado, who chaired the State Planning Committee of the National Governors Conference, worked to spread the message and recommendations across the fifty states. The message also may have influenced Florida Governor Claude R. Kirk, Jr., who had been a member of the committee.

Broadening the Scope of State Planning

Interest in the potential of state planning as a policy management tool began to surface in the 1950s, so by the early 1960s, it was evident that a movement was underway. The importance of placing state planning in close proximity to a state's governor was discussed at the American Institute of Planners (AIP) Conference in 1963. The following year, a Council of State Planning Agencies had been created, and it held its first meeting at the AIP annual conference in Toronto.[37] By the mid-1960s, a movement had coalesced among governors and, in some cases, state legislators, around the proposition that state planning needed to be formally tied to a state's chief executive. Wise expressed this view in a paper presented at a 1966 conference of Midwestern governors:

> ... the planning officer must be part of a triumvirate of functions that are directly available and controllable totally by the executive head of the state government, the governor. These three functions must have a constructive and creative interplay, as they are the basic tools of policy development available to the governor. I am referring, of course, to the budgeting function, the program or legislative development function, and the state planning function. These are the tools of management available to the governor.[38]

But the kind of state planning Wise espoused was different from the municipal land use planning model used by the federal 701 planning assistance program. Thus, in some states the initial 701 generated state comprehensive planning approach was replaced by a policy oriented planning model. What resulted was a shift in emphasis from a plan as a product, to a plan as an ongoing set of policies. This approach to state planning seemed more in tune with the interests of the governors.

Although state planning traces back to the 1930s, a new era began in 1961 when Hawaii passed a state land use law,[39] the first modern-era instance of state involvement in broad land use management. Urban and resort development had begun to spill into agricultural areas, and the state moved to protect those important components of its economic base.[40] Hawaii had taken the first step in what eventually became known as "The Quiet Revolution in Land Use Control."[41] Following Hawaii, Massachusetts (in 1963) adopted a critical areas program to provide for the management of all shoreland areas 250 feet from a high water mark,[42] and Wisconsin (in 1965) passed a law providing minimum statewide shoreline zoning standards over lands around lakes and waterways.[43] In 1969, Oregon enacted Senate Bill 10, which required local governments to adopt comprehensive land use plans. Massachusetts took another step in an unexplored direction when it passed a statewide zoning appeals act, popularly called the "anti-snob zoning law," in 1969.[44] State government land use planning and management initiatives peaked in the late 1960s and early 1970s when Colorado, Delaware, Florida, Maine, Michigan, Minnesota, Nevada, New York, Oregon, South Carolina, Texas, Vermont, West Virginia, and others joined the fold in passing or considering state land use or state policy legislation.[45] Florida was among the laggards in joining this national movement, but when it did, it did so with a quantum leap (which will be discussed in the following chapter). Things were beginning to take on a tint of the 1930s again, except that this time around governors realized planning could be used as a tool for managing policy. This time, planning would be to the advantage of the states, not just something that had to be done because the federal government wanted it done.

Occurring at about the same time the governors were focusing attention on planning as a policy tool, another new policy management tool called a "planning, programming, and budgeting" system (PPB) was devolving from the federal level to the state and local levels. In the 1960s, the PPB system and policy planning were two evolving thrusts in administrative theory.[46] The National Governors' Conference Committee on State Planning felt there had not been enough planning in the budget process—nor was there sufficient budgeting in the planning process, and programming was seen as providing a bridge between planning and budgeting.[47] Leaders in the planning and the budgeting professions were beginning to hearken to the idea.

Joining budgeting and planning functions was so replete with conflicts of interest, however, that the marriage failed to occur. S. Kenneth Howard, then state planning director for the State of Washington and one of the leading proponents for marrying planning and budgeting, cut right to the core of the issue:

> Reduced to their essentials, the planning process and the analytical approach to budgeting rely on the same model of rational behavior: define the goal, find alternative ways to achieve that goal, evaluate those alternatives, and select the most appropriate one ... But those who tried to use PPB to carve out a role in the administrative process encountered a political movement for which they were not totally prepared at a time when traditional budgeting was undergoing its own metamorphosis, and direct conflicts between planners and budgeters over the new system ensued.

> Not surprisingly, budgeters who sought to make the budget more useful to key executives ran into planners trying to demonstrate that their skills could be useful in policy formulation and decision-making ... What emerges is a clear battle in systems politics—that is, a struggle over the process (system) by which decisions or policies will be made rather than over the substance of those decisions ... In trying to shape the emerging PPB system, the planners have operated at a disadvantage in many jurisdictions. They have not had easy access to key decision-makers ... Budget staffs have been more able than planners to accommodate themselves to the time perspectives of politicians—perspectives that often do not extend much beyond the next election.[48]

George A. Steiner, known for his work in management policy and strategy, underscored the problem of access of planners to key decision-makers when he wrote,

> A genuine managerial problem arises because the budgeting process is rather well institutionalized. Over a long period of time, procedures, practices, and roles have been established. This is not true with a central planning unit. These groups are new and their roles and functions are not well established.[49]

In the late 1960s, planning was still an unproven tool in state policy-making circles.

The PPB concept also devolved to some cities and counties. For example, Miami-Dade County, Florida, was part of a federally funded "5-5-5" project where five cities, five counties, and five states were selected to initiate pilot projects.[50] They were to serve as models for other city, county, and state governments. There may have been a modicum of success to some of these efforts, but, for the most part, the marriage of planning and budgeting failed to occur at these levels, too. The PPB system has since disappeared as a usable concept.

Whereas a management tool such as budgeting tends to focus on immediate issues, planning deals primarily with uncertainties of the future. It is human nature for immediate problems to be more attention generating than future problems, even though decisions based on future consequences are often likely to have more positive and lasting impacts. This is especially true for elected officials faced with possibly negative reactions from voters if they fail to act on immediate issues.

The transfer of state planning authority to governors' offices continued until at least 1971, at which time a survey by the Council of State Governments disclosed that thirty-three state planning agencies were located in the office of the chief executive.[51] This was indicative of a general shift of state planning away from its early focus on classical land use planning based on the municipal model to a process of executive policy management. Even so, the transfer of location to a governor's office did not always result in a redefinition of function. In some of these states, preparation of a state-wide land use plan remained the principal mission, and policy management was no further advanced than it had been in the 1930s.

By the beginning of the 1970s, there was a creative tension revolving around the position, functions, and mission of state planning.[52] As planning professor Michael P. Brooks noted:

> A string of criticism, much of it internally generated and some of it long voiced by advocates of planning as a continuous, administrative process, had eroded faith in what one commentator would later call 'the classical model.' This executive approach, as it would become known, while drawing its proponents closer to the levers of power, implicated them in the short-range, shifting policies of day-to-day governance.[53]

Was it to be the land use oriented planning derived from the municipal model but brought to a higher plain or was it to evolve into the policy-oriented process espoused by Terry Sanford and others? Florida was one of the states that struggled mightily with this issue, and the decade of the 1960s was only the beginning of the struggle.

Regional/Metropolitan Planning:
Seeking to Become a Significant Player

Given the rapid expansion of urban sprawl, many types of public services, long regarded as strictly local responsibilities, were becoming regional in demand. In some metropolitan areas, the logic of cost-effective economics compelled service areas for water supply, sewage disposal, storm water management, parks and recreation, and especially highways and mass transit to expand beyond municipal boundaries, resulting in increased demands for intergovernmental planning and coordination. Cities had sprawled beyond their confines, suburbs were splitting off like amoebas, and balkanization of local governance was growing with abandon. However, localism has always been a prominent national ideal,[54] which makes it difficult to achieve regional objectives. Addressing this reluctance to act regionally, the Council of State Governments pointed out that, "Although the roles of local governments and the national government are indispensable, the key to solving the complex difficulties which make up the general problem of urban regional growth lies with state government."[55] Nevertheless it was the federal government—not the states—that confronted local governments with the need to think beyond their boundaries: language was inserted into many federal grant-in-aid programs requiring regional plans to be prepared before local jurisdictions became eligible for a variety of federal grants which required a regional perspective.

A number of specialized regional planning functions arose because of federal prerequisites for a regional perspective; an example was the requirement to prepare economic development district plans in order to qualify for certain grants from the U.S. Economic Development Administration.[56] In some states, such as Kentucky and Georgia, economic development district planning and 701 regional planning assistance were merged. In Georgia, nineteen area planning and development commissions were formed between 1966 and 1971, with only four counties out of 159 not participating.[57] The same sort of regional emphasis was happening regarding health, sewer, water, air pollution, and other federal aid programs.

Across the nation, the effects of unmitigated suburban land speculation, energized by the spreading Interstate Highway System, began to take its toll in never-ending demands for new infrastructure, especially new roads. Transportation needs in rapidly sprawling metropolitan areas were not being resolved by simply building more roads. This led to an amendment of the Housing Act of 1961, which, in part, provided grants for both mass transit and metropolitan transportation. Hence, federal aid for metropolitan-wide transportation planning initially came not from the federal Bureau of Public Roads (BPR) but from the Housing and Home Finance Agency. This circumvention occurred because the BPR was so closely allied with state highway departments, which at the time were dedicated to roadway construction.[58] A basis for contemporary metropolitan transportation planning was established in the BPR the following year when a new metropolitan transportation planning process required what became known as the "three-C planning process."[59] The three-C's referred to continuing, comprehensive, and cooperative transportation planning. This requirement resulted in the creation of a number of new or restructured metropolitan transportation organizations (e.g., the Connecticut, New York, and New Jersey Tri-State Regional Planning Commission), yet these organizations never rose beyond an advisory role.[60] This typically kept transportation decision-making in the hands of the highway-oriented personnel of state highway departments, most of which, by the early 1970s, had changed their titles to state departments of transportation. But most often, the change was in name only.[61] A start on broadening the focus of transportation agencies beyond that of just roads had been made, but it would prove to be a slow, incremental process.

When local governments confronted the necessity of engaging in regional planning in order to become eligible for some types of federal grants, they usually did this by creating regional planning agencies of one sort or another. While traditional regional planning commissions were helpful in preparing the required regional plans and in providing technical assistance to their constituent local governments, they were nonetheless little more than powerless halfway houses to true region-wide decision making. Technically competent regional plans were prepared, but implementation of these plans was dependent on the cooperation of the numerous local governments represented on the regional planning commission. This seldom occurred, since the principal responsibility of the true decision makers—local elected officials—was not to the region but to the self-interest of the local communities they represented.

State governments rarely attempt to influence their local governments to move toward anything approaching regional governance. An exception is the Twin Cities Council, created by the Minnesota legislature in 1967 to deal with issues that overlapped the boundaries of the more than two hundred local jurisdictions that existed in the Twin Cities metropolitan area.[62] Its initial purpose was to coordinate planning and development within the metropolitan area, but over the years its responsibilities expanded to include operational services such as a transit system, parks and open space, wastewater collection and treatment, water quality, and water management. The governor appoints the members, with approval of the State Senate. Though the council represents the metropolitan area, and is highly influenced by local interests, it is, at its core, a state-created entity. Hypothetically, the creation of a metropolitan council can be more easily accomplished in a state like Minnesota with its single large, dominating metropolitan area than in states that have multiple metropolitan areas. In Minnesota, a large proportion of the state legislators came from districts within the Twin Cities region, and this offered a unique opportunity for unifying interests on urban issues.

Other notable large-scale regional commissions created in the 1960s and early 1970s include the Association of Bay Area Governments (ABAG), the San Francisco Bay Conservation and Development Commission (BCDC), the Lake Tahoe Regional Compact and the New Jersey Meadowlands Commission. The Association of Bay Area Governments, established in 1962, is the comprehensive planning agency for the San Francisco Bay Area, and it deals with regional issues such as economic development, education, environment, housing, and transportation. On the other hand, the San Francisco Bay Conservation and Development Commission, which calls itself the nation's first coastal management agency, has a more geographically fixed focus. The commission, created in 1965, is charged with the protection and enhancement of San Francisco Bay. The Lake Tahoe Regional Compact is a unique entity in that it required co-enacted laws in California and Nevada, and authorization by the U.S. Congress in 1969.[63] The interstate compact administers the Tahoe Regional Planning Authority, which has prepared a long-range plan for the basin and administers regulations enforcing the plan. The New Jersey Meadowlands are located in a lowland area north of Newark and Jersey City. The commission, formed in 1968, is responsible for economic development, environmental protection, and solid waste management. In all of these cases, recognition of the need to balance short-range economic gain with long-term environmental protection overcame the pressures of developer's with a "bulldozer mentality." This happens all too infrequently.

Significant steps toward forms of metropolitan governance were also taken in Florida. As previously mentioned, voters in Miami-Dade County adopted a home rule charter in 1957, which created a county commission with broad legislative powers to the extent the commission was granted authority to enact local laws that were not in direct conflict with Florida general law. A different and more complete approach to regional governance occurred in Jacksonville and Duval County. In 1966, voters in Duval County, the City of Jacksonville, and some of the smaller cities within the county passed a referendum creating the City of Jacksonville consolidated government. Only the town of Baldwin and the small cities of Atlantic Beach, Jacksonville Beach, and Neptune Beach chose to remain independent of the consolidated government. Whereas Jacksonville is a consolidated government, Miami-Dade County is a federation: a strong county in a union with semi-independent municipal governments.

Elsewhere in Florida, a variety of approaches to regional thinking—at least in regard to "comprehensive" planning—were surfacing throughout the state;[64] for example, the Miami-Dade County Charter provided for countywide planning. A boost to regional planning occurred in 1959 when the legislature enacted Chapter 59-369, *Acts of Florida*,[65] allowing the organization of regional planning councils. The initial draft of the law was prepared by the Center for Practical Politics at Rollins College.[66] A year earlier, the Center had convened a Conference on Metropolitan Regionalism in Florida, chaired by Franklin Albert of Orlando. John T. Howard, head of the Department of City and Regional Planning, Harvard University, helped plan the conference, and Charles Haar of the Harvard Law School served as a consultant for the conference, along with Paul G. Watt of the National Capital Regional Planning Council and Carl Feiss, at that time a planning consultant operating out of Washington, DC.[67]

Five multi-county regional planning councils were created in the 1960s under this authorization. The first two were organized in 1962: the East Central Florida Regional Planning Council (which at that time included Brevard, Indian River, Orange, Osceola, Seminole, and Volusia counties) and the Tampa Bay Regional Planning Council (initially organized by representatives from the municipalities of Bradenton, Clearwater, St. Petersburg, Sarasota, and Tampa).[68] These were followed in 1964 by the Escarosa Regional Planning Council (which paired Escambia and Santa Rosa counties), and in 1969 by the Jacksonville Area Planning Board (which included Duval and Nassau counties) and the South Florida Everglades Area Planning Council (covering Broward, Collier, Dade, Monroe, and Palm Beach counties). The organization of the South Florida Everglades council was a political reaction to the now defunct plan to build a jetport in the Everglades.

Though not a multi-county operation, a consolidated Hillsborough City-County Planning Commission was established in 1959.[69] It consists of Hillsborough County and the cities of Tampa, Plant City, and Temple Terrace, all served by a single planning commission but with each participating government independently implementing its own plan and development regulations. Across the bay, a Pinellas Planning Council was formed by the cities of St. Petersburg and Clearwater, and the Pinellas County Board of County Commissioners in 1964; its structure and responsibilities were broadened by special acts of the state legislature in 1965, 1970, 1971, and later.[70] Further north, a Tallahassee-Leon County Planning Commission was created in 1967 as a joint city-county partnership. The city and county share the planning commission and planning staff, and operate from the same comprehensive plan and set of land development regulations (though much of the time, the administration of the regulations has been administered by separate city and county agencies, which results in different interpretations of implementation). The current North Central Florida Regional Planning Council began somewhat the same way, when, in 1968, Alachua County and five or six of the cities within it, including Gainesville, joined to become eligible for federal metropolitan planning grants.[71] The council later expanded to include surrounding counties. Municipalities and counties in Florida were beginning to look regionally (i.e., multi-county or at least countywide), even if most of the time it was merely to take advantage of federal 701 planning assistance funds or other federal grants requiring a regional perspective.[72]

Following the Federal Dollar—with Exceptions

Most local government comprehensive planning activity in the 1960s existed only because federal 701 planning assistance money could be used to meet the eligibility requirements of a variety of federal grant programs. Local plans were prepared in conformance with the planning guidelines set up by the U.S. Housing and Home Finance Agency (which later became the Department of Housing and Urban Development). Once the federal requirements were satisfied, most of the local governments placed their plans on a shelf, seldom to be used again.

Bypassing the constraints of the 701 approach to planning, a small cadre of local governments began to pioneer new approaches to planning and plan implementation. Ramapo, New York, is credited with being one of the first local governments to develop an innovative tool for managing future growth. This suburban community, on the urban fringe about twenty miles northwest of Manhattan, more than doubled its population in the 1960s. Along with its rapid growth, "the typical suburban concern for fitting growth to public facilities arose," said Israel Stollman, former executive director of the American Society of Planning Officials.[73] Concerned specifically about the timing of the availability of public facilities, Ramapo amended its zoning ordinance in 1969 to include a residential permit use, which established a point system based on the availability or planned availability of public services. Meanwhile, on the West Coast another locally initiated growth management program was emerging. Petaluma, California, was experiencing pressures similar to those of Ramapo. In 1972, Petaluma, an urban edge community located about twenty-five miles north of San Francisco, adopted a residential development control system that limited residential building permits to five hundred a year. Like Ramapo, the new ordinance supplemented existing land use regulations and, in Petaluma's case, created an urban growth boundary. Innovative growth management initiatives like these were gradually beginning to appear at the local government level, but they were too few, too scattered, and too localized to harness the sprawling, rapid growth that was occurring around them.

Events at the federal level gradually raised the consciousness of local and state governments about the need to plan. Though most plans, whether assisted by federal 701 financing or not, were ignored once completed, the planning idea was having an educational impact. The concept gradually permeated the consciousness of progressive elected officials, administrators, and citizens intent on finding new ways to meet the challenges of the decade. Though somewhat late in coming, this permeation of consciousness was as true for Florida as it was for any other state, the major difference being that Florida was in greater need given the massive, uncontrolled growth it was experiencing.

Florida Begins to Respond to the Need for Planning

In *Baker v. Carr*, the U.S. Supreme Court, in 1962, set in motion changes in the representative apportionment of state legislatures.[74] The court required all state legislatures or general assemblies to be apportioned to the population represented in each legislative district by a ratio of one-man, one-vote. The decision changed the characteristics of state houses across the nation: legislative bodies were thenceforth required to be representative of a state's demography. In Florida, for example, the State Senate and House of Representatives by 1967 consisted mostly of representatives from urban counties such as Miami-Dade, Broward, Orange, Hillsborough, Pinellas, and Duval for the first time in the twentieth century. The logjam had been broken, but not easily; it had resisted until the U.S. District Court in Miami ruled that the 1967 session of the legislature could not begin until all incumbents were out of office and an election held within court-approved districts.[75] As David R. Colburn and Lance deHaven-Smith point out, the result was that, "The most significant advances in the modernization of Florida government occurred in the late 1960s and the early 1970s."[76] The change brought a new breed of state legislators to Tallahassee, men like Frederick Shultz of Jacksonville, Richard Pettigrew and Talbot D'Alemberte of Miami, Robert Graham of Miami Lakes, and Terrell Sessums of Tampa. They and other urban legislators were mostly young, professional urban dwellers, enthusiastic about the opportunity to address both urban problems and the outdated 1885 state constitution.

A new constitution, adopted by Florida voters in 1968, limited the executive branch of state government to no more than twenty-five departments, other than those provided for in the constitution itself. This restriction was implemented through the Executive Reorganization Act of 1969.[77] Thus, in a bold stroke, over 200 state commissions, boards, and agencies, which had evolved in the long history of the antiquated constitution, were abolished. The new constitution also provided home rule for local governments, supposedly (but not actually) eliminating the well-established tradition of "special acts" which had been necessary for local governments to engage in planning, land use regulation, and other initiatives.

It also gave the legislature and governor specific responsibility to protect natural resources and the environment.

Throughout most of its history the executive branch of Florida's state government has operated—and continues to operate—under a *plural* executive. Since the state constitution of 1885, the people of the state have been reluctant to put all of the powers of the executive branch in the hands of one person, the governor. Some powers of the executive branch were (and still are) divided between the governor and a number of other independently and constitutionally elected officials. Combined, they are called the Governor and Cabinet; but be sure, it is not the "governor's" cabinet. The governor, though not *officially* a member of the cabinet itself, chairs meetings and is authorized to vote. In the 1960s, the cabinet consisted of the attorney general, the secretary of state, the comptroller, the treasurer, the commissioner of agriculture, and the commissioner of education, all elected independently statewide.[78] Most state agencies operated under the supervision of the governor, but the cabinet officers supervised their own agencies, and the Governor and Cabinet shared executive responsibility for some agencies or functions.[79]

Florida's chief executive had another significant weakness: until the *Constitution of the State of Florida* was revised in 1968, it denied the governor the authority to prepare a budget. This power lay instead with a budget commission composed of the Governor and Cabinet. Given the compromises required in such a plural executive system and the challenges generated by a rapidly growing population, it is not surprising that a survey taken in 1967 showed that most of the people surveyed identified government reorganization/constitutional revision as the biggest problem facing the state.[80] The omnibus 1968 amendments to the constitution did strengthen the hand of the governor, but it was still necessary to act in concert with the cabinet members on many matters. Nevertheless, the effort initiated by Governor Millard Fillmore Caldwell (1945-1949) two decades earlier to reorganize and streamline state government, only to be quashed by rural legislators reluctant to strengthen the governor's office,[81] had finally produced a positive result.

Florida was among the last states to respond to the state planning movement that took hold in the 1960s. At that time, the Florida Development Commission (FDC) had five professional planners on its staff, but they were not involved in state planning; their job was to administer 701 planning assistance program grants for local government planning.[82] In 1965, the FDC expanded its planning horizon when it applied for 701 funds to undertake a population study and a statewide recreation study. However, the U.S. Department of Housing and Urban Development (HUD) denied the application, refusing to fund specialized studies until the state had at least initiated a program design for statewide comprehensive planning.[83] When the FDC submitted a revised 701 application to design a comprehensive state planning program, as well as inventory planning resources in the functional departments of state government, HUD approved a grant of $27,568. The program had two parts: the design aspect, contracted to Harold F. Wise, a state planning consultant of national repute, and an inventory segment under the direction of David Godschalk, then a faculty member of the Department of Urban and Regional Planning at Florida State University. In the meantime, a second locus of interest in state planning was building in the legislature, an interest that foretold an expanded role for planning, a role to help guide the state in its growth while at the same time improving the management of Florida state government.

Frederick H. Schultz, the speaker-elect of the Florida House of Representatives, introduced legislation in 1967 to set up a state commission of planning and budgeting. He was interested in improving the effectiveness and efficiency of state government, especially in controlling spending. Schultz had been introduced to planning when he attended a special program sponsored by the IBM Corporation in which the importance of planning to private corporations was discussed; he felt the same process should be applicable to state government.[84] The speaker-elect envisioned a state law that would require each incoming executive branch administration to abide by the objectives of a state plan.[85] To help him in writing a bill, he sought aid from the Atlantic Test Center of the Boeing Company at Cape Kennedy, and Boeing assigned their director of planning, Paul Busse, to assist him.[86] A new planning and programming act was in the making.

Initially, Governor Claude R. Kirk, Jr., the first Republican governor in Florida in the twentieth century, was not interested in the bill, primarily because he felt he could accomplish much of what it proposed by executive order. This may have seemed a bit strange since he had been a member of the State Planning Committee of the National Governors' Conference, but it more likely was his way of saying he opposed the proposal that the director of the planning office be appointed by the cabinet.[87] However, Kirk threw his support behind the bill when Democratic leaders agreed to a compromise enabling him, not the cabinet, to appoint the director. He held the position that the governor should be the chief planner and that the director of the state planning agency should be someone who should report directly to him. He apparently saw this as a way to strengthen his management hand within Florida's plural executive system. However, there was a stipulation in the compromise: the cabinet could veto the governor's appointment if they did not concur.

The bill passed with near unanimous support and became a progenitor of Florida's current state planning law. The act, signed into law on June 7, 1967, created an Office of State Planning (OSP) and an Office of Budgeting within a State Planning and Budget Commission (the Governor and Cabinet).[88] The budget function was transferred from the former Budget Commission (also the Governor and Cabinet) and the authority for state planning was brought over from the Florida Development Commission.[89] The act designated the governor as the chief planning officer, required a state plan, and directed the head of the office to coordinate all state planning and programming. The act further stipulated that the OSP formulate overall goals and objectives, prepare annual development programs, develop financial schedules for accomplishing the plans and programs, and prepare a six-year schedule of capital improvements. To accomplish these tasks, the OSP was organized into five sections: planning operations, community affairs, comprehensive health planning, information, and programming. The initial staff also included an economist, a federal programs specialist, and a planning-programming specialist.[90]

Florida had adopted a state-of-the-art state planning act, and it seemed to be off to a good start managing state responsibilities in development and growth. As speaker-elect Schultz said, for the first time "the state will be able to know where it is and where it is going."[91] The new law made long-range planning the responsibility of the governor, who could then oversee the preparation of a state plan and ensure that the plan was adhered to, at least by the agencies directly responsible to him. The act also required state agencies to plan and, as part of programming, prepare financial schedules. In addition, the OSP was charged with being the principal staff agency of the executive branch in the planning of matters concerning the resources and development of the state. In this capacity, it was to be the lead agency in confronting the growth problems inundating Florida, but the OSP never exercised this responsibility. Furthermore, the office was to be responsible for harmonizing the planning activities of federal, state, regional, and local agencies, another task that was unachieved.

A noteworthy state planning act had been created by the legislature and the baton of responsibility had been passed to the executive branch, but Florida's plural executive system became an obstacle: the cabinet could veto a governor's nominee to head the planning office. The act failed to achieve its lofty goals because it was enacted at a time when the legislature and the cabinet, traditionally controlled by the Democrats, were confronted by Governor Kirk, a Republican—a perfect setting for the play of partisan politics. The effect of the veto provision became evident after the cabinet rejected first one and then another of Governor Kirk's nominees, until after several months, the late Homer E. Still, Jr., who had been director of planning and evaluation for the Board of Regents, was named to head the new agency in May 1968.[92] Homer Still was a respected high-level administrator who had once worked for state budget director Wallace Henderson—but he was not from Kirk's inner circle.[93] He knowingly accepted the challenge to walk the "thin political line" between the governor and the cabinet.[94]

Having lost the opportunity to name a planning director of his own preference, the flamboyant governor, who had dubbed the Governor and Cabinet as "Governor Kirk and the Six Dwarfs,"[95] lost interest in the OSP. Orphaned from the governor, Homer Still directed the staff of the newly created OSP to focus on developing the programming component of the new planning, programming, and budgeting (PPB) system. This was fortuitous for Henderson who was in the midst of trying to convert the budget process into a PPB system. Thus, it was possible for senior budget people to influence the direction of the planning program. To them, this seemed to be an opportunity to have the SPO orient the program component of the PPB system to budget needs. The SPO thereafter attended to an important but more bounded focus that did not appear to address problems relating to the state's rampant growth. The initially intended state planning responsibilities evaporated under constraints similar to those mentioned earlier by S. Kenneth Howard regarding the tension between planning and budgeting. Very little attention was placed on the state's spatial patterns, its urban growth, and the land use responsibilities of the OSP. As Fred Williams, former senior planner for education in the SPO, indicated, "The program budget was viewed as 'the plan,' thus getting in the way of any concerted effort to prepare a long-range, comprehensive state plan as called for in the 1967 act."[96] Meanwhile, the overall PPB effort was meeting with its own set of frustrations.

Installing a PPB system at any level of government was a formidable task, made even more complex in Florida because of its pluralistic executive branch.[97] Even under normal circumstances, it would take considerable time to design a system, educate the actors in the process, and work out the many kinks likely to arise, but time and education were not luxuries afforded to personnel in the State Planning and Budget Commission. They had the responsibility of attempting to institutionalize a PPB system in a time of turmoil and organizational change. Turmoil was a corollary of the volatile political atmosphere during the Kirk administration and organizational change was a consequence of, first, the Planning and Budgeting Commission Act of 1968, then the adoption of a new state constitution that same year, and finally a state reorganization act that followed a year later. According to a case study on the Florida PPB experience, "the reorganization act had a profound influence upon the relationship between the governor and state planning and budgeting activities."[98] The act abolished the State Planning and Budget Commission and transferred its planning and budgeting functions to a new Department of Administration, directly under the governor. The functions were placed in a Division of Planning and Budgeting, which consisted of the Bureau of Planning[99] and the Bureau of Budgeting. Despite finally coming under the direct hand of the governor, both the state planning function and the PPB system (still a responsibility of the budget staff) were not utilized by him. Lacking commitment from the governor, most state line agencies ignored the PPB process.[100]

In spite of Governor Kirk's withdrawal of interest in state planning (and the PPB system), John M. DeGrove later credited him as having "set the stage for what was accomplished in the early 1970s."[101] DeGrove, never a political supporter of Kirk, commended the governor for appointing Nathaniel Pryor Reed, former assistant secretary of the U.S. Department of Interior, under President Richard Nixon, as an unpaid chief advisor for environmental affairs. Reed was instrumental in assisting the governor in taking action to stop the Miami-Dade County Port Authority from completing an international airport in the Everglades and initiating steps to halt construction of the Cross-Florida Barge Canal.[102] These projects would have caused irreparable damage to Florida's environment had they been completed. Reed also was to be instrumental in helping to shape Florida's growth management program in the coming decades.

Florida's attempt to address state planning achieved less than what had been intended, and within four years, a new set of progressive thinkers joined together to try to find a way to effectively manage the state's rampant growth. The initial effort had become myopic, and to break the shackles that bound it so closely to the budget function, the reformers of the early 1970s concluded that it would be better to rewrite the state planning act than to just amend what already existed. Therefore, progressive thinkers like Richard Pettigrew, speaker of the House of Representatives, and John DeGrove from Florida Atlantic University, who came with the newly inaugurated administration of Governor Reubin O'Donovan Askew, set out to completely readdress the matter of planning at all levels of government in Florida—state, regional, and local.

Incremental Expansion of Interest in
Local and Regional Planning

In the 1960s, the majority of Florida jurisdictions were too rapt with growth to think about any need for planning.[103] Planning was not something most local government leaders thought they needed to do and, furthermore, to do so would be politically unpopular. They did not want to do anything to jeopardize population growth, especially with something that, in their perspective, could lead to regulation of land and possibly "impair" development. Most local leaders failed—or refused—to recognize there might be a down side to uncontrolled growth—and, hence, local and statewide growth machines operated unhindered.[104]

A tentative step toward considering matters regionally surfaced in a resolution of the Florida State Planning and Budget Commission in 1968, which recommended a set of uniform regional districts.[105] A more significant step came a year later with the enactment of the Interlocal Cooperation Act of 1969.[106] This statute provided general enabling legislation for local governments (counties, cities, special districts) to engage in planning at their own initiative, and it permitted them to voluntarily cooperate with other localities or private entities to provide services and facilities in meeting the needs of local governments, including the creation of regional planning councils. Responding to the opportunity provided by this act and to the home rule provisions of the new Florida constitution, cities and counties gradually bent to the winds of change and began to engage in local planning. It was the culmination of years of effort by professional planners like Fred Bair and Ernest Bartley in Gainesville, Frank Branan in Tallahassee-Leon County, and other members of the Florida Planning and Zoning Association, the American Institute of Planners, and the Florida Association of the American Institute of Architects.[107] A gradually increasing number of municipalities and counties in Florida prepared comprehensive plans with assistance from the federal 701 planning program, but, as the 1960s closed and the 1970s opened, most cities and rural communities in Florida—even if they were growing—were still not interested in what planning had to offer beyond making themselves eligible for federal grants.

There were exceptions to this general disinterest in effective planning, however. For example, in metropolitan Miami-Dade County, the Board of County Commissioners adopted a general land use master plan in 1965 and revised its zoning map to be consistent with the plan. The county planning department made an analysis of each land use change proposed and the report became part of the record during county commission hearings.[108] In addition to Miami-Dade County, a few other local jurisdictions in Florida—located in rapidly growing suburban or recreation areas—seized the opportunity and not only took planning seriously, but took *plan implementation* even more seriously. For example, the city of Coral Gables continued to adhere to its 1926 master plan with strict interpretation of its land use designations. The people of the city were not satisfied with the prevailing tendency to disregard an adopted plan and rely on the vagaries of zoning as a land use control. Coral Gables had enough concern about its appearance and long-term welfare to continue its practice of rigorous architectural review of proposed new developments. Today, Coral Gables is regarded as one of the finest places to live in south Florida.

Summary

The nation experienced tumultuous change during the decade of the 1960s. New technologies, growth, migration, urban unrest, national unrest with the Vietnam War, and urban sprawl all combined to change the economic, social, environmental, and political face of America. When the decade opened, the cities were incapable of contending with this change on their own, and the states, for the most part, were still underplaying the needs of their urban jurisdictions or critical environmental areas. State governments were still in the hands of malapportioned legislatures dominated by rural legislators, who believed they were not elected to take care of urban issues. The urban areas needed help, and since they were not getting it from the states, the federal government addressed the challenge. Late in the decade, with reapportionment taking hold, many states began to respond to the new needs by updating their constitutions, strengthening the management capabilities of the governors, and responding to urban needs by creating departments of urban or community affairs. But more than this was going to be needed.

With progressive leadership on the part of some governors, state legislators, and citizen-leaders, plus a huge nudge from the *Baker v. Carr* decision, the states, including Florida, began to rejuvenate their role in the federal system. First came the need to strengthen the management hands of the governors and then for the states to assume their responsibilities to their urban populations. It appeared that state planning would become one of the principal tools for strengthening a governor's management capability. However, was it to be the land use oriented planning derived from the municipal model and brought to a higher plane, or was it to evolve into the policy-oriented process espoused by the National Governors' Conference and others? And what about acting regionally? Some regional planning councils were involved in planning, but primarily in order for their constituent local jurisdictions to become eligible for federal grants. As for local government planning, becoming eligible for certain federal grants was the principal, and sometimes only reason they too were involved in planning; there were exceptions to this attitude, but not many.

Florida, in the face of massive, rapid, and basically unmanaged growth, struggled mightily with these issues, and the struggle was far from over when the 1970s began. Ahead were questions of how state planning could best serve state government. Could a comprehensive state plan be a meaningful guide to decision making? How could threatened natural resources be protected? What role could regional and metropolitan planning councils play beyond persuasion and technical assistance? Could urban sprawl be contained? How could local jurisdictions use planning to manage more effectively their growth? How should the state be a better steward of its natural and environmental resources? In addition, how could citizens play a more significant role in the planning process and plan implementation?[109] The period from the early 1960s to the early 1970s posed many questions, and Florida would find the challenges were only beginning to be addressed.

NOTES FOR CHAPTER V

1   Van Horn, Carl E., ed., "The Quiet Revolution," in *The State of the States*, Washington, DC: CQ Press, 1989, p. 2.

2   Kennedy, John F., *Inaugural Address*, January 20, 1961, Washington, DC.

3   The Florida legislature in 1967 created the Reedy Creek Improvement District, a public corporation of the state (Ch. 67-764 *General Laws of Florida* & Ch. 67-1104 *General Laws of Florida*), which provided Disney World with broad governmental powers making it "self-governing," virtually independent of the local governmental units around it. The second of the acts listed above created the City of Bay Lake (later renamed the City of Lake Buena Vista), a Disney controlled municipality within the district.

4   Mormino, Gary R., *Land of Sunshine, State of Dreams: A Social History of Modern Florida*, Gainesville, FL: University Press of Florida, 2005, pp. 50-55.

5   Ibid, p. 50.

6   Ibid, pp. 53-55.

7   Grad, Frank P., "The States' Capacity to Respond to Urban Problems," in Alan K. Campbell, ed., *The States and the Urban Crisis* Englewood Cliffs, NJ: Prentice-Hall, Inc., 1970, p. 30.

8   Advisory Commission on Intergovernmental Relations, "The Federal Role in Regionalism," in Kent Mathewson, ed., *The Regionalist Papers*, Detroit: Metropolitan Fund, 1977, p. 192.

9   Joyner, John R., "The Coordination of Federally Required Functional Plans Prepared by Counterpart State Agencies," *Planning and the Federal Establishment*, proceedings of the AIP Fourth Biennial Government Relations and Planning Policy Conference, Washington, DC: American Institute of Planners, 1967, p. 10.

10   Ibid, as quoted on p. 10.

11   Council of State Governments, *State Responsibility in Urban and Regional Development* Chicago: Council of State Governments, 1962, p. 51. The states were Alaska, California, Colorado, Connecticut, Hawaii, Illinois, Maine, Minnesota, New Jersey, New Mexico, Oregon, Pennsylvania, Rhode Island, Tennessee, Vermont, Wisconsin, and Puerto Rico. All were listed in this reference, except Vermont, which was added by personal experience of Richard RuBino.

12   U.S., Title 40, Ch. 10, § V, s. 531.

13   U.S., 42 U.S.C. 1450, s. 104, Public Law 89-754.

14   Circular A-95 superseded Circular No. A-82, and built upon the review process established under Section 204, and related to Circular

No. A-80, which encouraged regional planning based on regions established by state governments. Federal programs assisting planning and development were required to conform to these regions, unless there was clear justification for not doing so. Circular A-82 also required that applicants identify related planning and development activities in the region and demonstrate how planning and development would be coordinated among them. In 1982, President Ronald Reagan issued Executive Order 12372 replacing Circular A-95 with a review and comment system that functioned in a somewhat similar manner.

15 Douglas, Marjory Stoneman, *The Everglades; River of Grass*, 50th Anniversary Edition, Sarasota, FL: Pineapple Press, 2005.
16 Carson, Rachel, *Silent Spring*, Boston, MA: Haught Miflin Company, 1962.
17 Udal, Stewart L., *The Quiet Crisis*, New York: Avon Books, 1963.
18 Carson, ibid, p. 16.
19 Ibid, p. 66.
20 Among other environmentally oriented programs were the Water Resources Planning Act of 1965 (P.L. 89-80, 42 USC 1962 et seq.), the Clean Water Restoration Act of 1966 (P.L. 89-753), the Air Quality Act of 1967 (P.L. 90-148), and the Clean Air Act of 1970 (42 U.S.C. 7401-7671q).
21 Reilly, William K., ed., *The Use of Land: A Citizens' Policy Guide to Urban Growth*, New York: Thomas Y. Croswell Company, 1973, p. 71.
22 U.S. Urban Mass Transportation Act of 1964, PL 88-365, Ch. 53, Title 49, U.S.C.
23 On November 13 1997 the Dade County Charter was amended to change the name from Dade County to Miami-Dade County.
24 Sanford, Terry, *Storm Over the States*, New York: McGraw-Hill Book Company, 1967.
25 Ibid, p. 164.
26 Wise, Harold F. and Bertram Wakeley, "The Practice of State Planning and Policy Development," *State Government* 57: 3, 1984, p. 87.
27 See for example: National Municipal League, *Model State and Regional Planning Law*, New York, 1955, p. 16.
28 Conant, James K., "In the Shadow of Wilson and Brownlow: Executive Branch Reorganization in the States, 1965-1987," *Public Administration Review* 48: 5, 1988, pp. 892-902.
29 Sanford, ibid, pgs. 123-143.
30 Wise, Harold F., from a paper presented at a panel on "The States Begin to Plan," *Proceedings of the AIP Conference*, 1963.
31 Sanford, ibid, p. 187.

32 Council of State Governments, *State Responsibility in Urban and Regional Government*, Chicago, 1962, p. 65.

33 Ylvisaker became the first commissioner of the New Jersey Department of Community Affairs, the model for other states to follow; he later became dean of Harvard University's Graduate School of Education.

34 James G. Richardson (1969-1971) was followed as secretary of DCA by Athalie Range (1971-1973), Edward J. Trombetta (1973-1975), William Ravenell (1975-1979), Joan M. Heggen (1979-1983), and others who are named in this and following chapters.

35 Former governor of New Mexico, Jack M. Campbell, was chairman of the Institute; Philip V. Maher, former director of the Missouri Office of State and Regional Planning, was its director; and Richard RuBino, who had been a planning consultant and later the director of the Vermont State Central Planning Office, was the institute's deputy director.

36 The State Planning Committee was created in 1962. In 1967, it consisted of John A. Love, CO, as chair; Harold E. Hughes, IA; Owen S. Aspinall, American Samoa; Manuel F.L. Guerrero, Guam; Otto Kerner, IL; Claude R. Kirk, Jr., FL; Robert E. McNair, SC; Ronald Reagan, CA; Roberto Sanchez-Vilella, Puerto Rico; John A. Volpe, MA; and Jack Williams, AZ.

37 Richard RuBino was a founding member of the Council of State Planning Agencies (CSPA), and presented a paper at the Toronto meeting. The CSPA later became the Council of Governors Policy Advisors in 1990 and was disbanded in 1997.

38 Wise, Harold F., "State Planning: An Executive Responsibility," a paper presented at the Fifth Annual Meeting of the Midwestern Governors' Conference, Cincinnati, OH, June 20, 1966, as reported in Tilden Curry, *The State Comprehensive Plan: An Evaluation of Its Relevance to Public Decision-Making and State Planning Methodology*, a dissertation accepted by the Department of Urban and Regional Planning, Florida State University, Tallahassee, FL, 1979, p. 8.

39 Hawaii, Ch. 205, *Hawaii Statutes*. The Hawaii law initially divided the state into three districts: agricultural, conservation, and urban; a rural district was added in 1963. The State had direct land management responsibilities akin to zoning in all but urban districts.

40 RuBino, Richard G., and William R. Wagner, *The States' Role in Land Resource Management* Lexington, KY: Council of State Governments, 1972, p. 9.

41　The term comes from a report of the same name prepared by Fred Bosselman and David Callies in 1972, for the Council on Environmental Quality.

42　Massachusetts, Ch. 131, s. 40, *Massachusetts General Laws*. The act is administered at the state level by the Department of Environmental Protection and at the local level by conservation commissions appointed by the selectmen or city councils.

43　Wisconsin, s. 59.692, *Wisconsin Statutes*. Counties are required to adopt and enforce zoning standards that meet or exceed the standards. The Department of Natural Resources is the responsible State agency.

44　Massachusetts, Ch. 40B, *Massachusetts General Laws*. This law empowers a State Housing Appeals Committee to override a local zoning decision if less than ten percent of a local government's housing is classified as affordable.

45　Colorado Land Use Act, Ch. 106-4, CRS, 1971; Delaware Coastal Zone Act, Ch. 70, T. 7, 1971; Florida Environmental Land and Water Management Act, Ch. 380, *Florida Statutes*, 1972; Maine state management of unorganized or de-organized townships (Title 12, s. 681-689, 1969), large site industrial or commercial developments (Ch. 3, s. 481-488, 1970), and critical areas (Ch. 424, s. 4811-4814, 1971); Michigan Shorelines Management and Protection Act, Act No. 245, *Public Acts of 1970*; Minnesota, policy oriented planning in governor's office*; Nevada, consideration by State Planning Board*; New York, Adirondack Park Agency Act, Article 27, *NYS Executive Law*, 1971; Oregon, Land Conservation and Development Act, SB 100, *Oregon Statutes*, 1973; South Carolina, studies by state transportation agency and special commission*; Texas, considered by Division of Planning Coordination, 1972*; Vermont, Environmental Control Act (10 *Vermont Statutes*, 1970), Shoreline Zoning Act (Act 281, 1970), and approval of site development in accordance with state land use plan (Ch. 151, 6001, 1970); and West Virginia, policy oriented planning in Office of Federal-State Relations, 1969. *Personal involvement by Richard RuBino.

46　Millward, Robert E., "PPBS: Problems of Implementation," *Journal of the American Institute of Planners* 34: 2, 1968, p. 89.

47　Institute on State Programming for the 70s, *Relevance, Reliance, and Realism*, prepared for National Governors' Conference, Committee on State Planning, University of North Carolina-Chapel Hill: Institute on State Programming for the 70s, 1967, p. 9.

48　Howard, S. Kenneth, "Some Thoughts About State Planning and Budgeting," a paper presented at the Council of State Planning Agencies

Biennial Conference on Governmental Relations and Planning Policy, Washington, DC, January 28-31, 1971. For further coverage of the same subject see S. Kenneth Howard, "Planning and Budgeting: Marriage Whose Style?" in Thad L. Beyle and George T. Lathrop, eds., *Planning and Politics: Uneasy Partnership*, New York City: Odyssey Press of Bobbs-Merrill, Inc., 1970, pp. 144-167.

49   Steiner, George A., "Problems in Implementing Program Budgeting," in David Novick, ed., *Program Budgeting: Program Analysis and the Federal Budget*, Cambridge, MA: Harvard University Press, 1965, p. 346.

50   The participating states were: California, Michigan, New York, Vermont, and Wisconsin (Florida's PPB program, discussed later in this chapter, was independent of this project); the counties were: Dade (Florida), Davidson (Tennessee), Los Angeles (California), Nassau (New York), and Wayne (Michigan); and the cities were Dayton (Ohio), Denver (Colorado), Detroit (Michigan), New Haven (Connecticut), and San Diego (California). The project, sponsored by Council of State Governments, the National Association of Counties, the National League of Cities, and the U.S. Conference of Mayors was under the directorship of Selma Muskin at George Washington University. This information was obtained, in part, from Harold F. Wise, "Planning-Programming-Budgeting Systems and the Planning Role," in *Planning and the Federal Establishment*, Proceedings of AIP's Fourth Biennial Government Relations and Planning Policy Conference, Washington, DC, January 27-29, 1967.

51   Council of State Governments, "Survey of State Planning Agencies' Activities," prepared for the Council of State Planning Agencies by the Council of State Governments, Lexington, KY, April 1971, p. 8.

52   Wise, Harold F., *History of State Planning: An Interpretive Commentary*, State Planning Series 1, Washington, DC: Council of State Planning Agencies, an affiliate of the National Governors' Association, 1977, pp. 18-20.

53   Brooks, Michael P., "Four Critical Junctures in the History of the Urban Planning Profession: An Exercise in Hindsight," *Journal of the American Institute of Planners* 54, Spring 1988, p. 243.

54   See for example, Richard Briffault, "Our Localism: Part I—The Structure of Local Government Law," *Columbia Law Review* 90: 1, 1990, pp. 1-115, and ibid, "Our Localism: Part II—Localism and Legal Theory," *Columbia Law Review* 90: 2, 1990, pp. 346-455.

55   Council of State Governments, ibid, p. 16.

56   U.S. Public Works and Economic Development Act of 1965, 42 U.S.C. 3141, s. 201, Public Law 105-393.

57 Youngquist, Jim, Carl Vinson Institute of Government, Athens, GA, obtained from a letter to Earl Starnes, dated April 29, 2004.

58 New Jersey Transportation Association, "History of MPOs – Part II," *NJTA Journal*, December 1996; obtained from http://www.njta.org/public_affairs/mpo_history/hist_mpo2.htm on June 7, 2004.

59 The three-C planning process was authorized by the Federal Highway Act of 1962; this often is regarded as being the start of what led to the metropolitan (transportation) planning organization (MPO) concept.

60 New Jersey Transportation Association, "History of MPOs – Part III," *NJTA Journal*, December 1996; obtained from http://www.njta.org/public_affairs/mpo_history/hist_mpo3.htm, on June 7, 2004.

61 Ashford, Norman and Richard G. RuBino, "The Role of the State in Transportation," *Traffic Engineering* 42: 4, 1972, pp. 13-17.

62 For greater detail see Arthur Naftalin, *Making One Community Out of Many*, St. Paul: Metro Council of the Twin Cities Area, 1986.

63 California Government Code 66801 (and a similar law in Nevada) and U.S. Public Law 96-551, 1980.

64 This paragraph refers to regional councils involved in the *comprehensive* planning of the time, and does not include reference to numerous *specialized* regional planning councils created in response to federally funded programs such as regional health planning councils.

65 Chapter 160, *Florida Statutes*.

66 Douglas, Paul, *Regional Planning Councils in Florida*, Center for Practical Politics, Rollins College, Winter Park, FL, c. 1969, p. 3.

67 Ibid, p. 2. Watt latter became the first planning director for Dade County.

68 Ibid, p. 8.

69 *Florida State Law*, HB 2027, 06, 1959.

70 Undated document by unknown author circa 1982.

71 Information provided by Charles F. Justice, executive director of the North Central Florida Regional Planning Council, in an email message on May 5, 2005.

72 One of the "other" federal programs requiring a regional approach was the popular Overall Economic Development District program administered by the U.S. Economic Development Administration; this more specifically-oriented program is not included in our discussion of broad-based regional planning.

73 Stollman, Israel, "Ramapo: An Editorial & the Ordinance as Amended," in Randall W. Scott, ed., *Management & Control of Growth*, Volume II, Washington, DC: The Urban Land Institute, 1975, p. 5.

74 U.S., *Baker v. Carr* (369 U.S. 186, 1962), brought by citizens of Memphis to improve urban representation in the Tennessee State Assembly.

75 Barnett, Cynthia, "Saving Florida: A History of Growth Management in the Sunshine State," a thesis for the Master of Arts Degree at the University of Florida, Gainesville, December 2003, p. 13.

76 Colburn, David R. and Lance deHaven-Smith, *Government in the Sunshine State: Florida Since Statehood*, Gainesville, FL: University Press of Florida, 1999, p. 78.

77 Chapter 20, *Florida Statutes*, 1969.

78 Effective January 7, 2003, the cabinet was, by constitutional amendment, reduced to three members: the attorney general, the commissioner of agriculture and consumer affairs, and the chief financial officer. This constitutional amendment provides that in the event of a tie vote the governor's vote shall prevail; *Constitution of the State of Florida*, Article IV, s. 4, see "History."

79 Beginning in 2005, the Governor and Cabinet hold executive responsibility for the following entities: Administration Commission, Board of Administration, Board of Executive Clemency, Board of Trustees of the Internal Improvement Trust Fund, Department of Highway Safety and Motor Vehicles, Department of Law Enforcement, Department of Revenue, Department of Veterans' Affairs, Division of Bond Finance, Electrical Power Plant and Transmission Line Siting Board, Financial Services Commission, Land and Water Adjudicatory Commission, and the Office of Insurance Regulation.

80 Institute on State Programming for the 70s, "A Survey of the Present Status, Effectiveness, and Acceptance of Planning and Advanced Programming in State Government," University of North Carolina-Chapel Hill: Institute on State Programming for the 70s, 1967. (Participants in the interviews were primarily state government and community leaders or persons assigned by those leaders.)

81 Colburn & deHaven-Smith, ibid, p. 36.

82 Heale, Jack, deputy administrator of 701 planning, Florida Development Commission, obtained from "A Summary of Planning Activities in Florida," an interview by Oliver Williams for the Institute on State Programming for the 70s, University of North Carolina-Chapel Hill, 1967, p. 26.

83 Williams, Oliver, ibid, p. 11.

84 Ibid.

85 Ibid, p. 13.

86 Busse eventually became the first assistant director of the State Planning Office.

87　Williams, Oliver, ibid, p. 17.

88　Chapter 67-157, *Laws of Florida.*

89　The Florida Development Commission continued to administer the federal Section 701 planning assistance program.

90　Clark, Erica, "Florida State Planning," report prepared for Planning Education Symposium, Institute on State Programming for the 70s, University of North Carolina-Chapel Hill, 1968, p. 6. According to Clark (p. 7), the creation of OSP's section on community affairs roughly coincided with a proposal for a cabinet level department of urban affairs.

91　Ibid, p. 2.

92　Still, Homer, obtained from a telephone interview by Richard RuBino, on June 12, 2004. Robert Rosche, coordinator of the Office of Economic Opportunity in the governor's office, had been Governor Kirk's earlier choice to head the OSP.

93　Wallace Henderson had held the job of budget director through three administrations. He is reported to have said, "the Florida arrangement, in effect, makes it hard for the governor to place in the budget office, a man of his own choice." This information is recorded in an interview with Henderson by Oliver Williams, ibid., p. 23.

94　Tin, Eastern W., "The Florida PPB Experience: A Case Study," Department of Urban and Regional Planning, Florida State University, May 28, 1971, p. 22.

95　Kirk, Claude R., Jr., stated in a telephone interview by Richard RuBino on March 4, 2004. This statement had also been reported by the news media during Governor Kirk's term of office.

96　Williams, Fred, taken from an interview as reported in Tilden Curry, *The State Comprehensive Plan: An Evaluation of Its Relevance to Public Decision-Making and State Planning Methodology*, a dissertation accepted by the Department of Urban and Regional Planning, Florida State University, Tallahassee, FL, 1979.

97　See Tin, ibid, for a description of activities and events in attempting to institutionalize a PPB system in the executive branch of Florida state government.

98　Tin, ibid, p. 25.

99　The initial employees (and their responsibilities) in the Bureau of State Planning were Wallace Henderson (director), Homer Still (chief), Wayne Lynch (assistant chief), Gene Crowe (PPBS specialist), John Davis (health), Henry Leland (transportation), Fred Williams (education), Gary McDaniel, John Wagner, and an additional person. This information was provided by Fred Williams on December 22, 2005.

100 Ibid, pp. 14 and 35.

101 DeGrove, John, obtained from an interview by Cynthia Barnett on behalf of the Samuel Proctor Oral History Program at the University of Florida, Gainesville, on December 1, 2001.

102 Kallina, Edmund F., Jr., *Claude Kirk and the Politics of Confrontation*, Gainesville: University Press of Florida, 1993, p. 157.

103 One of the exceptions was Sun City Center, a self-contained retirement community developed near Tampa Bay, in 1960.

104 Molotch, Harvey, "The City as a Growth Machine: Toward a Political Economy of Place," *The American Journal of Sociology* 82: 2, 1976. Molotch observes that local decision-making centers on land development and he describes a growth machine as a politically powerful pro-growth coalition capable of influencing local decision-making to its advantage. Also see Terry Christensen, "Land-Use Policy: The Politics of Growth," in *Local Politics: Governing at the Grassroots*, Belmont, CA: Wadsworth Publishing, 1995, pp. 306-321; John R. Logan and Harvey Molotch, "The City as a Growth Machine," *Urban Fortunes*, Berkeley: University of California Press, 1988, pp. 50-98; and John R. Logan, Rachel Bridges Whaley, and Kyle Crowder, "The Character and Consequences of Growth Regimes: An Assessment of 20 Years of Research," *Urban Affairs Review* 32, 5, 1997, pp. 603-630.

105 Council of State Governments, "Sub-State District Systems," report of the National Governors' Conference Committee on Executive Management and Fiscal Affairs Advisory Task Force, Lexington, Kentucky, 1971, p. 17.

106 Ch. 163.01, Part 1, *Florida Statutes*.

107 The Florida Association of the American Institute of Architects "Red Flag Charrettes" initiative during the early 1970s identified both environmental and urban problems as the consequences of poor and sporadic local and state planning throughout the state.

108 Earl Starnes, who served on the Miami-Dade County Commission during the 1960s, contributed this information.

109 For typologies of participation, see Sherry R. Arnstein, "A Ladder of Citizen Participation," *Journal of the American Institute of Planners* 35: 4, pp. 45-54 and Elizabeth M. Rocha, "A Ladder of Empowerment," *Journal of Planning Education and Research* 17, pp. 31-44.

CHAPTER VI

A NEW PLANNING STRATEGY

The Early 1970s

> There are no other Everglades in the world ... The miracle of the light pours over the green and brown expanse of saw grass and of water, shining and slow-moving below, the grass and water that is the meaning of the central fact of the Everglades of Florida. It is a river of grass. (Marjory Stoneman Douglas, 1890-1998, from *The Everglades: River of Grass*, 1947, in *Bartlett's Familiar Quotations*, 2002.)

The population grew across Florida during the 1960s from just under 5 million to almost 6.8 million, a gain of 38 percent.[1] This growth was preceded during the 1940s by a 46.1 percent population increase and during the 1950s by a 78.7 percent increase. This rapid rate of growth placed a large demand for housing, roads, and schools, and administrative and financial stress on Florida's governments: cities, counties, school boards, and the state itself. In addition, as critical as the stress on the quality of municipal and urban county services and capacities was, the stress on Florida's environmental resources was even more critical. Wetlands, upland forests, beaches, bays and bay bottoms, rivers, streams and springs were experiencing perilous damage due to poorly regulated environmental and resource protection.

Problems resulting from rampant growth and inadequately considered local planning were statewide, but nowhere as severe as in the southeast coastal counties of Miami-Dade,[2] Broward, and Palm Beach, and the southwest coastal counties of Collier, Lee, and Charlotte. These counties were growing at a decennial average rate of 87.9 percent. This was over twice the rate for Florida statewide.[3] Coupled with this historic population growth, state and local political and business leaders of Florida were beginning to recognize the need for building a more relevant and effective system of state government with intergovernmental cooperation and coordination.

Contributing to this argument for state government and intergovernmental reform were participants in meetings across America organized by Columbia University's American Assembly during the late 1960s and early 1970s.[4] In his introduction to *States and the Urban Crisis*, Alan K. Campbell observed "that state governments have been both the whipping boy and scapegoat of the American governmental system."[5] In addition, Campbell, with Donna E. Shalala, noted that, "State governments have been described as 'the key stones of the American governmental arch.'"[6] "States sit between local governments and the federal government, which constitutionally possesses only delegated powers."[7] Theirs and other similar research efforts provided necessary data and information brought to the attention of state and local leaders, both in and outside of government to consider the need for governmental reform in Florida. During 1968, an American Assembly was held in Palm Beach County. The assembly chair, John DeGrove of Florida Atlantic University, and the organizing committee invited local and state political and business leaders to consider the state of Florida and its relevance and capacity to deal with urban issues. This discussion, in part, was an extension of the growing urgency for state governmental reform and much needed local planning reform. State government reform was driven by the U.S. Supreme Court in *Baker v. Carr*, which mandated reapportionment of the legislature[8] and by the general perception across the state that growth in Florida was out of control. Added to these concerns was the realization that local and regional planning did not exist, or if it did, the practice lacked any planning standards or political support. Some local governments were visionary in coping with population growth and demands for planning and public services, while most of Florida's local governments were languishing in the lap of localism and a persistent and pervasive belief in the prosperity of growth.

Miami-Dade County adopted a General Land Use Master Plan in 1960 and revised the plan in 1965.[9] Some interesting changes in 1965 to the 1960 plan were the deletion of two causeways planned to cross Biscayne Bay. One causeway had been planned to provide north-south automobile transportation up the middle of Biscayne Bay from downtown Miami to North Miami. The other causeway proposed a connection between Turkey Point in the Homestead area in south Miami-Dade County to Elliot Key, eighteen miles across Biscayne Bay. This proposed causeway was planned to open up the northern most Florida Keys to development. As a consequence of the later change in planning for causeway building, the Dade County keys were never developed and today are an integral part of the Biscayne Bay National Park. In general local plans did not have the force and effect of law as would be the case in years after 1975.[10] However, planning was a mandatory provision of the Dade County Home Rule Charter adopted by electors of Miami-Dade County in 1957. The home rule charter was authorized by an amendment to the Florida Constitution adopted by a statewide referendum in 1956. The inclusion of planning as a charter provision was then unusual, particularly, in view of the fact that planning was of little concern to many of Florida's local governments.

The majority of local governments may not have been concerned about planning, but along with Miami-Dade, some were concerned and took innovative steps toward improving the effectiveness of planning and plan implementation. Among these were the cities of Boca Raton and Coral Gables, and Broward, Collier, and Pinellas counties. Boca Raton, which 1920s architect and developer Addison Mizner had said would become a "Mediterranean-style Venice", ventured into innovative planning a little *too* ambitiously, however. In 1972, a citizen referendum imposed a population cap of 100,000 on the city. Within a few years this ambition fell victim to the courts, which ruled it would unnecessarily shift the burden of low and moderate-income housing on neighboring communities.[11] Nonetheless, Boca Raton remains a relatively exclusive and well-planned community.

At about the same time Boca Raton established its growth cap, Pinellas and Broward were taking steps to introduce countywide coordination of planning over both their unincorporated areas and municipalities. Their purposes were similar, but their approaches were different. The legislature established a countywide planning council for Pinellas County by a special act in 1973.[12] One important power of the council not shared by other coordinating entities enacted before or since is a special taxing authority—one sixth of a mill."[13] As John DeGrove and Nancy Stroud pointed out,

> Broward County included in its new 1974 Charter a model that goes even further than Pinellas in assuring city-county planning coordination. The Broward County model features a planning council of fifteen members, all appointed by the County Commission in accordance with certain requirements to ensure a representative balance of the county constituencies. Seven members must be municipal officers chosen from among the many municipalities in Broward County.[14]

Collier County took an entirely different approach to managing development. In October 1974, the county adopted a zoning overlay district called Special Treatment Overlay District. It was designed specifically to protect environmentally sensitive lands from indiscriminate use and development through a transfer of development rights (TDR) program.[15]

In this way, Collier County took its place among the first local governments in Florida to implement an innovative planning and development management tool.

There were only five multi-county regional planning organizations in Florida during the 1960s, but by 1977 the number had increased to eleven. Prior to 1972, participation in regional planning organizations was voluntary. However, by 1973, it became mandatory for every county to participate in a regional planning council in order to meet the development of regional impact review process requirements of the Environment Land and Water Management Act passed in 1972 (to be discussed later in this chapter). Though no county was to be excluded, participation by municipalities was voluntary. Each of the first five regional planning organizations was continued into the 1970s, though the counties they represented changed considerably in most instances.

The eleven regional planning councils, their constituent counties (as of November 2000), and the year the council was originally established are listed on page 252. A map of the current councils is shown on page 253.

Environmental Setting

In Chapter V we discussed the prominence of the environmental movement as articulated by Rachel Carson and Stewart Udall. In Florida, the important work of Marjorie Stoneman Douglas in her book, *The Everglades: River of Grass*, and environmental activists including Marjorie Harris Carr of Micanopy leading the Florida Defenders of the Environment, the Florida Chapter of the American Institute of Architects and its "Red Flag Charrettes" and the Florida Chapter of the Audubon Society added to the movement. These writings and activities among many other Floridians, local and statewide heightened the awareness of public and private leaders and the press to the environmental degradation that was resulting from growth and the sprawl of new development across the state, particularly in south Florida and the new Disney World development near Orlando.

In south Florida, degradation of estuaries was specifically a major intrusion to the maritime ecosystems of bays and inlets. Each year forests of mangroves and thousands of acres of bay bottom were lost permanently. The prevailing method of waterfront development beginning as early as the 1920s and into the 1960s in both southeast and southwest Florida was simple. A developer simply got an all-too-easy permit from a county government authorized by special acts to consider and issue dredge, fill, and seawall permits. In this way, the developer was permitted to use state owned bay bottom by establishing a surveyed bulkhead line, building a bulkhead, and dredging the adjacent bay bottom to fill the area to the elevation of the bulkhead. Islands in Biscayne Bay, Fort Lauderdale, Palm Beach, and many other coastal communities were created in this manner. The resulting islands, connected by bridges, were platted with lots for sale. Often these waterfront developments were located in former mangrove forests that were cut and left to rot under the newly manmade island. Estuarine land was disappearing and being replaced by dredged up bay bottom providing waterfront developments. During the 1950s and 1960s, nearly 170,000 acres of coastal ecosystems were lost to dredge and fill throughout Florida. It was an alarming statistic that indicated Florida's local governments with their riding partners, land speculators aided by minimal state oversight, were plundering Florida's resources.

In 1970, the Florida legislature enacted a law that authorized Florida's governor and cabinet, sitting as the Trustees of the Internal Improvement Commission, to review, permit, or reject applications for dredge and fill permits for any area of the state.[17] This action overrode the special acts and severely restricted the practice of building land from bay bottoms. Review of the applications fell to the analysts and regulators in the office of the Trustees of the Internal Improvement Trust Fund.

These early initiatives were clearly reactive to proposals rising from water to land speculation along estuaries and other natural waterfronts. These experiences built an information base within the state bureaucracy that recognized the need for state, regional and local planning. This was an early step in environmental and planning management of Florida estuarine shallow bay wetlands in the Gulf and Atlantic waters. The destruction of the waters and bay bottoms was stopped in Biscayne Bay, Fort Lauderdale, Lake Worth, Boca Ciega Bay, the Florida Keys and many other estuarine systems, particularly in south and southwest Florida. The demand for building on waterfront property had not reached Florida's Big Bend or Panhandle, in the late 1960s, but without effective local, regional, and state planning it would be a certainty in coming years.

In addition to unconstrained coastal development and land speculation, the Florida interior was subject to large-scale real estate schemes. As an example, Golden Gate Estates developed by Gulf American Corporation in the late 1960s and bordering on Everglades National Park, and the Fakahatchee Strand in Collier County, covered approximately 173 square miles. This was an old-style Florida real estate project with lots to be sold to 50,000 buyers worldwide.[18] Edward A. Fernald and Donald J. Patton observed,

> When the project's 813 miles of roads and 173 miles of canals were built, it complied with all local, state and federal land use and environmental requirements. No provisions were made for public facilities of any kind. Much of the development is either flood-prone or wetlands.[19]

The canals designed to drain the wetlands stressed the natural cypress communities. The Faka Union Canal system was completed in 1971 and for the next thirty years the State of Florida, the South Florida Water Management District, and the U.S. Corps of Engineers studied, planned, and developed a Hydrologic Restoration Plan[20] to mitigate the water management problem. Building large-scale residential developments in sensitive wetlands and environmental communities was common during this period of rapid population growth in Florida and concomitant real estate boom. There were also large land sales schemes in Port Charlotte in Charlotte County and Beverly Hills and Spring Hill in Citrus County. Planning was not considered or engaged at local, regional or state levels. Planning for such projects was essentially an engineering problem with little, if any concern for environmental impacts, or a concern for the infrastructure, or adjacent neighborhoods or jurisdictions. The decisive factors included maximizing the number of residential lots and minimizing the cost of road building. Road building usually consisted of graded roadbeds, a rolled rock sub base with no finished paving. No other public facilities were planned for the projects. Essentially these were land sales operations with no intent to build viable and working communities.

Federal Statewide Planning Requirements

In Chapter V, we discussed the influence of federal programs related to planning and management at the state level monitored by means of the required review of grant-in-aid projects using the A-95 mandatory state, regional, and some local review of proposed projects. This was an attempt by the U.S. Office of Management and Budget to resolve conflicts and duplication of federal programs within states and among local and regional agencies. Now we will consider federally required statewide plans. The requirements were based on the premise that in order to have access to federal program and grant support, a state plan for the functional area of the program must be in place. This has often been referred to as the "carrot and stick" approach to federal assistance.

Among the areas requiring state and regional or metropolitan plans were health, transportation, criminal justice, coastal zone management, civil defense, outdoor recreation, housing, and environmental protection. The thrust of these plans was to assure administrators of federal programs that goals of the agencies were consistent with federal program goals and planned state and regional objectives. In Florida, newly organized departments of state such as transportation, commerce and natural resources were assigned the responsibility of planning, management and operations of the various public functions. The State Planning Office was organized to place a senior planner responsible for coordination with each departmental planning officer. This organizational effort had the *potential* to provide a comprehensive overview of the various systems as a basis for assimilating and communicating data, information, and plan objectives and goals to affect state plan coordination. The system formed the foundation later of a more formally adopted state comprehensive planning model. It was an effective organizational strategy developed by Homer Still, chief of the Office of State Planning during the late 1960s and early 1970s. This also permitted a more effective means of integrating functional plans with the state budgeting process and led to the state's attempt to establish a planning, programming and budgeting system (PPBS). However, the PPBS program was only marginally successful in view of the habit of legislative bodies to want less programmatic information, but definitive fiscal information on costs, revenues, and staffing commitments. Legislators tended to be analysts with the "bottom line" as a politically important conclusion.

Health Planning

With the enactment of the federal Comprehensive Health Planning and Service Act of 1966,[21] health planning was to be accomplished by a coordinated and cooperative system of planning for all personal health services, manpower (Later to become human resources), facilities, and environmental health concerns. The partnership envisioned was to be multifaceted: among local, regional, state, and federal government; between the public and private sectors; between providers and consumers of health services,[22] and, between various health-related programs and other education, welfare, and rehabilitation programs. It was a comprehensive health planning system with regional or metropolitan agencies called "b" agencies. These were voluntary public or not for profit organizations and they functioned to prepare regional health plans, "to guide the coordination and development of new and existing health services, facilities, and manpower."[23] Each state had an "a" agency. In Florida, the "a" agency was the Florida Health Planning Council.[24] The council, as required by law, included consumers, providers, health professionals, nongovernmental and governmental organization and agencies. The council was responsible for a statewide health plan. It was appointed by the governor with staff provided by the State Planning Office and planners in the Department of Health and Rehabilitative Services.

Regardless of the lofty legislative language, the plans of the state and regional councils began on shaky ground.[25] Perhaps the lack of federal guidelines and evaluation of the planning process and plans led to the lack of perceived success. In 1972, the U.S. Department of Health, Education and Welfare "began to identify performance expectations for health planning agencies."[26] Following these evaluations, it was determined that with no authority other than review and comment on federal projects and programs, it was necessary to amend the provisions of health planning. Authority was strengthened with the passage of the 1972 amendments to the Social Security Act.[27] This change provided for the agency permitting authority to expand its reviews and comments to include federal expenditures for health related capital improvements. This has been and is today referred to as the certificate of need regulatory function. Both "a" and "b" agencies had this authority. Health planning in Florida thus became an important program with the capacity to modify capital expenditures and delivery of health related services. This included the approval of hospital expansions, new hospitals, and expenditures for expensive laboratory and diagnostic equipment.

Transportation Planning

During the 1950s, several large metropolitan area studies pioneered the development of planning methodologies for the collection of data and information, analysis and forecasting travel demand. Transportation models were promulgated to simulate and represent future transportation system demands and needs. The Chicago Area Transportation Study was the original model emulated in many metropolitan areas after the mid- 1950s. In addition, in 1956, the National System of Interstate Highways was established. The Federal Aid Highway Act of 1962 made transportation planning mandatory for urban places equal to or exceeding populations of 50,000.[28] Metropolitan transportation planning was to be guided by the "3 Cs" process: comprehensive, coordinated and continued planning.[29] This planning program included plans for all transportation modes. It was the first time all transportation modes received consideration in the emerging field of transportation planning. The Florida State Road Board was responsible for guiding and overseeing the statewide planning effort. Five-year plans were first approved by each of the five district engineers and State Road District Board members, then forwarded for review and approval by the transportation planners in Tallahassee, and finally sent to the State Road Board representing the five districts. All federally funded planning projects were also subject to the A-95 review managed by the Office of State Planning, which distributed the project description to relevant state and relevant regional agencies for comment and recommendation. Furthermore, all federally funded road projects were subject to the National Environment Policy Act and environmental impact analysis. The five district plans were adopted and revisited each year for updates and changes. These plans provided the direction for all multi-modal transportation projects within the transportation districts. Local governments did have input in the planning process, but so few had effective local comprehensive plans that the transportation plans became 'the driving force for development'. Political persuasion and political "cherry picking" were often the characteristic of transportation projects.

Some projects were built by the State of Florida with no, or certainly minimal, local attention or review. One example of such a project was the planning and building of North Kendall Drive in Miami-Dade County during the early 1960s. This project was a multi-lane highway connecting U.S. Highway 1 in south Miami-Dade to State Road 27. The construction of this three-mile arterial facility did not appear on any county plan nor was it anticipated by the county. It was built to respond to real estate interests holding winter croplands that were in the anticipated high growth corridor for development demands of south Miami-Dade County. This happened repeatedly in other parts of Florida during those days of minimal to no local planning.

As part of Florida's state reorganization plan, in 1969 the State Road Board was abolished and moved into the new Florida Department of Transportation (FDOT) with its four divisions: Transportation Planning, Road Operations, Public Transportation Operations, and Administration. The five transportation district boundaries remained the same. (There are seven districts and the Florida Turnpike Authority today.) In addition to the new state organization, state and regional transportation planning was reinforced by federal transportation planning initiatives. The initiatives and funding were a product of the Federal Aid Highway Act of 1970.[30] Action plans were required to assure consideration of environmental and multimodal issues. However, as then State Representative Vernon Holloway, Chair of the Florida House Transportation Committee cautioned, "It should not be surprising that reluctance to bring about a coordinated departmental approach [to inter-modal transportation] is encountered on the part of some officials who currently control the individual agencies."[31] Reluctant officials or not, by 1970, the Florida legislature had appropriated $5,000,000 for public transit. With these state funds, the FDOT could attract matching funds from the Urban Mass Transportation Administration and Federal Aid to Airports Program to assist local governments in public transit and airport projects. This represented the planning and capital assistance grants available for airports and public transit projects.

Transportation planners have often been faced with the inability to cope with the many separate governmental entities found in most metropolitan areas. This was partially remedied in 1973 when federal Department of Transportation agencies—the Federal Highway Administration, Urban Mass Transportation Administration (now the Federal Transit Administration), and the Federal Aviation Administration—focused on metropolitan planning organizations (MPOs) to receive support and some funding in every urban area. These new MPOs were often housed with urban area planning or regional planning councils. MPOs are required to be linked to county metropolitan statistical areas rather than all the counties in a multi-county regional planning district. Some of the MPOs and their staffs were co-located with regional planning councils and remain so today. Planning in Florida for transportation was beginning to be a well-funded and significant intergovernmental activity. The Florida State Transportation Five Year Plan and the MPO plans then became important elements in an emerging interest in both state and regional comprehensive planning. Transportation planning and transportation projects continued to be a major force in the growth plans of Florida's urban and rural communities.

Criminal Justice Planning

Another critical element in the steady flow of federal interest in state and regional planning was embodied in The Omnibus Crime and Safe Streets Act of 1968.[32] In Florida, the criminal justice state planning office was located in the Governor's Office during Claude Kirk's administration. A state plan was prepared by criminal justice planners each year with the advice of the Criminal Justice Advisory Council that usually met quarterly. The annual plan included topics ranging from neighborhood crime and delinquency, improving police operations, white-collar crime investigation and programs, reducing trial court delays, improving prosecutorial process and victim and witness assistance, improving correction programs and facilities, providing coordination among agencies, and developing statistical and evaluative systems. The planning and programming mission was comprehensive and required intergovernmental and interagency coordination and cooperation that had seldom been experienced in Florida. State criminal justice planning was supervised by the U.S. Law Enforcement Assistance Administration. The criminal justice plan was action-oriented, directly affecting the courts, the police, prosecutors and public defenders as well as state and local governmental correctional systems. Additionally, planning and programming for criminal justice supported research and educational projects in public education and university-level activities. Criminal justice planning became a specialty in many graduate programs and departments across the country, and in Florida both at the Florida State University and the University of Florida. Criminal justice planning was another element in the unintended consequence of the progression toward state comprehensive planning and intergovernmental coordination and cooperation.

The "Almost" National Land Use Planning Act

A federal proposal that would have had nearly every state moving toward a state land use policy was the National Land and Water Resources Planning bill.[33] Introduced by U.S. Senator Henry Jackson, of Washington, the legislative author of National Environmental Protection Act, the bill caught President Richard Nixon's interest. Jackson's bill, introduced first in 1970, proposed federal funding for state land use planning.[34] The administration had its own bill in 1971 (National Land Use Policy Act),[35] which drew heavily from a draft model land development code prepared by the American Law Institute.[36] Among other things, Jackson's bill would have funded states to prepare land use regulatory programs to protect areas of critical environmental concern.[37] A compromise bill was passed by the Senate in 1972, but the House of Representatives did not adopt it.[38] The union of Senator Jackson and the administration appeared to promise eventual success, but the president's support for a national land use policy succumbed to disruption of the Washington D.C. political landscape by pressures of Watergate.

Coastal Zone Management

The Coastal Zone Management Act vied for attention with the proposed National Land Use Policy Act but met with less controversy and garnered enough support to be enacted in 1972.[39] The Coastal Zone Management Act of 1972 provided that each state with seashores or shores along the Great Lakes prepare a coastal zone management plan.[40] In anticipation of the federal initiative, the Florida legislature created a Coastal Coordinating Council in 1970 and required the surveyed establishment of a coastal setback line. The council's plan for the coastal zone in Florida was prepared by the Office of Coastal Zone Management in the Department of Natural Resources with the advice of the council. Completed in 1971, there was also a regional coastal management plan called ESCAROSA affecting the counties of Escambia and Santa Rosa. A plan was also prepared for the Florida Keys in 1973. The Keys' plan provided much needed data and information for the later designation of the Florida Keys as an area of critical state concern. By 1975, the coastal planners had completed a statewide, generalized planning atlas and several additional detailed regional atlases.[41] After 1972, this planning activity was supported by federal grants from the U.S. Department of Commerce through its Office of Coastal Zone Management. These data, information, goals, and plans provided a significant step toward the future of planning in Florida. The Coastal Zone Management Plan was, however, not comprehensive planning and its only action space was the coastal zone. It certainly provided a planning and procedural model for future statewide planning and development management efforts soon to come along in the 1970s and 1980s.

Emergency Management

The Federal Civil Defense Administration was located in the Executive Office of the President in 1950 and successor agencies through the 1950s, 1960s and on to 1972 when it became the Office of Civil Defense (OCD). The OCD was located in the Department of the Army in the Department of Defense. According to a report by the Defense Civil Preparedness Agency (DCPA), the OCD, "Coordinated and directed federal, state, and local civil defense program activities, including fallout shelters; chemical, biological, and radiological warfare defense; emergency communications and warning systems; postattack [sic] assistance and damage assessment; preparedness planning; and government continuity."[42] A state civil defense and preparedness plan in Florida was developed under this federal program and included mapping, policy directives to state agencies and local governments and training programs, emergency government facilities in every county; facilities which were stocked with necessary communications equipment, survival supplies and related conveniences. This was a time when the DCPA expanded their initial concept of response and recovery to include prevention through planning. The plan included emergency governmental organizational structures and appropriate authority. The OCD was succeeded by the Federal Emergency Management Agency (FEMA), which carried on with the planning efforts. This again was an example of a federal initiative that essentially mandated states to make statewide and local plans; however, the plans tended to stand alone and were not necessarily coordinated with other state and local plans and often conflicting goals and objectives among other plans.

In the early 1970s, the DCPA had two major tasks: one was directed at emergency preparedness for a peacetime environment and the other for a possible wartime environment (i.e., nuclear attack). This was during the Cold War between the United States and the Soviet Union. Civil defense personnel in Florida had to plan for both possibilities. In fact, Florida was the setting for one of the most comprehensive wartime evacuation plans in the nation—and possibly the only one completed. Because MacDill Air Force Base was located in Tampa, the area was one of the likeliest places in the U.S. to be attacked. Under contract with the DCPA, one of the authors (RuBino) co-directed the preparation of a crisis relocation plan for the evacuation of Hillsborough and Pinellas counties to facilities in counties north of Tampa Bay.[43] Workers in critical industries (e.g., port facilities) were expected to go back to work in the targeted area each day and return to the host area upon completion of their shifts. Would the plan have worked? This is doubtful since this pilot plan was never put to a test. Practice evacuations were held in some Soviet cities, but never in the United States (even the thought of evacuating large cities under threat of a huge hurricane was new in those days), but typical to the chess game of the Cold War, what the Soviets did, the U.S. did, too. Nonetheless, these "games" introduced an extreme form of comprehensive planning to Florida, at least temporarily.

Other Federal Initiatives

There were other federal initiatives requiring statewide planning, including among others, outdoor recreation, housing, and environmental protection. These state and local plans were prepared to provide the basis for federal grant-in-aid programs. Each had to be in preparation or completed when state agencies or local governments applied for discretionary grants for such projects as recreational lands acquisition. Even entitlement programs such as public housing, required plans indicating need, location, and governmental responsibility; usually prepared by a local public housing authority. Federal environmental protection encouraged states to prepare land and water management programs in coastal areas. Each of these federal actions had a significant impact on the practice of planning in Florida. At the same time Congress was considering the proposed National Land Use Policy Act, it did propose several more geographically and specific systems approaches to managing land and water use. Planners at the local, regional, and state levels accommodated and adjusted to each new initiative as they felt necessary. The federal intent to propagate a need for planning seemed to be working, but was it something state and local governments wanted or only as a prerequisite to become eligible for federal grants? The former was the wish and the latter was the reality, but, undeniably, the federal government did lay the groundwork that shaped the practice of planning in Florida and elsewhere during the 1960s and early 1970s.

Other State and Regional Initiatives

States also had initiatives worth noting here before leaving the subject of federal planning requirements. The early 1970s brought a wave of innovative state and regional initiatives directed at managing growth. There were at least 18 initiatives enacted in 13 states across the nation (see Figure VI-1). Some of these were directed at critical geographic areas, such as shorelines, the Adirondacks Mountains of New York, and Massachusetts' Martha's Vineyard; others, like the Florida and Oregon programs, were more comprehensive and statewide. Many of these were influenced, to one degree or another, by the model code being prepared by the American Law Institute; others were the outcome of seeds planted years before. Combined, they gave body to what Fred Bosselman and David Callies identified as "The Quiet Revolution in Land Use Control".[44]

Figure VI-1
Selected Chronology of State and Major Regional
Land Use or growth Management Programs
1970-1974

1970   Maine – Approval of large-site industrial or commercial developments
        (38 Maine Revised Statutes Annotated, §§ 481-88. / Ch. 3, § 481-88)
        Michigan – Shorelands management and protection act (Act No. 245,
        Public Acts of 1970)
        Vermont – Environmental Control Law (Act 250, 10 Vermont
        Statutes Annotated, Ch. 151, §§ 6001, et. seq.)
        Vermont – Shoreline zoning act (Act 281)
1971   Colorado – Land use act (Ch. 106-5, C.R.S.)
        Colorado – State to prepare subdivision regulations for counties
        where no regulations exist (Ch. 106-2, C.R.S.)
        Delaware – Coastal zone act; state management of industrial
        development in shore zone (Ch. 70, T. 7)
        Georgia – Atlanta Metropolitan Area Planning and Development
        Commission
        Maine – Critical area program for all shoreland areas 250 feet from
        high water mark (Ch. 424, § 4811-4814)
        New York – Adirondack Park Agency Act
        Washington – State Land Planning Commission
1972   California – California Coastal Zone Conservation Act (Prop 20)
        Florida – Environmental Land and Water Management Act
        Florida – State Comprehensive Planning Act
1973   Oregon – Senate Bill 100 creates Land Conservation & Development
        Commission, includes an oversight role for the state
1974   Colorado – Land use act
        Massachusetts – Martha's Vineyard Commission Act
        North Carolina – Coastal Area Management Act
1978   Hawaii – Hawaii State Plan, Ch. 226, HRS, amends 1960 planning
        law.
1979   San Diego – Enacted a law to redirect new development inward from
        its rapidly urbanizing fringe.

Lessons Learned?

All of the actions listed in Figure VI-1 contributed to the Quiet Revolution, but we will elaborate on only some of the more significant ones, chronologically beginning with Vermont and ending with North Carolina. Because of increasing second-home development, Vermont had been moving toward planning since 1963, but the historically Republican legislature was not about to allow a Democrat, Governor Philip H. Hoff, to lead the state into an intergovernmental development management program. Hoff, with the assistance of nationally known land use lawyers Norman Williams, Jr. and Allen Fornoroff, had been especially aggressive in moving in the direction of scenery preservation.[46] Yet, it was not until a Republican governor, Deane C. Davis, was elected in 1969, that the legislature truly got serious about statewide land use planning and control. With Governor Davis' leadership, the legislature had enacted an Environmental Control Law. David G. Heeter compared the law to coastal zone legislation enacted in some other states, in that it established "interim or continuing development approval systems to secure compliance with the policies contained in adopted land development or coastal zone management plans."[47] The law created an Environmental Board, with regulatory jurisdiction over seven statewide district commissions.[48] The commissions' decisions were expected to be guided in their decision-making by a statewide land use plan.[49] However, after being distributed to every household in the state, the statewide plan (and map) ran into considerable citizen opposition and it was put aside.

Directly across Lake Champlain, New York State took a different approach to environmental protection. This was in the Adirondack Park area, a sparsely inhabited mountainous area that had been established as a state park in 1892 and subsequently protected by the state constitution.[50] The park was interlaced by private land holdings, and second home development was increasing. Environmental degradation was increasing, and this led to the creation of the Adirondack Park Agency in 1971. The agency was charged with preparing a land use plan and administering regulations over private and public lands to protect the "forever wild" nature of this environmentally critical area.[51]

Three times in 1970, 1971, and 1972—environmentalists interested in protecting California's rapidly developing coastline had bills introduced in the legislature; however, each time the bill passed the assembly but died in the senate due to opposition from business and commercial interests.[52] Frustrated by the senate's inaction, the California Coastal Alliance resorted to a ballot initiative in 1972; this initiative became known as Proposition 20.[53] The model for coastal regulation was taken from the San Francisco Bay Conservation and Development Commission, which came into existence in 1965.[54] Proposition 20 was approved by voters by a 55 to 45 percent margin. The proposition thus enacted into law established regional bodies covering the entire 1,100 miles of coastal area; these new regional bodies were "largely independent of state government apparatus to oversee coastal development and to initiate coastal zone planning."[55] The coastal zone act was amended and extended in 1976, and is now known as the California Coastal Commission Act.[56]

As Oregon's population began to climb to over two million people—most of them in the Willamette Valley—people became concerned that the negative impacts of uncontrolled growth they had fled from or heard about in California was also about to happen in Oregon. A popular slogan that began to circulate at that time, "Let's not 'Californicate' Oregon," says it all. Oregonians, mostly those in the Willamette Valley, were not about to let happen in Oregon what had happened in California. "Oregon leaders," said Gerrit Knaap and Arthur C. Nelson, "were quick to recognize the sensitivity of the state's environment to the urbanization trends of the 1960s and 1970s."[57] The result was the preparation of

Senate Bill 100 (not to be confused with 1969's Senate Bill 10 referred to in Chapter V), a proposal that would allow state government to oversee local government planning. The bill was enacted into a 1973 law,[58] but not until it was substantially compromised.[59] Among other things, the compromise removed the regulatory authority vested with the state in areas of critical state concern and the creation of fourteen regional planning districts. What remained was a requirement that county and municipal plans be consistent with statewide goals which would be developed by the Land Conservation and Development Commission. Even after the compromise, this was a significant step toward managing growth.

In 1974, fearing unchecked development, the residents of Martha's Vineyard and Cuttyhunk, islands off the upper arm of Cape Cod convinced the Massachusetts legislature to create the Martha's Vineyard Commission to protect the unique qualities of the islands.[60] The law enabled the commission to serve as the regional planning agency for Martha's Vineyard and to assist all eight of the towns in regulating developments of regional impact. Development pressure has continued to increase, however, leading to a fear of "suburbanization" of the Vineyard.[61]

North Carolina created its own coastal management act in 1974.[62] The program, which is jointly enforced by the state and local governments, is administered by the Coastal Resources Commission under the secretary of the Department of Environment and Natural Resources. It became the first Southern coastal management program to receive financial support from the federal Coastal Zone Management Act.[63] A somewhat similar bill that would have covered the mountainous western third of the state failed to make it through the legislature.

The growth management stars were properly aligned. The federal planning requirements of the 1960s and early 1970s, the forcing of state legislatures to be constitutionally apportioned[64] and the consequence of revitalizing executive branches of state governments were important events as the stars aligned. In addition, the rapid spread of interest in the American Law Institute's Draft Model Land Development Code, and, especially, the peaking of national environmental consciousness coalesced to set in motion a number of federal, state, regional, and local initiatives directed at better management of development. In turn, this peak period of activity in the early 1970s set the foundation for related actions over the following two decades. Florida was one of the major contributors to this foundation.

Initiatives in Florida

During the reorganization of Florida state government in 1969, the Department of Community Affairs (DCA) was included among the new state agencies. This agency, with James G. Richardson, former mayor of Gainesville, as its first secretary, was viewed as a link between state government and local governments. Creation of the agency was strongly supported by urban counties, particularly Miami-Dade County. The perceived need to have an agency in state government solely directing its programs and interests toward providing local governments with technical assistance, coordination among local governments, needed research and a presence in Tallahassee were arguments offered for support. After Secretary M. Athalie Range, former commissioner of the city of Miami replaced Richardson, the DCA also acted as staff to the Governor's Task Force on Housing and Community Development. The task force was chaired by John E. Smith, with Robert Mitchell of the Department of Urban and Regional Planning at Florida State University serving as its executive director.[65] The task force prepared Florida's "First Annual Report on State Housing Goals"[66] and "Housing in Florida," a state housing assessment study, which later led to programs of technical assistance to local governments.[67] In addition, the assessment study was updated annually to provide an ongoing source of data and information regarding the housing needs of the state. The DCA was also responsible for veteran's services, elder affairs, and coordination among all state agencies in matters related to local governmental issues and policies and the state's appropriate participation in community issues.

Until 1969, Florida's local governments were not authorized by general law to engage in city planning, unless special authority was enacted by the state legislature. There had been general enabling legislation (passed in 1939, but later repealed) to authorize land use zoning, but not planning. A local government wishing to engage in planning found it necessary to seek a special act from the Florida legislature to authorize such an activity; that is, in those few local governments which elected to plan at all. In 1969, with the sponsorship of then State Senator D. Robert (Bob) Graham, general enabling legislation for local planning was enacted.[68] Four years later, only about a dozen local governments had taken advantage of the new legislation. Local planning in Florida was definitely not a well-established practice with only a few of the nearly 400 local governments engaging in it at all; instead, the politics of localism were dominated by growth machines.[69] Political scientist Terry Christensen argues that growth machines, identified by Molotch,[70] self-adapt to the requirements of managed growth and often successfully influence public policy-making to achieve their own development-oriented ends.[71] To Christensen, the action of the growth management movement caused a reaction by growth machines, which through the private property rights movement and other avenues found ways to adapt to the changes in public management of development. With Florida growing in population at a rate of almost 6,000 persons each week,[72] the opportunities for growth and development seemed endless. Sprawling housing development, in part financed by the Federal Housing Administration with its low density housing subdivision requirements, was sprawling into the open lands surrounding Florida's urban areas. Local planning had no significant role in the market driven need for housing and the sprawling developments created in fringes of Florida's growing urban places.

A Shift Toward Environmental Protection and Statewide Planning

In 1970, a large field of Democrats entered the primary in hopes of unseating Republican Governor Claude Kirk in the general election. The traditional dominance of the Democratic Party in Florida had been upset by the election of a Republican governor in 1966. Thus, a large field of hopefuls emerged to "take back Tallahassee". Emerging during the primary was a little known state senator from Pensacola. Reubin O'Donovan Askew. He served a total of twelve years in both the Florida House of Representatives and the State Senate. His campaign was built upon the concept of a corporate income tax and his personal integrity. He won the primary and went on to win the general election in the fall. Interestingly, most of the environmental and planning interests in Florida had supported Governor Claude Kirk's reelection based on his record in this particular area of governments' environmental responsibility. In large part because of Nathaniel Pryor Reed, Kirk's advisor on environmental issues, the Kirk administration had an impressive record, including shutting down the South Florida Jetport in the Big Cypress swamp. Other initiatives in protection of the Everglades and in state level planning. Miami-Dade County with more than 1.2 million people had never been home to a state park. During the Kirk administration, Miami-Dade County got its state park when the state purchased the southern part of Key Biscayne, an area of 400 upland acres including the historic Cape Florida Light House. The park was named for the late editor of the *Miami News*, Bill Baggs.

Askew took advantage of the environmental impetus built by the previous administration by naming Reed as Director of the Department of Pollution Control. One of Reed's first actions found a paper mill in Pensacola, Governor Askew's hometown, in violation of state pollution regulations. Reed, along with Askew's governmental coordinator, Ken Woodburn, and others, helped continue Florida's path to environmental protection.

Legislative Initiatives in Florida

Before and during the 1971 session of the Florida legislature, several legislative staff members were instructed by committee chairs and Speaker of the House, Richard Pettigrew, to work on the issue of state and regional comprehensive land use planning including the mechanisms for enforcement.[73] Several bills relating to land use were introduced.[74] These incremental approaches did not survive the legislative process, but they did heighten the political debate regarding state policies and programs that might in the future address the impacts of growth, development management and environmental degradation. Following the 1971 session, the Florida House Committee on Governmental Affairs drafted a bill that somewhat reflected the state zoning approach taken by Hawaii ten years earlier. After further analysis, the approach was considered too extreme for Florida, and no further action was taken. Nonetheless, even to consider statewide zoning for Florida showed the depth of concern the leadership of the Florida House of Representatives had for addressing the problem of uncontrolled growth. Unforeseen at this point was an event that would eventually lead to other options.

Reorganization of the Department of Administration into planning and management functions was proposed, including a system of sub-state planning districts. Water resources were also on the Speaker's agenda, and the committee, chaired by Representative Jack Shreve, was instructed to "study existing water policies and programs and to prepare recommendations for a comprehensive state water management program."[75] During the late 1960s, Dean Frank Maloney of the University of Florida Law College and co-authors, Sheldon J. Plager and Fletcher N. Baldwin, proposed a model code for water management and administration.[76] Another Joint Committee of the House and Senate was studying a comprehensive regional organization for all of south Florida. Both the Florida House and Senate were actively involved in the emerging interest in interposing of the state into regional and local water and land use planning. About the same time, the Askew administration was moving on its own initiative to understand issues of growth and planning. It sought a course of action that would have the potential of dealing with competent, propitious, comprehensive, and constitutionally sound policies, programs, and governmental organization articulating and defining the state's role in growth and development management.

Governor's Conference on Water Management in South Florida

During the waning months of 1970 and into 1971, south Florida experienced a historic drought, its most severe in the 20th century.[77] Water for that rapidly growing part of the state was in short supply, and severe water use restrictions were imposed. Responding to the issue, Governor Askew called for a Conference on Water Management in South Florida. The governor expanded the call to include state level policies regarding growth and development management issues. The conference, chaired by John M. DeGrove, professor of political science in the Florida Atlantic University, and Arthur Marshall, was composed of 150 Floridians representing business, academia, and state, local and federal governmental agencies. James W. May, in his graduate research paper at the Florida State University in 1974, observed, "In short, it was a cross section of some of the most knowledgeable and experienced people in the field of land and water management, from a variety of perspectives, who assembled late in September of 1971 to hammer out the answers to their charge from the Governor."[78] That they did; this conference, said DeGrove, "marked the end of Florida's uncritical love affair with growth."[79] Among the conferees' conclusions was a far-reaching recommendation that water management not only needed to be coordinated at the federal, state, and regional levels, but also coordinated among regional water management and regional land management agencies. They went so far as to suggest that a combined regional comprehensive land and water use plan be prepared and implemented.[80] Though the conference recommendations were directed at south Florida, in later months, the basic idea was considered statewide. Thus was initiated a more advanced movement for statewide planning and statewide water management. Both the executive and legislative branches were beginning to respond to the water crisis and the rapid rate of population growth, and the countless impacts of uncontrolled growth upon the environment, urban services, and the often enigmatic "quality of life" across the state.

In plenary session, the conference recommended the creation of a "managing agency for the south Florida region."[81] Such an agency would geographically include "the Kissimmee River Basin (historically known as the 'Kissimmee River Valley'), the Okeechobee Basin, the Everglades, and the Big Cypress Watershed, including all adjacent coastal and estuarine areas."[82] Water quality, water supply and quantity, land reclamation, population, ground water and geography were specifically thought to be in such an agency's mission. In addition, thinking as planners, the conference saw the need and recommended, "At state level, there must be an agency or board that has all power necessary to develop and ensure implementation of a comprehensive land and water use plan for the state."[83] This was an important and far-reaching concept. It provided the springboard to tie land and water use planning together and to address all of Florida, not just the southern part of the state. The conference also recommended that regional plans for south Florida must be consistent with the envisioned state land and water use plan. The plan should address population levels, density of development, and availability of resources to support the future populations of the region.

It was timely that the Florida Association of the American Institute of Architects had been organizing a series of "Red Flag Charrettes" in several regions of the state to identify regional and local environmental and urban development issues, or "crises". These educational events created considerable interest among the state's news media and involved other groups with particular interests in planning and growth. Meanwhile, professional planners, previously focused mostly on local planning concerns, began to see a need for state level and greater regional level involvement in the management of development.

Governor's Task Force on Resources Management

What began as an initiative by the governor to seek solutions to the water management problem in south Florida gradually expanded to include other policy areas. The governor's initiative merged with the on-going state planning interests of the Florida legislature to form a framework for a broadly based intergovernmental approach to statewide management of growth. The bond between water management and state planning, previously somewhat independent efforts was provided when Governor Askew's Conference on Water Management in South Florida astutely observed that water management and coordinated control of land use were inextricably related. This put solving water problems into a broader framework. It also brought the water-land use relationship to the attention of legislative leaders.

The Florida legislature and the governor's office were now heavily committed to investigating and identifying crucial issues of growth, management of growth, and more effective management of natural resources. There were citizen activists and organizations such as the Florida Audubon Society, the Florida Defenders of the Environment, the Sierra Club, and groups representing many concerned citizens pressing for statewide action to deal with growth and environmental degradation. These citizen groups viewed state government incapable, incompetent, or politically unable to cope with Florida's future and its burgeoning population. To most political observers, the governor's initiative in south Florida might have appeared to be an adequate response, but Governor Askew was not a governor to leave things unresolved. In the months following the water conference recommendation, he appointed a Task Force on Resource Management (at first known as the Task Force on Land Use Planning). The task force was charged with the responsibility of preparing legislation designed to implement the recommendations of the Conference on Water Management in South Florida.

The task force met in November of 1971 for its first session. John DeGrove, always a leader in such emerging matters, had been appointed chair by the governor. Joining him were fourteen other members representing considerable expertise in planning, local, regional and state government administration, and legislative experience.[84] The Bureau of Planning in the Division of Budgeting and Planning in the Department of Administration staffed the task force.[85] Jay Landers, representing the governor, indicated that, "Governor Askew considered land use planning a problem of immediate concern."[86] The task force viewed this as a statewide mandate that, historically, would be a challenging change from the permissive local planning and zoning laws of the past.

During the first meeting, issues were proposed for discussion. As James May reported, "There were four major issues: state land use management; state comprehensive planning; environmental reorganization; and regional planning."[88] During the next meeting in December of 1971, working from draft papers developed by staff, the task force focused on the role of the governor as chief state planning officer acting by means of a state planning agency. Also among the issues were consideration of a single environmental and pollution control agency, sub-state regional planning agencies, and a state level and statewide land use and comprehensive plan. This was a large order. The task force sorted out its charges, and focused on the state land use and planning aspects of the issues, leaving the matter of environmental reorganization for future discussions in a different venue and by a different set of participants. Before their work was finished, when the task force met at River Ranch, it prepared or endorsed a package of ten related bills setting the initial framework for an intergovernmental growth management strategy:

1. Environmental Land and Water Management Act (CS for SB 629, HB 4248)

2. A $200 Million Bond Issue to but critical environmental lands (SB 982, HB 4228)

3. State Comprehensive Planning Act (CS for SB 778, HB 3801)

4. Water Resources Act (HB 4060)

5. Regional Planning bill (SB 1100, HB 3975)

6. South Florida Regional Planning Act (SB 1052, HB 4237)

7. Flood Control District Board Membership Act (SB 877, HB 4155)

8. Land Reserve Act (SB 961, HB 4224)

9. A $20 Million Outdoor Recreation Bond Issue (CS for SJR 292, HJR 4216)

10. Environmental Reorganization Act (HB 3650; this bill was killed on reconsideration)[88]

The task force worked through the fall of 1971 and into the winter months of 1972 and was able to send along to the governor a comprehensive set of bills that clearly reflected his deep concerns for the environment and for managing growth. Governor Askew forwarded these draft bills to the 1972 session of the Florida Legislature, where leaders in both houses were already committed to seeing this legislation through to completion.

Environmental Land and Water Management Act

The history of planning in Florida was incremental, disjointed, and fraught with the political vagaries of localism, land speculation, a contagious sense of resource abundance and an aphorism that growth paid for itself. Given this history, task force discussions led to an analysis of the existing system of land use decision making. Like most states, Florida had abdicated any responsibility it might have had for planning and land development, and delegated this legislative and police power to local governments. The process into the early 1970s had been based on the models prepared by the U. S. Department of Commerce in its recommended Standard City Planning Enabling Act in 1928. However, this model was outdated and no longer sufficient to meet Florida's needs. In Florida, the permissive quality of planning and zoning legislation had resulted in a patchwork of weak, localized efforts of development management.

Despite numerous commentaries, little fundamental research had been undertaken concerning the effectiveness, accountability, and quality of local governmental planning after nearly fifty years of employing the U.S. Department of Commerce's model acts for planning and zoning. However, in 1968, the Institute of Training in Municipal Administration[89] sponsored the publication of a seminal book on city planning and the Council of State Governments was also contributing to state and local planning research. In addition, there was broad agreement among many planning professionals and land use lawyers that existing planning authority was archaic. It did not meet the needs of modern America. Thus, the American Law Institute (ALI) began its examination of the existing framework of local control of land development. The Institute considered, "...proposals for change in both the form and substance of this legislation, clarifying the authority conferred, improving the procedure for its exercise and seeking, within limits, to encourage planning as an incident of local regulation..."[90] One of the major premises of the Institute's research was, "...that total localism in the regulation of land development has now become anachronistic, calling for imaginative recourse to the State's authority to safeguard values that ought not to be subordinated to competing local interests."[91] The institute called for change and greater state government involvement.

Early drafts of ALI's proposed Model Land Development Code were brought to the attention of the Task Force on Resource Management by one of its members, Gilbert Finnell, a professor in the College of Law at Florida State University. Finnell recognized the work as a new and creditable source of prescriptive design in land development planning and regulation. The reporters of the Institute were proposing a new generation of state, regional, and local policies, including creative administrative mechanisms at the state level and an intergovernmental process to address the issues. In framing its deliberations the task force was guided by the ALI, and its generalized inquiries are rephrased here:

Is there a machinery or process for Florida's state governmental machinery which offers more promise of ensuring planning and forethought than do other possible governmental procedures?

Are there in fact some governmental planning and land use decisions so fraught with undesirable consequences if made irrationally, locally, parochially, or prejudicially that the decisions reviewed or denied to certain levels of government altogether?

Is there an optimum level of government for allocation of responsibility for planning with regard to projects that may be larger in impacts that spill over into another jurisdiction?

The task force, with its view to the future, considered it necessary for the state to consider reorganizing to ensure its administrative structure was equipped to cope with planning and development management. If a new intergovernmental system of planning and development management were to be in Florida's future, then the state as the constitutional source of legislative authority must be able effectively to develop, encourage, and manage such an initiative.

With these essential questions and issues framing its deliberations, the task force proceeded to utilize the well-developed work of the ALI. It provided a new—though untested—approach to intergovernmental planning and development management for Florida, and eventually led to the task force adopting parts of Article 7 of ALI's proposed State Land Development Regulations. These parts contained passages on districts of critical state concern and developments of state and regional impact.[92] The task force chose to call these "areas of critical state concern" and "developments of regional impact". Tentative Draft No. 3 of the ALI Model Land Development Code contained two articles: the first, Article 7, pertained to state land development regulation, and the second, Article 8, related to state land development planning. The task force made greater use of Article 7 than it did of Article 8.

In preparing the draft legislation, the task force asked Fred Bosselman, associate reporter for the ALI, to provide legal and related services. This was an important step in moving on with the work of crafting an intergovernmental planning, development, and growth management framework for Florida. The recommended state land development regulating process did three basic things consistent with the task force assumptions. It provided for:

1.   The state to interpose its interest in land development when these issues are of more than local or regional concern;

2.   a new systematic process of intergovernmental relationship between state and local government, and

3.   the activation of regional planning agencies as instrumentalities of the state's policy in land use when land use issues are of more than local concern.

The draft might have been called the "land use management act", but the words environmental and water were added for practical and perhaps political reasons. RuBino observed that land use "is not solely an environmental matter; the way in which land is used has an impact on economic and social factors as much as it does the environment."[93] True enough, but using the term "environmental" in the title took advantage of the then prevailing interest in protecting Florida's environmental resources. He also noted that the term "water" was added because, "an adequate water management system (as authorized by the Water Resources Act) could not be insured without an adequate land management program." As had already been pointed out by the Conference on Water Management in South Florida, water could not be effectively managed without also managing land.

The 1972 Florida legislature enacted the recommendations of the Task Force on Resource Management supporting the Environmental Land and Water Management Act[94] (ELWMA) with three major modifications from the American Law Institute Model Land Development Code:

1.   The provision for interim development moratoria in areas of critical state concern was deleted,

2.   the ability of the state land planning agency to make rules was obviated by vesting this authority with the Governor and Cabinet,[95] and

3.   in the definition of development, a specific exemption for agricultural operation was made during the legislative process.[96]

The third modification was an essential compromise made in the Florida Senate in order to move the legislation through for a final vote. This change exempted agricultural operations from the definition of development, a change that had little impact upon the implementation of the act.

The ELWMA provides for designation of areas of critical state concern by the Governor and Cabinet.[97] The designation in the ELWMA provided that a finding of critical state concern be demonstrated to show that future development or proposed development could cause environmental degradation, degradation of historic or archeological resources, or the degradation of major public investments.[98] In doing so, the state land planning agency is required to demonstrate that one or more of the impacts upon the environment, historic and/or archeological resources, and public investment. Areas designated for new communities were also a provision, but it has never been used. In addition, the land planning agency[99] was required to show that appropriate local governments were not capable of managing development to prevent such degradations shown and the agency was required to provide guidelines for development in the proposed area if designated by the Governor and Cabinet.

The second substantive part of the ELWMA provided authority for the state to define substantive standards for developments of regional impact[100] and establish procedural methods and guidelines for administering their review. Developments of regional impact (DRIs) include any development that because of its location, magnitude, or character when developed would impact the people of more than one county in Florida. This provided the statutory presumption of developments that could be DRIs. The state land planning agency (the Division of State Planning) drafted the guidelines and standards for DRIs with the advice of the Environmental Land Management Study Committee (ELMS). The ELMS committee was also created by the ELWMA and had a predetermined life of two years.

In the reorganization of the Department of Administration, the Bureau of State Planning was separated from the Division of Planning and Budgeting and, in 1972, was made the Division of State Planning (DSP) in the Department of Administration.[101] The executive director of the ELMS Committee was Daniel O'Connell. One of the authors (Starnes) was Director of DSP and with Eastern Tin, John Alexander, Linda Frazier and John Davis provided the research necessary to formulate the standards. The definition of "regional" was a critical finding and, with the help of attorney Fred

Bosselman, the search led to definitions found in both national laws and regulations such as the description of regional airports and a definition of shopping centers suggested by the Urban Land Institute. The DRI standards and guidelines were submitted to the Governor and Cabinet in early 1973 and to the Florida Legislature for its consideration during the regular 1973 session. More about the promulgation of the DRI standards and guidelines is discussed in the following chapter.

Land Conservation Act of 1972

The 1972 Land Conservation Act provided for $200 million in general obligation bonds for the state to acquire environmentally endangered lands and $40 million to acquire and improve recreational facilities.[102] The bond issue was authorized by a statewide referendum in November 1972 and was adopted by a seventy percent favorable vote. The purpose of this act was to fulfill a policy requirement for purchase of endangered lands. The Task Force on Resourc Management anticipated there would be instances where land development regulations could not protect important environmental resources, and in the alternative the state needed the capacity to buy the land for preservation. One of the major strategies of the 1972 legislation was to implement land use planning management through regulation where and when possible, but the alternative to regulation was acquisition if such regulations could not be reasonably imposed—a policy squarely in the middle of the constitutional issue of "taking".

In addition to the referendum for general obligation bonds, there was another key provision on the ballot directly related to the vote. The provision, if passed with the bond referendum implemented the critical area provisions of the Land and Water Management Act of 1972.[103] This part of the ELWMA limited the designation of critical areas to no more than five percent of the land area of the state, or 1,950,000 acres. The state acquisition program was a step in the direction of development management that added another strategy to the growing bag of tools for Florida's move toward managing growth and development. The Department of Natural Resources (DNR), headed by the Governor and Cabinet, was the agency administering the program. The DNR made its recommendations for acquisition based on the deliberations of a multi-agency land acquisition advisory committee chaired by the Executive Director of the DNR, Randolph Hodges. This acquisition of lands was voluntary (i.e., "a willing seller") for the Governor and Cabinet announced that it did not intend to use eminent domain as a forceful means of acquiring endangered lands.

State Comprehensive Planning Act of 1972

This State Comprehensive Planning Act set forth the state comprehensive planning process and in broad terms described the comprehensive plan and its adoption procedures.[104] The DSP in the Department of Administration was thus an executive planning agency responsible to the governor, whom the act named as the chief planning officer. The Task Force on Resource Management believed this new state planning agency should be considered "first among equals" among state and regional agencies participating in planning. A provision of the act required each state agency to appoint an agency planning officer, thus forming a state level planning advisory group to assist in the comprehensive planning process. According to Robert M. Rhodes, the state comprehensive plan was expected to "provide needed policies for Chapter 380 programs and directions for related programs."[105]

Consensus among task force members was that the state planning agency should be located in the executive office of the governor. Governor Askew did not agree, thus the DSP was placed in the Department of Administration, which was the management arm of the governor administering planning, budgeting, personnel and the state employee retirement system. Askew's view of the governor's office was that it should be devoid of any of the functional agencies and planning activities which had accrued during the term of Governor Claude Kirk. Governor Kirk was not entirely responsible for the build-up of functions in his office, however. The federal government had created many new state programs in response to the domestic policies of the Nixon administration and, in an understandable desire to get these programs up and running at state level, they landed strategically in the governor's office. A significant example was planning and management of the large grant program of the U.S. Law Enforcement Assistance Act (often called the Safe Streets Act).[106] The planning and management staff of this program alone quickly grew to more than twenty professional personnel. Governor Askew was not disposed to have such large staff in his executive office.

Water Resources Act of 1972

The Task Force on Resource Management soon recognized the importance of the research completed by the College of Law at the University of Florida,[107] and referred it to the legislature. The outcome was the Water Resources Act (WRA), which, among other things, provided policy and planning interfaces with the land management policies of the ELWMA, as well as the Florida State Comprehensive Planning Act, in providing for statewide water use planning and management.[108]

Water use planning is a two-level effort: state oversight at one level and five sub-state water management districts at regional level, all created by the act. The WRA provided generally for hydrological district boundaries. The final boundaries were to be established by the Division of Geology in the Department of Natural Resources. Wisely, the boundaries were selected along surface water regimes and drainage basins not recognizing existing political boundaries of counties. The districts are the Northwest Florida Water Management District (WMD), the Suwannee River WMD, the St. Johns River WMD, the Southwest Florida WMD, and the South Florida WMD. With the approval of a statewide referendum held in 1973, the districts were authorized to have taxing authority. Each of the nine district governing board members are appointed by the governor and affirmed by the Senate. This was the final element of the 1972 legislation which, when taken together, are considered by the authors to be the threshold to Florida's next thirty years of coping with its rapid population growth through planning.

Summary

The early 1970s experienced a wave of innovative statewide and regional planning and development management initiatives. The wave of activity was the consequence of—to borrow a term from Donald A. Krueckeberg—four "converging ideas" of modernizing the practice of planning and development regulation. One was the permeating effect of the federal planning requirements of the 1960s and early 1970s, a second was the movement to revitalize state governments, the third was the rapid spread of interest in the ALI's Draft Model Land Development Code, and lastly the peaking of national environmental consciousness. All four of these movements entwined, especially in Florida, to contribute to the "Quiet Revolution" of the early 1970s.

The cooperation, coordination, and, above all, the political success of Florida's legislative and executive branches in promulgating such sweeping change in attempting to manage growth was a revelation and a learning experience. Seldom had such a comprehensive assessment of Florida's growth and future been brought together and promulgated in state laws creating a potentially meaningful intergovernmental system of planning and regulatory measures. Except for a few loose ends, the work appeared to be done. In the following chapter, we will discuss the implementation of the 1972 legislation, beginning with the work of the Environmental Land Management Study Committee and work of the Division of State Planning including organizing for the new intergovernmental framework for planning and the promulgation of the mandatory local government planning law.

NOTES FOR CHAPTER VI

1 1998 Florida Statistical Abstract, 32nd edition, Bureau of Economic and Business Research, University of Florida, Gainesville, FL, 1998, p 7.

2 Formerly Dade County. The name was changed by the county electorate to Miami-Dade in 1997.

3 Ibid., pp. 6-8.

4 Campbell, Alan K., ed., *The States and the Urban Crisis*, Englewood Cliffs, NJ: Prentice-Hall, Inc., 1970.

5 Ibid., p. 1.

6 Ibid., p. 6, quoting Elazar, Daniel J., "The States and the Nation," in Herbert Jacob and Kenneth N. Vines, eds., *Politics in the American States,* Boston, MA: Little, Brown and Company, 1965, p. 449.

7 Ibid., p. 6.

8 U.S., *Baker v. Carr* (U.S., 369 U.S. 186, 1962).

9 Information provided by staff of the Miami-Dade County Planning Department by telephone interview, January 29, 2006 with Earl Starnes.

10 In 1975, Florida's first mandatory local government planning was enacted by the Florida legislature, Ch. 163, Part II, *Florida Statutes*.

11 Meador, Toni L., "Managing Growth on Florida's Gold Coast: Boca Raton and the Growth Cap," *Florida Environmental and Urban Issues* VI: 3, 1979, pp. 10-13 and 17.

12 1973 *Florida Laws* 594.

13 DeGrove, John M. and Nancy E. Stroud, "New Developments and Future Trends in Local Government Comprehensive Planning: Florida's Growth Management System in the National Context," *Stetson Law Review* XVII: 3, 1988, p. 601.

14 Ibid., p. 602.

15 Spagna, Neno J., "Transfer of Development Rights: The Collier County Experience," *Florida Environmental and Urban Issues* VI: 3, 1979, pp. 7-9 and 15-16, this reference is on p. 7.

16 Florida Department of Administration, Division of State Planning, "The Green Plan", Doc-DSP-10-75, Tallahassee, FL: 1975, p. 6.

17 Ch. 70-375, *Laws of Florida*, later codified as Ch. 273.1281 *Florida Statutes*.

18 Fernald, Edward A., and Donald J. Patton, eds., *Water Resources Atlas of Florida*, Tallahassee, FL: Florida State University, 1984, p. 265.

19 Ibid.

20 Southern Golden Gate Estates, Watershed Planning Assistance Co-operative Study, Final Report, South Florida Water Management District and the U.S. Department of Agriculture, Natural Resource Conservation Service, October 2003.

21 Public Law 89-749. For an excellent discussion of the history of health planning in the U.S., see Ann Suter Ford, "Health Planning" in *The Practice of State and Regional Planning*, So, Frank S., Irving Hand, and Bruce McDowell, eds., Chicago: American Planning Association, 1985, pp. 519-567.

22 Ibid., p. 527.

23 Ibid.

24 Additional information regarding statewide health planning in Florida: Governor Hayden Burns assigned the federally initiated health planning responsibility to the Budget Commission (i.e., the Governor and Cabinet) in 1966; when Governor Claude Kirk assumed office in 1967, he moved the function to the budget office; the 1967 State Planning Act designated the State Planning Office, in the new State Planning and Budget Commission, as the state agency for health planning; and, in late 1967, Kirk appointed a Florida Health Advisory Council. This information was obtained from a report on Florida—Comprehensive Health Planning, prepared for the Institute on State Programming for the 70s, at the University of North Carolina-Chapel Hill, NC: 1968.

25 Ibid., p. 529.

26 Ibid.

27 Ibid.

28 *Public Law* 87-866.

29 Federal Highway Administration, Planning Process Memorandum, 50-9, 1965; Planning Process Memorandum 90-3, 1974.

30 *Public Law*, 91-605.

31 Ashford, Norman and Richard G. RuBino, "The Role of the State in Transportation," *Traffic Engineering,* 42: 4, 1972, p. 15.

32 *Public Law* 90-351.

33 S. 632 and H.R. 2173.

34 One of the authors (Starnes) testified to Congress regarding the potential need for state and local funds to adequately implement the Jackson legislation, and he also served on a Department of Interior Land Use Task Force empanelled to frame regulations designed to implement the legislation.

35 S. 992, H.R. 4332.

36 The code was not formally adopted by the American Law Institute until 1975.

37   Reilly, William K., ed., *The Use of Land*, New York, NY: Thomas Y. Crowell Company, 1973, p. 73.

38   Jerold S. Kayden has since classed this as "a toothless" attempt to enact a national land use policy. See "National Land-Use Planning in America: Something Whose Time Has Never Come," *Washington University Journal of Law and Policy* 445, 2000, p. 448.

39   U.S., Coastal Zone Management Act of 1972; Public Law 92-583. For other examples of geographically specific approaches to managing land and water use see RuBino, Richard G., and William R. Wagner, *The States' Role in Land Resource Management*, Lexington, KY: Council of State Governments, 1972.

40   *Public Law* 92-583, as amended by *Public Law* 109-58; the law covers all states along the Atlantic and Pacific coasts, as well as the states along the Great Lakes.

41   This information was made available by email from Lynn Griffin of the Florida State Library, Tallahassee, Florida to Starnes, February 10, 2006.

42   Records of the Defense Civil Preparedness Agency, The U.S. National Archives & Records Administration, Record group 397, 397.1 Administrative History, obtained by Earl Starnes, 10 February 2006.

43   In 1977, Richard G. RuBino, William Olsen, and Andrew Dzurik, professors with the Department of Urban and Regional Planning at Florida State University, along with Alan Pearman, research associate, completed the "Tampa-St. Petersburg Crisis Relocation Plans" for the U.S. Defense Civil Preparedness Agency, Region 3 office in Thomasville, GA. In 1980, RuBino and Olsen, under contract with the Federal Emergency Management Agency in Washington, DC, finished work on regional and state food distribution planning for crisis relocation for the eight states in the southeastern U.S. Soon after, the Cold War began to thaw and crisis relocation planning was no longer a priority.

44   Bosselman, Fred and David Callies, *The Quiet Revolution in Land Use Control,* Washington, DC: Council on Environmental Quality, USGPO, 1971.

45   Multiple sources: Bosselman, Fred and David Callies, *The Quiet Revolution in Land Use Control*, Washington, DC: Council on Environmental Quality, 1971; Burby, Raymond J. and Peter J. May, *Making Governments Plan*, Baltimore: Johns Hopkins University Press, 1997; Conners, Donald L., Anne Rickard Jackowitz, and Miriam A. Widmann, "State and Regional Planning: Summary of Selected Recent Acts and Initiatives," in Douglas R. Porter, *State and Regional Initiative for Managing Development*, Washington, DC: Urban Land

Institute, 1992; DeGrove, John M., *Land Growth and Politics*, Chicago: Planners Press, American Planning Association, 1984; DeGrove, John M. with Deborah A. Miness, *Planning and Growth Management in the States*, Cambridge, MA: Lincoln Institute of Land Policy, 1992; Healy, Robert G. and John S. Rosenberg, *Land Use and the States*, Baltimore: Johns Hopkins University Press, 1979; Knaap, Gerrit and Arthur C. Nelson, *The Regulated Landscape*, Cambridge, MA: Lincoln Institute of Land Policy, 1992; Leonard, H. Jeffrey, *Managing Oregon's Growth*, Washington, DC: Conservation Foundation, 1983; Pelham, Thomas G., *State Land-Use Planning and Regulation*, Lexington, MA: Lexington Books, 1979; Popper, Frank J., *The Politics of Land-Use Reform*, Madison: University of Wisconsin Press, 1981; RuBino, Richard G. and William R. Wagner, *The States' Role in Land Resource Management*, Lexington, KY: Council of State Governments, 1972; Squires, Jeffrey F., "Growth Management Redux: Vermont's Act 250 and Act 200," in Porter, ibid.

46 See *Vermont Scenery Preservation*, Montpelier, VT: Vermont Central Planning Office, 1966; and *The Preservation of Roadside Scenery*, Montpelier, VT: Vermont Central Planning Office, 1966. For skillful coverage of these activities see Harrison, Blake, *The View From Vermont*, Burlington, VT: University of Vermont Press, 2006.

47 Heeter, David G., "Almost Getting It Together in Vermont," in Daniel R. Mandelker, ed., *Environmental and Land Controls Legislation*, New York, NY: Bobbs-Merrill Company, 1976, p. 324.

48 The original seven district commissions were later divided into nine district commissions.

49 See Bosselman and Callies, ibid., pp. 54-107 for detailed coverage of these early activities in Vermont.

50 *New York State* Constitution, Article XIV, sec. 1.

51 Adirondack Park Agency Act, 1971, Executive Law, article 27, sec. 801-820; also see the Wild Scenic and Recreational Rivers System Act (Environmental Conservation Law, article 24) and the Freshwater Wetlands Act (Environmental Conservation Law, article 24 and article 15, respectively).

52 Healy, Robert G. and John S. Rosenberg, *Land Use and the States*, second edition, Baltimore, MD: Johns Hopkins University Press for Resources for the Future, 1979, p. 85.

53 Ibid.

54 Ibid.

55 See Mogulof, Melvin B., *Saving the Coast: California's Experiment in Intergovernmental Land Use Control*, Lexington, MA: Lexington Books, 1975, p. xi.

56 California Coastal Act, California Public Resources Code, sections 30000 et seq.

57 Knapp, Gerrit and Arthur C. Nelson, *The Regulated Landscape: Lessons on State Land Use Planning from Oregon*, Cambridge, MA: Lincoln Institute of Land Policy, 1992, p. 18.

58 SB 100, Oregon Land Conservation and Development Act, 1973, *Oregon Statutes*.

59 Leonard, H. Jeffrey, ibid, Among other things, the compromise removed the creation of fourteen regional planning districts and granting regulatory authority to the state in areas of critical state concern.

60 Ch. 716, Massachusetts Acts and Resolves.

61 Martha's Vineyard Commission, "Looking at the Commission," March 11, 2003, p. 5; obtained from www. mvcommission.org/doc.php on April 16, 2007.

62 North Carolina Coastal Management Act, Article 7, §§ 113A-100-134.3.

63 Healy and Rosenberg, ibid. pp. 203-204.

64 U.S., *Baker v. Carr* (369 U.S. 186, 1962), brought by citizens of Memphis to improve urban representation in the Tennessee State Assembly.

65 Information obtained during an interview with Hugh Macmillan on June 25, 2007.

66 Florida Office of the Governor, "The First Annual Report on State Housing Goals: A Message from Reubin O'Donovan Askew," 1973; the report was prepared by the Task Force on Housing and Community Development, with Jim Tait serving as the governor's representative.

67 Florida Office of the Governor, "Housing in Florida," c. 1973, prepared jointly by the Task Force on Housing and Community Development and the Department of Community Affairs; the lead writers of the report were Gilbert Bergquist, Gary Cooper, Henry Depew, Dorothy Kyle, and Diane Dzurik.

68 Ch. 163, Part II, *Florida Statutes*.

69 See Molotch, Harvey with John Logan, *Urban Fortunes: The Political Economy of Place*, Berkeley, CA: University of California Press, 1987, for a discussion of growth machines.

70 Molotch, Harvey, "The city as a growth machine: Toward a political economy of place," *American Journal of Sociology* 82: 2, 1976, pp. 309-332.

71 Christensen, Terry, *Local Politics: Governing at the Grassroots*, Belmont, CA: Wadsworth Publishing, 1994, pp. 306-321.

72 Dennis, James M., Staff Report on Planning and Growth Policy,"
    Governmental Operations Committee, Florida House of Represen-
    tatives, September 18, 1973, unnumbered p. 2.
73 Though a number of committees were instructed to address the growth
    issue, most of the attention focused on the work of the House Com-
    mittee on Community Affairs. John Wesley White was staff director,
    major contributors to the work of the committee were Robert Rhodes
    (aide to Speaker Pettigrew), Representative Donald Crane, and James
    Dennis (an analyst from the House Governmental Organization and
    Efficiency Committee); author Richard RuBino served as consultant
    to the committee. See pp. 12-16 of James W. May, referenced in the
    following footnote, for an account of this legislative activity.
74 May, James W., "The Florida Environmental Land and Water Man-
    agement Act of 1972: Planning and the State Legislative Policy-Mak-
    ing Process," a research paper prepared in fulfilling requirements for
    the degree of Master of Science in Planning, Department of Urban
    and Regional Planning, Florida State University, Tallahassee, FL.
    March 29, 1974, p. 10. This paper provides an excellent record of the
    entire planning-related executive and legislative experience in Florida
    during 1971 and 1972.
75 Ibid, pp. 13-14.
76 Maloney, Frank E., Sheldon J. Plager, and Fletcher N. Baldwin, Jr.,
    assisted by William Haddad, *Water Law and Administration, The
    Florida Experience*, Gainesville, FL: University of Florida Press,
    1968.
77 Fernald and Patton, ibid., p. 132.
78 May, ibid., p. 12.
79 DeGrove, John M., "Florida's Growth Management Legislation:
    1969-2000," paper presented at the Richard E. Nelson Symposium
    on Florida's Growth Management Legislation, October 13, 2000, p.
    1.
80 Governor's Conference on Water Management In South Florida,
    "Statement To Governor Reubin O'D. Askew," 1971.
81 Ibid.
82 Ibid, p. 7.
83 Ibid, p. 6.
84 The task force was chaired by professor John DeGrove of Florida
    Atlantic University; the other fourteen originally designatred mem-
    bers were State Representative Don Crane of St. Petersburg, law pro-
    fessor Gilbert Finnell of Florida State University, State Senator Rob-
    ert "Bob" Graham, Bruce Johnson of the Coastal Coordinating Council
    in the FL Department of Natural Resources, State Representative Ray

Knopke of Tampa, Jack Malloy of the Central and Southern Florida Flood Control District, Art Marshall of the Center for Urban Studies at the University of Miami, Don Morgan of the Central and South Florida Flood Control District, urban planning professor Richard RuBino of Florida State University, architect Nils Schweizer of Winter Park, State Senator Jack Shreve of Merritt Island, Earl Starnes of the Division of Mass Transit Operations in the FL Department of Transportation, Homer Still of the Bureau of Planning in the FL Department of Administration, and Norm Thompson of the Tampa Bay Regional Planning Council.

85 The staff members of the Bureau of Planning included planners Eastern Tin and John Davis.

86 May, ibid, p. 16.

87 Ibid, p. 18.

88 Obtained from a sheet titled "Legislation Prepared or Endorsed by Governor's Task Force on Resources Management, Status of Bills as of 3-17-72."

89 Goodman, I. Gordon, ed. and Eric C. Freund, assoc. ed., *Principles and Practice of Urban Planning*, Published by The International City Manager's Association, Washington, D.C., 1968.

90 Wechsler, Herbert, Foreword, "A Model Land Development Code", The American Law Institute, Tentative Draft No. 3, April 22, 1971, Philadelphia, PA.

91 Ibid.

92 Ibid, pp. 7-47.

93 RuBino, Richard G., "An Evaluation: Florida's Land Use Law," *State Government* XLVI: 3, 1973, p. 173.

94 Ch. 380, *Florida Statutes*.

95 The authority of the Florida Governor and Cabinet is established in the Constitution of the State of Florida; it establishes the Administration Commission, and the 1972 Land and Water Management Act creates the Florida Land and Water Adjudicatory Commission as a cabinet function. The latter commission is the final administrative appellate forum regarding appeals from local, regional, or state entities, and citizens regarding land development decisions.

96 § 380.04(3)(e), *Florida Statutes*.

97 This authority was later found unconstitutional and an unlawful designation of legislative powers in a case styled as *Askew v Cross Keys Waterways*, 372 So.2d 913 (Florida 1978).

98 American Law Institute, ibid, p. 293.

99   The land planning agency is designated in Ch. 380, *Florida Statutes.* In 1972, The Division of State Planning was the designated agency. In 1980, this designation was changed and today the Land Planning Agency is Department of Community Affairs.

100 § 380.06, *Florida Statutes.*

101 Ch. 23, *Florida Statutes*

102 Ch. 259, *Florida Statutes.*

103 § 380.05, *Florida Statutes.*

104 Ch. 23, *Florida Statutes.* This chapter was later amended and the comprehensive plan was moved to Ch. 186, *Florida Statutes.*

105 Rhodes, Robert M., "Growth Management in Florida 1985 and Beyond," *Florida Environmental and Urban Issues* XIII: 2, 1986, p. 2.

106 *Public Law* 89-197, 1965.

107 Maloney, ibid.

108 Ch. 373, *Florida Statutes.*

109 Krueckeberg, Donald A., *Introduction to Planning History in the United States*, New Brunswick, NJ: Center for Urban Policy Research, Rutgers University, 1983, p. 6.

CHAPTER VII

IMPLEMENTING FLORIDA'S 1970S PLANNING LAWS

Mid 1970s to About 1980

In the construction of a country it is not the practical workers but the idealists and planners that are
difficult to find.[1] (Chung-shan Ch'lian-shu, 1936.)

The purposes and policies of land use planning in
Florida are best stated in the Environmental Land and Water
Management Act of 1972 (ELWMA):

It is the legislative intent that, in order to protect the natural resources and environment of
this state as provided in §7, Art. II of the state
constitution, insure a water management system
that will reverse the deterioration of water quality and provide optimum utilization of our limited water resources, facilitate orderly and well-
planned development, and protect the health,
welfare, safety, and quality of life, of the residents of this state, it is necessary adequately to
plan for and guide growth and development
within this state.[2]

The act goes on to say:

In order to accomplish these purposes, it is necessary that the state establish land and water
management policies to guide and coordinate
local decisions relating to growth and development; that such state land and water management policies should, to the maximum possible
extent, be implemented by local governments
through existing processes for the guidance of

growth and development; and that all the existing rights of private property be preserved in accord with the constitutions of this state and of the United States.

It is our intention in this chapter to discuss the implementation of Florida's 1970s planning laws. We start by examining the organization of the Division of State Planning (DSP) in the Florida Department of Administration. The DSP was organized to respond to the explicit operational functions declared in the State Comprehensive Planning Act of 1972,[3] the ELWMA, and related planning initiatives. The preamble above establishes the state's statutory purpose, policies, and authority. Our intent is to show how the DSP implemented these new state imperatives.

It is clear the legislature intended building an intergovernmental system of planning and development management, which did not exist in 1972. Thus it was necessary to establish a local, regional, and state institutional operational framework and complete it by July of 1973. The ELWMA visualized a greater involvement of local governments and regional agencies, as well as new roles for state agencies. There were constraints to implementing planning and development management strategies which would become apparent as work unfolded at local, regional, and state levels. Those included financial resources and competent staffing of state agencies, the lack of "wall to wall"[4] regional planning agencies, and assessing competence of local governments. There were additional constraints derived from constitutional protections of due process and private property rights. This new state initiative of land and water management, or as we have been using the term, "development management", envisioned that planning strategies and policies should to the maximum possible extent, be developed by local governments. In doing so, those governments were required to employ often unused permissive planning authority and existing or new local planning agencies and practices.

Organizing for Implementation

With these legislative objectives and constraints, the purposes and policies of land use planning and water management were clearly set forth. The first step was to analyze the ELWMA and understand the mandatory operational strategies implicit and explicit within the language of the law. There were three sections of the act requiring attention and implementation by July of 1973. First, creation of the Environmental Land Management Study Committee (ELMS);[5] second, the authority of the state to designate areas of critical state concern (ACSC);[6] and third, the authority of the state, regional and local governments to determine what proposed developments meet the definition of developments of regional impact (DRI)[7] and to formulate standards, guidelines and procedures for the monitoring of DRI and land use and environmental regulation of such developments. Following the format of the ELWMA, the DSP organized into three bureaus: Comprehensive Planning, Land Management, and Intergovernmental Coordination. In addition, the DSP included an Office of Information Systems. Later, as programs were assigned by the Governor's Office to the DSP, other bureaus were created, such as Criminal Justice Planning and Highway Safety.

The first set of planning strategies engaged by the DSP dealt with the ACSC program. The strategies included procedures and ramifications of designation, boundary descriptions, coping with local governments, and analyses to determine critical planning and environmental issues to be addressed. Finally, the DSP was responsible for promulgating development management and land planning rules for designated areas.

Areas of Critical State Concern

The ELWMA provided for the interposition of state interests in areas that could be declared areas of critical state concern.[8] Such declarations could be made by the Governor and Cabinet sitting as the Administration Commission, based on findings and recommendations of the DSP. The DSP findings had to include a report with a convincing explanation why designation of an ACSC was of critical importance to state interests. The DSP planners were required to make the case for designation based on future development of an area identifying the potential threat to natural or environmental resources, the threat to archeological or historic resources, or the decline of the effectiveness or efficiency of existing public investments. In addition, a finding was required to show a lack of local government planning and land use regulations were not capable of protecting the identified state interests, thus making state interposition necessary.

As an example, we can look at the designation of the Florida Keys, which covers the archipelago of Monroe County. In 1974, the DSP cited that each of the planning principles and criteria noted above were found to exist. Continued unrestricted development was envisioned to impact negatively the upland environmental habitats of the Key deer and other endangered species unique to the Florida Keys. The continued employment of cess-pits[9] on individual properties would be certain to destroy the only natural archipelago of tropical reefs along the east coast of the North American continent. In addition, the reefs had been designated by the state as John Pennicamp State Park, a public investment of great environmental importance. There were also historic resources to be protected, particularly in the Key West Historic District previously designated by both the state of Florida and the U.S. Department of the Interior. Additional existing facilities of significant public investment threatened by unconstrained development included the U.S. Navy water main that originated in south Miami-Dade County well fields and supplied the unconstrained demand for public water along the entire reach of the Florida Keys. The other facility of significant public investment was the Key West Naval Air Station. The later was threatened by urban development sprawling into its safe fly zone. The DSP determined that Monroe County, the city of Key West, and other municipalities were ineffective in exercising planning and development management authority in protecting threatened environmental and public resources. Findings concluded that declaration of the Florida Keys as an ACSC was necessary to protect state and federal resources.[10]

In addition to findings for declaration, recommendations included strategies for protecting the resources in the Florida Keys. A crucial recommendation was to develop a comprehensive planning process, with the assistance of state planning and operational agencies and federal agencies having an interest and jurisdiction in Monroe County. The Florida Department of Community Affairs, in becoming the state land planning agency in 1980, received state funding for planning with onsite planners to prepare a comprehensive plan for Monroe County and its municipalities. Other planning issues emerged over time in regard to affordable housing, hurricane evacuation, the widening of U.S. Highway 1, and the carrying capacity of the Florida Keys. State funds were also appropriated to assist in the acquisition of specific lands to preserve habitat and recreational lands. The designation of the Florida Keys ACSC continues to be a statewide political issue and a struggle between state interposition and localism.[11]

There were other ACSC designated during the 1970s; the Green Swamp in parts of Polk and Lake counties, and the Big Cypress Swamp (designated by the Big Cypress Conservation Act of 1972)[12] and finally in the 1980s, an area covering the coastal area of Franklin County, including the city of Apalachicola, was designated an ACSC.[13]

The critical area program was brought into question by a suit against Governor Askew and others in 1978.[14] In this suit, the Florida Supreme Court affirmed the lower court's opinion and found that "The standard by which land development regulations were to be measured was not articulated by the legislature but was determined as the sole province of the administrative agency through formulation of principles." The court went on to say, "This violated the doctrine of no delegation [sic] of legislative power." It essentially found that the legislature must set at least minimum standards and guidelines for an administrative agency to make a determination regarding land development regulations. Too often the construction of statutory language and the language of local land development codes leave the administrative agencies or code enforcement officers without clear legislative directions. Without clear definitive language, rule making or development permitting is often subject to much discretion causing inconsistent and confused policy execution. A lesson learned.

Developments of Regional Impact

A second group of strategies pertained to organizing the developments of regional impact (DRIs) program.[15] The first effort was to promulgate standards and guidelines for describing a DRI and the procedures for administering the program. Procedurally, a determination is made following the appropriate local government's review of a developer's application for development approval. A complete description of the planned development and all future impacts upon urban and environmental systems is required. Following determination of the development as a DRI or not, the local government must then chose to act upon the application, whether this action is for approval, denial, or modification. Next, the regional planning agency analyzes the DRI application for approval or rejection or modification, and reports to the initiating local government the potential impact of developments on the resources of the region. The regional planning agency could appeal the local decision if it were inconsistent with its findings. The local government's decision is also subject to appeal by the developer, or the state land planning agency.[16] Such appeals are then heard before the Florida Land and Water Adjudicatory Commission, consisting of the Governor and Cabinet. The commission usually appoints a hearing officer for the first round of appeals. The effect of this process was to broaden the awareness of local governments in considering the stresses and impacts upon their own and neighboring urban resources as well as the impacts on the geographic and natural systems of the region. It encourages the appropriate employment and competence of land use decisions among local governments, regional agencies, and the state land planning agency.

The planning objectives of the ELWMA were hopefully to be realized by interposing the state's interest as articulated in the act.[17] The intergovernmental process of reviewing, commenting, and decision making related to DRIs would become common in Florida's planning discourse regarding land use, zoning, and growth management. It would also become a component of educational benefit to the public; a lesson learned.

When a development is determined to be a DRI, a regional review is imposed which results in a finding by the regional agency identifying regional impacts. The DRI process of review and comment, with conditions and information coming back to local governments from regional planning agencies, is thought to provide for orderly growth and development for such large-scale developments. At the time (1972), DSP staff considered it a short-term measure until local comprehensive plans could be promulgated and adopted by the many local governments in Florida lacking such plans.

As a second Environmental Land Management Study Committee declared some years later, "The DRIs expensive, time-consuming and duplicative process encouraged many developers to do small projects [sized under the DRI thresholds] in order to avoid the process."[18] In addition, another source considered the DRI review program to be only "partly effective without a regional growth-management strategy against which to measure its decisions."[19]

DRI standards and guidelines

Of specific interest was the mission of the DSP's Bureau of Land Management (BLM). The planners in the BLM were assigned the responsibility of drafting standards and guidelines for DRIs. The purpose was to define a "DRI", track the statutory language, and develop a protocol for administering the process of local decision making, regional review, and state oversight, plus an appellate procedure. The ELWMA defined a DRI as any development, which because of its magnitude, character, or location would impact the people of more than one county.[20] Other than the language in the ELWMA, definitions and standards did not exist in information available to the BLM staff. The term "DRI" emerged as a style, or term of art characterized as a more *controlled* approach to development, a theme that flowed through the 1972 land use legislation. The lack of local planning, the lack of any state agency oversight, coupled with significant growth, sprawl, and environmental degradation drove the political and legislative process in promulgating the ELWMA.

The DSP was required, and eagerly sought, to work closely with the Environmental Land Management Study (ELMS) Committee.[21] A significant advantage was that the ELMS committee provided an open forum across the state for citizen participation and input. It is too often typical that Tallahassee-bound agencies, such as DSP, lack resources to conduct or shape statewide public forums comparable to what the ELMS committee offered. The relationship was valuable, and as DSP continued its research in developing standards for DRIs, the committee became a vital partner in review and assessment. The committee's provision of statewide and regional public meetings elevated the new planning initiatives to an arena of greater public awareness and participation.

The DRI standards and guidelines were drafted by the DSP staff in consultation with attorney Fred Bosselman of the American Law Institute, professor Gilbert Finnell of the Florida State University College of Law, and attorney Daniel W. O'Connell, Executive Director of the ELMS committee. In addition, Governor Askew was represented by attorney Jay Landers, the governor's environmental advisor, and James Apthorp the governor's chief of staff. Many organizations shared useful information with the DSP, including the Florida Audubon Society, the Urban Land Institute (particularly related to definitions of shopping centers), the U.S. Federal Aviation Administration (in regard to its classification for regional airports), and the Florida Planning and Zoning Association, represented by Ernest Bartley, professor of Political Science from the University of Florida. Bartley also served as a consultant to the ELMS committee. ELMS chairman Alan Milledge and member John M. DeGrove of Florida Atlantic University were also contributors to the DSP research and compilation of the DRI standards. This was a unique and demanding planning and drafting effort. The DSP completed its work and moved the DRI standards and guidelines through the approval process. The process began with the ELMS committee, the Governor and Cabinet, and finally the 1973 Legislature. As James W. May observed, "A modification to the Environmental Land and Water Management Act was related to the approval of these guidelines which the legislature enacted,"[22] but reserving oversight authority for any future changes in the DRI standards and guidelines.

In July 1973, following adoption of the DRI standards and guidelines, the DSP found it necessary to prepare binding letters of determination as to whether a development was in fact a DRI or would be exempt from the review process. This resulted in the gathering volumes of data from many large-scale existing and partially completed developments. The DSP planning staff served as critical reviewers of the data and their analyses formed the basis for determining the DRI status of many proposed and ongoing developments. As an example, Palm Coast then a new planned community in Flagler County was partially complete. Palm Coast with a planned build out population of 250,000 was found to be partially exempt because of substantial investment in street paving, water, and sewer extensions and development of some of the properties, all based on its reliance on existing permits. The non-exempt status of large parts of the project resulted in an agreement with the developer, International Telephone and Telegraph Company and its Community Development Company. The agreement led to partial exemption and resulted in the employment of the well-known planner and landscape architect, John Simmons. His charge was to re-design and re-plan many areas of Palm Coast. Another favorable result prevented the connection of a canal system to the Inland Waterway. Given these accomplishments, the community plan was revisited and many significant changes were made. Today Palm Coast is a thriving community, a direct result of the DRI standards and guidelines. However, these letters of determination resulted in early legal challenges testing the constitutionality of the ELWMA and the rule making authority of the DSP. The act was found defensible, but the division was found to lack specific or general rule making authority. These deficiencies were later visited and revised by the legislature.

The measure of growth at the end of the first year of the DRI program was significant. In 1973, the DRI review process yielded 73 cases, with 23 of these acted upon by local governments modifying development orders. Local governments were thus responsive to regional reviews in mitigating regional impacts of the proposed development. Documenting the volume of DRI activity certainly provided empirical evidence of the pressures of development in Florida.

Growth Policies and Comprehensive Planning

There continued to be major state planning initiatives during 1973, 1974, and 1975, by both the Askew administration and the Florida legislature. In 1973 and into 1974, there were many "growth" conferences held across the state. One observer said, "The problem today in Florida is so many growth conferences."[23] In October of 1973, Governor Askew called his own Conference on Growth and the Environment. The place designated was Orlando near Walt Disney World. In charging the conferees, Governor Askew stated, "It is my hope that out of the conference will come recommendations for action by both government and the private sector that can work for a better Florida for all."[24] It is worth noting that concurrent with other activities and DSP planning efforts, the Florida legislature, under the leadership of Speaker of the House Terrell Sessums and Representative Kenneth H. (Buddy) McKay, Jr., in 1974 adopted its own policy resolution on growth which stated, "It shall not be the State's policy to stimulate further growth generally, but to plan for and distribute such growth as it may develop."[25]

The stimulation of growth was not the policy of the state as expressed in the legislature's adopted growth policy. It was an earnest attempt to require each legislative committee to consider all legislative proposals in terms of probable impact on growth. It was intended to be passed early in the session, but Sessums and McKay could not get final action on it until the last days of the session. By then it was useless, especially since there was a change in legislative leadership the following year. We ponder what future might have evolved if the state's growth policy had been more effectively used as anticipated by its sponsors. However, the DSP made use of the legislature's growth policy and the report of the Governor's Conference on Growth and the Environment as guiding references and considered visions of Florida's future in the promulgation of the state plan authorized by the State Comprehensive Planning Act of 1972.[26]

Among the early assignments of the Bureau of Comprehensive Planning in the DSP was to develop several documents. The first document, called "*Florida 10 Million, A Scenario of Florida's Future Based on Current Trends*," contained a projection of growth in Florida.[27] The projection was unconstrained by any envisioned state policies that would affect growth. In 1973, the population was estimated at 7.8 million.[28] The DSP utilized the advice of a distinguished panel of academics from the state university system including professors Edward McClure and Kosmos Balkus of the Florida Sate University, Howard T. Odom and Madelyn Lockhart of the University of Florida, and leading experts in education, transportation, environmental protection and others from state agencies. The document included statistics and descriptive sketches all in a very graphic presentation comparing the Florida of that time (1973) to a Florida with a projected population of 10 million. The Bureau of Business and Economic Research at the University of Florida had projected that the 10 million mark would be reached by 1982.[29]

The advisory panel and DSP planners analyzed the demographics of Florida's people, its urban and infrastructure, its environment, and the projection of probable impacts upon these systems with a Florida population of 10,000,000. They also studied Florida's socio/economic systems. The structures and systems included the economy, governments, cities, transportation alternatives, water and sewer, health and health services, education, leisure, justice and safety, employment and income, agriculture, housing, transportation, communications, energy, and settlement patterns, and urbanization. Data describing these systems were projected in the scenario to view a Florida with ten million people. The DSP planners were trying to understand both quantitative and qualitative dimensions of Florida's physical and social structure, as well as the interrelationships among systems as an unfolding process of the future. The *Florida 10 Million* study was employed as an educational instrument and distributed statewide through libraries, schools and governmental offices.

The State Comprehensive Plan

The DSP continued to focus on its responsibility to prepare the first state comprehensive plan for Florida. The task included the development of a planning and plan model for the state comprehensive plan. The DSP carefully examined Florida statutes, the organization of state agencies, and the general structure and character of city and county governments. From this analyses, a state plan model emerged with elements reflecting the organization of state government, its agencies' functions and additional substantive elements, including housing, urbanization, and land use. This land use element provided an opportunity for DSP to think about the spatial implications of Florida's future land development pattern, which led to a second study.

The second study, *The Florida Green Plan,* provided a model for land use study.[30] It was compiled from a group of studies prepared by state planners and state environmental scientists who formed a project team representing several state agencies. The team worked through 1974 and 1975 to produce the document. In 1974, "the Division [DSP] expanded its work program from one concerned primarily with regulation of land and water management to a broader program of land use planning."[31] In so doing, the DSP found it necessary to assess the distribution, quality, and measure of the state's water resources, coastal resources, rare and unique natural resources, recreational resources, forest resources, agricultural resources, mineral resources, historical and archaeological resources, public investments, growth, and development. *The Green Plan* included snapshot of a central Florida region, portraying existing land uses, land covers, and natural resources in 1974 and the future. This work helped develop a working model for the future state land use plan and state comprehensive plan.

Among the other documents published by the DSP from 1973 to 1976 was the *State of Florida Land Development Guide*.[32] This document was designed to "guide development by the use of all planning, legislative and management techniques in order to help achieve the highest long term quality of life for Floridians at the lowest social and economic costs."[33] The format of this guide included policies drawn from the statutes, with an explanation of the purpose of the laws. The guide was prepared by the DSP and planners representing all of the state agencies and the ten recently organized regional planning councils. Yet another document designed to provide guidance in land use planning was *The Florida Land Use and Cover Classification System: A Technical Report*".[34] Again, planners and representatives of all state agencies formed an interagency committee. The leading soils scientist was Earl VanAtta[35] of the U.S. Soil Conservation Service, who served as a state planner in the interagency personnel transfer program. The transfer of personnel between federal and state agencies was authorized by the U.S. Interagency Personnel Act.[36] These technical reports were essential in meeting "the need for a coordinated land data classification system as a first step to the creation of an adequate information program,"[37] and became useful in assisting local governments fulfilling their responsibilities under the 1975 Local Government Comprehensive Planning Act (LGCPA).[38] A common plan language and nomenclature would be needed in land use descriptions necessitated by the soon to be required local land use plans and the intergovernmental review and comment process mandated by the ELWMA and the LGCPA.

By early 1976, the DSP had a new director, Randy G. Whittle, who had been serving as Assistant Director. He was appointed by the secretary of the Department of Administration, Kenneth Ireland. Helge Swanson was chief of the Bureau of Comprehensive Planning (BCP). The BCP moved forward with the state comprehensive plan and "a plan for planning" during 1974 and 1975. Swanson states, "The goal was actually to create a planning process from which annual plan updates could be extracted. So the idea of comprehensive coverage and integration of levels in the annualized process made sense."[39]

The approach to the plan brought together advisory groups representing the general public, state agencies (usually the agency's planning officer), representatives of each agency's constituencies, Governor Askew's office, federal agencies, water management districts, and representatives of regional planning councils and local governments. Swanson recalls, "a count of over 1,500 direct participants in plan preparation."[40] The elements of the plan included agriculture, education, growth management, health, housing and community development, land development, recreation/leisure, social services, and transportation. Each element included goals, objectives, and policies. The status of the policy was indicated as current if the statutes supported it. If the actions recommended were new, studies and responsibilities for implementation were mentioned in the plan and designated as action steps.

The plan was slow in coming as noted by the DSP: "The relative absence of a model program to base the work on initially posed a hindrance to this ambitious project."[41] In his letter of submission to the Florida Senate and House of Representatives, Governor Askew noted, "This plan is intended to be a valuable tool as we address the many complex problems and needs of the State and seek to guide its future growth and prosperity."[42] These nine elements of the plan were a real beginning to statewide planning, but the Florida legislature did not adopt the plan. In fact, the DSP and the governor's office recommended that the plan serve as an executive plan, and thus become a guide to agencies in preparing budgets and implementing policies. Even though it lacked the imprimatur of state law, the plan remained an important document. Although the DRI program, in particular, required a finding that developments were consistent with the goals, objectives, and policies of the state comprehensive plan, this requirement was more often than not obviated by more local considerations and determinations.

Environmental Land Management Study Committee

The ELWMA created the Environmental Land Management Study Committee (ELMS) for a two-year period from 1972 through 1974.[43] The charge to the committee was "to encourage environmental protection consistent with a sound and economic pattern of well-planned development."[44] Led by its chair, Alan Milledge, an attorney from Miami, along with its executive director, Daniel W. O'Connell, the committee studied matters of state planning, local land use planning and regulation, environmental protection, and other development and growth issues in Florida. The contents of its final report of December 1973 can best be described by the broad range of its recommendations to the governor and legislature. The committee recommended actions to: (1) establish regional planning agencies geopolitically as coterminous with the five new water management districts as possible, (2) encourage the study of planning manpower and the role and capacity of planning education within the state, (3) establish state new communities policies, (4) consider recommendations regarding Florida's tax system, (5) reorganize state agencies to better deal with growth and environmental protection, and (6) promulgate and enact the new local government comprehensive planning bill they had prepared. The last was perhaps the most important and long-term recommendation of the ELMS committee.

This final recommendation was not enacted in 1974, but it did become the Local Government Comprehensive Planning Act (LGCPA) of 1975. The principal research and writing of the LGCPA was accomplished by Ernest Bartley of the Department of Political Science in the University of Florida. The LGCPA was scheduled on the calendar of the legislature in 1974, and it was passed by the House of Representatives and sent to the Senate where it was placed on the "consent" calendar the morning of sine die. When the LGCPA and related planning bills came up for a vote, one objection on each bill was raised by Panhandle Senator W.D. Childers, and the bills died.[45] Revived in 1975 they were enacted. In the adopted state budget for 1974-1975, $10 million had been included to implement the proposed LGCPA of *1974*, but it could not be used. In *1975*, the act was adopted, but *with no state financial support* for local planning. This has been a ploy of the Florida legislature through the years. It has been common practice to require local governments and boards of education to implement new laws without additional funding, often called "unfunded mandates".

The Local Government Comprehensive Planning Act

Regardless of funding, the passage of the LGCPA in 1975 was a major step forward in support of *statewide* planning and offered an opportunity to overcome years of no or unenthusiastic planning among local governments. As the ELMS committee noted, "60% or more of the land area of the state does not come under a comprehensive planning program."[46] The LGCPA provided statutory guidelines and requirements setting up procedures for plan preparation and adoption by the local planning agency and the local governing body. In addition, the act established submittal deadlines and plan reviews by neighboring local governments, regional planning agencies, and the state land planning agency. Substantive requirements included plan elements, optional plan elements, and element formats. The new state initiative also required that the plan and its elements, goals, objectives, and policies representing choices made by the local planners and governing bodies must be grounded in appropriate data and analysis. Finally, the LGCPA established that the locally adopted plan and any amendments, when found in compliance with the act, had the force and effect of a local law.

The LGCPA did not originally require land use or any other kind of plan maps. We believe that was a weakness in the act, but we recognize the political difficulty associated with future land use maps. Still the legal requirements of the law meant that any development order issued by the local government must be consistent with the local adopted plan. Compliance of the local plan was a result of the review of the state land planning agency. The legal standing of the plan was a new and interesting distinction for local governments and developers to cope with in Florida. Of course, that required interpretation and enforcement by officials who were politically willing and competent to enforce provisions of the law. This was not always the situation in many local governments.

In its final report, the ELMS committee provided a significant new direction for state and local planning. Its recommendations and the lasting effects of its deliberations and accomplishments institutionalized a recurring political process of thoughtful debate and consideration of Florida's development and growth management future. The role of state planning, the roles of state agencies, water management districts, regional planning agencies, and local governments continued to be the focus of this emerging intergovernmental system of planning. The committee provided a model for future public forums for planning, land use, and development management. The ELMS model of citizen involvement was used many times following the initiatives 1974 and 1975.

Regional Planning Agencies

In 1973, Florida had only the few regional planning agencies previously mentioned in Chapter VI. The DSP, through its Bureau of Intergovernmental Relations whose chief at the time was Don Spicer, a former mayor of St. Petersburg, found it necessary in implementing a statewide planning program to organize multi-county regional planning agencies. The ELWMA required review of DRI by regional entities. The ELMS committee recommended that water management district boundaries and regional planning boundaries be made coterminous wherever possible. The stress placed here by the ELMS committee was to "...establish close working relationships to share expertise, avoid duplication, and combine resources through such mechanisms as; A, regional planning agency consultation with water management districts concerning the water related portions of the DRI review process, and B, inclusion of water management districts in the areas of critical state concern process."[47] This, however, did not work out as the ELMS envisioned.

The Florida Department of Natural Resources, Bureau of Geology, was given the responsibility of drawing boundary lines of the five water management districts. Its director, Robert Vernon, analyzed data from the U.S. Geological Survey of Florida and identified five major surface water drainage basins, or related systems of basins. The basins identified were: (1) the St. Johns River basin; (2) the Suwannee River basin; (3) the southeast Florida basin, beginning with Lake Tohopekaliga, just south of Orlando, and following the Kissimmee River and Lake Okeechobee with its canalized rivers to the Atlantic Ocean; (4) the southwest basin including the Peace River Valley and a series of river basins along the Gulf of Mexico including the Hillsborough

River and north to the Withlacoochee River; and (5) the Florida Panhandle with a series of rivers and streams beginning in the east at the St. Marks River basin and west to the Alabama-Florida state line at the Perdido River. Respectively, these are now called the St. Johns River Water Management District (WMD), the Suwannee River WMD, the South Florida WMD, the Southwest Florida WMD, and the Northwest Florida WMD (see Figure VII-1).

Only in a few instances were these basin boundaries commonly shared with county boundaries. This approach resulted in water management and supply responsibilities for a metropolitan area like Orlando, which lies at the rise of three drainage basins, being shared by separate water management districts. This placed undue burdens on urban planning for Orlando and the other communities within its metropolitan area. Hence, due to the surface hydrologically validated option chosen by the Department of Natural Resources, any attempt to make regional planning districts co-terminus with water management districts was foreclosed. The management of water and the management of land development tend to be institutionally focused on the very real differences and areal characteristics of natural and manmade urban and geopolitical boundaries.

The DSP was therefore faced with the creation of another set of boundaries and jurisdictions for regional agencies responsible for reviewing DRI proposals that would soon be coming along after July 1973. At the time, there were five multi-county agencies which had been organized primarily for regional planning purposes. There were no completed regional plans and no genuinely effective regional planning programs. At that point in time the existing regional planning councils (RPC) were merely collecting data and providing a forum for discussing regional issues, and little else; however, there was one exception, the East Central Florida Regional Planning Agency had employed renowned planner Carl Feiss

Figure VII-1

WATER MANAGEMENT DISTRICTS
1992

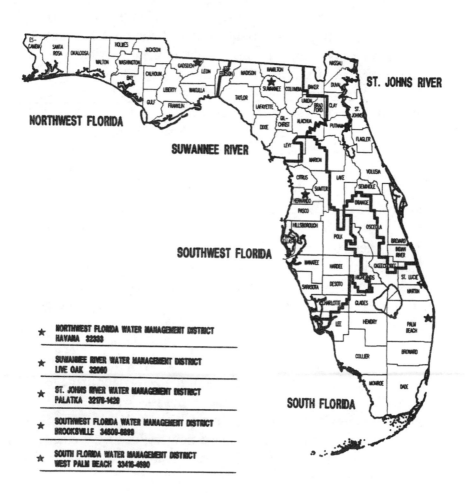

ST. JOHNS RIVER

NORTHWEST FLORIDA

SUWANNEE RIVER

SOUTHWEST FLORIDA

SOUTH FLORIDA

★ NORTHWEST FLORIDA WATER MANAGEMENT DISTRICT
HAVANA 32333

★ SUWANNEE RIVER WATER MANAGEMENT DISTRICT
LIVE OAK 32060

★ ST. JOHNS RIVER WATER MANAGEMENT DISTRICT
PALATKA 32178-1420

★ SOUTHWEST FLORIDA WATER MANAGEMENT DISTRICT
BROOKSVILLE 34609-8899

★ SOUTH FLORIDA WATER MANAGEMENT DISTRICT
WEST PALM BEACH 33416-4680

Source: Florida Chapter of the American Planning Association

to consult in preparing a regional vision. This was a unique opportunity for the Orlando, Daytona Beach, and Deland areas to discuss and thoughtfully consider their future. Unfortunately, this did not include Walt Disney's vision of central Florida and little came of the effort.

In the early 1970s, Homer Still, chief of the Bureau of Planning, the predecessor to the DSP, had completed a study of sub-state districts and regional planning in Florida. This study provided a source of data and analysis to permit the Bureau of Intergovernmental Relations (BIGR) to begin its analysis. The purpose of the analysis was to create a system of regional planning districts "wall to wall" within the state. In addition, it was necessary to understand the political history of cooperation between adjacent counties, any significant common geographical characteristics such as Tampa Bay, connectivity of transportation and road systems, cultural traditions, significant multi-county development patterns, and finally, newspaper circulation patterns. Another important characteristic was analyzing patterns of economic and business activity. The DSP was criticized for an inadequate analysis of business patterns; yet, the BIGR did interview many county officials, planners, and economists across the state in an attempt to bring adjacent counties into some thoughtful division of the state into planning districts. There were considerations of using the new and yet not organized water management districts as an interim measure, but this was not politically popular with the counties simply because local concerns would not be represented by these new water management agencies of the state. The DSP made recommendations for the boundaries.

Governor Askew issued an executive order requiring the counties to organize into ten regional planning districts. The structure of each regional planning council was organized using an inter-local agreement mechanism provided in Chapter 163, Part I, *Florida Statutes*. Existing regional planning agencies were subsumed into the new RPCs. It was a significant task and time was short. The RPCs were supported by voluntary county membership fees later authorized by state law. The DSP provided some start-up support using funds from the state's U.S. Safe Streets Act (discussed in Chapter VI), because regional criminal justice plans were a requirement of the federal law. Later, funding for the RPCs, at least for administering the DRI program, was made available from state appropriations.

In the months following the original designation of the RPCs, Sarasota County appealed and was granted a move from the Tampa Bay RPC to the Southwest Florida Regional Planning Council (later popularly called the *Promised Land*). Then an eleventh RPC (initially called the "Gold Coast") was formed by shifting Martin, Indian River, St. Lucie and Palm Beach counties from East Central Florida RPC and the South Florida RPC respectively (see Figure VII-2). This was indeed a significant step in creating regional forums for the deliberation of regional land use issues, regional transportation issues, and the many related social, urban, and environmental issues in a state under great growth stress.

The eleven regional planning councils, their constituent counties (as of November 2000), and the year the council was originally established are listed in Figure VII-2. A map of these councils is shown in Figure VII-3.

Environmentally Endangered Lands Acquisition Program

In addition to the planning laws of the 1970s, the first major state of Florida land acquisition program was initiated. Chapter 259, *Florida Statutes* provided $200 million for acquisition of environmentally endangered lands and $40 million for acquisition of recreation lands.[48] The funds came from revenue bonds funded by real estate transfer taxes (documentary stamps) approved by the state electorate in the fall of

Figure VII-2

Florida's Regional Planning Councils

Regional Planning Council	Member Counties	Year Established
Apalachee	Calhoun, Franklin, Gadsden, Gulf, Jackson, Jefferson, Leon, Liberty, Wakulla	1977
Central Florida	DeSoto, Hardee, Highlands, Okeechobee, Polk	1974
East Central Florida	Brevard, Lake, Orange, Osceola, Seminole, & Volusia	1962
North Central Florida	Alachua, Bradford, Columbia, Dixie, Gilchrist, Hamilton, Lafayette, Madison, Suwannee, Taylor, Union	1969
Northeast Florida	Baker, Clay, Jacksonville-Duval, Flagler, Nassau, Putnam, St. Johns	1977
Tampa Bay	Hillsborough, Manatee, Pasco, Pinellas	1962
Treasure Coast	Indian River, Martin, Palm Beach, St. Lucie	1976
South Florida	Broward, Monroe, Miami-Dade	1977
Southwest Florida	Charlotte, Collier, Glades, Hendry. Lee, Sarasota	1973
West Florida	Bay, Escambia, Holmes, Okaloosa, Santa Rosa, Walton, Washington	1964
Withlacoochee	Citrus, Hernando, Levy, Marion, Sumter	1973

Source: Florida Regional Councils Association, November 2, 2000.

1973. This referendum also activated the state's critical areas program.[49] Administration of the acquisition program was assigned to the Department of Natural Resources headed by former Florida Senate President Randolph Hodges, of Cedar Key. The DNR was a state agency headed by the Governor and Cabinet. An advisory panel was established to set regulations and guidelines in evaluating potential sites for acquisition.

The guidelines included acquisition of lands to conserve and protect environmentally unique lands, to protect and conserve lands within designated areas of critical state concern, to conserve and preserve native species habitat, to conserve important ecosystems, to promote water resource development, and to protect lands that may not be adequately protected by land development regulations.[50] The program was

Figure VII-3

REGIONAL PLANNING COUNCILS
1992

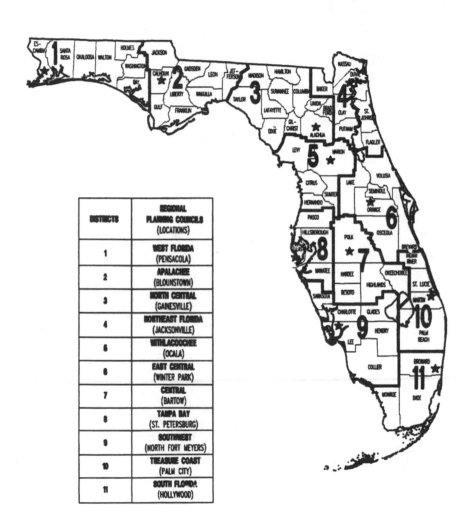

DISTRICTS	REGIONAL PLANNING COUNCILS (LOCATIONS)
1	WEST FLORIDA (PENSACOLA)
2	APALACHEE (BLOUNSTOWN)
3	NORTH CENTRAL (GAINESVILLE)
4	NORTHEAST FLORIDA (JACKSONVILLE)
5	WITHLACOOCHEE (OCALA)
6	EAST CENTRAL (WINTER PARK)
7	CENTRAL (BARTOW)
8	TAMPA BAY (ST. PETERSBURG)
9	SOUTHWEST (NORTH FORT MEYERS)
10	TREASURE COAST (PALM CITY)
11	SOUTH FLORIDA (HOLLYWOOD)

Source: Florida Chapter of the American Planning Association

Lessons Learned?

slow to mature due to the necessity of establishing an administrative system and establishing criteria for managing acquired properties. However, the first purchase was made in 1974 of what has become the Three Lakes Wildlife Management Area located in central Florida, east of the city of Lake Wales.

Summary

Relying on the fundamental assumptions of Governor Askew's Committee on Natural Resources in 1971 and 1972, Florida provided a framework in planning for land use and development management. The model recognized the existence of instrumentalities of government and the necessity of improved intergovernmental relations in the comprehensive planning and land management process. Planning in Florida progressed through the 1970s recognizing the need for state, sub-state, and local planning, and the importance of citizen participation in the process. The model recognized historically delegated authority, as well as established new administrative practices in state agencies and local governments. The new regional planning councils (RPCs) added another governmental presence in the intergovernmental planning framework. The growing presence of the RPCs provided public forums for envisioning regional transportation systems, environmental systems, regional growth patterns, and land use planning. This capacity was a much-needed view with the incumbent authority of the RPCs as they reviewed local plans, DRIs, and participated in other regional programs. In addition, the RPCs often provided valuable professional planning and technical assistance to smaller local governments. The effectiveness and credibility of this system of sub-state planning may be viewed as uneven; some RPCs have been sound and effective leaders and planning partners in the intergovernmental framework of Florida planning, whereas others have been less effective, but yet essential partners.

The 1970s Florida model was the beginning of a concept of horizontal and vertical deployment of authority integrating the three levels of governmental institutions in a planning-related decision making process. The opportunity for intergovernmental comment and assessment review of compliance among the state, regional and local planning agencies is an important product of the Florida model.

We will visit the evolution of this intergovernmental model in the chapters to follow. The model did not halt stresses and strains of population pressure on the state's natural and urban resources. However, it placed the state in a more hopeful and realistic posture to cope confidently with the planning problems of the future. One of the most valuable experiences of the 1970s, in addition to the area of critical state concern and development of regional impact programs, was the educational experience gained by hundreds of Floridians while serving on state required local and regional planning agencies and commissions. A vital and long-range program of land acquisition was a major contribution. With the election of Robert D. Graham, as governor in 1979 the planning model and systems which he, as a state senator, had so carefully shepherded through the Florida Senate were soon to be refined and changed to provide a more significant and well defined role for state, regional, and local planning.

NOTES FOR CHAPTER VII

1   Chung-shan Ch'lian-shu, 1936, Volume II in Bartlett, John, *Bartlett's Familiar Quotations*, Emily Morrison Beck ,ed., Boston, MA: Little, Brown and Company, 15th edition, 1980.

2   § 380.021, *Florida Statutes.*

3   § 23.01 *Florida Statutes*, 1972.

4   For years the U.S. Department of Housing and Urban Development strongly urged states to organize regional planning agencies and the term "wall to wall" represented its accomplishment.

5   § 380.09 *Florida Statutes.*

6   § 380.05 *Florida Statutes.*

7   § 380.06 *Florida Statutes.*

8   § 380.05 *Florida Statutes.*

9   Cesspits were and are to a great extent still existing today in the Florida Keys. A cesspit is simply an augured hole made into the sedimentary rock which form the land in the Florida Keys. The hole is approximately three feet or more in diameter and deep enough to reach tidal water. Raw sewage is simply piped into this cavity and tidal waters flush it.

10   The City of Key West was originally a part of the Florida Keys Area of Critical State Concern (ACSC), but it has since been split out as an ACSC separate from the Florida Keys ACSC.

11   For a recent analysis and status of the Florida Keys Critical Area see Department of Community Affairs, "Florida Keys Area of Critical State Concern, 2005 Annual Report to the Administration Commission." The Florida Governor and Cabinet, at that time included the Governor, Commissioner of Agriculture, the Attorney General, the State Controller, the Secretary of State , the Commissioner of Education, and the Treasurer.

12   Ch. 259, *Florida Statutes.*

13   Except for the city of Apalachicola, the remainder of the Apalachicola Bay Area of Critical State Concern was de-designated in 1993.

14   *Askew v Cross Key Waterways*, 372 So. 2nd 913; 1978 Fla Lexis 5100, 22 November 1978.

15   § 380.06 *Florida Statutes.*

16   In 1972, the Division of State Planning was the state land planning agency, however, this function was shifted to the Florida Department of Community Affairs in 1981.

17   § 380.06 *Florida Statutes.*

18 Environmental Land Management Study Committee, "Final Report of the Environmental Land Management Study Committee," February 1984, Tallahassee, FL, p. 40.

19 RuBino, Richard in A Framework for Growth Management in FL, testimony to the ELMSII committee, April 26, 1983.

20 § 380.01, *Florida Statutes*.

21 § 380,09(1), *Florida Statutes*. The Environmental Land Management Study Committee made interim reports during its two year legislative authorization.

22 May, James W., "The Florida Environmental Land and Water Management Act of 1972: Planning and the State Legislative Policy-Making Process," a research paper prepared in fulfilling requirements for the degree of Master of Science in Planning, Department of Urban and Regional Planning, Florida State University, Tallahassee, FL. March 29, 1974, p. 93.

23 Author unknown.

24 Starnes, Earl M., "An Explicit Growth Policy—Now What?" Florida Case Study, Council of State Governments, November, 1975. This unpublished document was part of a growth policy study by the Council of State Governments sponsored by the U.S. Department of Housing and Urban Development.

25 CS/HCR 2800 of the 1974 session of the Florida legislature.

26 § 23.01 *Florida Statutes*, 1972. This law was later repealed and its provisions moved in 1984 to the State and Regional Planning Act, Ch. 186, *Florida Statutes*.

27 *Florida 10 Million, A Scenario of Florida's Future Based on Current Trends*, Division of State Planning, Department of Administration, Document, DSP-BCP-S-1-8-73, Tallahassee, FL, First Printing, September 1, 1973.

28 *Florida Statistical Abstract 79*, Thompson, Ralph B., Ed., Bureau of Economic and Business Research, College of Business Administration, University of Florida, Gainesville, FL: The University Presses of Florida, 1979.

29 Ibid, p.3. The authors of this book estimated that Florida eclipsed ten million people by 1981, one year before the estimated year of 1982.

30 "The Green Plan," The Florida Department of Administration, Division of State Planning, Bureau of Comprehensive Planning, DSP-BCP-10-75, Tallahassee, FL, October 1975.

31 Ibid, p. 26.

32 State of Florida Land Development Guide, DSP-BCP-16-75, Tallahassee, 1975.

33 Ibid. p 2.

34 "The Florida Land Use and Cover Classification System: A Technical report," DSP-BCP-17-76, Tallahassee, FL.

35 VanAtta also compiled a state soils classification system showing level of development potential and constraint.

36 5 USC §§ 3371-3375.

37 Ibid, The Florida Land Use and Cover Classification System., p. 1.

38 Ch. 163, Part II, *Florida Statutes.*

39 Swanson, Helge, E-mail correspondence with Earl Starnes and Richard RuBino, November 29, 2007.

40 Ibid.

41 State Comprehensive Plan, Element Compendium, Governor Reubin O'D. Askew, May 4, 1977, Tallahassee, FL, p. ii.

42 Letter of enclosure from Reubin O'D. Askew to the Florida legislature, dated May 4, 1977.

43 § 380.09(5), *Florida Statutes.*

44 From a letter to Governor Reubin O'D. Askew, President Mallory Horne and Members of the Senate, and Speaker Terrell Sessums and Members of the House of Representatives, from ELMS Chairman, Allan Milledge, Tallahassee, FL, December 1973.

45 Earl Starnes observations from the Senate Gallery at the time. A senate vote on a bill on the consent calendar at the time could be stopped by one objecting member.

46 Florida Environmental Land Management Study Committee, "Final Report to the Governor and Legislature by the Environmental Land Management Study Committee," December 1973, p. 21.

47 Ibid.

48 Ch. 259, *Florida Statutes.*

49 § 380.05, *Florida Statutes.*

50 These criteria can be found in § 259.032(3)(a.i), *Florida Statutes.* The original criteria in the 1972 act have been subsequently amended to expand the state's program to include trails, greenways, and Florida Everglades restoration.

CHAPTER VIII

TRYING TO PUT THE
PIECES TOGETHER—AGAIN

Early 1980s to Mid 1980s

> It is the intent of this Act that adopted comprehensive plans shall have the legal status set out from this Act and that no public or private development shall be permitted except in conformity with comprehensive plans or elements, or portions thereof, prepared and adopted in conformity with the Act.[1]
> (Florida Local Government Comprehensive Planning and Land Development Regulation Act, 1985.)

John M. DeGrove, one of the principal contributors to Florida's development management system, attempted to remove a blanket of delusion when he pointed out that, "During the 1970s Florida still moved in a kind of fool's paradise in which it was believed that growth paid for itself, and that sooner or later the new growth itself would cause all the needed infrastructure to be put in place to support the impacts of that growth." This notion, he said, is "fundamentally false."[2] It took this and similar bold statements by other leaders to bring the state to comprehend the shortcomings of the 1970s development management laws and to readdress the negative aspects of still rampant growth.

In the 1970s, Florida put together a statewide intergovernmental development management system, but only some elements of the framework conceived by Governor Reubin Askew's Committee on Natural Resources were put in place. Undeniably, these were major accomplishments, but they alone were not enough to contend with the state's still under-controlled growth. Among the shortcomings were that the state plan was being ignored and no steps had been taken to improve planning at the regional level. Furthermore, the local planning law failed to provide state government with any *teeth* to enforce effective local government planning and, equally important, the mandate was not supported by state financing. As the decade closed, Florida found itself with only a partially integrated intergovernmental system for managing growth: critical elements of the intended system were illusionary or missing. Meanwhile, rapid, ill-managed growth continued to inflict environmental and economic harm, especially to the public trust.

By 1980, Florida's population had climbed to over 9.7 million people, an increase of 32.4 percent during the decade, enough to make the Sunshine State one of the nation's largest in size of population. Even greater growth was to occur in the 1980s: the state's population increased by 874 new faces a day, the highest numerical rate of growth in Florida's history. Most of the growth since World War II had been along the southeast and southwest coasts; it was to Florida's southeast coast that the Mariel boatlift brought 120,000 Cubans. However, as the decade of the 1980s dawned, central Florida also was feeling the pressure of population growth. The Orlando area, spurred by development at Disney World and other tourist attractions, was spreading out, and growth tentacles from the Tampa and St. Petersburg-Clearwater areas were beginning to move northward into Pasco county and eastward into Polk County along the Interstate 4 corridor to Orlando. Adding to the buildup in the mid-section of the state was the U.S. 27 corridor running from Ocala to Sebring. On the other hand, north Florida, the originally settled part of the state, was growing more slowly.

Development in south and central Florida sprawled across the countryside, replacing orange groves, cattle lands, forests, and swamps with urban-related residential housing.

Trip-to-work distances climbed significantly and roads clogged with traffic. Demand for water use increased exponentially, and water wars between Pinellas and Pasco counties and other local governments loomed. Local governments were not able to keep up with the demands for urban services placed upon them. A jurisdiction's increase in population size was mystically supposed to provide a similar or greater increase in property tax and other revenues to pay for the growth, but the disparity between the benefits of growth and the public costs needed to support that growth was ever-widening. The development management actions of the early 1970s had placed the first rein on the feral beast of growth, but it was far from tamed. Positive steps had been taken, but the task of managing growth in Florida had only started—much more needed to be done.

In this chapter, we will discuss changes in the intent and direction of federal policies vis-à-vis the states and local governments in the 1980s. We also will refer to growth management initiatives pursued in other places across the nation. Following the discussion of national activities during the third decade of the "Quiet Revolution,"[3] our attention will turn to problems generated by still ineffective development management in Florida. The foundation for management of growth put in place in the 1970s was found to be incomplete and uncoordinated. Further actions were needed; the *revolution* had become *evolution*.[4] State executive and legislative leaders again stepped into the breach, and by mid-decade Florida enacted one of the most far-reaching planning and growth management programs in the nation.

State of the Nation

Florida was growing more rapidly than most states, but it was not alone. To one degree or another, growth was *almost* everywhere, but it was particularly evident in certain areas. Numerically, only California and Texas added more people than Florida in the 1970s; no other state was even close to the numeric increases experienced by these three states. Given the convenience of improved transportation, many people were moving from places of high-density population to places of lesser density, often seeking a more pleasant living environment. Sometimes this meant from the city to the suburbs and other times into the rural countryside: exurbia. But each relocation added to a process that began to change the very environment it sought and place another brick in the pavement of urban sprawl.

Federal level activities

Not everyone wanted to leave the metropolis or urban area in which she or he lived, though many who might have liked to leave could not afford to do so. Central cities were still headed in a downward spiral and newly emerging cities were cultivating their own problems. However, the 1980s brought a major change in intergovernmental affairs: the federal government, in implementing President Ronald Reagan's policy of devolution, began to reduce its financial aid to states and local governments. Politics had changed in Washington, DC. The federal establishment began to move back toward its pre-New Deal position regarding intergovernmental relations. It began to cut back or eliminate aid programs to local governments under the principle that this was a state government responsibility. This devolution would have a major effect on state and especially local programs.

The federal 701 planning assistance program was one of the programs rescinded by Reagan and Congress. Actually, annual appropriations for the 701 program had been dropping since 1975.[5] It was commonly accepted that this program had out-served its usefulness, but the unanswered question was would the states step in and provide the policy direction and state aid needed to contend with growth and redevelopment? Or would the decision to continue to plan or not plan return to the discretion of local governments themselves? The answer was obvious: for most local governments, comprehensive planning dropped to a far lower rung in the ladder of local priorities. This was not true in every case, however; educational by-products of years of 701 assistance had in many places led to greater citizen awareness and acceptance of planning as a component of good civic management. Regardless, public planning needed to find new sources of support.

State and regional level activities

The Quiet Revolution in employing state government responsibilities in land use control was waning as the 1980s opened, but several states initiated programs or expanded on existing programs early in the decade. Among them was a joint program involving Maryland and Virginia, and individual programs in New Jersey and Florida.

In 1978, a Maryland-Virginia Chesapeake Bay Legislative Advisory Commission found that greater interstate coordination would be needed if the escalating rate of pollution entering the bay was to be stemmed. The result was an interstate agreement creating the Chesapeake Bay Commission, made up of representatives from the commonwealths of Maryland and Virginia; Pennsylvania became a participating member in 1985. In response to the commission's recommendation, Maryland enacted a specific law for the protection of Chesapeake Bay in 1984. The intent of this critical area law was to reverse the deterioration of the bay caused by continual population growth along its shores.[6] The act created a resource protection program for the bay and its tributaries, implemented on a cooperative basis between the state and affected local governments. Twenty years later, a study criticized the program by saying it "isn't working very well."[7] Another critic said somewhat the same thing, only more directly: the law "lacks teeth ... because local jurisdictions don't have enough resources to enforce it and [they] often side with development over environmental protection."[8] If these commentators are correct, then the cooperative approach of this program may be admirable but not practical in that it appears difficult to implement.

In the late 1970s, New Jersey, along with the federal government, took a major step in protecting an important ecological region when it created the Pinelands Commission. The National Parks and Recreation Act of 1978 established the Pinelands as a national reserve. The reserve covers an area of about 1.1 million acres, which includes parts of seven counties and all or parts of over fifty municipalities.[9] The federal act called for the adoption of a management plan to preserve, protect, and enhance the natural and cultural resources of the area. Preparation of the plan became the principal responsibility of the newly created state commission. Membership on the fifteen-member commission is allotted to seven gubernatorial appointees, one from each participating county, and one appointed by the U.S. Secretary of the Interior. A Pinelands Municipal Commission, representing the municipalities, works in concert with the Pinelands Commission. Included in the powers of the Pinelands Commission is the authority to certify municipal master plans and zoning ordinances for consistency with its management plan and to administer a transfer of development rights program.

The New Jersey legislature adopted a State Planning Act in 1985,[10] which was an outcome of the state Supreme Court's decision in *Southern Burlington County NAACP v. Township of Mount Laurel,*[11] addressing the obligations of local governments to provide affordable housing. In deference to the court's decision, the legislature further found that an adequate response regarding housing for low and moderate-income persons requires good planning to prevent sprawl and promote suitable use of land. Because New Jersey was becoming "a state of suburban sprawl,"[12] the legislature declared that sound and integrated state planning was needed to meet housing and public service needs and conserve its remaining natural resources, while also promoting economic growth and renewal. The law required that a state development and redevelopment plan be prepared and adopted, and that the plan was to include a long-term infrastructure needs assessment. The law also required a "cross-acceptance" process. This, in essence, was a collaborative, participatory process to compare planning policies of the different levels of government in an effort to attain compatibility among differing policies.

One way of achieving greater efficiency at the local level of government is through merger of local governments, a form of which is consolidation. This is not a popular option among local governments, but it is a choice and can be exercised in a variety of ways—including state legislative initiative. Apparently, the last state legislature-mandated city-county consolidation was that of Las Vegas and Clark County, Nevada, in 1975; another of relatively recent vintage was Indianapolis and Marion County, Indiana.[13] In the twenty-five years between 1960 and the mid-1980s, twenty-three mergers of one sort or another occurred, including Jacksonville-Duval County, Florida.[14] Of four mergers that took place in the early 1980s, the consolidation of Battle Creek city and township is the most telling, because initially neither the city nor the township were interested in merging. Battle Creek is home to the Kellogg Corporation, however. At the time, Kellogg wanted to construct a new headquarters building, but it was hesitant to rebuild in Battle Creek because bickering between the two local governments was crippling local economic development. Hence, the corporation threatened to move its headquarters elsewhere unless the two communities merged into one. Not surprisingly, voters in the city approved the union by a margin of 12 to 1, and support in the township was 2 to 1.[15] This illustrates the importance a nationally known business corporation placed on local government consolidation.

Florida: Fixing a House Half Built

The set of development management-oriented laws enacted in the 1970s were intended to place Florida in a position to guide its growth rather than continually respond to problems created by uncontrolled growth. The laws reflected a conviction that too many local governments were disinclined or incapable of protecting natural systems without state imposed planning requirements.[16] As it turned out, only pieces of a development management system had been put together. Furthermore, there was little or no cohesion between the parts that were created. At the state-level, a number of specialized development management programs had been set up, as was a state planning process. However, at the request of Governor Askew and the planning staff in the Division of State Planning, the state planning law was amended in 1978 to reduce the state comprehensive plan to executive advisory status only.[17] Other then for involvement in the DRI process, virtually no actions had been taken regarding regional planning, and most local planning efforts under the 1975 mandate were floundering. Thus, given these partial achievements, development remained uncontrolled—and so did the problems generated by growth.

John DeGrove, addressing "The Quiet Revolution Ten Years Later," listed three ingredients essential to successful state growth management programs: (1) no program is likely to get off the ground unless there is a reasonably widespread perception that serious problems require a new look at how state and local governments manage growth, (2) the ability to keep the land and growth management issue free of partisan politics, and (3) support from the top (e.g., the governor and the legislature).[18] To DeGrove's three essential ingredients, we add adequate funding to support the planning, implementation, and monitoring stages of a growth management program.[19] DeGrove might consider the topic of funding to be part of his third point, but we believe it is significant enough to be highlighted as a fourth essential ingredient. DeGrove has, in fact, espoused the same on numerous occasions. For example, he pointed out that "in the early 1980s *new growth paid for less than 40 percent of what it required in public services* [italics added]."[20] This means the taxpayers provided much of the other 60 percent of what was required.

DeGrove's three ingredients, plus one, should be kept in mind as we trace the evolution of Florida's intergovernmental system of managing development in the decade of the 1980s and into the following chapters. Unfortunately, financial support has continuously been the weakest link in the quartet. To use a metaphor: being without financial support is like being without the lead singer in a barbershop quartet; there is little harmony. To DeGrove, Florida's system was "reactive rather than proactive."[21] Robert M. Rhodes, a leading land use attorney who participated in growth management issues from both public and private perspectives, affirmed this view when he stated, "The goal of effective planning at each level of government had not been achieved."[22] To this declaration, Rhodes added that this failure nurtured a need for further action.[23] Further action was not long in coming.

Florida: State-level Activity in Planning

D. Robert (Bob) Graham, who as a state senator had played a key role in the planning legislation of the 1970s, became governor in 1979. During his two terms as governor, he proved himself a continuing advocate of good government and an exceptional defender of the environment. His tenure saw the enactment of outstanding environmental programs such as the Save Our Rivers, Save Our Coasts, and Save Our Everglades acts. These programs provided money to purchase endangered lands in all three areas. Graham rightfully recognized that the surest way of countering ecological destruction was through public acquisition.

One of Governor Graham's first steps in improving government was taken in 1979 when he replaced the 1972 state comprehensive planning process with, in the words of Stroud and Abrams, "a program planning and budgeting system more akin to" a management model which emphasizes "the planning process as an ongoing component of other management tools such as budgeting and program evaluation."[24] The Division of State Planning was eliminated and its functions, including state planning, were transferred to a new Office of Planning and Budgeting. "The merging of planning with the budgeting responsibilities in one office was intended," as Stroud and Abrams observed, "to ensure that planning had a greater influence on the relation to the budget process."[25] This brought Kenneth Howard's "Marriage Whose Style?" back into play (see Chapter 5), but *maybe* this time the merging of planning and budgeting would work. Would this be a lesson learned?

Many of the local governments were either unable or unwilling to manage growth effectively. DeGrove, who became secretary of the Department of Community Affairs in 1983, felt that, "Plans were changed willy-nilly virtually every time a city council or county commission met."[26] Furthermore, a comprehensive regional perspective was needed since the negative affects of much of this uncontrolled growth spilled beyond municipal boundaries into other jurisdictions and into formerly rural countryside and agricultural lands. Given this situation, there was no recourse other than for state government to elevate the role of planning at all levels of government, and enhance vertical and horizontal consistency of plan preparation and plan implementation. By necessity, this also meant added state oversight of development management programs at the local and regional levels.

The perception of a need for more effective management of growth snowballed; at least three independent special committees or task forces were created from 1979 to 1982.

The first was Governor Graham's Resource Management Task Force; a second was the House Select Committee on Growth Management, created by House Speaker H. Lee Moffitt; and a third was another Environmental Land Management Study Committee (ELMS II), this one created by Governor Graham. Once again, the executive office and the legislature were marching toward the same objective.

Governor's Resource Management Task Force

Dissatisfied with the lack of progress of the 1970s planning-related laws Governor Graham appointed a Resource Management Task Force during his first year as the state's chief executive. The task force was chaired by Tampa area homebuilder Jim Shimburg, with Nancy E. Stroud as staff coordinator.[27] Graham charged the task force with a broad mission, including reviewing the areas of critical state concern and developments of regional impact programs, assessing the lack of a comprehensive regional perspective and chronic under-funding for regional planning, and appraising the quality of local government plans.[28] The task force also deliberated over agricultural lands preservation, coastal management, water resources, and state, regional, and local planning relationships.[29] Despite the breadth of its charge, it was equal to the task and soon came forth with recommendations.

In its first year, the task force produced an interim report that resulted, in part, in a legislative amendment to the process for defining areas of critical state concern. The amended law featured the creation of advisory resource planning and management committees consisting of state, regional, and local members.[30] The committees provided a more cooperative and less controversial way to achieve the policies of the critical areas process and to avoid many of the limitations of the earlier "more top-down process"[31]. Advisory committees had no authority to enforce their recommendations; that authority remained in the hands of the Governor and Cabinet.

The recommendations of the task force also resulted in the first major rewrite of the DRI review process.[32]

The following year, the task force won legislative approval of a proposal relating to regional planning: the Regional Planning Act of 1980.[33] In reporting on the weak role of regional planning in policy-making, the task force claimed that, "Regional management continues as a fragmented and virtually invisible means of influencing resource decisions."[34] Hence, they sought to give regional planning more influence and visibility by strengthening the regional role in policy guidance. Central to the improvements in the new act was giving the governor authority to appoint one-third of the membership of regional planning councils (RPCs); in theory, this gave state government a more influential role. The new act also required RPCs to prepare comprehensive regional policy plans. However, the bane of Florida's planning-related programs struck again: the legislature enacted a mandate for regionalism but failed to fund it adequately.[35] A lesson never learned? True—but as far as regionalism is concerned, it may have been an indication of a refusal to *want* to learn!

The final report of the task force restated the need for an integrated policy framework to shape the nature of Florida's development management system.[36] This set the stage for further actions by the about-to-be-created House Select Committee on Growth Management, ELMS II, and legislative actions of the mid-1980s.

House Select Committee on Growth Management

The need for improving the state's development management system was being discussed in the legislative branch as well as in the executive branch. The first formal legislative action came in 1982 when H. Lee Moffitt, Speaker of the House of Representatives, created a House Select Committee on Growth Management.[37] This was one of the earliest direct uses of the term "growth management" in Florida. Representative Ray Liberti headed the committee, with staff assistance provided by the late George H. Meier, staff director, and the late James W. May, staff analyst.[38] This indicated a turn-around of interest in growth management by the new leadership in the chamber given that the speaker's predecessor had failed to move a proposal submitted by the Florida Department of Community Affairs during its session in 1982.

Like Governor Graham, Speaker Moffitt recognized the shortcomings in the structure and implementation of the 1972-1975 planning laws, and he made growth management one of his priorities; in fact, he rated growth management as the top issue facing the 1984 legislative session.[39] The governor, the speaker, and Senate President Curtis Peterson were of the same accord. A few months earlier, October 1983, they had joined in sponsoring a conference in Pasco County called "Change, Challenge, and Response: Facing Florida's Future". This later became known as the "Saddlebrook Conference". James May, who coordinated the conference, reported that a wide cross-section of Florida's leaders came together "to develop specific growth management recommendations for the 1984 session."[40] As recounted by one of its participants, "A question placed before the gathering at Saddlebrook was, 'How does Florida become the third most populous state in the union at the turn of the century and still remain a desirable place to work, retire, live and raise our children?'"[41] This was similar to a question put before Governor Reubin Askew's Committee on Natural Resources at the River Ranch retreat a decade earlier (see Chapter VI), a question answered but not fully implemented. Recommendations generated at both conferences in large part were forerunners of actions taken in later legislative sessions. At Saddlebrook, varied interests had been brought together, a consensus was reached, and the stage for action was set.

Environmental Land Management Study Committee II

About the same time Speaker Moffitt created the House Select Committee on Growth management, Governor Graham ratcheted the action lever up another notch by appointing his own study committee. It was given the same name as the Environmental Land Management Study Committee formed in 1972 and on which Graham served while he was a state senator. To differentiate between the two committees, the new committee became known as ELMS II. The twenty-one member committee was chaired by Robert M. (Bob) Rhodes, by then a partner in the law firm of Messer, Rhodes & Vickers; Robert C. Apgar, also an attorney, served as its executive director.[42] Daniel W. O'Connell, executive director of the first ELMS committee wrote that, "ELMS II chairman, Bob Rhodes, has succinctly stated the basic planning issue: The state of Florida is an $11 billion operation. No enterprise of this magnitude and importance can competently manage its resources and policies without an effective planning system."[43] Rhodes set the challenge, and it was up to the committee to find a way to manage competently the state's resources and policies.

Graham charged the committee to review the Environmental Land and Water Management Act of 1972 (ELWMA) and all related programs, and to prepare a blueprint to guide development for the 1980s and beyond.[44] The committee's first report, issued in April 1983, recommended improved enforcement and funding of the areas of critical state concern and developments of regional impact programs created by the ELWMA. Most of the committee's recommendations were enacted into law during the 1983 legislative session, though the final report of the committee was not submitted until February 1984. Committee member John DeGrove, who had been one of Graham's professors at the University of Florida,[45] said the final report "put into one package in clear and strong language a recommendation for an integrated policy framework to shape and guide the future of Florida into the twenty-first century."[46] This catalyzed action for Florida's second try at managing its rampant growth.

The recommendations in the final report fell into three categories: the first dealt with the existing intergovernmental planning framework, the second covered further revisions to the developments of regional impact (DRI) review process, and the third stressed a need to strengthen the coastal management program. The first category "found that local government comprehensive plans, alone, cannot adequately address Florida's needs."[47] Thus, the cornerstone recommendation of this category was a legislatively adopted state plan, which would be implemented through state agency long-range program plans, regional plans, and local comprehensive plans; in other words, the creation of a fully integrated, intergovernmental system for managing massive growth. An additional adhesive, to ensure the workability of the system, was provided by a recommendation to establish procedures for individual citizens to enforce a local government's growth management responsibilities.[48] These recommendations, for the most part, were enacted into law by the legislature, but unifying the system was to prove difficult to accomplish.

The second category of recommendations proposed ways to improve the continually contentious DRI process and integrate it into the proposed statewide planning framework.[49] The third set of recommendations addressed the need to strengthen the coastal management program by providing state funding, requiring state approval of the coastal protection elements of local comprehensive plans, and obliging state agencies to implement regulations for critical areas in the coastal zone.

The committee's final point reiterated the warning that growth problems would not be solved by *piecemeal solutions*.[50] This was a warning as appropriate to the future as it was to that time. Thus, the final report of ELMS II put into one package recommendations for an integrated policy framework to shape the future of Florida.[51] The report also put "strong and extensive emphasis on the need to fund whatever new systems and programs were called for in its recommendations, stating flatly that if the state could not or would not fund the proposed system adequately, it ought not to adopt it at all."[52] With this statement, the committee defined what was—and still is—the intergovernmental development management system's weakest link.

Coordinating closely with its executive counterpart, the House Select Committee on Growth Management prepared a bill that incorporated most of the ELMS II recommendations. With the support of both the speaker of the House of Representatives and the president of the Senate,[53] that measure (and an accompanying bill in the senate) was, over three consecutive sessions, enacted into law putting Florida in the forefront of states attempting to gain control over inadequately guided growth.

Putting the Pieces Together, Once Again

The product of the cooperative—though not easily achieved—executive and legislative initiatives of the mid-1980s is the most complex intergovernmental development management system in the nation. The system is complex because virtually every type of local, regional, and state public entity involved in any aspect of development is in some manner tied to the development management process. Adding to this complexity is that Florida's development management system does not stem from a single law: it is a combination of several associated laws and administrative rules enacted over time. These laws and rules affect private and even public development proposals.

The principal components of the development management system at that time were the:

- State Comprehensive Planning Act,[54]
- State Comprehensive Plan,[55]
- Environmental Land and Water Management Act,[56]
- State Capital Facilities Planning and Budgeting Process,[57]
- Regional Planning Council Act,[58] and
- Local Government Comprehensive Planning and Land Development Regulation Act.[59]

Other laws closely tied to the development management system through consistency requirements included:

- transportation planning,[60]
- metropolitan transportation planning organizations (MPOs),[61] and
- state water resources planning, including water management districts.[62]

It was assumed that consistency requirements referenced in these acts would tie plans and programs together somewhat like the strands of a spider's web, each theoretically communicating with and supporting the other.[63] Though the web exists, some of the interconnecting strands are still missing, weakly adhered, or somewhat battered.

A New State and Regional Planning Act

The first of the new set of development management laws was enacted in 1984. Like the 1972 law, it dealt with both state and regional planning.[64] This advance unit of the new intergovernmental system of development management called for the governor's office to prepare a state comprehensive plan, which, among other things, was intended to provide direction to the budget process and state agency long-range program plans, and act as a reference for comprehen-

sive regional policy plans. It was to be completed and submitted to the Governor and Cabinet within five months of the
enactment of the law, and to the legislature two months later.
Completing a state comprehensive plan within a relatively
short timeframe was a lesson learned from the unfortunate
fate of the drawn-out (though technically correct) process used
in preparing a state plan a decade earlier.[65] Accordingly,
Florida's fast-track deadlines were met, and the new state plan
was enacted into law in the 1985 legislative session.

This state plan was visualized as the mooring point
for the intergovernmental statewide development management
system. The law states that the plan is intended to be a direction-setting document: virtually all public planning is to be
consistent with and further the attainment of the plan. The
plan consists of twenty-five goal areas, each having one or
more objectives,[66] about three hundred policies, and a multitude of sub-policies. It is an omnipresent document, dealing
with more than just the management of growth.[67]

The 1984 State and Regional Planning Act also called
for additional actions to support the state plan: one was to
constitute the growth management portion of the state plan,
another called for state agency long-range program plans, and
a third required a separate portion related to the long-term
infrastructure and capital outlay needs of the state.[68] The
growth management portion of the state plan was to emphasize the management of land use, water resources, and transportation system development. Although a state agency plan
was prepared for each of these three topics, Richard RuBino
cautioned, "… there is little evidence that the plans are being
coordinated and that they will be used to 'drive' growth management decisions as intended."[69] The caution was justified;
the growth management portion of the state plan became lost
in the muddle of state goals and policies. Thus, the state comprehensive plan is viewed by the authors as not specifically

relevant to the day-to-day local growth management process and substantive choices in urban growth patterns or land use.

State agencies were required to adopt agency long-range program plans (sometimes referred to as functional plans), which contained policies and objectives consistent with the state comprehensive plan. The act further required the governor's office to review all state agency long-range program plans and regional policy plans for consistency. If an inconsistency existed, the matter was to be sent to the Florida Land and Water Adjudicatory Commission (the Governor and Cabinet) to be resolved.

The required long-term infrastructure and capital outlay needs portion had a somewhat better fate, however. The act required state agencies to develop long-range program plans annually;[70] these program plans were to provide a framework for state agency budget requests.[71] A related measure, the Capital Facilities Planning and Budgeting Act,[72] created as a companion to the state planning act, provided a means for "implementing a planning and budgeting process for state capital facilities.[73] According to George Meier, this was to be the major way "in which the state will manage growth since it is to contain recommendations for directing state expenditures for infrastructure investments to different regions of the state."[74] He anticipated that the state plan would provide the policy framework for decisions about state infrastructure investments.[75] This remained an elusive dream, however.

Strengthening Regional Planning

Making effective use of regionalism is one of the most perplexing aspects of Florida's development management system. Regionalism in Florida—as least as far as land use is concerned—consists of three major, yet independent regional programs, loosely tied together by consistency language. However, the consistency language is couched in a bevy of ambiguous terms, such as "to the maximum extent feasible."[76]

Theoretically, the state comprehensive plan sets the initial reference point for propagating consistency of planning between the three subsystems: regional planning councils (RPCs), water management districts, and metropolitan (transportation) planning organizations. However, the RPCs are the only areawide entities that have specific responsibility for addressing *broad, multi-jurisdictional* problems. All three of these regional entities have been discussed in preceding chapters, but our focus here will be on changes in RPC authority.

Prior to 1980, RPC responsibilities had been primarily directed at providing technical assistance to local governments, meeting the regional requirements of certain federal programs, and administering the development of the (DRI) program. In 1980, they received authority to prepare comprehensive regional policy plans.[77] Four years later, the 1984 State and Regional Planning Act changed the organizational structure of regional planning. The 1984 act provided that one-third of the membership of an RPC be appointed by the governor, subject to the approval of the senate. The remaining two-thirds of the members included at least one member from each county, plus representatives from some of the municipalities within the county.[78] Other than at least one member from each county, the precise number of municipal representatives was left for the local participants to decide. Despite the addition of gubernatorial appointees, the most significant regional planning council activity continued to be that of administering the DRI process.

Each RPC was required to prepare a comprehensive regional policy plan as a long-range guide for physical, economic, and social development of its planning area. Under the then new legislation, it was the responsibility of the Executive Office of the Governor to review the regional goals and policies for their consistency with and furtherance of the state comprehensive plan. Hypothetically, the regional goals and policies were to be used to develop a coordinated program of regional actions directed at resolving identified problems and needs. Upon adoption by an RPC, the regional policy plan serves as the primary reference for regional review of DRIs, regional review of federally assisted projects, and other regional overview and comment functions.

A general-purpose bill that would have provided for an alternative form of regionalism in Florida was introduced during the 1984 legislative session. It would have allowed counties to establish countywide planning councils involving both a county and the municipal governments within it.[79] The structure and responsibilities would have been similar to the Pinellas Planning Council, created by a special act in 1973 (see Chapter VI). Steve Seibert, then an assistant Pinellas County attorney (later a county commissioner and eventually secretary of the Florida Department of Community Affairs), said in support, "A countywide multi-jurisdictional body with 'over-sight' land-use authority makes sense ... the countywide planning entity is a most reasonable alternative to the state's growth management dilemma."[80] Though the bill was not seriously considered, the concept of permitting countywide multi-jurisdictional planning through a general enabling act might resurface again in Florida as the state and local governments seek new and better ways of managing sprawling developments. Some counties, through special acts and locally adopted charters, already practice some form of countywide planning. These include Broward, Hillsborough, Jacksonville-Duval, Leon, Miami-Dade, and Pinellas counties. Palm Beach County had been a member of this group, but only temporarily. In 1985, a coalition of Palm Beach County retirees and environmentalists succeeded in getting a countywide charter passed that made changes to the existing structure of government by creating a countywide planning council with the power to make decisions about zoning in the cities as well as in the county.[81] However, within two years, as Colburn and deHaven-Smith note, "city leaders rebelled and succeeded in getting voters to repeal the planning council's enabling authority."[82] Once established, municipalities are protective of local authority, even if it is not in the best interest of the citizens of a county as a whole. Localism is a powerful inhibitor of things smacking of regional interest.

The 1985 legislature had adopted several alternative approaches that added flexibility to the development of regional impact (DRI) review process; these were Florida Quality Developments (FQD), the Downtown DRI Program, the Local Government Certification Program, and the Areawide DRI Program.[83] The FQD program was intended to encourage developers to create projects that were compatible with the environment and surpassed some of the criteria for DRI approval.[84] The first four projects to be eligible were in Broward, Clay, Hillsborough, and Lee counties; the Pace Island development, located on 977 acres in northern Clay County, became the first approved FQD; others (e.g., in Tampa and Fort Myers) soon followed.[85] Under the Downtown DRI program, large-scale developments located within the boundaries of a downtown development authority or community redevelopment agency were facilitated in an effort to encourage in-fill development. The first six projects approved were in Altamonte Springs, Boca Raton, Jacksonville, Lakeland, Miami, and Tampa. If local governments meet the eligibility requirements of the Local Government Certification Program and receive approval of the Florida Administration Commission (the Governor and Cabinet), they can assume the responsibility for reviewing DRIs. Like the Downtown DRI program, the Areawide DRI program would allow approval of development over a larger area than a single project DRI. It also would offer a shortened review time and greater flexibility to accommodate changes to an already approved plan. The first two applications for this program came from Santa Rosa County for its Navarre Beach area and the City of St. Petersburg for an in-town area. Over time, the DRI review program probably has generated the most controversy and thus experienced the greatest number of adjustments.

Local Level Mandates

Proposals to improve the 1975 local planning act, many of which were initiated by the Florida Department of Veteran and Community Affairs (DVCA)[86] under Secretary Joan Heggen, were submitted to the legislature in 1981. The department's proposed amendments were primarily intended to clarify procedural and legal questions; few substantial amendments were proposed.[87] Perhaps the most substantial amendment, according to John Corbett, former attorney with the DVCA, would have provided "standing to citizens or local governments to seek injunctive or other relief against a local government for taking action on a development order or land development regulation which is not consistent with its adopted plan."[88] The bill, though approved by the Senate after removal of an enforcement section, never made it through the House. However, as we will see, the desire for a more efficacious local government planning law would not go away.

Consequently, some of the amendments proposed by the department reappeared in the 1984 legislative session. However, as James May, at that time staff analyst of the House Select Committee on Growth Management, observed, "When the smoke cleared, there were no local planning revisions enacted into law."[89] In reference to the package of growth management bills, he went on to say, "1984 was a mixed year for legislative initiatives in growth management. … [b]ut if past is prologue to the future, the education, discussion, debate, and adoption process will continue during the 1985 legislative session on the unfinished growth management agenda."[90] This was an unerring prediction, because revision of local government planning and development regulation took center stage during the 1985 legislative session.

What materialized during the session was an omnibus new local planning law: the Local Government Comprehensive Planning and Land Development Regulation Act.[91] This is an accurate title for what is embodied in the law, but too wordy for common reference, thus this act became popularly known as the "Growth Management Act." The title is a misnomer, however, because it leaves the impression that it is the only act that attempts to manage growth in Florida, when, in fact, the state has an intergovernmental system consisting of numerous integrated acts directed at managing growth.

Though the new local planning law built upon the base laid by the 1975 local planning act, it went beyond it in placing the Florida Department of Community Affairs in a relatively strong oversight role to insure proper implementation of the act. This was a lesson learned: the legislature had refused to give the department such powers in the 1975 act. We use the term "relatively strong" because the real strength in state oversight is during plan preparation and plan amendments; state oversight is weaker concerning plan implementation, which is primarily dependent on local citizen initiative. This omnibus act required all local governments to prepare comprehensive plans under rules and schedules set by the DCA. The plans had to meet the requirements of the act, be consistent with and further the state comprehensive plan, and be adopted as *law* by the local jurisdictions. In addition, all actions taken in regard to local development orders are required to be consistent with the adopted plan.

Plans had to meet the requirements of the Department of Community Affairs' Rule 9J-5, *Florida Administrative Code* (F.A.C.), "Minimum Criteria for Review of Local Government Comprehensive Plans and Determination of Compliance," that was mandated by the 1985 legislation. Earl Starnes emphasized the importance of Rule 9J-5 when he identified it as being as vital as the State Comprehensive Plan and the local planning act itself because, "it has the function of making these new standards stick."[92] Rule 9J-5 became the measuring stick for determining whether local comprehensive plans met the requirements of the new mandatory local planning act. One of the other administrative rules that came into prominent play at the time was Rule 9J-11, F.A.C., "Procedure for Review of Local Government Comprehensive Plans and Amendments." Rule 9J-5 set the technical guidelines for preparing a local plan and Rule 9J-11 laid out the review process.

Aside from planning, a concept of increasing interest to local governments was the application of impact fees. This would provide them a point-source opportunity to help pay for the costs of infrastructure generated by new developments. A few local governments proactively adopted impact fee ordinances, but most were reluctant to do so because the state legislature had shied away from enacting general legislation. Things became more flexible in 1983, however, when court decisions in *Hollywood Inc. v. Broward County* and *Homebuilders and Contractors Association v. Palm Beach County* supported the application of impact fees to help pay for the costs of growth.[93] Yet, general application of impact fees was slow to grow until the state legislature enacted a law authorizing the practice.

The Glitch Bill

When the Local Government Comprehensive Planning and Land Development Regulation Act was passed in 1985, executive and legislative leadership knew it needed readjusting and polishing. Therefore, it had been agreed that a bill addressing the act would be brought back in 1986 to work out oversights or glitches. When a "glitch bill" was introduced in 1986, it primarily contained corrections to technical flaws.[94] However, by the time the bill passed through committee hearings in both houses, several substantive changes had been made. Despite the substantive changes, the basic thrust of the 1985 local planning law was unchanged. The most significant additions fell into four broad categories: local government comprehensive planning, agreements between developers and local governments, coastal management, and the development of regional impact program.

Not surprisingly, municipal and county officials exerted considerable pressure for major revisions to the 1985 act. Westi Jo deHaven-Smith and Robert Paterson reported that, "Both the State Association of County Commissioners and the Florida League of Cities have expressed concern about the State usurping local governments' authority in land use planning/regulation."[95] Given the history of localism, this reaction of the municipal and county associations was predictable. This concern and others were addressed by the legislature, resulting in what was called a more balanced policy framework where, according to deHaven-Smith and Paterson, "Local governments have greater discretion, allowing policy to flow 'up' as well as 'down,' while a clear and meaningful state and regional framework is maintained."[96] Other studies classified Florida's intergovernmental development management system as being in the process of shifting from a relatively centralized, top-down approach to a more cooperative, state-local partnership approach by 1992.[97] These findings were true to one degree or another, but centralizing state policies on compact development, concurrency, consistency, and minimum criteria remained in effect.

The legislature took the opportunity to clarify the meaning of some of the terms and requirements (e.g., compliance, consistency) in the 1986 act often to the point of striving for a "balance" between competing interests. For example, one change provided local governments with the opportunity to challenge regional policy plans under Chapter 120 procedural due process guarantees.[98] Another change was in the schedule for submitting local plans to the DCA. Priority was placed on the coastal areas—where most Floridians live. Completed plans for coastal counties and municipalities were to be submitted between July 1, 1988 and July 1, 1990, whereas submissions by non-coastal counties and municipalities would be delayed until between July 1, 1989 and July 1, 1990.[99] The Glitch Bill also created the Florida Local Government Development Agreement Act, which allowed local governments to create, by ordinance, procedures and requirements for entering into agreements with developers.[100]

The Local Government Comprehensive Planning and Land Development Regulation Act required every county and municipality to prepare a comprehensive plan and update it at least once every five years. Local comprehensive plans must be consistent with the state comprehensive plan and the appropriate regional policy plan. After the local plan has been adopted and found in compliance by DCA, all local land development regulations and orders must be consistent with it. Though the local planning agency (popularly called the local planning commission) is responsible for the conduct of the comprehensive planning program, final responsibility for the plan, including its adoption, rests with the local governing body (the city or county commission or council).

Comprehensive plans must include the following elements: a future land use plan; a traffic circulation element; a general sanitary sewer, solid waste, drainage, potable water, and natural aquifer recharge element; a conservation element; a recreation and open space element; a housing element; a capital improvements element; and an intergovernmental coordination element. Local governments in the coastal zone must prepare a coastal management element. In addition, local governments having populations greater than 50,000 must prepare, as part of their circulation element or as a separate element, a mass-transit element; plans for port, aviation, and related facilities; a plan for circulation of recreational traffic (e.g., bicycle facilities); and an element for the development of off-street parking facilities. These larger local governments also must prepare elements for public buildings and related facilities, community design, general area redevelopment, safety (e.g., regarding hurricane protection), historic and scenic preservation, and economic considerations. All of the elements are required to include data and analysis, goals, objectives and policies, and some of them must include a map or a map series (e.g., a future land use map, topographic maps), something not required by the earlier local planning law.

An important lesson learned from a major inadequacy of the 1975 local planning law was that mandates are usually not taken seriously unless backed by sanctions or at least incentives. Whether using a stick or a carrot is better depends on the scope and criticalness of what is being mandated. If the mandate deals with an "absolute need," then sanctions are required; if it supports a "desire," then incentives may be sufficient to accomplish the purpose. It is the difference between "we must have" as opposed to "we would like to have". In Florida's case, rampant growth was so out of control that the situation demanded "an absolute need" response. If a local government failed to prepare and adopt all the elements required by the act, the regional planning agency having responsibility for the area was to complete the task(s) and be compensated by the local government for the cost(s) involved.[101] Should the local government fail to compensate the regional planning agency, the chief financial officer of the state is authorized to make payment from unencumbered revenue or other tax sharing funds due that local government from the state.[102] The threat of this sanction has been sufficient to assure compliance except in a handful of cases.

To make certain that local planning programs are an ongoing process, the law requires that local comprehensive plans be updated through an evaluation and appraisal report (EAR). At least once every five years (now extended to seven years) following the adoption of a plan, a local government must submit to the DCA a report that evaluates and appraises the success or failure of its comprehensive plan. The EAR is subject to the same review requirements that apply to the plan adoption process. Any amendments to the comprehensive plan recommended in the report must be adopted within one year of when the report is adopted by the local governing body.

Local comprehensive plans are implemented primarily by means of the administration of a capital improvements program and land development regulations (LDRs).[103] At a minimum, LDRs must provide regulations for the subdivision of land, development standards and boundaries of land and water use (zoning) and open space, protection of potable water well fields, regulation of areas subject to flooding, ensuring proper drainage and storm water management, protection of environmentally sensitive lands, regulation of signage, ensuring that public facilities and services meet standards set in the capital improvements element (as part of the concurrency requirement), and the provision of safe and convenient onsite traffic flow and required parking. Local governments must also adopt historic preservation and design standards if such elements are included in the comprehensive plan. Although a zoning ordinance is not included in the requirements, it remains embodied within the LDRs of most local governments.

Local governments were required to adopt LDRs within a year after submitting a draft of the comprehensive plan to the DCA for determination of compliance. However, the DCA does not oversee the LDR process once it has been duly established, unless it requires a change in the future land use element. The DCA may require a local government to submit its LDRs for review only if it has reasonable grounds for believing that the local government did not adopt the required regulations. A review can be instituted only to determine whether there has been a failure to adopt the required regulations; this does not involve determining if LDR actions are consistent with the local comprehensive plan. However, no action is taken by the DCA until it receives a letter alleging non-adoption. Thereafter, the DCA must determine whether it has reasonable grounds to believe the local government has failed to adopt one or more of the required LDRs.

Only a substantially affected person can challenge the lack of consistency of an LDR with a local comprehensive plan. A challenge goes first to the DCA. If the DCA finds that the LDR is consistent, the petitioner can continue the challenge by requesting a hearing from the Florida Division of Administrative Hearings (DOAH). On the other hand, if the DCA finds the LDR inconsistent, it may request a hearing with the DOAH. If the hearing officer finds the LDR inconsistent, his or her determination is forwarded to the Administration Commission (the Governor and Cabinet) to take final action, which can include the imposition of a sanction.

Another aspect in implementing a local government comprehensive plan is that of concurrency management, one of the most controversial aspects of the law. This provision, called the "concurrency requirement", states that public facilities and services meet or exceed levels of service established in the capital improvement element of a local plan and that adequate infrastructure is *concurrent* with development.[104] The facilities and services covered by this requirement are sanitary sewer, solid waste, drainage, potable water, parks and recreation, schools, and transportation facilities, including mass transit, where applicable.[105] John DeGrove helped convince the legislature to add this requirement to the Glitch Bill.[106] Years later, DeGrove was to say that the statement should have read "*development* concurrent with infrastructure, not *infrastructure* [concurrent] with development."[107] This was a play on words meaning that development should be predicated on the availability of infrastructure.

Concurrency turned out to be a concept before its time. It is theoretically sound, but extremely complex—and it never went through the rigors of a pilot study before being made operational. As Robert Rhodes said in an interview with Cynthia Barnett, "It was not tested on a smaller scale to make sure it would work statewide."[108] Furthermore, the law imposed its standards "on an already overburdened and deficit-ridden service system without a strategy to cure past neglect and accommodate new needs."[109] Such a strategy should have included state financial assistance to local governments to help them mitigate their infrastructure needs—a double failure caused by local government neglect of the deficit side of growth and state government paranoia about tax increases to support the provision of local services. The concurrency requirement also has been accused of slowing growth in urban areas and contributing to sprawl, especially regarding its transportation system standards. In part, it may have contributed to urban sprawl in Florida, but it has not been a principal cause of sprawl. To argue otherwise is to ignore the fact that sprawl has occurred in every state (with the possible exception of Hawaii), absent the help of a concurrency requirement.

The principles of consistency and concurrency, along with the policy fostering compact development, are considered the major policies "driving" the requirements of local planning. To one degree or another, these principles are assumed to be ingrained in all local government plans, although how well ingrained is possibly more veneer than in depth. For example, local governments sometimes manipulate concurrency requirements to mitigate their impact on politically popular development.

Summary

As the 1980s opened, state leaders recognized that the planning initiatives of the 1970s were successful in some ways, but, for the most part, were woefully inadequate in contending with Florida's continuing escalation of growth. Florida continued to move in "a kind of fool's paradise".[110] The whole issue needed to be revisited. Therefore it was.

Given a continuing environment of executive and legislative cooperation, state leaders set out to address how to improve Florida's approach to managing growth. The end product was an intergovernmental development management system involving all three levels of Florida governance. An ambitious expansion of planning at the state level began, with a new comprehensive state plan as a mooring point. Planning at the regional level was improved, though not to the extent some decision makers would have liked. Planning at the local level, however, was vastly changed by a new, higher-demand, sanction-backed, and partially state-supported local planning program. Some—but not all—of the lessons learned from the missteps of the 1970s were applied, but given the complexity of the new system and its components, more lessons needed to be learned.

NOTES FOR CHAPTER VIII

1   § 163.3161(5), *Florida Statutes*, Florida Local Government and Development Regulation Act of 1985.

2   DeGrove, John M., ed., "Florida: A Second Try at Managing Massive Growth Pressures," *Planning and Growth Management in the States*, Cambridge, MA: Lincoln Institute of Land Policy, 1992, p. 9.

3   The Quiet Revolution began with Hawaii in 1961; hence, the 1960s constitute the first decade.

4   Powell, David L., "Growth Management: Florida's Past as Prologue for the Future," *Florida State Law Review* 28, Spring, 2001, p. 520.

5   Feiss, Carl, "The Foundations of Federal Planning Assistance: A Personal Account of the 701 Program," *Journal of the American Institute of Planners* 51: 2, p. 183.

6   *Maryland Laws*, Ch. 794, 1984. The program is currently called the Chesapeake and Atlantic Bays Critical Area Protection Program; *Maryland Code*, s. 8-1801-1817.

7   Lutz, Lara, "Critical Areas Act not working well, report concludes," *Bay Journal*, Alliance for the Chesapeake Bay, June 2006, reporting on a study by the University of Maryland Environmental Law Clinic, obtained from www.bayjournal.com/article.cfm?article=2830 on January 22, 2007.

8   Furgurson, E.B., III, "Enforcement of Critical Area law lacking, report says," South River Federation, obtained from www.southriverfederation.net/CriticalAreaLawStudy5-3-06.php on January 22, 2007.

9   Obtained from The Pinelands National Reserve, www. state.mj.us/pinelands/reserve/ on July 15, 2007.

10   *New Jersey Statutes Annotated* 52:18A-196 *et seq.*

11   92 N.J. 158 (1983) is known as *Mount Laurel II*; it created a fair share formula to measure a municipality's obligation to provide affordable housing.

12   Obtained from www.njlegallib.rutgers.edu/mtlaurel/aboutmtlaurel.php on April 29, 2007.

13   Glendening, Parris N. and Patricia S. Atkins, "City-County Consolidations: New Views for the Eighties," *Municipal Yearbook 1980*, Washington, DC: International City Management Association, 1980, p. 70.

14   RuBino, Richard G., "Comparison and Comments on Service and Taxing Districts in Consolidated Governments," submitted to the Tallahassee-Leon County [Florida] Consolidation Charter Commission, May 1991.

15 Breckenfeld, Gurney, "Kellogg's Battle of Battle Creek," *Fortune*, November 29, 1982, p. 122.

16 DeGrove, John M. and Nancy E. Stroud, "New Developments and Future Trends in Local Government Comprehensive Planning," *Stetson Law Review* XVII: 3, 1988, p. 604; see also Turner, Robyne S., "Intergovernmental Growth Management: A Partnership Framework for State-Local Relations," *Publius: The Journal of Federalism* 20, Summer 1990, p. 82.

17 Ch. 78-287, *Florida Laws* 814, 1978.

18 DeGrove, John M., "The Quiet Revolution 10 Years Later," *Journal of the American Planning Association*, November 1983, p. 25.

19 See, for example, DeGrove, John M., "Florida's Growth Management Legislation: 1969 to 2000," paper prepared for the Richard E. Nelson Symposium on Florida's Growth Management Legislation, October 13, 2000, p. 8; obtained from http://lic.law.ufl.edu/~nicholas/GMsem/DeGrove.htm on July 27, 2005.

20 DeGrove, John M., as quoted in Al Burt, *The Tropic of Cracker*, Gainesville, FL: University Press of Florida, 1999, p. 221.

21 DeGrove, John M., "The Proposed Florida State Plan: Issues, Options and Process," *Florida Environmental and Urban Issues* XII: 3, 1985, p. 4.

22 Rhodes, Robert M., "Growth Management in Florida 1985 and Beyond," *Florida Environmental and Urban Issues* XIII, 2, 1986, p. 1. Among his past associations with growth management are as staff representative of House Speaker Richard Pettigrew to Governor Askew's Committee on Natural Resources, chief of the Bureau of Land and Water Management at the Florida DCA, chair of Governor Graham's ELMS II Committee, and executive vice president and general counsel of the St. Joe Company.

23 Ibid.

24 Stroud, Nancy E. and Kathleen Shea Abrams, "A Report on a Proposed State Integrated Policy Framework," prepared for the Office of Planning and Budgeting, Executive Office of the Governor, by the Joint Center for Environmental and Urban Problems, Florida Atlantic Univeristy/Florida International University, Boca Raton, FL, 1981, p.15.

25 Stroud and Abrams, ibid, pp. 15-16.

26 DeGrove, John M., ed., "Florida: A Second Try at Managing Massive Growth Pressures," *The New Frontier for Land Policy: Planning & Growth Management in the States*, Cambridge, MA: Lincoln Institute of Land Policy, 1992, p. 10.

27 The task force members, in addition to Shimberg, were Kathleen Shea
Abrams, Jack P. Brandon, John R. Buckley, Robert K. Butler, Charles
E. Cobb Jr., James B. Duncan, R. Ray Goode, Art Harper, Helen Hood,
Dennis P. Koehler, Mary Kumpe, Bobbie Lisle, John R. Middlemas, R.
L. Price, Jr., Phillip E. Searcy, John O. Simonds, Shirley Taylor, and
Louis E. Larson, Sr. In addition to Stroud, the staff, which represented
a variety of agencies, included Tasha Buford, James W. May, Daniel W.
O'Connell, Sam Shannon, and George Willson.

28 "Final Report to Governor Bob Graham of the Resource Management Task Force," January 1980.

29 Stroud, Nancy E., "Regional Planning Council Reform in Florida,"
chapter 12 in Gill C. Lim, ed., *Regional Planning: Evolution, Crises, and Prospects*, Totowa, NJ: Allensheld, Omman Publishers, 1983,
p. 142.

30 Ch. 380.045, *Florida Statutes*.

31 Marlow, Kimberly A., "The Expanded Role of Resource Planning
and Management Committees," *Florida Environmental and Urban
Issues* XII: 1, October 1984, p. 12.

32 Stroud, Nancy E., "The Second Generation Legislation for Developments of Regional Impact," *Florida Environmental and Urban Issues* VIII, October 1980, p. 3. For a review of Florida's DRI process,
as of 1985, see Alfred Lloyd Firth, "Florida's Development of Regional Impact Process, Practice, and Procedure," *Journal of Land
Use and Environmental Law* 1: 2, 1985, pp. 72-104.

33 Ch. 180, *Florida Statutes*.

34 "Final Report to Governor Bob Graham of the Resource Management Task Force, ibid.

35 Rhodes, Robert M., ibid, p. 2.

36 DeGrove, "Florida: A Second Try at Managing Massive Growth Pressures," ibid, p. 10.

37 The members of the committee were Ray Liberti as chair, Patricia L.
Bailey, Samuel P. Bell III, Beverly B. Burnsed, Carl Carpenter, Jr.,
Peter M. Dunbar, Elaine Gordon, Tom Gustafson, Mary Ellen
Hawkins, Gene Hodges, Robert M. Johnson, Ronald Clyde Johnson,
C. Fred Jones, Dexter W. Lehtinen, Sidney Martin, Jon L. Mills,
Herbert F. Morgan, Steve Pajcic (speaker pro tempore), R. Dale
Patchett (minority leader pro tempore), Charles R. Smith, James
Harold Thompson, and Eleanor Weinstock.

38 Richard RuBino served as staff consultant to the committee.

39 RuBino, Richard G., "Growth Management Initiatives in Florida: From
River Ranch to Saddlebrook," *Florida Environmental and Urban
Issues* XI: 2, January 1984, p. 4.

40 May, James W., "Growth Management: A 1984 Update," *Florida Environmental and Urban Issues* XII: 2, 1985, p.1.

41 RuBino, Richard G., "Growth Management Initiatives in Florida: From River Ranch to Saddlebrook," ibid, p. 3.

42 The members of the committee were Robert M. Rhodes, Jean Beem, Jack Chambers, John M. DeGrove, Edgar M. Dunn, Jr., Alan S. Gold, Porter J. Goss, Bill Gunter, Joan M. Heggen , John H. Hankinson, Jr., Stanley W. Hole, Wade L. Hopping, Ray Liberti, Lenore N. McCullagh, Bobby F. McKown, Jon Mills, Pat Neal, Robert L. Parks, Nathaniel P. Reed, Sam Shannon, and Gerald F. Thompson.

43 O'Connell, Daniel W., "Growth Management in Florida: Will State and Local Governments Get Their Acts Together?" *Florida Environmental and Urban Issues* XI: 3, 1984, pp. 1-5, p. 2.

44 Environmental Land Management Study Committee, *Final Report of the Environmental Land Management Study Committee*, Tallahassee, Florida, February 1984, p. 1.

45 Interview with John DeGrove by Cynthia Barnett, Samuel Proctor Oral History Project, University of Florida, December 1, 2001.

46 DeGrove, "Florida: A Second Try at Managing Massive Growth Pressures," ibid, p. 10.

47 Environmental Land Management Study Committee, ibid, p. 2.

48 Ibid, p. 3.

49 See endnote 19 above.

50 Environmental Land Management Study Committee, ibid, p. 4.

51 DeGrove, John M., "Florida's Growth Management Legislation: 1969 to 2000," paper prepared for the Richard E. Nelson Symposium on Florida's Growth Management Legislation, October 13, 2000, p. 5; obtained from http://lic.law.ufl.edu/~nicholas/GMsem/DeGrove.htm on July 27, 2005.

52 DeGrove, "Florida's Growth Management Legislation: 1969 to 2000," ibid, pp. 5-6.

53 DeGrove, "Florida: A Second Try at Managing Massive Growth Pressures," ibid, p. 11.

54 §§ 186.001-186.031, 186.801-186.911, *Florida Statutes*.

55 Ch. 187, *Florida Statutes*.

56 §§ 380.012-380.12, *Florida Statutes*.

57 §§ 216.015-216.0162, *Florida Statutes*.

58 §§ 186.501-186.515, *Florida Statutes*.

59 §§ 163-316-163.3215, *Florida Statutes*.

60 §§ 338.223(1)(a), 339.135, and 339.155, *Florida Statutes*.

61 § 339.175, *Florida Statutes*.

62 Ch. 373, Part I, *Florida Statutes*.

63 Planning for location of local educational facilities, though loosely mentioned in both the 1975 and 1985 local planning laws, did not become a significant factor until the 1990s.

64 Ch. 186, *Florida Statutes*.

65 As Jack Campbell, former governor of New Mexico, had warned (in regard to another situation), "In far too many cases state planning just plain takes too long!" He went on to point out that, "State planning is not an aid for the paleontologist ... any process that takes too long to produce a useful product cannot really be regarded as being very helpful." From Jack Campbell, "Planning is on Trial," *Planning 1968: Selected Papers from the ASPO [American Society of Planning Officials] National Planning Conference*, Chicago: American Society of Planning Officials, p. 258.

66 The original goal areas (in mostly alphabetical order) were agriculture, air quality, children, coastal and marine resources, cultural and historical resources, education, the economy, the elderly, employment, energy, families, governmental efficiency, hazardous and non-hazardous materials and waste, health, housing, land use, mining, natural systems and recreational lands, property rights, public facilities, public safety, tourism, transportation, water resources, and plan implementation.

67 RuBino, Richard G., "Can the Legacy of a Lack of Follow-Through in Florida State Planning be Changed?" *Journal of Land Use & Environmental Law* 2: 1, 1986, p. 38.

68 Respectively, s. 186.007(4) and s. 186.007(5), *Florida Statutes*.

69 RuBino, "Can the Legacy of a Lack of Follow-Through in Florida State Planning be Changed?" ibid, p. 39, footnote 74.

70 § 186.021, *Florida Statutes*.

71 § 216.013, *Florida Statutes*.

72 §§ 216.015-216.031, *Florida Statutes*.

73 May, James W., ibid, p. 2.

74 Meier, George H., "Capital Facilities Planning and Budgeting: Is a State CIP Possible?" *Florida Environmental & Urban Issues* XII: 3, 1985, p. 19.

75 Ibid, p. 20.

76 For a discussion of this term, see letters from Representative C. Fred Jones to Governor Bob Martinez (January 25, 1989) and from General Counsel Peter M. Dunbar, acting in response for the governor (February 7, 1989).

77 Chapter 160, *Florida Statutes*, the Regional Planning Council Act.

78 Authority for two or more local governments to create councils of local officials also exists under s. 163.02, F.S.

79 The bill was introduced by State Senator Mary Grizzle.
80 Seibert, Steven M., "The Countywide Planning Council: A Growth Management Alternative?" *Florida Environmental & Urban Issues* XII: 2, 1985, p. 15.
81 Colburn, David R. and Lance deHaven-Smith, *Government in the Sunshine State*, Gainesville: University Press of Florida, 1999, pp. 106-107.
82 Ibid.
83 Florida Department of Community Affairs, *Technical* Memo 3: 2, Summer 1988, p. 13.
84 Ibid, *Technical Memo* 1: 2, July 1986, pp. 2-6.
85 Ibid, *Planning Notes* 1: 4, November 1988, p. 4.
86 The title Florida Department of Veteran and Community Affairs was the official name of the agency from 1980 to 1982 only; before and after these years it has been called the Department of Community Affairs (DCA). Veterans' Affairs was a division within DCA prior to 1980, but the function became a department under the Governor and Cabinet in 1982.
87 Corbett, John, "Proposed Revisions To Florida's Local Government Comprehensive Planning Act," *Florida Environmental and Urban Issues* IX: 2, 1982, p. 17.
88 Ibid, p. 20.
89 May, James W., ibid, p. 2.
90 Ibid, p. 4.
91 §§. 163.3161-163.3215, *Florida Statutes*.
92 Starnes, Earl M., "Florida's Minimum Criteria Rule," in John M. DeGrove and Julian Conrad Juergensmeyer, eds., *Perspectives on Florida's Growth Management Act of 1985*, Monograph 86-5,Cambridge, MA: Lincoln Institute of Land Policy, 1986, p. 73.
93 Juergensmeyer, Julian Conrad, "Impact Fees after Florida's Growth Management Act," in DeGrove and Juergensmeyer eds, ibid, pp.183-189.
94 Florida Department of Community Affairs, *Technical Memo* 1: 2, July 1986, p. 2.
95 deHaven-Smith, Westi Jo and Robert Paterson, ibid, p. 4. See this article for a review of actions taken relative to the "Glitch Bill".
96 Ibid.
97 Bollens, Scott A., "State Growth Management: Intergovernmental Frameworks and Policy Objectives," *Journal of the American Planning Association* 58: 4, 1992, pp. 454-466. For other interpretations of Florida's conjoint approach, see Richard G. RuBino and Frank LaRosa, "Alternative Approaches to Intergovernmental Planning and

Growth Management Systems," pp. 103-118, in Lance deHaven-Smith and Dena Hurst eds., *Charting Florida's Future*, Tallahassee: Florida Institute of Government, 1999; and Turner, ibid, who uses the term "state-local partnership" rather than "conjoint".

98 deHaven Smith and Paterson, ibid, p. 6.
99 Florida Department of Community Affairs, *Technical Memo* 1: 2, ibid, pp. 2-3.
100 Ibid, p. 5.
101 § 163.3167(3), *Florida Statutes*.
102 § 163.3167(6), *Florida Statutes*.
103 §§ 163.3201-163.3243, *Florida Statutes*, and Rule 9J-24, *Florida Administrative Code.*.
104 § 163.3202(2)(g), *Florida Statutes*.
105 § 163.3180(1)(a), *Florida Statutes*.
106 Barnett, Cynthia, "Saving Florida: A History of Growth Management in the Sunshine State," a thesis for the Master of Arts Degree at the University of Florida, December 2003, p. 38.
107 DeGrove, John M., during the "Twenty-Year Retrospective of Growth Management in Florida," sponsored by the Florida Department of Community Affairs and held at the University of Florida, Gainesville, on February 10, 2005.
108 From interviews with Robert Rhodes by Cynthia Barnett on August 22 and September 12, 2003; as shown in footnote number 3, p. 38, in "Saving Florida: A History of Growth Management in the Sunshine State," master's thesis, University of Florida, Gainesville, December 2003.
109 Rhodes, Robert M. "Concurrency: Problems, Practicalities and Prospects," *FSU Journal of Land Use and Environmental Law* 6, 2, 1991, p. 244.
110 DeGrove, "Florida: A Second Try at Managing Massive Growth Pressures," ibid, p. 9.

CHAPTER IX

IMPLEMENTING THE NEW INTERGOVERNMENTAL DEVELOPMENT MANAGEMENT SYSTEM

Late 1980s to Early 1990s

> Through effective growth management, we must build a competitive Florida. We must not just regulate. Our reluctance to pay for growth, our reluctance to provide the resources that both state and local governments need to meet the demands of growth, only increases the need to regulate—and keeps us from competing successfully with other states and other nations.[1] (Zwick Committee, 1987)

Florida had just put together an integrated, intergovernmental development management system in the mid 1980s, and it was the time to put words into action. The system was on a fast track of change, but a lot still needed to be accomplished, and accomplished with competent people at all three levels of government: state, regional, and local. However, many of these people had little experience in dealing with such a complex and broadly based system. Planners and people in planning related fields were experienced in their particular specialty or level of practice, but little working knowledge of the innovative and varied aspects of the new system. A lot of rapid learning was in order.

An underpinning of planners had gained experience with the planning programs of the 1970s, but their number was insufficient to meet the demands of the new development management system. The state had three universities (Florida State University, University of Florida, and University of Miami) turning out master's level planners, but their combined number of graduates fell far below the need.

Robert M. Rhodes pointed at this issue when he wrote, "There is a continuing challenge to find and train competent and dedicated administrative personnel to administer the new and expanded programs."[2] The challenge was met as professional planners from across the nation and graduates from other planning schools found jobs in Florida. Nonetheless, despite ratcheting up the number of planners, the task of implementing Florida's complex new intergovernmental development management system was going to be daunting.

Meanwhile, the eruption of problems due to uncontrolled growth continued to spread. Florida needed to confront the costs of growth through fundamental changes in the way infrastructure is financed, and thereby lessen the dependence of local governments on regulation as a means of attempting to manage growth and development.[3] Population growth during the 1980s increased from 810 to 874 persons per day. By end of the decade, Florida's population had climbed to 12.9 million people, and even long-bypassed north Florida was beginning to experience growth. Jacksonville had always been a large population center, but places like Tallahassee and Panhandle cities such as Pensacola, Fort Walton Beach, and Panama City were beginning to face rates of growth that had assaulted south and central Florida cities and counties in the preceding decades. The neck of the bottle was beginning to fill up and overflow into Georgia, Alabama, and beyond.

Significant Development Management Initiatives in Other States

Unlike the governors (and legislators) of the 1960s, so many of whom were focused on improving the role of state governments in the federal system, the states' chief executives in later years were more concerned with specific issues than they were about a need for reorganization. In that the federal system issue had apparently been solved, the "golden era of state reorganization" had ended.[4] More compressed issues took top priority. "Today's issue-oriented, planning and policy development model is a strategic planning model," Harold F. Wise and Bertram Wakeley pointed out in 1984.[5] The strategic planning model was becoming the new *modus operandi* at both state and regional levels of planning. "With this shift of emphasis from management improvement to substantive issues," Wise and Wakeley added, "has come a series of changes in the practice, organization and methods of state planning and policy development offices."[6] This even resulted in changing the name of the national organization of state planning officials from Council of State Planning Agencies to Council of Governors' Policy Advisors. In sum, this reflected a shorter-range orientation to state planning and policy-making than the more long-range, all-encompassing model that came to the fore in the 1960s (see Chapter V).

Despite the changes in orientation going on in governors' offices, the late 1980s saw a resurgence of interest in development management not only in Florida but also in states across the nation. However, none of these, except Hawaii and Oregon, was as far-reaching as the Florida system. Most were more narrowly focused, and suffered from being severely under-funded and underpowered. As with the Florida local government planning programs of the 1970s, the enacted laws were "feel good mandates" without adequate financial support and based solely on weak incentives and without the backing of sanctions.

State Initiatives

Some earlier state development management initiatives were ineffective because they had been thoroughly compromised in getting through the legislative process—so compromised that they had to be strengthened a decade later. Some states stepped lightly into the arena with courageous dialogue but with less than substantive structure; these programs were due to underachieve from the beginning. Nonetheless, at least nine states took some form of action toward initiating or improving development management programs in the late 1980s and early 1990s. Four of the nine were New England states (Maine, Massachusetts, Rhode Island, and Vermont), two were Mid-Atlantic states (Maryland and New Jersey), Florida and Georgia represented the South, and Washington the Northwest.

Maine, under assault from the outflow of suburban growth from the Boston area, passed a Comprehensive Planning and Land Use Regulation Act, in 1988.[7] Municipalities were to complete their plans by specified target dates, depending on their rates of population growth. The Boston metropolitan area was also sprawling southward and melding with the Providence area. Rhode Island, which had long-standing involvement in statewide planning, passed a new Comprehensive Planning and Land Use Act in 1988.[8] The new planning law strengthened planning by providing for state overview of sixteen plan elements and updating local planning, zoning, and subdivision laws. Vermont, an early entry into managing development, added to its Act 250 (passed in 1970) when it enacted a Growth Management Act in 1988 (Act 200).[9] The earlier act authorized issuance of state land use permits for development projects over certain specified sizes or above 2500 feet elevation if the projects conformed to specified statewide criteria. The intent of Act 200 was to correct deficiencies in Act 250, especially by encouraging statewide regional growth management plans—even though it provided no mechanism to require local government plans to be consistent with the regional plans.[10]

In the Mid-Atlantic region, Maryland, always innovative, passed a set of Economic Growth, Resource Protection, and Planning Act amendments in 1992.[11] Among other things, the amendments required local plans to be guided by seven visions listed in the act, streamline local development regulations in areas designated for growth, and prepare a local planning element to protect sensitive areas from undesirable development. The Maryland approach relied primarily on incentives to attain local plan consistency with non-local goals.

New Jersey actions in the mid-1980s included passing a Fair Housing Act in 1985 and a State Planning Act in 1986. The first action was a direct result of the *Mount Laurel* decision promoting regional fair share affordable housing[13] and the second was supportive, though institutionally broader in scope. The 1986 act created a State Planning Commission and an Office of State Planning within the Department of Treasury. The principal responsibility of the commission and staff was to prepare a state development and redevelopment plan; however, the act did not require local plans to be consistent with the state plan. A preliminary plan, called "Communities of Place," set forth, among other things, a tier system (identifying levels of urbanization as well as agricultural and environmentally sensitive lands), a voluntary intergovernmental process known as "cross-acceptance," and a monitoring and evaluation system.

Georgia, along with Florida, represented the only significant development management action in the South. In 1987, Governor Joe Frank Harris appointed a Growth Strategies Commission to study and recommend growth management and economic development policies. The proposal failed to be enacted in 1988, but, as Earl Starnes observed, "The commission continued its efforts ... stressing the need for growth management in coastal and mountain regions, and Atlanta."[14] The Georgia planning program was designed to be plan making built from the local level, with general guidelines prepared by the Georgia Department of Community Affairs. Regional and state level plans were expected to evolve from a synthesis of local plans.[15]

In the far Northwest, Washington state passed a Growth Management Act in 1990,[16] then amended it in 1991 to create three growth management hearings boards. The intent of the 1991 act was to designate urban growth areas and protect critical areas and natural resource lands. Fourteen state goals served as guidelines for planning in fast-growing cities and counties. Twenty-nine counties are participating in the full extent of the program, whereas the remaining ten counties must at least plan for critical areas and natural resource lands.[17] A unique feature of the program was that state agencies were required to comply with the plans and development regulations of the jurisdictions operating under the act.

Elsewhere, states showed either no interest in joining the second wave of the Quiet Revolution or proponents in those states could not muster enough support to enact legislation. Local government interests continued to resist state government intrusion into what they considered their prerogative. On the other hand, the Quiet Revolution-joining states were reassuming state constitutional responsibilities they had long ignored. In the face of sprawling development, local governments acting alone can no longer effectively control growth.

Regional Initiatives

Noteworthy regional initiatives were passed in Connecticut, Massachusetts, and New York. Connecticut, a state with no county governments, enacted an ambitious law requiring fair share affordable housing agreements between Hartford and the twenty-five surrounding municipalities in the Capitol Region Council of Governments.[18] Though it was a commendable action, in the end, little progress was made in achieving its goals. The same could be said for a growth management initiative started in San Diego, California, in the late 1970s. San Diego adopted an infill strategy in 1979, but according to development policy researcher Douglas R. Porter, it might receive an "A" for effort, but deserved only a "C" for accomplishment.[19]

The Bay State assembly passed a Cape Cod Commission Act in 1989.[20] The Cape Cod Commission, an organization covering all of Barnstable County, is both a planning and a regulatory agency. As a regulatory agency, it administers minimum performance standards for developments of regional impact.[21] In a weak-county state like Massachusetts, providing a county commission with coordinative powers is a progressive but chancy experiment in addressing localism.

Another regional effort was at play in the lower Hudson River area. In the early 1990s, the New York Regional Plan Association was involved in a collaborative program of negotiating interlocal watershed management agreements between New York City (NYC) and the counties and municipalities in the Catskill, Delaware, and Groton watersheds. The negotiated agreements were a consequence of resistance by outlying counties and municipalities to the application of a state health law enacted in 1953 whereby NYC is authorized to employ extraterritorial regulations to protect its watersheds. Forced by the U.S. Environmental Protection Agency to either improve watershed management or filter its water supply, NYC produced a set of development requirements and announced that the communities in the watersheds must abide by them. This brought the Regional Plan Association (see Chapter III) into the mix as a negotiating agent, and a settlement was eventually reached.[22]

The second surge of the Quiet Revolution may not have been as pervasive as the first, but it does reflect the continuing recognition of some states that management of growth is better accomplished via a coordinated whole. Each of the regional initiatives during the late 1980s to early 1990s also attempted to achieve this, sometimes successfully, sometimes not. Nevertheless, each success was a measured step toward better governance.

Meanwhile In Florida

The late 1980s to the early 1990s saw two different governors overseeing the implementation of Florida's inter-governmental development management system as amended in 1985. The first, Governor D. Robert (Bob) Graham (1979-1987), a Democrat, had a great stake in the system since he was a leader in "shepherding" it into existence.[23] The next governor, Robert (Bob) Martinez (1987-1991), had no prior stake in the system, but he continued to support it. Given that such a system had never been put in place anywhere, support from the chief executive was essential. Nonetheless, additional research and allowance for citizen input was needed. Foremost among the blue-ribbon citizen groups charged with doing so were the Growth Management Advisory Committee, the State Comprehensive Plan Committee, the Affordable Housing Study Commission, and the Task Force on Urban Growth Patterns. Each played a role in shaping Florida's new intergovernmental development management system, though some more than others.

Growth Management Advisory Committee

In August 1985, Governor Graham announced the creation of a twenty-three member Governor's Growth Management Advisory Committee to oversee the implementation of the new laws.[24] In the announcement, Graham said, "Florida has neither the ability nor the desire to halt its growth; instead, our goal is to manage that growth in a manner that enhances our economy and our quality of life."[25] Thus, the tone was set: Florida welcomed continued growth, but it needed to be managed effectively.

Tampa developer Jack Wilson headed the committee and Daniel W. O'Connell, director of the first Environmental Land Management Study Commission, was its executive director. The task of the committee was to (1) review programs of the state to ensure citizen and private organization involvement in development management matters; (2) work to integrate state, regional, and local concerns in carrying out the development management legislation; and (3) recommend incentives to promote quality development that protects the state's environment. The final report of the committee was issued the following year, the last year of the Graham administration. They recognized that Florida's complex system would generate conflicts between varying interests, so among the committee's recommendations was the need to create a consortium of conflict resolution experts to help resolve the conflicts.

The legislature responded to this need in 1987, by establishing the Florida Growth Management Conflict Resolution Consortium. Edward A. Fernald, Director of the Institute of Science and Public Affairs at Florida State University (FSU) organized the consortium. It opened an office at FSU, with Robert Jones as the consortium's director and Tom Taylor as assistant director. Field offices were opened first at the University of Central Florida and later at Florida Atlantic University. The consortium provides assistance by facilitating mediation of growth-related disputes for public agencies. It also provides information on dispute resolution and training in mediation.

State Comprehensive Plan Committee

The legislature also sought advice regarding the new planning system when, in 1985, they appointed a twenty-one member State Comprehensive Plan Committee—or what came to be better known as the Zwick Committee. It was named after its chairman, Charles J. Zwick, who was chairperson of the Southeast Banking Corporation in Miami and earlier had been budget director in President Lyndon B. Johnson's administration. The committee's charge was to calculate the costs of implementing goals and objectives in the State Comprehensive Plan and recommend specific ways of paying for those costs.[26] In the course of its work, it noted that growth brought many positive things to Florida, including an increase in employment of about 58 percent between 1975 and 1985; but they also found that:

> ... as our economy grows, and as our population grows, so too grow the stresses and the strains on our public facilities, our governmental services, and our fragile environment. And so too grow the constant pressures on our leaders to produce new and imaginative ways to help each of us secure our fair share of Florida's dream.[27]

Not surprisingly, the Zwick Committee reported that transportation was creating the most stress in Florida:

> Almost 6,000 lane miles of highways—nearly 18 percent of all our highways—are in need of resurfacing or repair. More than 1,300 bridges—about 24 percent of all the bridges on state highways— are deficient. More than 9,000 lane miles of state highways—about 27 percent of all state highways—are congested. About 60 percent of the highways in Florida's urban areas are extremely congested. And traffic jams are getting longer every day.[28]

Transportation was not the only contributor to stress, however. The committee also called attention to other demands that rapid growth was placing on the state and its citizens. As a measure of growth, the committee observed that *each day* the state needs two more miles of roads, two new classrooms, two new police officers, one more jail cell, 111,108 gallons of additional potable water, management of 94,560 more gallons of waste water, management of 3,546 more pounds of solid waste, and other public services to support these growing daily needs.[29] Multiply these figures by the number of days in a year and the totals become overwhelming; for example, over a year, this would mean 730 more miles of roads, over 40 million gallons of potable water, and 645 tons of solid waste. This clearly illustrates that growth has costs as well as benefits—and if growth is managed poorly, the former can easily outweigh the latter. Moreover, recognize that the figures in the quotation were based on 1985 data; the figures would be even greater today.

The Zwick Committee pointed out that, *Florida's greatest failure in effectively managing its high rate of growth was the failure to pay for growth*; this, they said, "leads to needless regulation that hinders private enterprise, stifles initiative and incentive, and diminishes our quality of life."[30] Over-dependence on regulation (i.e., use of the police power) is a weak, erodible, and ineffective means of implementing a plan, any plan—state, regional, or local.

Neither the state nor its local governments absorbed the costs of growth *as it occurred*. They were content with facilitating growth and "hoping" it would eventually pay for itself. They thereby have been digging themselves into financial deficits regarding public infrastructure and service costs. The Zwick Committee pointed its finger at how "our low tax rates and our undue reliance on a narrow-based sales tax keep us from having the stable and reliable flow of governmental revenues that is needed to attract and accommodate quality growth."[31] It noted that Florida ranked last—50th among the 50 states—in per capita spending on human services, it ranked 47th in state and local taxes as a percentage of state personal income, and that Florida was [and still is] engaging in the functional equivalent of deficit financing.[32] The committee believed that Florida could *afford* to improve its standings and become more economically competitive with other states. But they asked the question: "Are we willing to pay the price for our state?"[33] The response to this question can be assumed to be, "Maybe sometime, but not on my watch." Politically, it always seems easier to leave "tough love" decisions to someone else to wrestle with later.

A New Face in the Governor's Office

"Keys to Florida's Future: Winning in a Competitive World," the final report of the Zwick committee, was submitted to the legislature in February 1987, a few weeks after Republican Bob Martinez became governor.[34] Not a promising scenario. Especially poignant in the report were the committee's recommendations about how to finance the development management system. It concluded that fundamental changes, particularly to the way government is financed, were needed to achieve the goals of the State Comprehensive Plan; the committee found that a fundamental change in the way government in Florida—both state and local—is financed is the more direct path to effectively manage growth.[35] It is also the most neglected path. In partial response to this and in a move that delighted some state leaders and greatly disturbed others, Governor Martinez proposed a sales tax on services to generate the revenues for a trust fund to support the infrastructure needs of local governments. The governor's proposal was endorsed by the legislature.

This appeared to be a direct path to effectively managing growth, but opposition to the tax grew. The state collected the tax for six months, but under pressure from the legal establishment and the media, Martinez, said Colburn and deHaven-Smith, "suddenly retreated and urged the legislature to repeal the tax."[36] It was repealed. Years later, John DeGrove called the repeal, "A tragedy for growth management."[37] Indeed it was.

People who had worked hard in putting together Florida's improved system for managing development feared that Governor Martinez would attempt to neutralize the fledgling system. Other than for reversing himself on the sales tax, this was not the case. Whether his experience as mayor of Tampa gave him the experience essential to backing the new system or the fact that the legislature was still in the hands of Democrats who had helped put the system together is unknown. We speculate that it was a bit of both, with hopefully greater weight attributed to the former.

Governor's Task Force on Urban Growth Patterns

Allen and Joan Perry Morris, in their 2005-2006 compilation of *The Florida Handbook* said, "To the credit of Republican Martinez was his carrying forward environmental programs of his Democratic predecessor, Governor Bob Graham."[38] He also tended to growth management matters. In 1988, Governor Martinez appointed a Task Force on Urban Growth Patterns, whose duty was to identify the public service costs of land development patterns. The task force, consisting of twenty members, was headed by Ron Rotella, a Tampa businessman.[39] In its final report to Governor Martinez in June 1989, it warned that,

> ... most of Florida's future growth will be accommodated through sprawling, low density development on raw land ... unless decisive action is taken at *every* [emphasis added] level of government and by the private sector to reverse this trend.[40]

This was a warning ignored—and a lesson still not learned. Among the task force's recommendations was a call for the designation of local government urban service areas and urban expansion areas.[41] The task force also recommended attacking urban sprawl through better intergovernmental coordination, and it suggested that local planning should be conducted from a *countywide* perspective. The concept of urban service areas was accepted by the governor and the legislature, as was improved intergovernmental coordination. However, both ignored the more adventurous notion that a county plan should gain ascendancy over a municipal plan. They left that matter to the initiative of counties aggressive enough to propose such action on their own.

State Planning, the State Comprehensive Plan, and Related Functions

At the pinnacle of the planning-related activities in the mid to late 1980s was the preparation of a state comprehensive plan, and its integrated and supportive pillars of state translational plans, state agency long-range program plans, and other significant endeavors related to development management. Below these functions—but not any less important— were implementation of regional level planning activities and the multitude of tasks related to local government planning and land development regulation.

The State Comprehensive Plan

The centerpiece of the Florida's intergovernmental development management system is the State Comprehensive Plan.[42] All local comprehensive plans are required to be consistent with and further the goals of the state plan. However, it does not require the same consistency of the activities and permitting decisions of state and regional regulatory agencies.[43]

The *Constitution of the State of Florida* includes a section that refers to *the state planning document*, which can be interpreted as a somewhat ambiguous reference to the State Comprehensive Plan. The relevant section of the Constitution reads:

> The Governor shall recommend to the legislature biennially any revisions to the state planning document, as defined by law. General law shall require a biennial review and revision of the state planning document, shall require the governor to report to the legislature on the progress in achieving

the state planning document's goals, and shall require all departments and agencies of state government to develop planning documents consistent with the state planning document.[44]

Getting both halves of the legislature and the governor to adopt a state comprehensive plan was an astounding feat, but getting similar language into the state constitution in 1992 was just as notable.[45] However, retaining the political will to sustain use of the plan is another matter. Like the legislature's short-lived Growth Management Resolution of 1974 (see Chapter 6), the new state plan faced the challenge of being relevant to the bureaucratic and political arenas. As history reveals, just because something is in the constitution does not automatically mean that it is followed to the letter—or even in part. Denying funding is always a naysayer's alternative.

 The architects of the State Comprehensive Plan intended it to be the pinnacle under which the remainder of the development management system rests. Theoretically, all state, regional, and even local actions were to conform to it through consistency requirements. It was to be the document against which the consistency of the governor's capital outlay recommendations, state agency long-range program plans, regional policy plans, and local government comprehensive plans could be measured. John DeGrove went so far as to call the consistency concept the backbone of all state planning and growth management systems.[46] However, consistency may be the Achilles' heel of the state plan.[47] A critical look at the state plan reveals that it may be impossible to determine whether any proposed action is inconsistent with the plan. The difficulty rests on a sentence the legislature added to the initial proposal:

> The plan shall be construed and applied as a whole,
> and no specific goal or policy shall be construed
> or applied in isolation from the other goals and
> policies in the plan.[48]

The plan, therefore, regards all goals and policies as equal, with no single goal or policy holding greater priority than another does.[49] The major culprit in neutralizing the state plan was the Florida House. Unlike the Senate, which created a special committee to review the plan, the House divided it amongst standing committees for review.[50] The result is that almost anything can be found to be consistent with some aspect of the plan. That single sentence in the state plan and the legislative committee changes that accompanied it crippled the potential of using the plan as a guide for effective policy-making. Colburn and deHaven-Smith see the plan as being "too long, too general, and too inclusive to provide meaningful direction."[51]

Adding to the fuzziness of the state plan is that it is formless: it is without a map of preferable futures for urban development, lands to be set aside for environmental protection, and lands suitable for agricultural use. We suggest that a set of state goals requires a complementary future land use map. However, such a map should be generalized, with the details left to lower levels of planning: state agency plans, regional plans, and local government plans.

Translational plans

The State and Regional Planning Act of 1984 required each state agency to prepare a long-range program plan, but the departments of transportation, community affairs, and environmental regulation were also required to prepare translational plans.[52] The translational plans were intended to offer a sense of priority to the three functions deemed to have the greatest influence on development: transportation facilities, water use, and land use. Thus, the idea was that if coordinated special plans (translational plans) were prepared for each of these functions then Florida would have a more definitive guide for managing development than the all-encompassing State Comprehensive Plan, which has been called "too comprehensive."[53] Combined, the set of three translational plans could have become the State's "growth management plan." However, despite good intentions, experience has shown that few policy decisions have been based on the translational plans.

The concept was commendable, but its execution flawed. There were at least three problems in attempting to arrive at combining translational plans prepared by three independent agencies. The foremost problem was that developing a *single* translational plan was not considered or at least not enacted. David L. Powell astutely pointed out that the state plan "did not segregate those topics into a specific part identified as the 'growth management portion' of the plan."[54] This contributed to a second problem: no single agency was responsible for overseeing the *coordination and consistency* of the translational plans. It was to be a cooperative effort. Developing them separately, despite some attempts at coordination, resulted in three less than effectively integrated translational plans, at least concerning managing statewide growth and development. For the most part, the agencies' program plans did double-duty, serving as both their required agency functional plan and their translational plan. Thus, the translational plans remained an underused part of Florida's state-level development management system.

State agency long-range program plans

Long-range program plans are department and agency planning documents. The 1984 State and Regional Planning Act[55] required each state agency to prepare a state agency long-range program plan. The program plans, along with a state capital improvements program created under a separate act,[56] were to be consistent with the State Comprehensive Plan. The agencies duly prepared their program plans, but because of a variety of circumstances, the plans were mostly under-utilized; the same fate befell the state capital improvements program.

As John M. DeGrove has noted, "Two fast track plans, the State Land Development Plan and the State Water Use Plan, had to be ready by January 1, 1986."[57] The first of these fast-track program plans was the responsibility of the Department of Community Affairs (DCA);[58] the second was prepared by the Department of Environmental Regulation. They were to be used as guides for the plans of other agencies.[59]

As of 1985, the DCA had a new head: Tom E. Lewis, Jr., former assistant secretary of the Department of Transportation, replaced John DeGrove as secretary. He had the immediate responsibility of implementing his agency's role in all three levels of Florida's new intergovernmental development system. The program plan provided a framework to guide departmental policy decisions, and included sections covering coordination with other state agency program plans and for regional planning councils in updating their regional plans. As for local governments, they were merely encouraged to consider the guidelines in DCA's program plan.[60]

The state agencies were to prepare their program plans by July 1, 1986. However, some state agencies were slow to warm to the idea of these plans. As James (Jim) F. Murley, later an agency head himself, noted, "The agencies duly prepared their functional plans, but because of a variety of circumstances the plans were mostly ignored."[61] In part, this may have been because of a lack of executive interest or ever-present bureaucratic inertia that so often tends to resist innovative change.[62]

Other Significant State Activities Related
To Development Management

Other significant state level development management-related initiatives that were enacted in the late 1980s include the Surface Water Improvement and Management Act (in 1987), Preservation 2000 (in 1990), and the Florida Communities Trust (1989). The Surface Water Improvement and Management Act (SWIM)[63] is a statewide program for restoring and protecting priority surface waters of state or regional significance. It requires the state's water management districts to develop plans to preserve water bodies in good condition and to restore some of the more significant rivers, lakes, estuaries, and bays within their geographic areas. The legislation specifically named the Everglades, Lake Apopka, Lake Okeechobee, Tampa Bay, and the Indian River Lagoon. Among other water bodies that have received assistance from the SWIM program are Lake Jackson in Leon County, the Winter Haven Chain of Lakes in Polk County, Alligator Lake in Columbia County, the St. Johns River, and the Kissimmee River.[64]

Preservation 2000[65] (P2000) was the 1990s offspring of the Environmentally Endangered Lands state land acquisition program of the 1970s and the Save Our Rivers and Save Our Beaches programs of the early 1980s. Its purpose was to protect the integrity of ecosystems, as well as acquire fish and wildlife habitat, recreation areas, and aquifer recharge areas. The program, administered by the Division of State Lands in the Department of Environmental Protection, was authorized to spend three million dollars a year over ten years to carry out its purpose. With funding from real estate documentary stamps, P2000 incorporated the earlier CARL and Save Our Coasts/Rivers/Everglades programs.[66]

The Florida Communities Trust was created to provide financial assistance to local governments for the preservation of parks, beaches, natural areas, and other green space.

According to the DCA, it was intended to "implement the conservation, recreation and open space, and coastal elements of comprehensive plans through land acquisition and preservation activities."[67] The DCA administers the program with funds from Preservation 2000 (which later became the Florida Forever program). The Trust and its local government partners from 1993 to spring of 2006 have purchased more than sixty-nine thousand acres of land.[68]

Regional Level Planning Activities

When regional level planning is mentioned in Florida, the first entities that come to mind are regional planning councils (RPCs), water management districts (WMDs), and metropolitan planning organizations (MPOs). Among other regional planning or development management efforts in the late 1980s, were the Wekiva River Protection program and the designation of the Myakka River as a Florida Wild and Scenic River. At the county level, Pinellas County initiated an intra-county consistency program. Each of these is briefly discussed below.

Comprehensive regional planning remained an area of mostly subsurface controversy. Proponents argued for a stronger role for regional planning councils (RPCs) vis-à-vis local governments. Opponents, principally local officials and district legislators, resisted attempts to give regions a stronger role in development management. There is an endemic political tendency—that we call localism—to resist the creation or expansion of any organization that appears to weaken or require locals to share perceived power. Unwarranted localism continues to contribute to problems of managing growth.

The late 1980s were busy years for the eleven RPCs. In addition to assisting local governments in addressing the new local planning mandates, administering the developments of regional impact requirements, and undertaking a variety of federally supported functional planning programs, they were required to complete comprehensive regional policy plans. The latter had to be submitted to the Office of Planning and Budgeting (OPB), in Governor's Office, by the end of November 1986.[69] The OPB had the responsibility for ensuring that the regional policy plans met the requirements of the State and Regional Planning Act of 1984. However, after the first round, the RPCs were no longer required to amend their plans according to recommended revisions from the OPB. This was an early step in weakening the consistency requirement between state and regional plans,[70] and it was a harbinger of things to come.

The five water management districts (WMDs) in Florida are agencies of state government responsible for designated major water drainage basins (see Chapter VI). They work with local governments and agricultural users in the course of regulating water consumption, but because they are responsible to state interests, they are not as subject to the confines of localism as are RPCs. They also issue wetland, dock, seawall, storm water, and other permits.[71] Thus, the WMDs with their permitting and taxing authority have greater power to influence development decisions than do RPCs.

Another regional organization with greater influence over development management decisions than an RPC is a metropolitan planning organization (MPO). A more descriptive name would be metropolitan "transportation" planning organization, because transportation is its area of responsibility. An MPO is an urban area organization required by the Intermodal Surface Transportation Efficiency Act of 1991 (ISTEA).[72] The act necessitates the existence of an MPO in every urbanized area with a population of over 50,000 people before the Federal Highway Administration can disperse federal funds for transportation projects to that area; other than for this requirement, the jurisdictions are designated by the governor. Twenty-five MPOs existed in Florida in 1992. However, an MPO is responsible for transportation system planning, not specific transportation projects.

In one sense, the MPO concept fosters a limited form of bottom-up planning because it puts additional decision-making weight for transportation planning in the hands of local elected officials. In addition, state law requires state transportation facilities to be consistent with local comprehensive plans to the greatest extent feasible.[73] The looseness of the term "greatest extent feasible" sometimes makes things a bit baffling, but the MPO process at least has the major actors communicating with each other. On the other hand, the process definitely has a top-down bias in that the program *mandates* transportation regionalism.[74] This is a lesson in why the federal government, in critical matters like transportation, must continue to intercede over parochial localism if federal expenditures are to be managed efficiently.

Among the more specialized regional actions taken in Florida during the late 1980s were the Wekiva River Protection program and the Pinellas Planning Council Countywide Consistency program. Both were initiated by local initiatives, and both required enactment of special state laws. The Wekiva River Protection Act of 1988[75] exemplifies an approach to managing an area of critical *regional* concern. The act was passed to protect the water quality and rural character of this scenic river system from the sprawling urban growth of the Orlando area. Within its designated protection zone, it required local governments to amend their comprehensive plans and development regulations to discourage intense residential development, and maintain wetlands and protect wildlife. The law did not attempt to stop development adjacent to the river, but to keep development rural in character.[76]

Four years earlier, the legislature had designated a 34-mile portion of the Myakka River as a Florida Wild and Scenic River. The provision called for the preservation and management of the river within Sarasota County; however, the law was not as specific as the later action for the Wekiva River. For the sponsors of the Wekiva River Protection program, this apparently was a lesson learned.

Further north along Tampa Bay, Pinellas County was also concerned about future urban development, particularly concerning the lack of horizontal consistency between local government comprehensive plans. Each of the twenty-four municipalities in Pinellas County had its own plan, but a lack of coordination between municipalities left the county to contend with inconsistencies not of its own making. When the Pinellas Planning Council found a startling number of inconsistencies in the 1989 Pinellas Countywide Plan, the county had nowhere to turn. In essence, the county plan was rendered ineffective due to a lack of coordination between governmental entities within it. Thus, it was time to make changes in countywide intergovernmental relations.

Pinellas County had tried to coordinate municipal plans as early as the early 1970s, but this effort ended when a court found that the appointed Pinellas Planning Council (PPC) was not authorized to make decisions independent of the county commission. This fault was rectified in 1989 when the PPC was reconstituted as a body acting in an advisory capacity to the county commission. Thereafter, the county commission, acting as the Countywide Planning Authority, was responsible for ensuring consistency between all local government plans (including the plan of the countywide school board) and development regulations in the county. Special state legislation provided for this, but it went into effect only after voters approved the action through a countywide referendum.

On the east coast, Palm Beach County also moved toward coordinating countywide planning when it created a Palm Beach County Planning Council in 1986. One of the chief tasks of the seventeen-member council was "to coordinate the land use planning process of all governments within the county."[77] Six members were appointed by the county commission, nine by the Palm Beach County Municipal League, and one each from the county school board and the South Florida Water Management District.

Planning Activities Related To Local Governments

The late 1980s to early 1990s were busy times for planners at the state and regional levels. The State Comprehensive Plan was completed by 1986, though the tough task of implementing it lay ahead. The regional policy plans were adopted by 1988, but they remained merely *advisory* documents. However, the period was even more chaotic for planners and other officials at the local level of government. Everything seemed new and untested—and it was. Additional staff had to be added to meet the demands of the new Local Government Comprehensive Planning and Land Development Regulation Act and the new administrative rules that flowed from it. It was an exciting time, a time of challenge—and a time of confusion. The unique and complex act had no predecessors. There was no history, there were no models, and there was too little experience upon which to develop the program and commence with planning. But despite these pitfalls, the act was implemented.

DCA responsibilities

Four different secretaries led the Florida Department of Community Affairs (DCA) in the formative years of the Local Government Comprehensive Planning and Land Development Regulation Act. John DeGrove, sometimes called the "father of growth management in Florida," was the first during this period. After helping to put the development management system together, he returned to his academic position at the Joint Center for Environmental and Urban Problems, at Florida Atlantic University-Florida International University. As mentioned earlier, Tom Lewis took DeGrove's place in 1985. However, when Governor Martinez took office in 1987, he named Thomas G. Pelham as secretary. Pelham was a Tallahassee attorney and author of *State Land Use Planning and Regulation: The Model Code and Beyond.*[78] Many significant planning and administrative policies were set during Pelham's tenure. When Lawton M. Chiles became governor in 1989, he appointed William Sadowski to head the department. Sadowski was a Dade County attorney and a former legislator known as an advocate for affordable housing. Given the changes in gubernatorial and DCA leadership, it is astonishing that the local government planning program came together as well as it did.

The local-level development management subsystem is centered on the requirements of the Local Government Comprehensive Planning and Land Development Regulation Act.[79] The local plans had to abide by the DCA's Rule 9J-5, *Florida Administrative Code,* "Minimum Criteria for Review of Local Government Comprehensive Plans and Determination of Compliance"[80] and Rule 9J-11, "Procedure for Review of Local Government Comprehensive Plans and Amendments."[81] (Though some requirements may have changed over the following years, the core of each rule remains the same.)

Upon receipt of a local government's proposed plan or plan amendment,[82] the DCA, acting as the state land planning agency (as it is called in the act), transmitted copies for comment to the Florida Department of Transportation, the Department of Environmental Regulation,[83] and the appropriate regional planning council and water management district. If the amendment was for a municipal plan, it was also sent to the county planning agency within which the municipality was located. The agencies had forty-five days to provide comments regarding the proposed plan or plan amendment to the DCA. Following this initial review stage, the DCA provided written comments, after which the local government had sixty days to adopt plan amendments. The adopted amendment was then re-submitted to the DCA, which had forty-five days to issue a notice of intent to find the amendment in compliance or not in compliance. Affected parties had twenty-one days to challenge a finding that the plan amendment was in compliance. If the DCA found an amendment not in compliance, it requested a hearing from the Florida Division of Administrative Hearings, which then assigned an independent administrative law judge to hear and make a recommendation regarding the issue.[84]

To ensure that local planning programs are an ongoing process, the law requires that local comprehensive plans be updated through an evaluation and appraisal report (EAR). At least once every five years following the adoption of a plan, a local government is required to submit to the DCA a report that evaluates and appraises the success or failure of its comprehensive plan.[85] The EAR was generally subject to the same review requirements that applied to the plan adoption process. Any amendments to the comprehensive plan recommended in the report must be adopted within one year of when the report is adopted by the local governing body.

Organization and personnel

In early 1986, the DCA was organized into three bureaus: the Bureau of Local Resource Planning (later called the Bureau of Local Planning), the Bureau of State Resource Planning, and the Bureau of Resource Management. The first bureau chiefs were Robert Kessler, who headed the Bureau of Local Resource Planning; James Quinn, the Bureau of State Resource Planning (he became chief of the Bureau of Local Planning in 1987); and Diana Sawaya-Crane, the Bureau of Resource Management. The local planning bureau was responsible for providing technical assistance and administering local planning requirements; the state resource planning team concentrated on administering the areas of critical state concern program and resource planning areas; and the third group, resource management, was concerned with the developments of regional impact program, areawide policy implementation, and intergovernmental project review. As an example of escalating workload, in addition to preparing publications, the Bureau of Local Planning was faced with reviewing some 2,100 local work products submitted in the last three months of 1987.[86]

A component of the DCA's technical assistance to local governments was in the form of publications prepared and distributed by the Bureau of Local Planning. These early guides were distributed to local officials, as well as to water management districts and regional planning councils.[87] In addition to publications, the bureau held technical assistance workshops throughout the state; in early 1987, one of these workshops attracted an interested crowd of 850 people.[88]

The DCA issued the first of its *Technical Memos* in March 1986. In it, Secretary Lewis wrote that the memos were to be distributed on a quarterly basis and they would "provide information of practical value in preparing, adopting and implementing local comprehensive plans."[89] The memos were a major aid to planners in local planning agencies and consulting firms, all of which were adding planners—and "wannabe" planners. The DCA also began issuing another somewhat less formal information publication, *Planning Notes*, two years later. The two publications kept people up-to-date on new developments or interpretations of law, especially emerging administrative rules.

Though most local governments in Florida already had plans dating back to the requirements of the 1975 Local Government Comprehensive Planning Act, their quality and structure varied greatly; therefore, *all* local governments had to comply with the minimum criteria provided by Rule 9J-5. Despite the guidelines, the bureau found significant weaknesses in many of the plans submitted during the early rounds.

These weaknesses were listed in one of issues of the *Technical Memo* as "lessons learned;" that is, faults that other local governments should avoid making. Among the problems found were:

- lack of consistency between parts of a plan;
- existing land use maps often fail to include natural resources, historic resources, and land uses of adjacent jurisdictions;
- failure to explain the methodology used to determine system capacity and establish level of service standards;
- local governments need to explain their methodology for projecting water needs and sources for the next ten years;
- for many local governments, the Intergovernmental Coordination Element consists [only] of a matrix or list of gov-ernment agencies with whom they coordinate; this approach does not fulfill the purpose of this element, which is to determine and, if necessary, improve the effectiveness of coordination between government agencies as a means of resolving conflict; and
- public participation procedures commonly fail to describe how the public is involved in the planning program.[90]

The DCA staff also mentioned that too many of the goal statements in the local comprehensive plans were adorned with, "Indirect statements containing verbs such as *promote, encourage, strive to, coordinate,* and *ensure* and qualifying phrases such as *wherever possible* and *to the extent feasible.*" The objection was that such indirect statements and qualifying phrases "fail to describe when and by what means a specific objective will be achieved."[91] However unavoidable, persistent and frequent use of *floating verbs* in statements of planning continues to provide opportunities for compromising goals, objectives, and policies.

The Three C's: Consistency, Concurrency, and Compact Development

Three precepts of Florida's intergovernmental development management system are consistency, concurrency, and compact development. The first of three C's, consistency, refers to the unity of the planning process, in both its vertical and horizontal senses.[92] The word "cooperation" was the popular jargon during the early years of planning, though it was more intention than execution. This was followed by the word "coordination," thought to have a stronger meaning than cooperation. This term was not any more successful, despite its frequent use in federal "701" planning assistance programs. It was not until the 1980s that the word "consistency" began to appear here and there, particularly in Florida planning legislation.

The consistency requirement was not restricted to lack of consistency between parts of a local comprehensive plan. The new system was designed to have state, regional, and local government entities marching down the same road toward a similar vision, in harmony, not in discord. As DeGrove and Miness point out, "Statutory consistency requirements bind the system together."[93] The degree of detail might be different for each level of governance, but the direction is to be the same. Thus, *consistency* between levels is a critical link in the system. Actually, two types of consistency are involved: one is the vertical consistency necessary *between* levels of governance and the second is horizontal consistency, *within* each of the three levels. At the state level, for example, the latter meant between the state plan and the agency long-range program plans. At the regional level, it meant between

RPCs, WMDs, and MPOs. Consistency was especially critical at the local level because it linked the goals of the local comprehensive plan to the required local land development regulations. Without a modicum of both vertical and horizontal consistency, there was a chance of system collapse.

Consistency is required between a local comprehensive plan and the land development regulations used to implement the plan. A precedent was set early in a 1987 Dade County case, *Machado v. Musgrove*,[94] when the Third District Court of Appeals ruled that a rezoning must conform strictly to the comprehensive plan and its elements.[95] The case was precipitated by a challenge to an amendment to the county's zoning map, which would have changed the zoning from estate residential to professional office. As noted by Terrell K. Arline in a later case but referring to *Machado*, "The requirement to act consistent with the plan, coupled with the meaningful standard of judicial review in the strict scrutiny standard furthers the state's integrated comprehensive planning process."[96] This coupled the importance of the consistency requirement to the intergovernmental development system.

Inconsistency with the State Comprehensive Plan and the Comprehensive Regional Policy Plans was identified as a problem common to many local plans submitted to the DCA for review. The relevant rule states that if a local government comprehensive plan is compatible with and furthers the goals of the state and regional plans, then it is consistent.[97] "Compatible with" is defined to mean that the local plan is not in conflict with the state or regional plans. "Furthers" is action in the direction of realizing the goals or policies of the state or regional plans. Consistency between local plans and the state and regional plans, wrote DCA, "is essential to make Florida's three-tiered integrated planning process work."[98]

<u>Concurrency</u>

As critical as the consistency requirement was to the intergovernmental development management system, even more attention has been paid to concurrency, at least in literature. Concurrency, according to the local planning act means that public facilities and services needed to support the impact of a development must be available *concurrent with* the impacts of the development (see Chapter VIII).[99] The facilities and services covered by this requirement are roads, drainage, potable water, sanitary sewer, solid waste, parks and recreation, and mass transit (if applicable). Level of service standards set the environment for concurrency management and a capital improvements element is a major tool in implementing it. Public facilities and services meeting or exceeding levels of service established in the capital improvement element of a local plan must be available concurrent with the actual impacts of the development. If the actual level of service of a facility drops below the level of service adopted in the local plan, the concurrency requirement is not being satisfied.

In discussing concurrency, Paul Bradshaw, then director of DCA's Bureau of Resource Planning and Management, pointed to Secretary Thomas G. Pelham's response to an inquiry from State Senator Gwen Margolis as becoming the state's definitive policy on concurrency. As Bradshaw noted, Senator Margolis wrote a letter in January 1988 "in which she asked several penetrating questions concerning the Department's interpretation of the concurrency requirement of the Development Management Act."[100] In his response, Pelham called the concurrency requirement the "teeth" of the Growth Management Act, and that it distinguished growth management from mere planning.[101] He earlier had added emphasis when he wrote, "... there remains one area where I will not compromise—the concurrency requirement."[102] Bradshaw reflected that "he [Pelham] and the Department will hold fast to a firm, but flexible, interpretation of the requirement."[103] Then, he went on to define what was meant by flexible: "Flexible, in the sense of the concurrency requirement, means that all necessary infrastructure need not be in place at the very moment a local government issues a development order."[104] He went on to say the requirement "may be satisfied through the staging or phasing of development and supporting services and facilities, just as long as development and supporting services and facilities are basically in sync."[105] "I will not compromise" may not have been quite the same as "firm, but flexible," but the latter was pragmatic because it was essential that some flexibility be written into the concurrency requirement.

Addressing concurrency, Robert Rhodes noted that, "the practical implications of this seemingly simple and politically seductive policy were not fully understood when it was enacted in 1985."[106] Therefore, "It was left to DCA, under the leadership of Secretary Thomas G. Pelham, to complete the weaving begun by the Legislature, utilizing both case-by-case adjudications and agency rulemaking."[107] Thus, pragmatism prevailed without losing sight of the intent of the law.

Brevard County was among the first to feel the effect of the concurrency requirement. Among DCA's objections regarding the concurrency issue was that the county adopted level of service standards for "state roads that were lower than those set by the Florida Department of Transportation."[108] The most difficult aspect in implementing a local government comprehensive plan was—and still is—that of transportation concurrency management. It has continued to be a thorn in implementing the concurrency doctrine.

Compact development

Compact development and redevelopment of existing urban places is also a standard expressed in the Local Government Comprehensive Planning and Land Development Regulation Act. As a counterpoint to urban sprawl, compact development provides for greater densities and intensities of land development and concentrates the efficiency of urban services and transportation.

Concerned that the debate over concurrency requirements was overshadowing the need for compact development, Secretary Pelham had the DCA publish a special issue of its *Technical Memo* devoted entirely to urban sprawl.[109] This was an attempt to get local governments to understand the importance of dealing with urban sprawl and the rationale behind the policies put in place by the department, especially "DCA's legal authority to find local plans not in compliance for failure to discourage urban sprawl."[110] The memo also identified indicators of urban sprawl (e.g., allocation of exurban residential densities, such as one to five dwelling units per acre, to large expanses of rural lands) and techniques for discouraging sprawl (e.g., designation of urban service areas).[111] Pelham described urban sprawl as "premature, low density development that 'leapfrogs' over land that is available for urban development."[112] Florida was already pocked with leapfrog indicators of urban sprawl, and Pelham was attempting to temper the practice.

For decades, urban sprawl, in large part, has been the consequence of the compulsive habit of many local government officials to ease the permitting of development proposals. This compulsion carried over into local comprehensive plans. For example, the DCA expressed concern that local governments were designating more land as low-density, single-family suburban areas than needed to support their projected increases in population.[113] This compulsion is more likely to occur in county governments than in municipal governments, though it occurs in both. We contend a covert, too often unstated problem contributing to urban sprawl is that, given the ability of motor vehicles to overcome problems of accessibility, county governments find they are in an advantageous position to be competitive with municipal governments regarding land use. Florida's anachronistic annexation law,[114] which is Byzantine in its electoral requirements, almost inhibits annexation when urban growth sprawls into the more permissive unincorporated surrounding county lands. In this way, localism exacerbates the problem of sprawl.

State Financial Assistance

Unlike the 1975 local planning law that had no financial backing, the 1985 local planning act was supported by state financial aid. This was a lesson learned—or at least temporarily learned. Despite the generous appearing support of a program designed to help local governments contend with the negative consequences of rapid growth, the $23 million provided from 1985 to 1989 was relatively insignificant when compared to the cost of transportation and other related urban services.

The $2.3 million provided in FY 1985-86 was distributed to all 67 counties, whereas most of the $8.8 million for the following fiscal year was directed to coastal counties and their municipalities, though certain interior counties also received some assistance and all local governments were eligible to compete for planning reserve funds.[115] Coastal counties initially were given higher priority because the greatest part of the state's population growth was along or near the coast. After most of the local governments had completed their plans or were working to bring them into compliance, the legislature reduced funding. However, the completed local comprehensive plans would have been virtually useless without the principal tools to implement them: land development regulations (LDRs). With the urging of the DCA, the legislature appropriated the bulk of the $7.6 million of financial aid in FY 1989-90 for completing the LDRs.

Compliance

In the course of reviewing comprehensive plans and plan elements, the DCA found that many of them did not comply with the requirements of the local government planning law and Rule 9J-5.[116] Though most of the submitted materials were basically sound, they failed to address important minimum requirements adequately. These failures generally fell into eight categories: concurrency management, level of service (LOS) for state roads, LOS for other facilities, financial feasibility of the five-year schedule of capital improvements, urban sprawl, affordable housing, resource protection, and consistency with the State Comprehensive Plan and regional policy plans. A local government was provided with opportunities to revise their plan or plan element and submit it for further review. However, if the local government continually failed to satisfy the requirement, it could be subject to sanctions applied by state government. The policy for imposing sanctions against local governments with plans found not in compliance was similar to the policy for non-submission.

Charlotte County failed to satisfy the DCA's charge that the county comprehensive plan did not control urban sprawl. Following a public hearing before a state hearing examiner, the Administration Commission (Governor and Cabinet) found the plan not in compliance with state law. Under the threat of state imposed sanctions, Charlotte County entered into a settlement with the DCA, agreeing to adopt tougher regulations in 1990. However, it took until 1994 before the Administration Commission finally approved the Charlotte County plan as being in compliance.

In April 1989, Broward County became the first county whose comprehensive plan was found to be in compliance; the Sarasota County plan was approved a month later. Secretary Pelham said, "The Broward and Sarasota experiences show that the planning process can work successfully in large urban areas if both the state and local government are committed to make it work."[117]

The Administration Commission, in October 1989, had adopted policies to withhold state revenue from local governments that failed to submit their comprehensive plans on time or have plans found not in compliance with planning requirements.[118] A local government could forfeit one day's worth of state revenue-sharing funds for each day the plan was late.[119] The Administration Commission could direct state agencies not to provide certain funds or they could declare the local government ineligible for certain grants.[120] In the early days of the program, the Administration Commission imposed sanctions on three cities: (1) Pembroke Park, a community in Broward County, was assessed $190,299, because its plan was submitted 160 days late; (2) Indian Creek Village, in Miami-Dade County, was assessed $3,146 since its plan was presented 167 days late; and Virginia Gardens, also in Dade County, was levied $92,767 because its plan was submitted 220 days late.[121] The differentiation in the assessments was primarily due to the difference in the population size of the community and other factors.

Affordable Housing

Though the environment and public infrastructure issues appeared to garner the most attention, housing was not being completely ignored. However, as the Florida DCA noted, "Few local governments which show a need for affordable housing have adopted specific policies which propose implementation activities or management techniques for addressing the need."[122] The state agency went on to point out that the policies were "not specific or measurable, such as one local government that indicated that it would 'encourage development by the private sector to address affordable housing.'"[123] The private sector, however, historically gravitates to building middle and high-income housing because the profits are greater. Without adequate state (or federal financial) aid, many communities were, once again, giving affordable housing short shrift—that is, for *low-income* families.

The concern was there, but the action was lacking. In 1986, an Affordable Housing Study Commission was created by the legislature to investigate programs to address the state's need for housing for low- and moderate-income people. In addition, Secretary Pelham appointed an Affordable Housing Task Force in 1988. His focus was more specific, however, for he charged the task force to make "specific recommendations to amend Key West's local government comprehensive plan and development management ordinance, as well as Monroe County's land development regulations, to better promote affordable housing."[124] Despite these efforts, finding answers for the problem of low-income housing remained less than a high priority.

Citizen Participation

A central component in the local government comprehensive planning process in Florida is citizen participation. Citizens not only need to understand the process, but to also have a meaningful opportunity to provide input to the planning, plan amendment, and implementation stages of the process to the fullest extent possible. The new planning law provided these opportunities.[125] It required the adoption of specific procedures including required public hearings; acceptance, consideration and responses to written comments; and notices to affected property owners and the general public.[126] These provisions could not guarantee that citizens *would* participate, but the *opportunity* was there. During the late 1980s and early 1990s, participation in the planning process or plan amendment proposals was high in some communities, disappointing in others.

Citizen participation is likely to be less during the formative stages of preparing a plan, but then increase as the plan nears consideration for adoption. This is frustrating to planners, since citizen input is as critical in the early stages of plan preparation as it is in the final stages. Early participation by citizens can help to increase their understanding of the purpose of planning, make them more aware of the importance of citizen input in the evolution of a plan, and provide a general feeling that it is "their" plan, not something prepared just by planning professionals and subject only to the approval of elected officials.

Despite widely ranging levels of citizen participation in the early stages of the new planning process, the idea of the importance of citizen participation began to take hold. Among the vehicles which helped to spread the importance of having an open process were the news media, public interest groups, professional organizations of planners and architects, and, most importantly, grassroots neighborhood organizations, such as the Council of Neighborhood Associations in Tallahassee. Some business groups, long accustomed to having singular, highly influential contact with local elected officials slowly became aware that this movement was beginning to put additional players around the table of land use decision-making. Planning, in Florida, was becoming a more *open* process, and citizen participation was beginning to exert political influence. The traditional partners in the *growth machine* (development interests, elected officials, and appointed bureaucrats) were obliged to consider a broader range of interests than before.

Special Interest Groups

Committees and task forces are usually created for specific tasks over limited periods, but some special interest groups are formed as permanent bodies dedicated to a particular cause. For example, the citizens watchdog group known as 1000 Friends of Florida (somewhat modeled after 1000 Friends of Oregon[127]) was organized in 1986 to further and support Florida's growth management laws. Nathaniel Pryor Reed of Hobe Sound, former environmental advisor to Governors Claude Kirk and Reubin Askew, was its first president.[128] The organization's first interim director was attorney Al Hadeed, then executive director of the Southern Legal Council. Hadeed was followed by Jim Murley, as executive director, then Patricia McKay, and later Charles Pattison. The group maintains a staff in Tallahassee that monitors the administration of planning and growth management laws, rules, and related activities. It also maintains statewide support for growth management, undertakes research, and involves itself in litigation in the interests of growth management. Because it is involved in so many growth management functions in Florida and so well tied to growth management activities in other states, it is a reliable source of information on past and present growth management activities. The success of 1000 Friends of Florida has encouraged the creation of similar, though more locally oriented groups throughout the state. Although these smaller groups are not directly affiliated with 1000 Friends of Florida, they are, in essence, ongoing citizen action groups supporting local planning and growth management.

Numerous other statewide special interest groups are concerned with or involved in growth management. These include good government oriented groups such as the Florida Chapter of the American Planning Association, the Florida Association of the American Institute of Architects, the Florida Planning and Zoning Association, the Florida League of Cities, the Florida Association of Counties, and the League of Women Voters. Environmentally oriented associations such as the Florida Audubon Society, the Florida Chapter of the Sierra Club, and Citizens for a Scenic Florida are among a league of other interested groups. The list of concerned organizations goes on to include the Florida Home Builders Association, the Florida Chamber of Commerce, and others, who from their perspectives have an interest in growth management.

Summary

Florida's growth in the late 1980s and early 1990s showed no signs of slowing. The frenzy of land speculation continued, and so did eruptions of problems resulting from insufficiently guided development. Likewise, the costs of growth continued to mount. In the mid-1980s, a major step in reining in the wild mustang of growth had been taken in the form of a number of significant planning laws, including the adoption of a State Comprehensive Plan and a Local Government Comprehensive Planning and Land Development Regulation Act. In short, an improved intergovernmental development management system had been put in place. It was now time to implement the system. A lot needed to be learned and accomplished in a relatively short period. The system was put together under two governors, a multitude of study commissions, and under four different secretaries of the Florida Department of Community Affairs. This was a difficult play to stage, particularly with a continually changing cast of leading and supporting actors who were learning how to participate in the system as it evolved.

The centerpiece of the state intergovernmental development management system is the State Comprehensive Plan. The rest of the system—translational plans, state agency program plans, various types of regional plans, and local comprehensive plans—is tied to it by consistency requirements. These requirements were applied to all levels, but it was at the local level where the requirement was most effectively enforced. In addition, it was at the local level (and to a lesser degree, the regional level) that the concurrency and compact development requirements were applied. Admittedly, most land use development decisions are made at the local level, and, therefore, it is essential that good (i.e., "smart") local government management be practiced. Nonetheless, it is also important for the state (and regional) levels of governance to conform to the dictums of consistency, concurrency, and compact development. However, it was the state level—the most organizationally fractured level of governance—that showed the greatest reluctance at implementing its own planning requirements. Furthermore, the state level failed to listen to the warning of the Zwick Committee when, in 1987, it addressed the state's greatest weakness: the need for a stable source of revenue to keep pace with the demands of a growing state. As the committee aptly put it, "We can pay now. Or we will surely pay more—much more—later."[129]

There were to be more development management committees named in the future and a change in state leadership, but the pointed warning of the Zwick Committee would continue to be ignored.

NOTES FOR CHAPTER IX

1   Zwick, Charles J., chair, State Comprehensive Plan Committee, *Keys to Florida's Future: Winning in a Competitive World—The Final Report of the State Comprehensive Plan Committee to the State of Florida*, February 1987, p. 5.

2   Rhodes, Robert M., "Growth Management in Florida 1985 and Beyond," *Florida Environmental and Urban Issues* XIII: 2, 1986, p. 2; also see Bruce Stiftel, "The Interpersonal/Organizational/Political View of Planning: Do Planners Believe It? *Florida Environmental and Urban Issues* XII: 3, 1985, pp. 24-29 and Richard G. RuBino, "Can the Legacy of a Lack of Follow-through in Florida State Planning be Changed?" *Journal of Land Use & Environmental Law* 1: 2, 1986, p. 39.

3   Zwick, ibid.

4   Conant, James K., "In the Shadow of Wilson and Brownlow: Executive Branch Reorganization in the States, 1965-1987," *Public Administration Review* 48: 5, 1988, p. 894.

5   Wise, Harold F. and Bertram Wakeley, "The Practice of State Planning and Policy Development," *State Government* 57: 3, 1984, p. 89.

6   Ibid.

7   30 *M.R.S.A.,* sec. 4960, *et seq.*

8   Title 45, Ch. 22.2, *Rhode Island General Laws*.

9   Act 200; 24 *Vermont Statutes*, Ch. 117; Development Management Act of 1988 and Amendments to Act 250, 1990.

10 In 1994, the Vermont legislature removed a consistency requirement that was in the original Act 200.

11 Article 66B, *Annotated Code of Maryland*.

12 *New Jersey Statutes Annotated*, §§ 52:18A-196 et seq. For a review of this program, see John W. Epling, "Growth Management in New Jersey: An Update," *Environmental and Urban Issues* XVII: 4, 1990, pp. 6-16.

13 In 1975 the New Jersey Supreme Court in *Southern Burlington County N.A.A.C.P. v. Mount Laurel Township* found that all municipalities are required to provide a fair share of affordable housing within their larger region.

14 Starnes, Earl M., "Substate Frameworks for Growth Management," in *Growth Management, The Planning Challenge of the 1990's,* Jay M. Stein, ed., Newberry Park, CA: Sage Publications, 1993, p. 82.

15 This failed to happen.

16 Chapter 36.70A *Revised Code of Washington*.

17 Obtained from www.mrsc.org/Subjects/Planning/compplan.aspx on June 17, 2007.

18 RuBino, Richard G., "Creative Intergovernmental Programs and the Roles Planners Play," prepared for the Division of Intergovernmental Relations, American Planning Association, September 1994, pp. 6-7, unpublished.

19 Porter, Douglas R., "San Diego's Brand of Growth Management: A for Effort, C for Accomplishment," *Urban Land* 48, 5, 1989.

20 Chapter 716 of *Massachusetts Acts and Resolves*.

21 Obtained from www.capecodecommission.org on August 22, 2006.

22 RuBino, ibid, pp. 9-10.

23 Lieutenant Governor (John) Wayne Mixson served as governor for four days in January 1987 when Governor Graham began his first term as a member of the U.S. Senate.

24 The committee members were Kathleen Shea Abrams, Harry C. Adley, Larry Y. Anchors, Bill Basford, George J. Berlin, Vera M. Carter, Armando Codina, Thomas Coward, John M. DeGrove, Robert F. Ehrling, William H. Griffith, Elaine R. Harrington, Helen H. Hood, Judy D. Johnson, Bobby F. McKown, Benjamin E. Norbom, Sergio Pereira, J.L. Plummer, Albert D. Quentel, James M. Rester, Barbara Sheen Todd, Jack Wilson, and Bernard J. Yokel.

25 Office of the Governor, "Graham Names Growth Panel to Oversee Implementation of Law," news release dated August 16, 1985, regarding Executive Order 85-162.

26 Zwick, ibid. The committee determined that the cost over the next ten years of implementing the State Comprehensive Plan would be $52.9 billion, over half of which would be for transportation needs, p. 3.

27 Ibid, p. 10.

28 Ibid, p. 13.

29 Ibid, p. 6.

30. Ibid, p. 2.

31 Ibid, pp. 2-3.

32 Ibid, pp. 22-24.

33 Ibid, p. 4.

34 Martinez later went on to become secretary of the U.S. Department of Housing and Urban Development.

35 Zwick, ibid, p. 4.

36 Colburn, David R. and Lance deHaven-Smith, *Government in the Sunshine* State, Gainesville: University Press of Florida, 1999, p. 71.

37 Burt, Al, *The Tropic of Cracker*, Gainesville, FL: University Press of Florida, 1999, p. 223.

38 Morris, Allen and Joan Perry Morris, *The Florida Handbook 2005-2006*, Tallahassee: The Peninsular Publishing Company, 2005, p. 325.

39 The members of the task force were Richard Bernhardt, Barbara Henderson Cawley, Jan Cummings, Gerald Dake, John M. DeGrove, David Denslow, Peter Dunbar, James Frank, Kaye N. Henderson, Thomas Kohler, Charles Lee, Dan McClure, Sr., Thomas G. Pelham, Ron Rotella, Xavier Suarez, Arthur E. Teele, Jr., Barbara Sheen Todd, Dale Twachtmann, Vince Whibbs, and Patricia Woodworth; L. Benjamin Starrett was project director.

40 *Governor's Task Force on Urban Growth Patterns: Final Report*, Tallahassee, FL, June 1989. For an analysis of the organization, deliberations, and recommendations of this task force, see L. Benjamin Starrett, "Concentrated Urban Growth: A Review of the Final Report of the Governor's Task Force on Urban Growth Patterns," *Environmental and Urban Issues*, Fall 1989, pp. 31-37.

41 Florida Department of Community Affairs, *Planning Notes* 2: 5, August 1989, p. 1.

42 Ch. 187, *Florida Statutes*.

43 Powell, David, "Managing Florida's Growth: The Next Generation," *Florida State University Law Review* 21: 2, 1993, p. 242.

44 *Constitution of the State of Florida*, Article III, § 19(h), Long-Range State Planning Document and Department and Agency Planning Document Processes.

45 It was proposed by a Budget and Taxation Reform Commission in 1992. The section was amended in 1998; the amended version appears here.

46 DeGrove, John M. "The Emergence of State Planning and Growth Management Systems: An Overview," in Buchsbaum, Peter A. and Larry J. Smith, eds., *State & Regional Comprehensive Planning: Implementing New Methods for Growth Management*, Chicago: American Bar Association, 1993, p. 4.

47 RuBino, ibid, pp. 39-40.

48 § 187.101(3), 1985, *Florida Statutes*.

49 RuBino, ibid.

50 O'Connell, Daniel W., "New Directions in State Legislation: The Florida Growth Management Act and State Comprehensive Plan," *Institute on Planning, Zoning, and Eminent Domain*, Dallas, TX: Southwestern Legal Foundation, 1986, p. 6-15.

51 Colburn and deHaven-Smith, ibid, p. 143.

52 § 186.007(4), *Florida Statutes*. The term "translational" refers to translating relevant sections of the State Comprehensive Plan into a coordinated set of development management plans.

53 RuBino, ibid, p. 37-39.
54 Powell, ibid, p. 240.
55 § 186.021, *Florida Statutes*.
56 Ch. 216, *Florida Statutes*.
57 DeGrove, John M., "Florida's Growth Management Legislation: 1969 to 2000," paper prepared for the Richard E. Nelson Symposium on Florida's Growth Management Legislation, October 13, 2000, p. 7.
58 It also served as the agency's functional plan.
59 DeGrove, ibid.
60 Florida Department of Community Affairs, *Planning Notes* 2: 4, June 1989, p. 3.
61 Murley, James , original source misplaced, but verified by Murley (in an email to RuBino on January 8, 2007) as having been said on a number of occasions.
62 Bureaucratic inertia is one of four impediments to state policy management identified by Richard G. RuBino, in "State Policy Management: A Question of the Will to Act," *Public Administration Review* 35, special issue, 1975, p. 772.
63 §§ 373.451-373.4595, *Florida Statutes*.
64 Morris and Morris, *ibid*.
65 § 259.101, *Florida Statutes*.
66 See James Farr and O. Greg Brock, "Florida's Landmark Programs for Conservation and Recreation Land Acquisition," *Sustain* 14, 2006.
67 Florida Department of Community Affairs, *Technical Memo* 4: 4, Fall 1989, p. 6.
68 Obtained from www.dca.state.fl.us/Fhcd/fct/about.cfm on October 23, 2006.
69 Florida Department of Community Affairs, *Technical Memo* 1: 3, October 1986, p. 3.
70 deHaven-Smith, Westi Jo and Robert Paterson, "The 1986 Glitch Bill—Missing Links in Growth Management," *Florida Environmental and Urban Issues* 14: 1, 1986, p. 6.
71 If a development exceeds a certain size (established by agreement) it must be submitted to the Florida Department of Environmental Protection, not a water management district.
72 § 134 of Title 23, *United States Code*.
73 § 339.135, *Florida Statutes*.
74 Acturally, the MPO program allows a somewhat fractured type of transportation regionalism; for example, the Tampa Bay metropolitan area consists of four separate MPOs.
75 Chapter 369, Part II, *Florida Statutes*.

76 Four years later, Governor Jeb Bush created a task force to find ways to build the Wekiva Parkway through the area; the parkway was the final segment of the Central Florida Beltway around the Orlando metropolitan area. In 2004, the Wekiva Parkway and Protection Act (Chapter 2004-384, *Laws of Florida*) was passed, permitting the design and future construction of the parkway. The act calls for local governments to adjust their comprehensive plans and development regulations to accommodate the stipulations of the act.

77 Palm Beach County ordinance number 86-30, § 2.

78 Pelham, Thomas G., *State Land Use Planning and Regulation: The Model Code and Beyond*, Lexington, MA: D.C. Heath Company, 1979.

79 Ch. 163, Part II, *Florida Statutes*.

80 Robert Kessler (as section head), Jan Ollry (planning), and Dana Minerva (legal) of the DCA did most of the initial writing of Rule 9J-5; among other DCA personnel directly or indirectly involved in the writing were Thomas Pelham (department head), Woody Price, Robert Kessler, Paul Noll, Diane Salz, and Dean Alexander; Patricia McKay, who moved from DCA to 1000 Friends of Florida also contributed. This information was obtained from Jan Ollry on November 5, 2003 and verified on November 2, 2007.

81 These were not the only administrative rules pertaining to local planning, but they were two of the most basic ones.

82 Most Florida local governments had completed some form of local plan as required by the 1975 Local Government Comprehensive Planning Act (even if they were not using them), therefore the new act and rules generally referred to planning amendments.

83 The name of this agency was later changed to Department of Environmental Protection.

84 See §§ 120.567d and 120.57(1), *Florida Statutes*.

85 § 163.3191, *Florida Statutes*. and Rule 9J-5.005 (6) and (8), *Florida Administrative Code*.

86 Florida Department of Community Affairs, *Technical Memo* 3: 1, March 1988, p. 3.

87 Among these technical publications were a data source guide, a population methodology guide, a comprehensive planning manual and a series of model comprehensive plan elements, methodologies for forecasting population growth, and suggestions for preparing a local comprehensive plan; the last mentioned discussed ways of organizing for comprehensive planning and major steps in the planning process. This information was obtained in part from Florida Department of Community Affairs, *Technical Memo* 2: 1, June 1987, p. 3.

88 Florida Department of Community Affairs, *Technical Memo* 2: 2, October 1987, p. 1.

89 Lewis, Tom, E., Jr., "An Open Letter from Secretary Tom Lewis," *Technical Memo* 1: 1, Florida Department of Community Affairs, March 1986, p. 1.

90 Florida Department of Community Affairs, *Technical Memo* 3: 1, ibid, pp. 4-7.

91 Ibid, p. 5

92 For a review of concepts and policies critical to implementing the consistency requirement see Robert Lincoln, "Implementing the Consistency Doctrine," in American Planning Association, *Modernizing State Planning Statutes*, numbers 462-463, Chicago: Planning Advisory Service, 1996, pp. 89-104. For a Florida specific discussion, see Kristine Williams, "Planning, Zoning, and the Consistency Doctrine: The Florida Experience, Center for Urban Transportation Research, College of Engineering, University of South Florida, 1995.

93 DeGrove, John M. and Deborah A. Miness, *The New Frontier for Land Policy: Planning & Growth Management in the States*, Cambridge, MA: Lincoln Institute of Land Policy, 1992, p. 162.

94 519 So.2d 629, 632, Florida 3d District Court of Appeals, 1987.

95 Florida Department of Community Affairs, *Planning Notes* 1: 2, June 1988, p. 3.

96 Arline, Terrell K., *The City of Jacksonville, et al, v. Charles Dixon, Jr., et al* (Case No. SC01-103, Florida Supreme Court), First Amended Brief of Amicus Curiae, 1000 Friends of Florida, Inc., in support of respondent, Charles Dixon, Jr., April 2002.

97 Rule 9J-4.021, *Florida Administrative Code.*

98 Florida Department of Community Affairs, *Technical Memo* 4: 3, Summer 1989, p. 5.

99 §§ 163.3177(10)(h), *Florida Statutes.*

100 Bradshaw, Paul, Florida Department of Community Affairs, *Technical Memo* 4: 1, Winter 1989, p. 1.

101 Florida Department of Community Affairs, *Technical Memo* 4: 2, Spring 1989, p. 4. For scholarly reviews of the concurrency requirement see Thomas G. Pelham, "Adequate Public Facilities Requirements: Reflections on Florida's Concurrency System for Managing Growth," *Florida State University Law Review* 19: 4, 1992, pp. 973-1052 and Robert M. Rhodes, "Concurrency: Problems, Practicalities, and Prospects, *Journal of Land Use and Environmental Law* 6: 2, 1991, pp. 241-254.

102 Pelham, Thomas G., Florida Department of Community Affairs, *Technical Memo* 4: 1, ibid, p. 2.

103 Bradshaw, p. 3.

104 Ibid.

105 Ibid.

106 Powell, ibid, p. 293, reference 414, citing Robert Rhodes.

107 Powell, ibid, p. 293.

108 Florida Department of Community Affairs, *Technical Memo* 4: 1, ibid, p. 3; and *Technical Memo* 4: 2, ibid, p. 5

109 Florida Department of Community Affairs, *Technical Memo* 4: 4, Special Issue, 1989.

110 Ibid, p. 1.

111 Ibid, pp. 11-14.

112 Florida Department of Community Affairs, *Technical* Memo 4: 2, ibid, p. 1.

113 Florida Department of Community Affairs, *Technical* Memo 4: 3, ibid, p. 8.

114 Chapter 171, *Florida.Statutes.*

115 Florida Department of Community Affairs, *Technical Memo* 3: 1, ibid, p. 2.

116 Florida Department of Community Affairs, *Technical Memo* 4: 3, ibid, p. 1.

117 Florida Department of Community Affairs, *Planning Notes* 2: 4, June 1989, p. 3.

118 § 163.3184(11), *Florida Statutes.*

119 Sanctions could not be imposed unless a plan was submitted more than ninety days after its due date.

120 Florida Department of Community Affairs, *Technical Memo* 1: 1, ibid, p. 9.

121 Florida Department of Community Affairs, *Technical Memo* 4: 4, ibid, p. 12.

122 Florida Department of Community Affairs, *Technical Memo* 4: 3, ibid, p. 7.

123 Ibid, p. 3.

124 Florida Department of Community Affairs, *Planning Notes* 2: 2, March 1989, p. 3.

125 In addition, §§ 163.3184 and 163.3213, *Florida Statutes*, provide affected persons with the right to challenge certain decisions regarding the local growth management act. In brief, affected persons include the local government; an adjoining local government; and persons who own property, reside, or own or operate a business within the local government (and submit comments).

126 Florida Department of Community Affairs, *Technical Memo* 1: 3, ibid, p. 7.

127 Reed, Nathaniel P. "A New Citizens Watchdog for Sound Growth Management," *Florida Environmental and Urban Issues* XIV: 3, 1987, p. 9.

128 Earl Starnes, a founding board member, served on 1000 Friends of Florida Board of Directors from 1986 to 1993.

129 Zwick, ibid, p. 45.

CHAPTER X

MOVING TOWARD FLEXIBILITY, FOLLOWED BY PARTIAL DISMANTLING

Early to Late 1990s

> If Florida is to secure the economic future it so
> desperately sought for much of the twentieth cen-
> tury, it will have to find a new way to come to
> terms with growth. To do so, state and local gov-
> ernments must be able and willing to regulate
> growth and limit or prevent its harmful effects. If
> they do not do this, Florida will suffocate economi-
> cally and environmentally.[1] (David R. Colburn, and
> Lance deHaven-Smith, 1999.)

What happened in the years immediately before the end of
the 20th Century was in some ways reminiscent of the years
toward the end of the 19th Century. A hundred years had passed,
but Florida and its people were still wrestling with self-made
problems. Moreover, planners and policy makers were still
trying to find ways to address those problems, while at the
same time ignoring the lessons that might been have learned
from the past. Public planning, in most places, is still subjected to the overpowering influences of the concepts of minimal government responsibility, rampant land speculation, and
minimal interference with private property rights. In the early
years of the 20th century, public planning was in its infancy,
and it had little or no meaning in places like Florida. However, planning has since become an accepted part of public
management in many places, especially Florida.

In this chapter, we address shifts and "spins," sometimes minor, sometimes major. As in other chapters, we begin with a review of what was happening across the nation
and then bring our focus to Florida. For example, nationally,

a private property rights protection movement arose as a backlash to the surge of environmental protection and growth management activity that had been occurring. At the same time, new approaches to confront ill-managed development were coming on the scene: concepts such as smart growth, new urbanism, visioning, and sustainable communities.

Some of these concepts are similar to growth management, but they radiate more positive-sounding terminology. For example, the term "smart growth" paints a somewhat more acceptable image than growth management. Smart growth tends to be interpreted as smart *thinking*, whereas growth management infers an element of *control*. Control appears to be an optional element in the former, but it is automatically present in the latter; thus, smart growth is more of a "feel-good" term. Smart growth, according to John DeGrove, "Make[s] efficient and effective use of land resources and existing infrastructure by encouraging development to areas with existing infrastructure of capacity to avoid costly duplication of services and costly use of land."[2] This definition also applies to growth management. Though a limited degree of control can be of enormous immediate and long-term gain for the general public, the idea is often repugnant to many Americans. Nonetheless, the success of either growth management or smart growth is dependent on convincing individuals as voters and consumers of "the long-term benefit of short-term adjustments and sacrifices."[3] Amongst the many new terms for planning and managing development, smart growth, predicted Andres Duany, "will win the race."[4]

Smart Growth

"Smart Growth," a movement encouraged by the American Planning Association and the National Governors' Association, seeks to help states and local governments to modernize statutes and ordinances relating to planning and the management of change.[5] It provides a new image replacing the timeworn concept of public planning that took root in the 1920s and has remained mostly static since then. Smart growth directs itself at policies designed to balance growth with conservation of the natural environment and farmland. It espouses compact, transit-oriented, bicycle conscious, walkable, mixed-use development, along with a wide range of housing choices.[6] Theoretically, it seeks to reduce sprawl by encouraging greater densities within urban boundaries. The term "smart growth" caught on so well that it has even migrated to other fields, such as references to "smart grids" when referring to updating the nation's electrical grid system.

New Urbanism

New Urbanism, a concept promoted by Miami architects Elizabeth Plater-Zyberk and Andres Duany, and others, surfaced as early as the mid-1980s. The concept is a version of traditional, early to mid-20th century neighborhoods with grid street patterns, alleyways, sidewalks, and neighborhood businesses. Though appealing in scale, intimacy, and pedestrian friendliness, many of the "traditional" neighborhoods of the 1940s and 1950s were themselves manifestations of suburbanism. (Ask us—we lived in them!) However, they were more dependent on public transit (at a time before the outright dominance of the automobile) and more socially oriented, markets and schools were in walking distance, and people on sidewalks exchanged greetings with neighbors sitting on screened porches. New Urbanism does not exclude a place for cars, but it calls for greater balance between the car, public transit, bicycle, and walkers. Its initial showplace development, Seaside, Florida, was designed with the intent of providing a mixed-use development with affordable, north Florida style housing. However, Seaside quickly escalated into something beyond "affordable" in cost, gaining further notoriety as the set for the movie *The Truman Show*. Celebration, another Florida new town using the New Urbanism concept, was developed by the Walt Disney Corporation in 1994. Located near Walt Disney World, it features compact urban design, a mixed-use core, walk-ability, bicycle ways, and open space, but, like Seaside, it lacks public transit in that it is relatively small and isolated from urban centers. Native Floridian and National Public Radio commentator Diane Roberts has called Celebration "high-calorie cute, a gingerbread village built on spare land Disney snagged in the 1960s."[7] Not surprisingly, these two communities became the domiciles of upper income and middle-to-upper income people.

Visioning

Visioning also gained popularity in the 1990s, particularly in Florida where the Department of Community Affairs funded communities engaging in visioning efforts. Visioning often, but not always, includes a charrette involving local citizens who meet for one or more days in an organized exploration of the community's future. This may include visual, social, economic, environmental, historic, and other characteristics as desired by the citizen assembly. The resulting community visions are then used as input for updating comprehensive plans. The exercises are valuable for their participatory process and educational experience, particularly for neighborhoods and smaller communities. However, they also have been used in broader, more regional scenarios, such as the committees for a Sustainable Treasure Coast and a Sustainable Emerald Coast, both of which were aided in their efforts by the Florida Growth Management Dispute Resolution Consortium at Florida State University and the Center for Urban & Environmental Solutions at Florida Atlantic University.[8]

Sustainable Communities

The sustainable communities movement is somewhat more associated with balancing human and natural resource needs. Like the other movements, it posits itself as contrary to sprawl, yet, despite its positive attributes, it often contributes to sprawl in a different form. In Florida, the most well known attempts at development of sustainable communities are in southwest Florida, notably the new developments of Ave Marie in Collier County and Babcock Ranch in Lee County (see Chapter XI). These are well-financed, ambitious undertakings, but whether sustainability can be maintained over the long run without aggressive and continuing participation of the county governments within which they are located is arguable.[9]

Private Property Rights Movement

As the United States grew and the industrial revolution attracted people to the cities, land ownership in urbanizing areas gradually became less secure.[10] Initially, squabbles over land use between neighbors were resolved under nuisance law, at least for those people who could afford to pursue litigation. However, rapid urbanization brought such an increase in conflicts over land use that nuisance law was no longer adequate. Rapid urbanization also brought conditions of urban squalor, and cries for urban reform arose from both the privileged and the underprivileged. Along with urban reform came gradual application of the police power, first ruled on by the U.S. Supreme Court in 1887.[11] Peter Wolf defines the police power as "government's obligation to act in the public interest, for wide public benefit."[12] The police power has its basis in the creation of the Union itself and may reflect the phrase "furthering the public welfare," part of the opening paragraph of the U.S. Constitution.

Use of the police power expanded as the nation urbanized. This, compounded by the inability or reluctance of balkanized local governments to generate funds needed to support the public services demanded by their citizens, accelerated dependence on using the police power to achieve public services that might otherwise have been obtained through some form of the purchase power. Thus began a noticeable shift from a guarantee of absolute property rights to increasing public influence over private property through use of police power.[13] Concern over the differing views of protecting private property and protecting the public welfare began to rise precipitously as the nation spread its suburban wings. Coupled with this, was the federal requirement that local governments must plan and develop land use regulations before grants would be awarded for infrastructure improvements (see Chapters IV and V). Next came the "Quiet Revolution" (Chapter VI) whereby states began to require reluctant local governments to prepare plans and enact land use regulations, things formerly left to the prerogative of the local governments. In combination, these events, designed to benefit the public welfare, spawned increasing conflicts over private property rights.

Protection of private property rights versus protection of the public welfare is not an either-or issue. Both have roots in the U.S. Constitution: the public welfare in the opening paragraph of the constitution and property rights in the fifth amendment. Supporters of property rights feared that public welfare advocates were carrying their end too far. In response, a so-called "wise use" backlash began, first in the West—as the Sagebrush Rebellion—and then spreading throughout the nation. "The wise use movement," wrote University of Wisconsin-Madison professor Harvey Jacobs, "taps into and exploits a cultural myth about private property that runs deep with the American people."[14] A core of libertarian-oriented property rights advocates appeared to want to do away with all governmental regulation over land use.[15] On the other hand, a detractor called it a movement on a mission, a wise *marketing* mission.[16] It was a sign of the times.

On the other hand, in a nation approaching three hundred million people, many property owners are concerned about protecting their property values from being reduced if a property next door becomes an incompatible land use. They cannot afford to let government out of its constitutional responsibility of protecting the general welfare. A balance is needed. Legislative battles were fought in many states, with advances for property rights protection in some states, rejection of similar attempts in other states, and some states, like Florida, reaching compromise positions. From 1991 to 1996, according to Kirk Emerson and Charles Wise, twenty-six states adopted some form of private property rights measure.[17]

In addressing the property rights movement initiated in the 1990s, we point out that, yes, everyone's home is his or her own castle, but each castle sits within a wide cluster of *interdependent* castles and, in the face of our growing population, acting for the good of the whole is as important as acting for personal good. Both must be accommodated; the profit motive *must not be* the sole determinant. As Scotsman William Drummond long ago wrote, "Property has its duties as well as its rights."[18]

Activities in Other States and Regions

A number of new state and regional initiatives occurred during the period covered by this chapter, notably in Maryland, Tennessee, and Utah. These may not have been the only initiatives, but they serve to illustrate the continuing interest in growth management and smart growth. By the end of the 1990s, twenty-six states had enacted either growth management or smart growth laws.[19]

A year after a so-called radical planning bill failed to be enacted by the Maryland legislature, a new, more cooperative-based planning law was passed.[20] The Economic Growth, Resource Protection, and Planning Act of 1992, involves state government, municipal and county governments, and the planning commissions created by the act.[21] Though the Maryland law calls for consistency between levels of government and between plans and development regulations, implementation is dependent on the voluntary cooperation of all parties involved; a set of visions, prepared by the Chesapeake Bay Commission, is expected to tie the separate planning efforts together.[22] Furthermore, Pennsylvania and Virginia, as partners in the Chesapeake Bay Commission, were expected to incorporate the commission's visions into law, but neither acted on the matter at that time.

Maryland also enacted a set of five initiatives in 1997 collectively known as "Smart Growth". To one degree or another, the initiatives are intended to deter sprawl, but as the Maryland Department of Planning recently stated, "Sprawl is still occurring" and "nothing in the 1997 Act prevents sprawl."[23] Given that this is from the state agency most involved in attempting to contain sprawl, it appears that much of the 1997 act may be largely smoke and mirrors, falling short in the state's cooperative approach to deterring sprawl. There may be some kind of lesson in this.

A relatively recent (1998) growth policy law requires municipalities and counties in Tennessee to develop joint plans for urban growth.[24] The joint plans must identify three types of areas: growth areas (for municipalities), planned growth areas (for counties), and rural areas (within counties). Plans are prepared by county/municipality coordinating committees, and ratified by municipal and county governing bodies. If agreement on a plan by a governing body and its coordinating committee cannot be reached, the secretary of state is authorized to appoint a dispute resolution panel. Failure to comply with the planning law could affect a governing body's ability to receive various state and federal funds. The Tennessee law is often portrayed as using the smart growth approach to planning; in other words, "a renewed emphasis on comprehensive planning and a departure from the way it historically was carried out."[25]

An Envision Utah Public/Private Partnership, which identifies itself as a partnership for quality growth, was created in 1997. Its task is to develop a visionary growth strategy to protect Utah's environment, economy, and quality of life. One of its even higher priority concerns, however, is to plan for the future development of the greater Wasatch (Ogden-Salt Lake City-Provo) area. The founding chair of the partnership, Robert Grow, discussed the program before committees of both houses of the Florida legislature in 2006.

Florida: Still Struggling to Catch Up with Problems of Rampant Growth, but with Waning Fervor

A national economic recession in the early 1990s led to a wave of bankruptcies in Florida and a slowing of land development. This event, paired with the excessive damage to the Miami area from Hurricane Andrew in 1992, reminded old Floridians of the circumstances of the bust of the late 1920s, which was preceded by devastating hurricanes in 1926 and 1928. On August 24, 1992, Hurricane Andrew, a Category V storm with surface winds reaching 165 miles per hour and a storm surge of up to eighteen feet, flattened the southern portion of Miami-Dade County, with a loss of 23 lives in Florida and Louisiana and $25 billion in property damage.[26] At the time, Andrew was the most destructive hurricane on record (this was surpassed by Katrina's swath of devastation from Louisiana to the western panhandle of Florida in 2005). In response to the devastation, the legislature acted to improve Florida's inadequate building code, but this was a partial response at best. The inadequacy of Florida's building codes to protect against strong hurricane damage had been known for a long time, but like so many political reactions, it took a disaster of major proportion for action to be taken. Even then, the Florida Panhandle was excluded from having to meet the new building standards; apparently the hungry eyes of a growth coalition were on the coastal area of the

Panhandle. Thus, including the Panhandle in the "statewide" building code was left for future hurricane disasters to demonstrate that it was as susceptible to hurricane damage as the Florida peninsula.

Hurricane Andrew was followed by seven more named hurricanes before the turn of the century: Gordon in 1994, Erin and Opal in 1995, Fran in 1996, Earl and Georges in 1998, and Irene in 1999.[27] The pace is not surprising. Between 1900 and 2000, Florida has been hit by 38.5 percent of the sixty-five most intense hurricanes to strike the U.S. mainland and 36.7 percent of the thirty costliest tropical storms (a category that includes hurricanes).[28] Hence, the dangers—and private and public costs—of building on the Florida coast are well known, yet coastal development continues to be carried on with intensity.

The interior of Florida is no less endangered by excessive development. No state had such an extensive proportion of wetlands. According to the *Water Resources Atlas of Florida*, satellite imagery from the early 1970s showed that "wetlands and their associated open-water areas accounted for almost a third of the total land area of the state."[29] Cynthia Barnett, in *Mirage: Florida and the Vanishing Water of the Eastern U.S.*, revealed that during the 1970s Florida had one of the most extensive losses of wetlands in the nation.[30] The U.S. Fish and Wildlife Service, she points out, found that between 1972 and 1980, over 24,000 acres of wetlands were drained for urban development and agriculture in south Florida alone.

Florida faces many different kinds of environmental problems, but one of the most serious, in terms of effect, is the depletion and pollution of its water. Many of its local governments are fast approaching a state of non-sustainability in this regard. Thus, water wars have emerged, between not only counties such as Hillsborough, Pasco, and Pinellas, but also an interstate battle between Florida, Georgia, and Alabama over water flowing into Apalachicola Bay. Three principal river basins drained by the Apalachicola, Chattahoochee, and Flint rivers feed the bay. The Chattahoochee and Flint supply much of Atlanta's water needs and those of other cities in southwestern Georgia and southeastern Alabama. At the Apalachicola end of the basin, the oyster industry in Apalachicola Bay, dependent on the quality and quantity of the riverine water flowing into the bay, faces a dire future as urban areas such as Atlanta, Columbus, and Dothan become more densely populated. At the other end of Florida, many people, according to historian Michael Gannon, are predicting "a dire future for the dying Everglades," whereas others claim it is already dead.[31] Gannon takes his comments a step further by adding, "The sad fate of the Everglades is only one example of the ecological consequences of Florida's modern growth-at-any-cost mentality."[32]

As we repeatedly have mentioned, an associated and continuing problem for Florida is urban sprawl. Despite attempts to discourage sprawl, it continues on, and on, and on. In 1993, Thomas G. Pelham felt the need to point out that the discouragement of urban sprawl is a central policy of Florida's growth management laws.[33] But his admonition had little effect on the development industry. Sprawl continued, especially into the rural countryside. Urban sprawl, water issues, and hurricanes, accompanied by transportation and housing problems, are but examples of Florida's continuing negative consequences of rampant and only partially managed growth. More problems were to come.

Making Changes: Creeping Toward the Edge of a Slippery Slope

In 1991, former U.S. Senator Lawton M. Chiles was elected governor of Florida; he served in this position until his death in 1998. For most of his years as governor, Chiles, a Democrat, had to work with a cabinet split between Republicans and Democrats, a State Senate split by both parties from 1991 until Republican control started in 1995, and a House of Representatives that in 1997 gained a Republican majority. This made policy leadership somewhat difficult for him. Most of the Chiles years were times of political compromise, marked by a redirection of state level planning activities, an overly ambitious attempt to pair the resolution of two distinct regional issues into one (the developments of regional impact review process and the intergovernmental coordination element of a local plan), and a gradual relaxation of state limitations on local planning. Though managing growth remained a matter of significant concern, slippage in zeal was evident.

Changes were made to all three levels of the growth management system during the 1993 legislative session. Agency planning at the state level shifted from its functional, long-range approach to a shorter strategic timeframe. Regional planning councils were made subject to a "sunset" review, the developments of regional impact program was redirected, and state control over local-level planning and growth management began to be addressed more in terms of a "partnership" with less aggressive state government direction setting.

Environmental Land Management Study Committee III

In the first year of his administration, Governor Chiles appointed a third Environmental Land Management Study Committee (ELMS III). The committee had 51 members, 45 of whom were elected officials or citizens representing various interests, and six were administrators of state agencies who served as ex officio nonvoting members.[34] James Harold Thompson, a Tallahassee attorney and former state legislator, was its chair; Linda Loomis Shelley, who had served as general counsel to Governor Graham and similarly with the Florida Department of Community Affairs, was vice-chair; and David L. Powell, who was a partner in a Tallahassee law firm, was its executive director. The two previous ELMS committees, the first appointed in the early 1970s and the second in the early 1980s, were instrumental in furthering the maturity of the state's development management system. The new committee was charged with providing the basis for the next generation of development management policy in Florida.[35] Powell wrote that the threshold issue before the ELMS III committee was to assess "the desired role of state government in growth management."[36]

The ELMS III committee conducted an overall review of Florida's intergovernmental development management system and suggested changes desired in the 1990s. The suggested changes covered eight topics: (1) the state role in planning and development management, (2) the regional role in planning and development management, (3) local planning and intergovernmental coordination, (4) evaluation and appraisal reports on local comprehensive plans, (5) concurrency and public facilities, (6) programs pre-dating the mid-1980s development management acts (e.g., areas of critical state concern program and the developments of regional impact review process), (7) coastal management, and (8) land preservation.

Most of the committee's final recommendations were adopted by legislature in 1992 without substantial modifications. The suggestions resulted in changes to all three levels of the intergovernmental system during the 1992 legislative session. Among the changes recommended by the committee was the need for and continuation of the state government's leadership role in development management. In addition, the ELMS III committee concluded that state agency functional planning should be redirected from a comprehensive approach to planning to a strategic approach, regional planning councils ought to be made subject to a "sunset" law (a requirement that was reversed in 1996), the DRI program should be relegated to local governments as part of the intergovernmental element of their local plans, and state control over local-level planning should move more toward a concept of "partnership." The major omission from the committee's recommendations was the legislature's refusal to enact a proposal "for a statewide motor fuel tax increase of ten cents per gallon to finance the transportation improvements necessary to implement local comprehensive plans."[37] This would prove to be a significant blunder for it retarded the potential success of Florida's development management system.

Other Commissions with Responsibilities Relating to Development Management

What started as a joint project by 1000 Friends of Florida and the Conservation Foundation found root when Governor Chiles created the Florida Greenways Commission in 1993. This study committee, co-chaired by Lieutenant Governor Kenneth Hood (Buddy) McKay, Jr. and Nathaniel Reed, was asked to make recommendations for a statewide system of greenways "that would link natural areas and open spaces, conserving native landscapes and ecosystems and offering recreational opportunities across the state."[38] The work of the commission culminated in the 1995 enactment of Senate Bill 1010, which created a Florida Greenways Coordinating Council and established the Office of Greenways and Trails (OGT) in the Department of Environmental Protection.[39] The creation of the OGT and funding from the Department of Transportation provided the means for preparing the Florida Greenways Plan, and establishing the Marjorie Harris Carr Cross Florida Greenway, the final solution to the proposed Cross Florida Canal that had been resisted for decades. The Florida Greenways Plan identifies greenway and trail connections throughout the entire state and provides a basis for future land acquisitions of ecologically connected natural systems and recreational trails. A lesson learned is that a meaningful statewide planning effort can be accomplished and adopted by the legislature with executive, political, and citizen support.

Governor Chiles' attention turned to the highly urbanized area of southeast Florida in 1994 when he created a Commission for a Sustainable South Florida. Richard A. Pettigrew, former speaker of the Florida House of Representatives, initially chaired the commission. Though much of their work was directed at finding ways to protect the Everglades, they also were charged with moving the region "toward long-term recovery of its natural systems and its decaying urban centers and enable them to be sustained at a level we would find appropriate for future generations of South Floridians."[40] The commission identified sustainable communities as those that believe today's growth must not be achieved at tomorrow's expense. Their vision had five broad principles: restore key ecosystems; achieve a clean, healthy environment; limit urban sprawl; protect wildlife and natural areas; and create quality communities and jobs.[41] The vision began to take form when James (Jim) F. Murley, then secretary of the DCA, and Linda Shelley, then chief of staff of the Governor's Office, succeeded in getting the legislature to enact a sustainable communities law.[42] The commission continued to June 1999 when Governor John Ellis (Jeb) Bush's Commission for the Everglades succeeded it.

Land use attorney Richard Grosso strongly supported the focus on this area of Florida because development activities were being allowed which had detrimental consequences. As examples, he pointed out that in the 1990s, decisions were "made to allow residential development in the Agricultural Reserve in Palm Beach County, to intensify residential densities in an area of western Broward County that is being studied for Everglades restoration options, and to widen Highway US 1 into the Keys from two lanes to four." Grosso charged the state with failure to seek reversal of these decisions. Because of such decisions, he felt, "The burden increasingly falls upon citizens to enforce the Act and turn growth management into a reality."[43] Enforcement is more logically the responsibility of the State (i.e., to protect the public welfare) than it is to burden citizens with the expense of attempting to reverse such detrimental decisions.

Linked to the sustainable communities initiative was a noteworthy experiment in growth management called the "Eastward Ho! Corridor" study, begun in 1996. The Governor's Commission for a Sustainable South Florida a year earlier had recommended the initiative. The commission concluded that a sustainable Everglades ecosystem was not possible without also creating a more sustainable urban system in south Florida.[44] Thus, a program to contain future development east of I-95 and keep it away from the fringes of the Everglades was begun. This effort has produced some notable work, but as Frank Schnidman, senior research fellow at the Florida Atlantic University Center for Urban and Environmental Solutions, pointed out, in Broward County "no major effort was undertaken to turn recommendations into required action" and "there is no more Everglades fringe to protect—it has all been committed to development."[45] So much for sustainability in Broward County.

Yet, sustainability has had some positive outfall that can be partially attributed to Eastward Ho! For example, a three-year land use battle (beginning in 2003) raged over the location of a proposed Scripps Biomedical Research Institute in Palm Beach County.[46] Three potential sites were selected in the county: the Briger Tract, the Florida Research Park, and the Mecca Farms site. The first and third sites drew the greatest debate. The Bridger Tract conformed to the Eastward Ho! goal of promoting economic development eastward of Interstate 95.[47] Further inland (west of I-95), the thousand-acre Mecca Farms site, located on an old citrus grove and adjacent to the J.W. Corbett Wildlife Management Area. posed significant environmental issues. An even bigger threat, however, was that owners of adjacent properties began to show interest in developing their lands. It was reported that up to

30,000 housing units on nearby properties might be developed around the Mecca Farms site. [48]This was counter to the Palm Beach County Comprehensive Plan, and it would have created an immense cost in providing supportive infrastructure. After the Palm Beach County Business Development Board supported the Mecca Farms site, the county commission voiced a similar preference. However, growth management watchdog, 1000 Friends of Florida, in partnership with other organizations, fought for the integrity of the county plan by supporting the Briger Tract. "This site—closer to existing development and infrastructure—makes the most sense for everyone involved," said Charles Pattison, executive director of 1000 Friends of Florida.[49] The county commission eventually approved a tract of land on the Jupiter Campus of Florida Atlantic University, adjacent to the new town of Abacoa.[50] The tract borders part of the northern edge of the Briger site. A win for Eastward Ho! and good planning.

During Governor Chiles' last year in office, the legislature created a Transportation and Land Use Study Committee.[51] The task of this twenty-five member committee, chaired by L. Benjamin Starrett of the Florida Department of Community Affairs, was to evaluate transportation and land use planning and coordination issues and recommend needed changes.[52] The final report was submitted to Senate President Toni Jennings, House Speaker John Thrasher, and newly installed Governor Bush in January 1999. Among its forty recommendations were the following needs: better community design, getting concurrency right, improving coordination of land use and transportation planning and processes, and fully funding the Florida intrastate highway system. Considerable time would pass before progress was made on these recommendations.

Land Acquisition/Preservation

If the money is available, outright purchase (i.e., fee simple) or even compensation under some kind of less-than-fee-simple program is usually preferable over use of the police power. Everyone wins that way, the property owner receives compensation and the public has greater assurance that the land or natural resource is protected for the public good. Florida has done relatively well in this regard—as long as dedicated money was available and funds were not shunted off for other purposes. Nevertheless, the State's land acquisition programs have been important tools in development management. It has been estimated that Florida now owns 5.7 million acres in protected environmental lands.[53] If this is added to federal lands, approximately 12 million acres are protected (nearly one-third of the land and water area of the state) in one manner or another.

The Ongoing Struggle between Protecting the Public Welfare versus Respecting Private Property Rights

"We're not against growth management, but the policies could have some unintended consequences," claimed Kathryn Stephens of the Claremont Institute's Florida Growth Policy Studies office.[54] This statement is representative of attacks backlash groups began making on Florida's development management system in the 1990s. These groups, conscious of the general statewide support for development management and environmental protection, adorned themselves with goals such as "wise land use" and names like the "American Environmental Foundation," but their primary interest was in protecting property rights from government intrusion.

The issue of private property rights was not new to Florida.[55] Things were changing rapidly and land use conflicts were cropping up from Key West to Pensacola. "Private property rights in Florida," claimed Peter Doherty of the James Madison Institute, "have suffered perhaps more than in any other United States jurisdiction."[56] On the other side of the ledger, few places in the nation have had the public welfare subjected to such a barrage of land use conversions. Both sides of the issue felt aggrieved. These differences eventually led to the Florida legislature, where they came to a head.

After a few aborted attempts, the state legislature, in 1995, created the Bert J. Harris, Jr., Private Property Rights Protection Act,[57] a law "designed specifically to undermine Florida's landmark Growth Management Act."[58] The Harris Act is based on the concept of an *inordinate burden*.[59] This concept, which Toby Brigham called "the heart of the Harris Act," creates a legal remedy for governmental regulatory actions that inordinately burden private property.[60] The act provides an alternative route to compensation or to negotiated compromise for a property owner who believes a governmental action has inordinately burdened an existing use or a vested right. If a government action is declared to have inordinately burdened a property owner, then the owner is entitled to relief, including compensation.

Relief under the Harris Act may be for the actual loss to the fair market value of the property at issue. However, the parties to the conflict must go through a negotiation process before such a decision can be reached. The negotiation process is designed to result in a settlement offer by the governmental entity that issued the action affecting the property. If the concept of inordinate burden is the heart of the Harris Act, then the negotiation process established by the act is its lifeblood. The negotiated settlement offer is an option to direct compensation; it puts a governmental entity in a continuing state of readiness to compromise a regulation. Thus, a settlement offer can be viewed as a compromise. To attorney Robert C. Downie, II, the potential "liability created by the Harris Act makes it more attractive for the government entity to grant exceptions to property owners."[61] As Powell and his co-authors observed, the negotiation process required by the act "signals a change in the way government will do business with land owners."[62] However, after an early chilling effect on initiating any new land development regulations, government regulators found smarter ways of doing things; thus, though the chilling effect was real, it was not as severe as anticipated.[63]

Though the Harris Act is the ensign of the property rights advocates, it has not rendered development management ineffective, as some of its more radical advocates had hoped. One of the reasons for this is that it has a fraternal twin, the Dispute Resolution Act, also passed in 1995.[64] The act provides a simpler option for property owners seeking relief from "burdensome" regulations. Section 70.001(8) of the Harris Act even encourages property owners and governmental entities to use alternative dispute resolution to augment or facilitate settlements. Ronald L. Weaver feels the Dispute Resolution Act offers an easier standard than the Harris Act; he points out that under the former, a property owner may seek relief from a development order that is unreasonable or unfairly burdens the use of his property, whereas the latter provides relief only for an inordinate burden.[65]

The two laws had different origins: the initial Harris bill was the product of a set of legislators and special interests intent on advocating strong private property rights protection, whereas the dispute resolution option was based on recommendations of a Property Rights Study Commission created by the Governor Chiles.[66] The dispute resolution bill was introduced in the hope that it would be passed instead of the Harris bill or one of the other measures being considered by the legislature. As it turned out, however, the legislature enacted both the Harris bill *and* the dispute resolution bill.

State-level Changes

As discussed in Chapter IX, the weak, non-directional Florida State Comprehensiveness Plan[67] is of little use as a guide for decision-making. As Jim Murley, when he was executive director of 1000 Friends of Florida, pointed out, "it was in need of overhaul."[68] However, the changes posited by Murley and others were not about to happen. Many people seemed and still seem content to let it to remain just the way it is. However, it could become the focus of many interesting and challenging debates if state government leadership gets truly serious about using the plan as a direction-setting tool for development management.

The Taxation and Budget Reform Commission[69] added to the probable prolongation of the state plan by tying a statement about a *state planning* document (alias the State Comprehensive Plan) into constitutional revisions adopted in 1992. Article III, section 19(h) of the state constitution is called "State Planning Document and Department and Agency Planning Documents." This elevated the state plan/state planning document from a statutory law to constitutional standing. This action may have secured the position of the state plan, but it did not make it any more relevant to executive and legislative decision-making. As Fred Bosselman so mercilessly put it, "the plan has rested in its sarcophagus unexamined while the world has changed dramatically."[70]

A controversy arose over a recommendation by the ELMS III committee regarding a strategic growth and development plan at a level immediately below the State Comprehensive Plan.[71] The idea was to develop a strategic plan directed at integrating land, water, transportation, and other state policies relating to physical development. Despite the spreading popularity of the concept of strategic planning, this proposal was redirected into becoming an improved "growth management portion" of the state plan.[72] The notion may have been good, but the process for implementing it was faulty.

Absent strong backing from the governor, it was given only perfunctory effort by most of the agencies involved. Though the growth-management-portion balloon was filled with the helium of high hopes, it eventually became as disregarded as had been the translational plans.

Governor Chiles expanded on the strategic planning approach initiated during the prior administration when he came into office in 1991. His transition task force labeled the state agency functional planning process a "disaster," and they called for its complete revision or abandonment.[73] Abandonment did not occur, but functional planning was replaced by strategic planning. The strategic approach to planning was codified into law during the 1992 legislative session, and all state agencies were required to make the switch.[74] A significant difference between a comprehensive plan and a strategic plan is that goals are often prioritized or at least given weights in the latter approach. Strategic plans are statements of the priority directions an agency will take to carry out its mission within the context of the state plan. State agency strategic plans are prepared with a five-year outlook and provide a framework for an agency's legislative budget request. Thus, state-level planning was subtly changed to include a growth management portion of the State Comprehensive Plan and agency planning was shifted to the strategic planning concept.

Regional-level Changes

Not so subtle was an attack on regional planning. Irritated by the role that regional planning councils (RPCs) play in areawide coordination and as lead agencies in administering the developments of regional impact review process, a coalition of local governments, farmers, and developers aggressively pressured the legislature to do away with regional planning. The coalition contended that RPCs are an unnecessary layer of bureaucracy due to the authority given to local governments and the Florida Department of Community Affairs by the Local Government Comprehensive Planning and Land Development Regulation Act.[75] The core of their argument was that RPCs have outlived their usefulness since almost all local governments by then had adopted comprehensive plans that had been found in compliance with the local planning act. This argument was successful in spearheading a bill to consider "sun setting" regional planning councils as of September 1, 1993.[76] The sunset review was to be undertaken by the Florida Advisory Council on Intergovernmental Relations (a legislative agency), in conjunction with ELMS III before being considered by the legislature. If the sun were allowed to set, the RPCs would have been stripped of their statutory growth management authority and funding.[77] In a separate but related legislative action, the Department of Community Affairs was directed to evaluate the developments of regional impact review (DRI) program and the comprehensive planning process, and to recommend whether the program should be replaced, repealed, or incorporated in whole or in part into the comprehensive planning process.[78] The agency was instructed to work with the ELMS III committee in making the evaluation.

The 1992 final report of the ELMS III committee proposed that the DRI program be terminated in the largest local government jurisdictions and replaced by an enhanced intergovernmental coordination element (ICE).[79] The thought was that since all local governments now had comprehensive plans, the intergovernmental coordination elements in larger (and assumedly well-staffed) jurisdictions could be broadened to ensure coordination with neighboring local governments regarding proposed developments that might impact more than one local government. However, the ELMS committee recognized that existing ICE requirements were weak and needed to be strengthened *before* DRI responsibilities could be incorporated into an ICE. Consequently, the 1993 legislature required that the DRI program not be terminated until 1997.[80]

Minor legislative and administrative improvements were made, but revisions to the ICE remained so controversial that the 1995 legislature directed the DCA to come up with recommendations by December of that year.[81] A technical committee appointed by the DCA reexamined the basic ideas behind the proposed changes; by their third meeting, serious questions were raised about the need to replace the DRI process.[82] The committee agreed that fitting the DRI review process into an ICE placed intergovernmental coordination and review too late in the process to result in meaningful improvements. In other words, the ICE element is a function of the plan preparation process, whereas a DRI review is part of the plan implementation process. The latter process is dependent on the guidelines provided by the first process, and therefore "follows" rather than occurs simultaneously. Hence, the technical committee recommended returning much of the ICE to its pre-ELMS III status and retaining the DRI process.[83] These recommendations were accepted and, other than for a few changes, everything fell back into its original place.[84] "In reality," according to Brian Teeple, chief executive officer of the Northeast Florida Regional Council, "the development community, wary of multiple jurisdictional enhanced ICE elements, opted to retain 'the devil they knew' in the DRI process."[85] Consequently, the legislature reinstated the DRI program in 1996.

Local-level Changes

A second prong of attack was directed at state government's imposition of planning requirements on local governments. "Growth management is damaging Florida's economy" became a straw man phrase for attacks, especially regarding state requirements placed upon local governments.

Among the more serious of these threats was that of Speaker of the Florida House of Representatives, T.K. Wetherell, who in 1992 told big city mayors that an answer to their money problems was to relax the growth management act.[86] Statements like this, when added to agitation of backlash groups, led to newspaper headlines such as, "Assault on Florida's future" (*Orlando Sentinel*), "Plot to kill growth management" (*Tampa Tribune*), and "Warning bells are ringing in the state's growth fight" (*St. Petersburg Times*).[87] The warning bells were ringing loud enough to encourage the introduction of eight bills designed to weaken or kill the local government growth management law. The Florida Chapter of the American Planning Association, in an issue of *Florida Planning* headlined the legislative session as "Growth Management Under Attack."[88] And indeed it was.

However, the allusion of growth as the cause of a depressed economy in Florida was blunted by retorts from observers such as Carol Taylor West, a University of Florida economist. She pointed out that growth management did not overbuild Florida, growth management did not pass the 1986 U.S. Tax Law, and growth management did not contribute to the failure of savings and loan organizations.[89] Nor, as revealed through media coverage, did growth management cause decreased home values in places like New Jersey and Massachusetts. More influential forces than growth management were causing the economic recession in Florida.

One of the more pervasive arguments for change was that which questioned the requirement for rural municipalities and counties to meet the same planning criteria as much larger cities and urban counties. The argument was persuasive because the concern about this issue was broadly based. In fact, state government officials were as concerned about the issue as were the representatives from rural areas. Under the leadership of Secretary William E. Sadowski, the Department of Community Affairs had already begun statewide hearings on revisions to Rule 9J-5.[90] A major segment of the proposed revisions dealt with ways to make the local comprehensive planning process easier for small counties and cities. Other proposed amendments pertained to urban sprawl, transportation concurrency management areas, concurrency management systems, and the processing of plan amendments.

Amending Rule 9J-5 was not enough for some rural counties, however, especially those in the Florida Panhandle. These counties apparently wished to have the same opportunity to develop as had rural south and central Florida counties before them. In other words, they preferred no, or very little, meaningful state involvement in local growth management. Spurred by a lawsuit initiated by Santa Rosa County against the DCA, opposition spread.[91] The suit, which centered on allowing growth in environmentally sensitive and traffic-congested areas, was settled when the DCA backed away from their initial rejection of the county's comprehensive plan. This resulted in what one opinion writer called "Sadowski's retreat," saying that, "The secretary may just be trying to defuse the anger in Santa Rosa, but the danger is that he will set off a much larger explosion."[92] The anger in this rural county was on display when buckets of tar and feathers greeted Sadowski when he arrived for a meeting with county officials one evening. Despite support of growth management from 1000 Friends of Florida and environmental groups,[93] opponents ignited enough of an outburst to add substantive amendments to a bill that was initially designed to make only non-controversial technical and procedural improvements to the local planning law.[94]

One of the substantive changes enacted by the legislature was that planning and development strategies, which address anticipated demands of continued urbanization of coastal and other environmentally sensitive areas, were permissible as long as they were *innovative*. The word "innovative" can cover a broad spectrum, however. In the earlier version of the law, urbanization of coastal areas (like barrier islands) and other environmentally sensitive areas had been discouraged. Now, innovative strategies that could facilitate the development of less populated regions of the state were allowed. The new language referred to innovative and flexible planning and development strategies and creative land use planning techniques as including urban villages, new towns, satellite communities, area-based allocations, clustering and open space provisions, mixed-use development, and sector planning. This broad interpretation of the term "innovative" has allowed some award winning developments, but at the same time, it has permitted development to extend sprawl and place irreversible urban-type demands on rural land and the natural environment along both the coast and inland areas.

The amendments also set up an optional plan amendment process that allowed local governments to avoid the burden of state sanctions when a plan amendment was found not in compliance with state requirements. This change altered the potency of the state's consistency requirement. Nevertheless, despite some success in weakening development management, the intergovernmental system was still in place. The strategic approach was now ingrained at the state and regional levels of planning, whereas the comprehensive approach continued to prevail at the local level. This appears to be a logical division of approaches. Nevertheless, some chinks in the armor of growth management had appeared and the state continued to be besieged with problems of growth that needed to be avoided or resolved. Yet, overall public support for development management remained relatively strong.

Summary

Changes were made to Florida's intergovernmental development management system in the 1990s. Some of them added needed flexibility, some appeared to erode the roles of state government and the regional planning councils, and some were just technical. The term "growth management" appeared to be losing some of its luster. When Joan, in a "Doonesbury" comic strip, asked Lacey why none of the young women today wants to be called a feminist, Lacey's response was, "Once a social transformation [e.g., growth management] is largely complete, the language that drove it loses both urgency and meaning."[95] This is a common phenomenon, terms become passé as they lose the excitement of newness—or as Lacey said, they lose their "urgency and meaning." In this time of change—and potential movement toward a slippery slope— the political scene was itself changing. The development management programs of previous administrations were gradually coming under siege.

The change to the political environment was just beginning during the brief period William Sadowski was secretary of DCA. Linda Shelley (1992-1995), who succeeded him after his death in an airplane crash, faced an increasing environment of change. Shelley was a Tallahassee attorney who had been vice-chair of the ELMS III committee. The rules to managing growth were under further stress by the time former 1000 Friends of Florida director Jim Murley became head of DCA in 1995. He was greeted not only by administrative and political change, but also by a bevy of natural disasters: forest fires, floods, and tornadoes. Murley remained in office until 1999, when he left to take over John DeGrove's position as executive director of the Joint Center for Urban and Environmental Problems at Florida Atlantic University/ Florida International University. Natural disasters and changes were to increase in intensity as the 1990s came to a close and the twenty-first century dawned.

NOTES FOR CHAPTER X

1   Colburn, David R. and Lance deHaven-Smith, *Government in the Sunshine State: Florida Since Statehood*, Gainesville, FL: University Press of Florida, 1999, p. 149.

2   DeGrove, John M., *Planning Policy and Politics, Smart Growth and The States*, Lincoln Cambridge, MA: Institute of Land Policy, 2005, p. 2.

3   Lorentz, Amalia and Kirsten Shaw, "What do builders, politicians, farmers, and environmentalists have in common? Amazingly, they're all talking about smart growth. ...,"*Planning* 56: 1990, pp. 5-9.

4   Duany, Andres, stated in an email message to Steven Seibert, secretary of the Florida Department of Community Affairs, January 23, 2007.

5   American Planning Association, *Planning Communities for the 21st Century*, Chicago: American Planning Association, 1994, p. 21. For a thorough recent history and discussion of Smart Growth, the seminal reference is DeGrove, ibid; also see Patricia E. Salkin, "Smart Growth at Century's End: The State of the States," *Urban Lawyer* 31, 3: 601-648, 1999.

6   James F. Murley, former secretary of the Florida Department of Community Affairs and currently director of Florida Atlantic University's Anthony James Catanese Center for Urban & Environmental Solutions, notes that smart growth at the state level was used to emphasize "a more strategic use of state infrastructure funding to support growth in target areas and to purchase environmentally sensitive lands." From an email message to Richard RuBino on December 10, 2007.

7   Roberts, Diane, *Dream State*, Gainesville: University Press of Florida, 2006, p. 312.

8   Murley, ibid.

9   RuBino, Richard G., "The Improbability of Attaining Sustainable Communities Without Urban Reform," a paper presented at the Annual Congress of the European Schools of Planning, Bergen, Norway, 1999. In a separate reference, James Murley (see Murley, ibid) recalls that when he was secretary of the Florida Department of Community Affairs, the agency made a significant effort in trying to sign joint agreements with some local governments on specified sustainable issues, but, "Unfortunately, the locals placed more weight on getting the oversight relief [from the department] and never really came to the table."

10   Much of this section is taken from Richard G. RuBino, "The chilling effect of Florida's private property rights protection act on growth management and environmental regulation," a paper presented to the

Land Tenure Center, North America Program, University of Wisconsin-Madison, June 1997.

11 Wolfe, Peter, *Land in America: Its Value, Use and Control*, New York: Pantheon Books, 1981, p. 86.

12 Ibid, p. 85.

13 Ibid, p. 81.

14 Jacobs, Harvey, ed., *Who Owns America? Conflict Over Property Rights*, Madison, WI: University of Wisconsin Press, 1998, pp. 40-41.

15 For example, see Peter Doherty, "The Unending Story of Property Rights Abuses," *Journal of the James Madison Institute*, Spring 2002, pp. 4-10.

16 Gallagher, Mary Lou, "Wise Use or Wise Marketing?" *Planning* 62: 1, 4-9, 1996.

17 Emerson, Kirk and Charles R. Wise, "Statutory approaches to regulatory takings: State property rights legislation issues and implications for public administration," *Public Administration Review* 57: 5, 1997, pp. 411-422.

18 Drummond, William (1585-1649), *The Oxford Dictionary of Quotations*, Oxford: Oxford University Press, 1979.

19 States that enacted so-called growth management legislation were: Florida, Georgia, Hawaii, Maine, New Jersey, Oregon, Rhode Island, Vermont, and Washington; states that enacted so-called smart growth legislation were: Arizona, California, Colorado, Delaware, Iowa, Illinois, Massachusetts, Minnesota, New Hampshire, New Mexico, New York, Ohio, Pennsylvania, Tennessee, Utah, Virginia, and Wisconsin.

20 Noonan, James T. and Gail Moran, "Implementation of Maryland's Economic Growth, Resource Protection, and Planning Act," *Environmental and Urban Issues* XXIII: 4, 1996, pp. 9-14.

21 Article 66B of the *Annotated Code of Maryland*.

22 Ibid.

23 Obtained from www.mdp.state.md.us/smartintro.htm on May 2, 2007.

24 Comprehensive Growth Policy Act of 1998, *Tennessee Public Chapter 1101*. The act does not apply to metropolitan governments like Nashville-Davidson County, however.

25 Obtained from http://eerc.ra.utk.edu/smart/chapter1.htm, on May 4, 2007.

26 Obtained from *NOAA News Online*, www.noaanews.noaa.gov/stories/s966.htm, on January 22, 2007. Andrew had originally been classified as a Category 4 hurricane on the Saffer-Simpson scale, but it was upgraded in 2002 by a review committee after a re-analysis of

the storm. It now is one of only three Category 5 storms to have struck the continental U.S.; the other two are the Florida Keys Hurricane in 1935 and Hurricane Camille in 1969.

27 Tropical storm Alberto (1994) was not classified as a hurricane, but it ranks 19th on the National Oceanic and Atmospheric Administrations's (NOAA) list of costliest tropical storms (which includes hurricanes) and 30th among the deadliest mainland tropical storms. Obtained from www.aoml.noaa.gov/hrd/ Landsea/deadly/, on May 10, 2007.

28 Compiled from "U.S. Hurricanes 1900-2000" (unadjusted), Tables 2, 3, and 4, at www..noaa.gov/ hrd/Landsea/deadly, on May 10, 2007.

29 Hampson, P.S., *Wetlands in Florida*, Florida Bureau of Geology Map Series 109, Tallahassee, 1984, referenced in Edward A. Fernald and Elizabeth D. Purdum, *Water Atlas of Florida*, Tallahassee: Institute of Science and Public Affairs, Florida State University, 1998, p. 78.

30 Barnett, Cynthia, *Mirage, Florida and the Vanishing Water of the Eastern U.S.*, Ann Arbor, Michigan: University of Michigan Press, 2007, p. 55.

31 Gannon, Michael, *The New History of Florida*, Gainesville: University Press of Florida, 1996, p. 427.

32 Ibid.

33 Pelham, Thomas G., "The Florida Experience: Creating a Comprehensive Planning Process," in Buchsbaum, Peter A. and Larry J. Smith eds., *State & Regional Comprehensive Planning: Implementing New Methods for Growth Management*, Washington, DC: American Bar Association, 1993, p. 105.

34 As of January 1992 the members of ELMS III were Clarence Anthony, Rick Bernhardt, Valerie Boyd, Linda Chapin, Seth Craine, Don Crane, Jr., Robert Davis, John DeGrove, Gail Easley, John Flicker, Rhoda Glasco, Casey Gluckman, Lex Hester, Maggy Hurchalla, John Infantino, Curt Kiser, Mary Kumpe, Ilene Lieberman, Carl Loop, Mel Maguire, Carrie Meek, Arsenio Milian, Jefferson Miller, Jon Mills, Jim Murley, Jack Osterholt, Sam Poole, Robert Rhodes, Kathy Rundle, Bill Sadowski, Linda Shelley (vice-chair), Jim Shimberg, Glenn Thomas, James Harold Thompson (chair), Alberto Vadia, Margaret Vizzi, Robert Wilhelm, Marlene Young, C. Fred Jones, and Peter Rudy Wallace. Ex-officio members were Carol Browner, Greg Farmer, Ben Watts, Bob Williams, and Virginia Wetherell.

35 Powell, David, "Managing Florida's Growth: The Next Generation," *Florida State University Law Review* 21: 2, 1993, p. 229.

36 Ibid, p. 233.

37 Ibid, p. 232 and ELMS III Report, recommendation 91, pp. 64-65.

38 Florida Department of Environmental Protection and the Florida Greenways Council, "Connecting Florida's Communities with Greenways and Trails," a summary report obtained from www.dep.state.fl.us/gwt on June 27, 2007.

39 Florida Department of Environmental Protection, *Final Report: Phase I*, prepared by the departments of Landscape Architecture and Urban and Regional Planning, University of Florida, memorandum from 1000 Friends of Florida Executive Director, James Murley, May 12, 1995, Appendix B.

40 Letter to The Honorable Lawton Chiles, signed by Richard A. Pettigrew, Chairman, October 1, 1995.

41 Preface to "South Florida: A Sustainable Vision For 2020, modified as of March 12, 2001.

42 DeGrove, John M., "Florida's Growth Management Legislation: 1969-2000," a paper prepared for the Richard E. Nelson Symposium on Florida's Growth Management Legislation, October 13, 2000, p. 11. The sustainable communities bill was HB 2705, in 1996.

43 Grosso, Richard, "Florida's Growth Management Act: How Far We Have Come and How Far We Have Yet to Go," *Nova Law Review* 20: 2, 1996, pgs. 591-659, pp. 658-659.

44 Governor's Commission for a Sustainable South Florida, 1995.

45 Schnidman, Frank, "Region Throws in the Towel on Eastward Ho!" *Palm Beach Daily Business Review*, June 8, 2005, obtained from www.floridacdc.org/articles/050617-1.html on June 2, 2007.

46 The land use battle over the Scripps' site occurred between 2003 and 2006, but it is covered here because of its relationship to one of the major goals of Eastward Ho!

47 Bowman, Janet, "County's attractions are obvious—at Bridger property," *South Florida Sun-Sentinel*, February 28, 2005.

48 Florin, Hector, "Planners face daunting task for tidy growth around Scripps," *The Palm Beach Post*, February 21, 2005, p. 1A.

49 Bowman, ibid.

50 A map of the area shows seventy acres of the Briger tract set aside for Phase II of the Scripps development.

51 § 30 of CS/SB 2474 (1998).

52 Florida Department of Transportation, *Transportation and Land Use Study Committee Recommendations*, January 15, 1999.

53 Telephone interview between Earl Starnes and Mark Glisson of the Bureau of State Lands in the Florida Department of Environmental Protection on January 28, 2007. Glisson reported on state lands acreage which today includes lands acquired before the Environmental Endangered Lands (EEL) legislation of 1972 and include EEL and

subsequent land acquisition initiatives of the state, water management districts and Florida Communities Trust.

54 Stephens, Kathryn, "Land-use group fights growth management," *Tallahassee Democrat*, May 11, 1992. The mission of this institute is to "restore the principles of the American Founding to their rightful, preeminent authority in our national life" Obtained from www.clearmont.org on May 25, 2007.

55 Powell, David L., Robert M. Rhodes, and Dan R. Stengle, "A Measured Step to Protect Private Property Rights," *Florida State University Law Review* 23: 2, 1995, p. 258.

56 Doherty, Peter, ibid, p. 7. The institute is "A Florida-based public policy organization dedicated to promoting economic freedom, limited government, federalism, traditional values ..." Obtained from www.jamesmadison.org on May 26, 2007.

57 § 70.001, *Florida Statutes*, hereafter called the Harris Act.

58 Henderson, Clay, "A dynamic opportunity to resolve land use disputes," *Environmental and Urban Issues* 23: 1, 1995, pgs. 23-24.

59 See Spohr, David, "Florida's takings law: a bark worse than its bite," *Virginia Environmental Law Journal* 16: 2, 1997, pp. 313-362.

60 Brigham, Toby, P., "The Harris Act—will it be enough?" *Environmental and Urban Issues* 23: 1, 1995, p. 21.

61 Downie, Robert C., II., "Property rights: Will exceptions become the rule?" *Florida Bar Journal* 64: 10, 1995, pp. 69-73.

62 Powell, et al, ibid.

63 RuBino, ibid, "The chilling effect of Florida's private property rights protection act ... ."

64 § 70.51, *Florida Statutes*.

65 Weaver, Ronald L., "Florida property rights protection: A background discussion and first year report card on the Bert J. Harris Act," presented at a seminar on regulatory takings, CLE International, Orlando, FL, June 5, 1995.

66 Powell, et al, ibid; see also Spohr, ibid, p. 326. Earl Starnes served on this commission.

67 Ch. 187, *Florida Statutes*.

68 Murley, James, "The 1992 legislative session: Time for a change?" *Foresight* 4: 3, 1992, pp. 1 and 12.

69 The Taxation and Budget Reform Commission was authorized under a 1988 revision to the state constitution. Its scope of responsibility is limited to budget, spending, and government operations (including planning). It met first in 1990, again in 1998, and will meet in 2007. Twenty-five members of the Taxation and Budget Reform Commission were named by Governor Charlie Crist (who took office in January 2007),

the President of the Senate, and Speaker of the House. The governor had eleven appointees and the president and speaker had seven each. Four others—members of the legislature—are ex officio members. This body has the authority to place questions on the state election ballot without legislative approval, including a question regarding the process of state-level planning.

70 Bosselman, Fred, "A Role for State Planning," *Journal of Law and Public Policy* 12, 2, University of Florida, 2001, p. 328.
71 Powell, "Managing Florida's Growth: The Next Generation," ibid, p. 240.
72 Ibid.
73 Porter, Douglas R., "Issues in State and Regional Growth Management," in Porter, ed., *State and Regional Initiatives for Managing Development: Policy Issues and Practical Concerns*, Washington, DC: The Urban Land Institute, 1992, p. 175.
74 CS/HB 497 (1992).
75 Ch. 163 Part II, *Florida Statutes*.
76 HB 1061 (1992). See Powell, David L., "Managing Florida's Growth: The Next Generation," ibid, for a review of this sun-setting proposal.
77 As noted by Brian Teeple, executive director of the Northeast Florida Regional Council, since most RPCs were organized under the Intergovernmental Cooperation Act of 1969 (Chapter 163, *Florida Statutes*) and created by interlocal agreements among participating counties, the RPCs could have continued as councils of government. The loss of state funding for growth management activities would have reduced the budgets of most RPCs by only a small percentage, since most of their funding comes from specialized federal programs (e.g., small business loan programs, maternal and child health care, domestic security) and other sources.
78 SB 1882 (1992).
79 Florida Department of Community Affairs, "The Intergovernmental Coordination Element: Report of the Technical Committee and the Department of Community Affairs," December 1995, p. 2. Section 163.3177(6)(h), *Florida Statutes*, addresses intergovernmental coordination element requirements.
80 Ibid.
81 Ibid, p. 3.
82 Ibid, p. 4.
83 Ibid.
84 In 1996, HB 2705 deleted the process for termination of developments of regional impact (DRIs).
85 Teeple, Brian, stated in email comments to RuBino on January 3, 2008.

86 Wetherell, T.K., in a presentation to the mayors of Florida's largest cities, in February 1992.

87 *Orlando Sentinel*, March 3, 1992; *Tampa Tribune*, March 26, 1992; and *St. Petersburg Times*, January 26, 1992.

88 Florida Chapter of the American Planning Association, "Growth Management Under Attack," *Florida Planning* IV, 1992, pgs. 1, 4, and 11.

89 West, Carol Taylor, remarks made to the ELMS III committee, in Tallahassee, on March 19, 1992.

90 Rule 9J-5, *Florida Administrative Code*.

91 Taken from an opinion editorial in the *St. Petersburg Times*, January 17, 1992 (author unidentified).

92 *St. Petersburg Times*, opinion editorial, January 17, 1992.

93 McKay, Patricia S., "Planning for Rural Florida: What's the Point?" in "Plan Review," c. 1992, pp. 4 and 10.

94 Senate Bill 1882 (1992).

95 Trudeau, Garry, "Doonesbury," as appeared in the *Asheville Citizen-Times* of July 16, 2006.

CHAPTER XI

ON A DOWNWARD SLOPE

Late 1990s to 2007

History is past politics, and politics present history.[1] (Sir J.E.B. Seely, a close friend of Winston Churchill.)

AND THE BEAT GOES ON. As we mentioned earlier, during the Scopes "monkey trial," which was over eighty years ago, a truck drove up and down the main street of Dayton, Tennessee, carrying signs advertising land for sale in Tampa, Florida. Despite the passing of eight decades, speculation in land development is still a dominant pursuit in Florida, though the medium of advertising has changed. When you turned on your television in 2006, you could see and hear Mel Tillis, country music star, smiling and saying, "Welcome to Steinhatchee, the best kept secret in Florida, a piece of paradise."[2] He then went on to say, "Come buy a piece of paradise, before it is gone." Thus, we can say goodbye to the *former* best kept secret in Florida—and say goodbye to "paradise" at the same time.

Though growth may be inevitable, even in out-of-the-way Steinhatchee, it need not be destructive. As President Eisenhower said in his farewell address to the American people,

> As we peer into society's future, we—you and I, and our government—must avoid the impulse to live only for today, plundering, for our own ease and convenience, the precious resources of tomorrow. We cannot mortgage the material assets of our grandchildren without risking the loss also of their political and spiritual heritage. We want democracy to survive for all generations to come,

not to become the insolvent phantom of tomor-row.[3]

Much of the development in Florida thrives on the impulse of making money today—right now! Future generations of Floridians, take heed, you may have to pay for the over-indulgent developments of today. But growth does not need to be as expensive to the public as we make it. Growth can be accommodated without plundering precious natural resources and without excessive cost to society, but it is becoming more difficult to accommodate with each passing year.

Entering the 21st Century

Paradises were being lost across the nation as the 21st century dawned. Multiple-lane highways and other so-called advances are making paradises more accessible. The continued urban and ex-urban sprawl put ever-increasing strain on provision of public services and threatened natural resources.[4] Problems mounted: a major blackout in the northeastern United States in 2003; severe hurricane strikes on intensive coastal development; and severe droughts or floods, perhaps associated with global warming. Our climate is changing, and so is the physical world it encompasses. Future conditions will require far wiser land management practices than we have used to date.

The U.S. Census Bureau estimated that almost 300 million people lived in the United States as of 2006, an increase of almost 18 million in the first six years of the new millennium. In terms of percent increase, most of this growth is occurring in the southeastern states and in a northwestward-tending band running from Texas to the state of Washington.[5] Rapid growth is expected to continue in these states.

With growth comes costly urban sprawl, because we have a national road system with access to anywhere. And "anywhere" is where land is cheaper, development regulations are minimal, and huge profits can be made. Sprawl in America is not restricted to the ever-enlarging rings of metropolitan areas: close observation will disclose forerunners of sprawl beginning to appear in heretofore relatively low density locations such as the coastline of Maine, the North Carolina mountains, the lakes of Minnesota and Wisconsin, the eastern slope of the Rocky Mountains in Montana, some of the once isolated valleys of Utah and Wyoming, and the Saguaro cactus lands of southeastern Arizona. Growth is welcomed—until rising land values and increasing taxes chase long-time, less affluent residents out and private and public infrastructure costs (e.g., water, roads, and schools) begin to weigh heavily. Many people fail to recognize that current residents, as well as new residents share the weight or cost of growth.

In a study of the cost of alternative development patterns, James E. Frank, professor of urban and regional planning at Florida State University, found that although many people prefer suburban or rural residential locations:

> ... such preferences are often partially subsidized by revenue paid from other area residents and business and from intergovernmental fund transfers. Development in these locations do not always pay their full share of the costs for providing their off-site public facilities and services.[6]

In growing communities, public service costs usually grow at a faster rate than tax revenues. In this situation, said one writer, "citizens are often asked to pay through higher tax rates,"[7] a situation that has contributed to a property tax problem in Florida.

Development Management Activities
in States and Regions across the Nation

The degree of new activity in land use reform has been replaced by a period of some advances and some retractions. A few states and regions have gone in new directions: for example, Georgia, with a strong push from the federal government, established a hopefully powerful regional program in the Atlanta metropolitan area and Wisconsin updated its antiquated planning law.[8] On the other hand, voters in Oregon virtually brought their nationally noted statewide growth management program to a standstill and Florida was on a slow slide of easing state government involvement in growth management.

As the Atlanta metropolitan area sprawled outward, "growing from 65 miles from north to south in 1990 to 110 miles in 1998,"[9] its traffic woes mounted. Atlanta has become known as the city that sold its soul to the car.[10] Consequently, the U.S. Environmental Protection Agency declared Atlanta out of compliance on ozone standards and thus ineligible for more money for new highway projects. This forced Atlanta to declare war on its urban problems because the EPA gave it no choice.[11] The Metro Atlanta Chamber of Commerce lobbied hard for a metropolitan solution; their conviction and strength resulted in the Georgia legislature creating the Georgia Regional Transportation Authority in 1999.[12] The governor appoints the members of this state-created body, which has sweeping authority over land use and transportation decision-making in the eleven-county metropolitan area, yet, like the Cape Cod Commission, seems reluctant to use its power.

In the Midwest, Wisconsin updated its local planning legislation in 1999 by redefining the content of a comprehensive plan and updating its process of plan preparation and adoption. Beginning in 2010, zoning and subdivision programs of communities must be consistent with their comprehensive plans. However, Richard A. Lehmann, a nationally known Wisconsin land use attorney, points out that the law does not clearly state that every community conducting land use regulatory programs must have a comprehensive plan. This, coupled with inadequate funding to support plan preparation and reliance on litigation to enforce the consistency mandate (rather than state government enforcement), may make the consistency rule a weak mandate.[13] By 2007, only three years short of the 2010 deadline, less than a third of the local governments had completed plans under the 1999 law. This well-intended Wisconsin law appears similar in some ways to Florida's unsuccessful local planning law of 1975.

Oregon suffered a setback in land use control when, in 2004, its land conservation and development program was abolished by Measure 37, a citizen initiative designed to roll back Oregon's land use protection laws. Under the measure, a regulation that reduces the dollar value of a property may be waived unless the owner is compensated for the economic loss.[14] By 2006, almost 6,400 claims had been submitted to the Oregon Department of Land Conservation and Development, totaling many billions of dollars for compensation,[15] but state and local governments have been hard pressed to find the money to cover all these requests. According to the Sightline Institute, "Taxpayers seldom have the resources to pay claims, so the laws simply get waived instead."[16] The institute says this is unfortunate because before Measure 37, "Oregon cities have flourished while they sprawled less rapidly and consumed fewer farms and forests than similarly sized cities in neighboring states."[17]

In an editorial, the *Oregonian*, Portland's leading newspaper, charged that Measure 37 "wasn't so much about righting wrongs as it was about razing farms and forest and enriching developers."[18] Advocates of wise conservation and development of land responded to this issue by initiating Ballot Measure 49 to moderate Measure 37 by clarifying the right to build homes, limiting large developments, and protecting farms, forests, and groundwater. This statewide measure modifying Measure 37 was approved by the voters of Oregon in November 2007.

In 2006, six other Western states surfaced initiatives similar to Oregon's Measure 37, although the measures were defeated in three of the states: California, Idaho, and Washington. Only Arizona approved its initiative, whereas measures in Montana and Nevada were invalidated by their state supreme courts.[19]

When someone mentions regional planning in Florida, it is usually in reference to one of its eleven regional planning councils, partners—albeit restrained partners—in the state's intergovernmental development management system. Yet, a new type of regional entity is surfacing; an entity "genetically" similar to the Regional Plan Association of the New York City metropolitan area (see Chapter III). At the forefront of this initiative is the ULI Florida Committee for Regional Cooperation, sponsored by the Urban Land Institute, located in Washington, DC. The purpose of the committee is "to identify what the State of Florida can do to promote regional collaboration to ensure the future economic competitiveness and livability of Florida and its communities."[20] The thirty-seven member committee is co-chaired by Peter S. Rummell and Nathaniel P. Reed; Rummell is CEO of the St. Joe Company, a development corporation, and Reed formerly served as environmental advisor to Florida governors Claude Kirk and Reubin Askew.[21]

After a year of fact-finding, the committee found that among the factors contributing to a lack of shared regional identities, visions, and goals are:

- the intense competition among cities and counties for development;
- current state and local governmental structures do not accommodate effective regional approaches; and

- regional programs and regional planning councils lack dedicated funding sources.[22]

Given this negative situation for successful regionalism, the report says, "Strong state leadership, starting with the governor, and a demonstrated statewide commitment to regional cooperation are essential."[23] The report goes on to recommend that state government "should allocate funds to support regional cooperation," and "there must be a change in the status quo that rewards local thinking."[24] The latter recommendation supports our concern about unbridled localism. Yet, what this overall, private-public regional collaboration means to Florida's current regional planning councils remains to be seen.

Florida: Still Growing, but With Indications of Increasing Outflow

The U.S. Census Bureau estimates Florida's 2006 population as being over eighteen million people, an addition of more than two million people since the census six years earlier. Florida probably will become the third most populous state in the nation before the end of the decade. Its 11.3 percent rate of growth since 2000 is greater than any of the other three most populated states: California, Texas, and New York. Florida probably may never catch—nor want to catch—California and Texas. Even more startling is that Florida's population growth over the *last twenty-five years* equals that of its entire population growth in the prior 142 years since 1845, the year it attained statehood.[25]

The Sunshine State continues on its lemming-like path toward massive population growth, urban and ex-urban sprawl, and loss of agricultural land and environmental resources. In the early 2000s, housing prices soared, the separation between income levels widened, and natural disasters took greater tolls than ever before. Problems of growth continued to weigh down Florida.

Florida has about 1,800 miles of coastline, all of it susceptible to hurricane strikes. From 2000 to 2006, seven hurricanes slammed into the state: Charley, Frances, Ivan, and Jeanne in 2004, and Dennis, Katrina, and Wilma in 2005.[26] The greatest period of activity was between August 13 and September 26, 2004, when four hurricanes struck parts of Florida. The first three resulted in the loss of 81 lives and $15-22 billion in *insured* damages.[27] The Federal Emergency Management Agency reports that the $860 million paid for national flood insurance program claims for Hurricane Ivan was greater than any other Florida disaster.[28] The great majority of these claims were from the coastal area. How often does this lesson need to be repeated? How many devastating hurricanes will it take before *truly* strong coastal land use controls or a coastal land purchase program is put in place?

Jeff Parker, cartoonist; permission granted by Bob Stover of Florida Today.

"Feed me! Feed me!" cries the growth monster.[29] Some land developers persist in their craving to over-develop fragile, storm-prone barrier islands. Briny Breezes is one such place. A proposal to intensely develop the island brought Thomas B. Evans, Jr., a former U.S. congressman from Delaware and now chair of the Florida Coalition for Preservation, to write that, "We must not play Russian roulette with people's lives and property."[30] He used the community of Briny Breezes, in Palm Beach County, as an example:

> The tiny South Florida town of Briny Breezes sits on just 600 feet of barrier island sand fronting the Atlantic Ocean. Today it's a quiet collection of single-story structures. ... Developers have proposed to jam tiny Briny Breezes with multiple high rise towers housing 900 condominium units, 300 timeshare units, a 349-room luxury hotel, restaurants, retail shops, parking facilities and a yacht marina—all on an environmentally fragile hurricane-vulnerable barrier island. ... That's why intensive, high-density over-development on our state's fragile, storm-prone barrier islands is risky at best and grossly negligent at worst.[31]

This scenario continues to be played along much of Florida's coastline.

Serious questions about the costs of over-developing (or improper development) along the coastline are being raised by residents of Florida's interior. Many of them feel their own taxes and insurance fees should not be used to help bailout coastal properties damaged by hurricanes. Evans succinctly points to this when he writes:

> Unfortunately, Florida taxpayers actually end up subsidizing such development by the coverage

extended by the state-supported Citizens Property Insurance Corporation that often grants coverage to new beachfront developments—even when risk-wary private insurance companies refuse to offer coverage. This irresponsible policy is made possible by the fact that even if a hurricane inflicts massive damage costing billions of dollars, taxpayers will always be there to provide a bailout for the system. The spirit of Citizens was meant to protect Floridians and enable homeowners to buy needed property insurance. It was not to enable irresponsible coastal development where it clearly does not belong.[32]

Unfortunately, prudent words like these fall upon denying ears.

Though hurricanes are more subdued once they track inland, the interior of the Florida peninsula also experiences their wrath. On the other hand, inland areas have their own special form of hazard: wildfires brought on by droughts. These conflagrations, even more common to Florida than hurricanes, have hit hard in recent years, causing major damage to homes and property. Forty-three fire management assistance declarations occurred between 1998 and 2001, a major wildfire raged in 2006,[33] and scores of wildfires spread through Florida during the drought of spring 2007. As buildup occurs in the interior of Florida more and more acres of residential and business development will be subject to this threat.

Given the losses from natural disasters, it is not surprising to find many retired and even pre-retirement Floridians making permanent moves to upstate Georgia and the mountains of North Carolina. As *Florida Trend* magazine journalist Cynthia Barnett wrote, in North Carolina's "cloud-laded mountains, Florida history is repeating itself in a dozen different ways."[34] For many Floridians, the prevailing reason for leaving is that the Florida they knew before is not the

Florida they know today. According to a newspaper report, "United Van Lines Inc. said for the first time in thirty years it moved more people out of Florida than in."[35] On another front, the Florida Senate Education Pre-Kl-12 Appropriations Committee reported that 2006-2007 was the first year to have declining enrollment since 1982-83.[36] These incidents may be only bumps in the road to further growth or they may be a harbinger that growth may not be quite as rampant as it has been for the past sixty years. A 2007 report referring to Standard & Poors' Case-Shiller Home Price Index lists five major housing markets in Florida as being among the thirteen riskiest markets in the United States.[37] This, too, may merely be a bump in Florida's economy, but the bumps may be adding up.

A Change in Political Ideology

As stated in the preface quotation to this chapter, "History is past politics, and politics present history."[38] This certainly holds true for the history of planning in Florida: its history has rested occasionally in the hands of progressive political will, but far more often as a handmaiden to political whims. Where, within these extremes, today's political actions (or inactions) will rest is dependent on the path of present history.

Florida state government still operates under a plural executive structure, even though the number of members in the elected cabinet has decreased. A state constitutional revision in 1998 reduced the cabinet from six to three members, effective in 2002. The cabinet now consists of the chief financial officer, attorney general, and commissioner of agriculture. Despite the reduction in cabinet members, the governor continues to be faced with a significant amount of shared policy-making: the Governor and Cabinet still jointly administer control of twelve state agencies.[39] The cabinet system "creates a power imbalance between the legislative and executive branches," argue David R. Colburn and Lance deHaven-Smith; this, they say, makes "it difficult for Florida to rise above regional concerns and address the long-term needs of the state as a whole."[40] A point to remember.

Working within a plural executive did not seem to hinder Governor John E. (Jeb) Bush (1999-2007), however. After eight years in office, this former land developer and former secretary of the Florida Department of Commerce under Governor Robert Martinez gained a reputation as being perhaps the most powerful governor since Andrew Jackson.[41] As author S.V. Dáte noted, "Generally what Jeb wanted, Jeb got, both in terms of actual policy objectives as well as the expansion of his own power."[42]

Still Functioning, but Accompanied by Subtle Dismantling

Governor Bush stepped into office intent on reducing the scale and influence of state government in general, including its oversight role in Florida's intergovernmental development management system. His strategy was to work toward a "smaller, more efficient government."[43] His approach was to privatize as many state government functions as possible, do away with certain programs or render them ineffective through attrition of personnel, and move 16,000 state employees into a classification that could allow them to be fired at will. In addition, he assumed the growth management system was not working and opted to devolve "the power down to local governments."[44] The intergovernmental development management system was under attack, and the Florida Department of Community Affairs (DCA) was to play a lead role in making changes.

The man chosen to do the job at DCA was Steven M. Seibert, a county commissioner from Pinellas County, who had played a major role in quelling a water war in the Tampa Bay area. Four years later (2003), Seibert was replaced by

Colleen Castille, who after a year became secretary of the Florida Department of Environmental Protection. Prior to these appointments, Castille had been the governor's chief cabinet aide. In 2004, Thaddeus Cohen, an architect from Palm Beach County and a member of Governor Bush's Growth Management Study Commission, replaced her. Cohen remained in office until Governor Bush's tenure ended in 2007.

During Governor Bush's two terms, he made a number of attempts to defuse the growth management system, but after being deflected, he set a strategy for taking tangential and incremental steps toward a makeover. This included severe cuts in funding and staffing of the DCA.[45] So, even here, Jeb got what he wanted. Nonetheless, he appeared to learn eventually that a state role in certain aspects of growth management had value, and he supported things like school concurrency. His philosophy was if a local government wants new schools and roads in outlying areas, then *they* should pay for the infrastructure to support them, otherwise the state should reject their requests to amend their land use plans.[46]

With a new governor in the executive office and a legislature controlled by members of the same party, it appeared that Florida's intergovernmental development management system was about to face a major overhaul. Was the system truly not working? Specifically what types of changes should be made? Were the citizens less supportive of growth management than they had been in 1985? These questions and others generated a spate of surveys directed at finding answers.

Secretary Seibert was determined to "revise how we deal with growth" and restructure the process of growth management.[47] Given similar, if not even stronger, determination by the governor and legislators, supporters of the existing growth management process feared that state oversight of growth management might be eliminated or, short of this, that there would be less involvement by state government. This, they assumed, would give local communities more control over their development (as they had prior to 1985). Yet, the administration's determination would be more difficult to achieve than anticipated.

Seibert was interested in reforming the growth management system because he felt that, "the same issues that led to the enactment of this [growth management] law continue to burden us today."[48] But since he was a fair-minded man and a born mediator, he wanted affirmation about what needed to be reformed. His own principles for reform turned out to be: leave matters of local concern to the local governments, delineate and vigorously protect interests and resources of state concern, improve citizen access to the system, and improve intergovernmental coordination.[49] Perhaps helping him to shape these principles were the responses to a 38-question survey designed to provide input for reevaluating Florida's growth management laws.[50]

Thousand of copies of the survey, conducted in 1999, were sent by the department to individuals and organizations throughout Florida.[51] The recipients included statewide associations, local governments, legislators and their staffs, developers, environmental groups, and citizens at large. The survey also was available on the department's website. Over 3,600 responses were received, a surprisingly high rate of return. The high return possibly reflected the fact that most copies of the survey were distributed to people or organizations closely involved in growth management. Standing out among the results was the belief that the general quality of life in Florida had changed for the worse and that the most serious problems were traffic congestion, urban sprawl, loss of wildlife and habitat, and limited water supplies.[52] In addition, many respondents felt that Florida governments were ineffective in addressing growth management issues. Furthermore, the survey showed there was broad support for providing incentives for *redevelopment*, as well as support for strengthening the links between transportation and land use, and that it was very important for the DCA to protect identified state interests. As Secretary Seibert reported, "They [the respondents] support a strong, wide-ranging role for the state, and expanded access for citizens."[53] The survey was not intended to be a scientific evaluation of public opinion, but it did succeed in receiving input from people and organizations most involved in growth management. Nonetheless, the support for the concept of growth management may have surprised the governor and his administration.

Step two in Seibert's review process was to conduct a series of regional forums throughout the state to gather additional public input on possible reforms. The results of the forums confirmed those of the statewide survey. During early 2000, Florida's eleven regional planning councils and the Department of Community Affairs hosted twenty-two forums in thirteen cities. Nearly 2,000 people attended the forums with more than one-quarter of them making statements to the secretary.[54] Speakers advocating less state control over local issues were in the minority, and most of the participants expressed concern that uncontrolled growth was still adversely affecting their quality of life. Listed in descending order, the most frequent views were that: state oversight should be strengthened; citizen involvement should be improved; regional planning councils should be strengthened to act as arms of the state; affordable housing, community revitalization, and mixed-use development should continue to be emphasized; agriculture and natural resources should be protected, while improving economic development in rural areas; intergovernmental coordination needed improving; and attention should be given to coordination among state departments to combat urban sprawl.

A few months later, 1000 Friends of Florida sponsored a telephone survey, the purpose of which was to measure awareness of Floridians to changes in growth management policy being considered by the legislature in 2000. The survey of 439 people, contacted by random digit dialing, found that "public opinion runs strongly counter to the changes in growth management policy currently being contemplated by the Legislature."[55] The respondents were particularly opposed to making it easier for developers to build new projects and making it harder for citizens to challenge new development, both items were under consideration by the legislature.

The surveys sponsored by the DCA and 1000 Friends of Florida uncovered considerable support for growth management, but how did this compare to citizen attitudes in the year the Local Government Comprehensive Planning and Land Development Regulation Act was initiated? This question was addressed in a study conducted by Tim Chapin and Charles Connerly.[56] From a representative sample of 983 residents taken in 1985 and 1,085 in 2001, the two urban and regional planning professors from Florida State University found that overall support for a state government role in managing growth slipped from 75.5 percent in 1985 to 63.7 percent in 2001. As the authors noted, however, in 1985 the growth management law was new and unblemished; it was "a vision of 'good planning' that had yet to be spoiled by the realities of day-to-day implementation." Nevertheless, this survey confirmed the findings of the previous two reports in that Florida's citizens still perceived growth to be a problem and that there was still substantial support for managing growth.

Growth Management Study Commission

A change in administration meant it was time for another review of Florida's intergovernmental development management system, so it was natural that Governor Bush appointed a Growth Management Study Commission (GMSC) in 2000. He charged it with assessing "the current effectiveness of the [growth management] system ... at all levels of government, to determine what revisions are needed to provide incentives for urban redevelopment, to give local government more flexibility to achieve state goals, and to reduce the complexity of the regulatory and enforcement process for citizens and localities."[57] The commission consisted of twenty-three voting members, chaired by former Orange County Commission Chair Mel Martinez.[58] "The governor clearly indicated to us that he would support less command and control in the growth process," Martinez said later.[59] Thus, the focus of their work was set. However, the commission would not be given much time: work was to be completed within six months, the completion date occurring just before the beginning of the 2001 legislative session in March.

Governor Bush said the focus should not be on managing growth, "It should be how do we create more livable communities ... make urban core areas more livable, more exciting ... and then the marketplace will help us achieve what we want.[60] He also felt it was "important to look at the funding of all this as well, because if we design a new system ... and we still have this issue about how we fund our infrastructure, we may be in trouble." Taking steps like these he believed would "free up some time and energy for the State to play more of a positive role, more of a mediator, more of a facilitator, more of a planning role, perhaps, than it is today." Within these statements lay charges not only to the commission, but also to the Florida Department of Community Affairs. These charges shaped the mission of the department as long as Bush remained in office. Martinez must have foreseen this when he told the commission, "There seems to be a sense that the proper role of DCA in the future is one of technical assistance."[61] This set the stage for subtle dismantling of the oversight responsibilities of the department.

Completing their final report within the timeframe allotted, the commission noted that the growth management process then in place should remain fully in effect. In general, their recommendations fell into eight categories: (1) revise the State Comprehensive Plan, (2) focus state review of local comprehensive plan amendments on those that involve compelling state interests (primarily in regard to disaster preparedness, natural resources, and transportation), (3) implement regional cooperation agreements for developments with extra-jurisdictional impacts, (4) develop a uniform methodology for reviewing the costs and benefits of local land use decisions, (5) require local government to adopt a financially feasible public school facilities element, (6) authorize incentives for an effective urban revitalization policy, (7) develop an incentive-based state rural policy, and (8) empower citizens to better participate in the process.[62] Many of these recommendations sounded similar to recommendations made by past commissions. Conspicuously missing was a recommendation to provide financial support for local government to relieve their infrastructure backlog.

These eight general headings were relatively palatable, but some of the eighty-nine specific recommendations within these categories caused considerable controversy. Even one of the commission's members reacted negatively to some of the recommendations in the final report. In explaining his reluctant, but nevertheless no vote on the final report, commission member Charles Lee, senior vice-president of Audubon of Florida, said one of his primary concerns was that linkage of school construction funding was "severely watered down by an amendment which requires that school boards ... exhaust all reasonable options to provide adequate facilities before a local government may reject or delay approval of a plan amendment or rezoning which increases residential density or intensity..."[63] Another of his objections was a "(l)ack of clear provisions recommending better protection for natural resources of 'compelling state interest', once these are defined." He expressed his final point as: "[I]n a sudden and unexpected move an amendment was inserted into the

Rural Lands portion of the report which appears to potentially preclude any density reductions from current levels at all by local governments." The governor expressed his disappointment in Lee's position, but commission member Paul Bradshaw responded angrily, "I thought your vote illuminated the self-defeating pathos that typifies the environmental movement: no deal is ever good enough, and given the choice between reasonable compromise and an inferior status quo that justifies your whining, you'll take the status quo every time."[64] Lee responded that he was not opting for the status quo merely that the commission's recommendations did not go far enough.[65] This possibly meant that the three recommendations had become *too compromised* to be effective.

Outside the commission, general reaction was guardedly congratulatory, though some groups expressed concern. For example, 1000 Friends of Florida, though supportive of many of the recommendations, expressed considerable unease over others. Among its concerns were the recommendations dealing with less State involvement in community planning and taking the state out of the mediation role on planning challenges by giving the responsibilities to already under-funded regional planning councils without increased funding. Others on their worry list were the narrowness of the scope of full cost accounting (i.e., because it excluded categories like the environment, natural resources, and social issues); the commission's failure to recommend funding needed to address backlogs for schools and infrastructure; its failure to finalize incentives to promote urban redevelopment and infill; ignoring the call to lower housing densities in rural areas; and a concern about providing density bonuses in rural areas which would make it more expensive for state government to purchase development rights.[66] The commission's attention seemed more focused on rural development than on urban redevelopment and infill—possibly because leaders of emerging growth coalitions felt there was greater profit to be made in the future from rural development than urban redevelopment and infill.

Century Commission for a Sustainable Florida

In 2005, the legislature created a Century Commission for a Sustainable Florida. Rick Baker, mayor of the City of St. Petersburg, chairs the commission, which has fourteen other members.[68] Steve Seibert, who had resigned his position as secretary of the DCA, is the executive director. Seibert's stance on sustainability is aptly put, "A sustainable Florida is one where our children and their children will desire to stay."[69] More broadly, the responsibilities of the commission are to envision Florida's future, develop a shared image of developed and natural areas, focus on essential state interests, serve as a repository of community-building ideas, and annually provide recommendations addressing growth management to the governor, the president of the senate, and the speaker of the house.[70]

One of the research projects the commission initiated during their first year was a project that reviewed twenty-nine earlier surveys regarding citizen attitudes toward growth management. Tim Chapin and Heather Khan of Florida State University undertook this encompassing study. The results showed that Florida citizens still had substantial concerns with the pace of growth, perceived the state's growth as negatively affecting the state and slowly compromising their quality of life, and that they also had concerns over transportation, environmental quality, provision of education, and the management of growth issues.[71] Other findings showed citizens were unhappy with the progress of government in managing growth and mitigating its impacts, and that there was a willingness to pay for amenities that contributed to the quality of life. This study and others provided the commission with a foundation for understanding the status of growth management in Florida. However, other people were not satisfied with the pace of the commission; they felt that action is needed now, not in terms of the 25 and 50-year time horizons assigned to the commission.

Recent Major Events

Threatening clouds loomed over Florida's intergovernmental development management system as the old millennium came to a close and the 21st century began. Growth management was not as effective in managing growth as people had hoped. Some people took this as a reason—or opportunity—to do away with growth management, whereas others wanted to try to find ways to improve the system. The early years of the first new decade were witness to a struggle, a struggle wherein the growth management system appeared to be gradually losing ground.

Legislative Changes to Chapter 163, *Florida Statutes*

Things looked bad for growth management. The governor was less than supportive and many legislators had soured on state oversight of local planning. In 2000, Representative George Albright led the attack by introducing a bill intended to reduce severely the review authority of the Department of Community Affairs.[72] The bill was designed to speed up the state review process and let local elected officials decide for themselves how much growth they could manage. This would have returned state-local planning relationships to where they were prior to 1985. The bill was threatening, but in the face of well-organized opposition, it failed to be enacted.

Representative Albright was term-limited out of office in 2001, but the attack on growth management was renewed: some of the recommendations from the Growth Management Study Commission surfaced in bill form.[73] Growth management's watchdog organization, 1000 Friends of Florida, called the 2001 proposal a "bad" bill.[74] They admitted the bill contained some good provisions, but they listed thirteen objectionable items, including "DRI exemptions for airports, marinas, and petroleum storage facilities ... a good idea, known as Rural Land Stewardship Areas, is promising but relies on local government control through a plan amendment process to achieve success ... school siting [is still] allowed to continue sprawl development patterns." As in the year before, supporters of growth management were able to thwart action on the bill, but the objectionable items would return later.

It was reported that since Governor Bush was not successful in getting the legislature to change the planning laws, his administration, "behind the scenes," was moving forward anyway by setting a goal for the DCA to "reduce the number of [local plan amendment] reviews by 50% by January 1, 2002."[75] Richard Grosso, general counsel for the Environmental & Land Use Law Center, and Charles Pattison, executive director of 1000 Friends of Florida, were suspicious. Grosso expressed it this way: "I see them trying to rewrite the Growth Management Act without actually doing so."[76] With a similar concern, Pattison felt, "they are chipping away at regulatory oversight."[77] "Gov. Jeb Bush's response to Florida's fast growth has been to cut funding and staff for the state's growth management agency," reported another source.[78] The rewriting and chipping away at growth management would continue throughout the years of the Bush administration.

Nevertheless, with the cooperation of the growth management community, a bill was enacted in 2002.[79] Two particularly critical features of the new law addressed school and water supply planning. Thenceforth, local comprehensive plans were to incorporate a potable water element, including a ten-year work plan for water facilities; this was intended to improve integration with the water supply plans of water management districts. Coordination between local governments and school boards was to be facilitated by an intergovernmental agreement prior to the preparation of a coordinated public educational facilities element. Among other things, the new law established a planning certification program for local governments with a history of good planning practices, which would allow them to plan with less State and regional oversight. This program succeeded the Sustainable Communities Pilot Project of 1996.[80] The new legislation also provided a new judicial review and optional special master process for challenges to the consistency of a development order with a local comprehensive plan. Cari L. Roth, then general counsel at DCA, and Laura J. Feagin called the changes more evolutionary than revolutionary.[81]

The new judicial review and optional special master process was in response to a 2002 decision by the Florida Supreme Court to let an appellate court decision stand, in *Pinecrest Lakes, Inc. v. Shidel*.[82] The suit arose after a developer obtained approval from the Martin County Commission to change a site plan from 29 single-family homes (at one unit per acre density) to 136 rental units in 19 two-story buildings (at a density of 6.6 units per acre). The site was adjacent to the home of Karen Shidel and other single-family homeowners who objected to the change in the intensity of land use from that shown in the comprehensive plan. The case was initially decided in favor of the developer, but upon appeal, that decision was overruled.

Reacting to the ruling by the appellate court, Tom Pelham, former secretary of the Florida Department of Community Affairs, wrote, "The Court observed that the consistency requirement [in the local growth management law] is a statutory command to local governments to comply with their own comprehensive plans...."[83] Adding to this, Richard Grosso noted that the appeals court "ruled that the integrity of a citizen's right to enforce a comprehensive plan prevails over the financial loss to a developer who acted in 'bad faith' in an attempt to preclude the Court's ability to enforce the law."[84] Eventually, the case was taken to the State Supreme

Court where the decision of the appeals court was unanimously upheld. The high court "found that the alleged inequity [i.e., the construction and subsequent costs] would have been avoided had the developer waited for the exhaustion of legal remedies before undertaking construction ... Therefore, it found no inequity in ordering the apartments to be removed."[85] The developer continued construction fully knowing—but apparently not believing—the risk he was taking. Grosso, who helped represent the plaintiffs, declared, "This was a victory for citizen enforcement of comprehensive plans."[86] Despite broad citizen concern over the lack of effective growth management, this decision illustrates that there is opportunity to right wrongdoings under the law. Such an opportunity, however, arises only rarely. The Shidel case took seven years to resolve, seven years of persistence, legal support, and considerable financial backing. It is immensely difficult and expensive to win one of these challenges.

Action on growth management law was relatively quiet during the next two years, but some noteworthy changes were made during the 2005 legislative session. Governor Bush (having found some features to his liking) ranked growth management reform as a top priority during that session.[87] When the smoke finally cleared and debate ceased, some major changes affecting growth management had been made. The bill (SB360) focused on school, transportation, and water concurrency, as well as changing the requirements for capital improvement elements of local government comprehensive plans. It also created the Century Commission for a Sustainable Florida (mentioned earlier). Senate President Tom Lee proclaimed, "The legislation includes meaningful safeguards and strong financial incentives to promote smarter, more efficient community planning in Florida."[88] Governor Bush noted his satisfaction with the linking of school capacity and water supply to development approvals.[89]

Additional changes affecting growth management were proposed during the 2006 legislative session. Environmental and planning interests were concerned enough about two of the bills that were enacted to urge the governor to veto them.[90] Their concern was that the first, the Agricultural Economic Development Act, "promotes sprawling development in rural, agricultural lands," and the second, the Hazard Mitigation for Coastal Redevelopment Act, "makes it easier to develop coastal lands ... particularly in the relatively undeveloped Panhandle."[91] Ignoring their concerns, Governor Bush signed both bills into law.

Further proposals to change growth management appeared during the 2007 legislative session. The initial bill drew such negative reaction that it was soon withdrawn. Another, HB 7203, appeared in the House of Representatives a couple of weeks before the session ended, and opposition groups had little time to organize resistance. But resist it they did: Marilynn Wills, first vice-president of the League of Women Voters of Florida, argued, "If passed, HB 7203 would make comprehensive plans useless."[92] Ever-watchful 1000 Friends of Florida sent out an action alert saying, "Stop this Train Wreck!"[93] Telephone calls and emails from concerned citizens across the state resulted in taking some sting out of the proposal, but the bill *was* passed. Among other things, it made "it easier for development to occur regardless of transportation concurrency issues," says 1000 Friends of Florida.[94] It also established pilot programs in Broward and Pinellas counties and the cities of Jacksonville, Miami, Hialeah, and Tampa, allowing them "to avoid state review for numerous development projects."[95] Thus, the downward slope of dismantling state government oversight of growth management initiated by Governor Bush (and supportive legislatures) continued beyond his final year in office.

Twenty-year Retrospective

While serving as secretary of the Florida Department of Community Affairs, Thaddeus L. Cohen decided he could learn from the experiences of the secretaries who preceded him. His idea led to a symposium titled a "Twenty Year Retrospective of Growth Management in Florida," held in Gainesville, on February 10, 2005. Each of the six former secretaries who attended was asked to present his or her view on what worked or did not work regarding growth management and how to correct weaknesses in the system.[96] Cohen served as moderator of the symposium.

Experiences were shared and wisdom offered by the former secretaries. They recounted successes, but more prevalent were regrets that far more could have been accomplished in implementing the state's "blueprint for growth." The greatest failure in the eyes of some of the former secretaries was the lack of money to do the job right, money that local governments should have generated on their own and financial aid that the state neglected to provide (e.g., infrastructure funding) or provided in insufficient quantity. One of the issues pointed out was the ever-increasing demands being generated by Florida's growing population while, simultaneously, its resources are being depleted. Among other items discussed was the need to protect the environment while promoting the economy, the significance of addressing matters inter-governmentally, the importance of an effective regional role in growth management, improved inter-agency coordination, and recognition that growth management continues to be supported by Floridians.

The Rural Land Stewardship Program

On the ostensible note of aiding agriculture and environmental conservation, attention drifted from compact urban development to facilitating development in rural areas. The term compactness, typically applied to existing urban areas, was inventively adapted to compact settlements in *rural* areas.

In keeping with the strong shift in political attention toward development in rural areas, the Growth Management Study Commission had introduced a fresh—but relatively untested—idea for developing rural areas while simultaneously preserving agricultural and conservation areas. This idea led to legislation in 2001 authorizing the Florida Department of Community Affairs (DCA) to permit up to five local government pilot projects, allowing them to designate all or a portion of lands classified in their "future land use element as predominantly agricultural, rural, open, open-rural, or a substantively equivalent land use."[97]

The intent of the legislation is that rural land stewardship areas (RLSAs) should be used to further the following principles of rural sustainability:

- restoration and maintenance of the economic value of rural land;
- control of urban sprawl;
- identification and protection of ecosystems, habitats, and natural resources;
- promotion of rural economic activity;
- maintenance of the viability of Florida's agricultural economy; and
- protection of the character of rural areas of Florida.[98]

To be eligible for designation, an RLSA needed be a minimum of 50,000 acres and be located outside of municipalities and urban growth boundaries. The law did not limit the size of RLSAs nor speak to how far from a municipality or urban growth boundary an RLSA should be. Like a sector plan, a stewardship area must be adopted as a plan amendment by the local government, and then submitted for approval to the DCA.

An RLSA program is similar to a transfer of development rights (TDR) program in that development rights are transferred from one or more designated sending areas to one or more designated receiving areas. Though based on the TDR concept, an RLSA is more complex; it provides landowners with an opportunity to enhance the value of land if public benefits are protected in some way. Thus, enhancement of value is a key feature of the RLSA program.

Land use credits from sending areas can be used to increase development density in receiving areas. A specified number of potential development rights (e.g., residential or commercial) are thereby lost to the sending area, whereas higher densities of residential or commercial development are then permitted in the receiving area over what is currently allowed under a county's comprehensive plan. The new density of development is dependent on the number of credits transferred and the value assigned to those credits.

The RLSA program grew slowly. In the first few years of the program, only the Collier County program could be loosely classified as an RLSA; we say "loosely" because it was not an "official" RLSA. However, in 2004, the requirements in the original law and related sections in other laws were relaxed, generating considerable new interest. The amendments included eliminating its pilot project status and extending the program statewide. In addition, the threshold size was reduced from 50,000 acres to 10,000 acres. Furthermore, RLSA amendments were released from the twice-a-year growth management act limitation on local plan amendments, and they were exempted from the developments of regional impact (DRI) review process. Within two years, Adams Ranch in St. Lucie County, was officially designated an RLSA. Aided by these amendments, along with growing concern over the development-inhibiting aspects of a potential statewide ballot to require voters to approve changes to local comprehensive plans, there was an explosion of proposals.[99] Table XI-1 lists the first two projects (named above) and five later proposals by county, short title, and size, as of spring 2007.

Table XI-1
Explosion of RLSA Proposals
Spring 2007

County	Title of RLSA	Size in Acres
Brevard	Farmton	10,364
Collier	Collier County	217,483
Glades	Lykes Property	258,633
Highlands	Lykes Property	67,424
Highlands	Blue Head Ranch	65,000
Osceola	South Osceola	96,082
St. Lucie	Adams Ranch	22,384
Volusia	Farmton	10,384

Source: Florida Department of Community Affairs, Division of Community Planning, 2007.

These eight RLSA proposals encompass a combined 781,343 acres of Florida's rural landscape or, put another way, a pooled area of 1,220.8 square miles.

Sometimes referred to as being the first rural stewardship-type project, Ave Maria, a new town surrounding a new university of the same name, is being built in rural Collier County. The development may have as many as 11,000 dwelling units at build-out.[100] Indications point to perhaps an additional six neighboring villages (e.g., the new town of Big Cypress, just west of Ave Maria), for an overall population of 60,000 in the RSLA. In exchange for approval to increase development intensities in the town and villages, the development company has agreed to preserve a minimum 17,050 acres in agricultural and conservation lands.[101]

An event in 1997 laid the foundation for this project. The DCA had found the Collier County evaluation and appraisal report not in compliance with state requirements, and after an administrative hearing, the issue rose to the Administration Commission (the Governor and Cabinet) for a decision. The Administration Commission held with the decision of the DCA, and directed the county to come up with a better way to "identify measures to protect agricultural areas, direct incompatible land uses away from wetlands and upland habitats and assess the growth potential of the area."[102] A "better way" was found—theoretically. The county government and stakeholder groups, working in concert, put together a concept of using stewardship credits to allow development while protecting agricultural and environmental interests at the same time. Following a study, funded by five major landowners, the concept was applied to the Ave Maria site and surrounding area.[103]

The first "official" RLSA project was the Adams Ranch-Cloud Grove pairing in St. Lucie County. Adams Ranch is the sending area, and Cloud Grove is the initial receiving area. This project has a growing number of critics statewide because it has more than tripled the amount of development initially allowed.[104] Locally, Doug Coward, a St. Lucie county commissioner, reportedly said he had "grave reservations" about how well the project was working.[105] Prior to the new legislation, large developments like Cloud Grove would have had to go through the DRI review process. This exclusion has prompted Charles Pattison, to deprecatingly call them, "DRIs with steroids."[106]

Environmentally conscious organizations such as 1000 Friends of Florida, the Nature Conservancy, and the Florida Wildlife Federation believe that, "it is critical that DCA establish some minimum guidelines before RLSA projects over-take the necessary comprehensive planning our rural areas require."[107] They list several substantive areas that need at-tention: open space, development acreage and separation dis-tances, surrounding lands, easements, planning timeframes, sending and receiving areas, and the review and implementa-tion process.[108]

Caution should be observed when an RLSA project is considered. Though "maintenance of the agricultural economy" is one of the principles of the program, RLSAs cannot guarantee that farming will be continued because main-taining farming is an inter-generational problem. This con-cern brought Lester Abberger, legislative representative of the Florida Chapter of the American Planning Association, to warn that RLSAs may be "a special interest issue that has implica-tions beyond the health of Florida's agricultural industry."[109] After a current farm owner passes away, his or her heirs may not be interested in farming, they may more interested in the urban development potential of the land. Additionally, as the University of Kentucky Cooperative Extension Service ad-vises, "Binding restrictions on future landowners and future land uses may become more controversial as population and development forces continue to pressure the land base."[110] Thus, there is a question of sustainability associated with RLSAs.

Rural land stewardship is a promising concept, but *sustainability* may be its weakest link. Stewardship-oriented developers may plan and assemble the stewardship areas, but who will serve as stewards for monitoring and backing up the conservation easements that will assure sustainability of the projects? Since subsequent landowners often are not inter-ested in upholding easement terms, the outcome of the pro-gram is dependent on a serious commitment to monitoring and enforcing conservation easements, The American Farm-land Trust includes concerns about monitoring and enforce-ment in its list of drawbacks to agricultural conservation easements.[111] In the same line of thought, Jeff Pidot, author of *Reinventing Conservation Easements*, says, "... far too much about conservation easements is left to chance."[112] And as everyone *should* know, Florida cannot afford to leave its remaining rural areas to chance.

Maintaining rural character and the economic viability of agriculture may be another weak link in the RLSA program. These positive features to Florida's visual and economic landscapes could disappear over time, if the location, number, and density of RLSAs are not controlled. Too many RSLAs could result in a blunderbuss splattering of sprawl, definitely contrary to the concept of building compactness around existing urban and town centers. If used in moderation and "sustainably" controlled, rural land stewardship is an admirable pursuit. If not, it could morph into an even greater urban area expansion-agent than the construction of the interstate highway system.

What will happen in ten to twenty years? The rural lands stewardship program could end up being one of the most significant of Florida's land development programs or the use of the word "stewardship" could become a horrendous misnomer. All the law mentions is that the use or conveyance of transferable rural land use credits must be recorded by the county "as a covenant or restrictive easement running with the land in favor of the county *and* [italics added] either the state Department of Environmental Protection, the state Department of Agriculture and Consumer Services, a water management district, or a recognized statewide land trust."[113] If the *cost* of monitoring the covenant or restrictive easement is not supported as well as the planning, development, and marketing phases of stewardship areas, then the program will fail to achieve its stated goals—and Florida will be in far worse shape than it is today. A patchwork quilt of urbanized areas, or what 1000 Friends of Florida calls "a sea of urbanization," could soon cover the whole state.[114]

The rural land stewardship concept appears to be the product of growth coalitions at work. The self-benefiting ties between political policy-makers and large corporate landowners are too prevalent to be purely coincidental. Given a sufficiently large profit motive, a growth machine will coalesce, and, with sizeable financial backing and political influence, find a way to work around existing public requirements.

Northwest Florida–A Plum in the Process of Being Picked

In line with state government's rush to develop rural areas, the St. Joe Company is pursuing its own versions of rural development. Much of northern Florida is owned by the St. Joe Company—which has been called "Florida's Land Czar."[115] In a paper called "Defining the New Ruralism," the company outlined a marketing approach for much of its acreage in the Florida Panhandle.[116] It intends to meet what it calls a growing demand for private retreat residences similar to its already created RiverCamps, WhiteFence Farms, and Florida Ranches. These are not RLSAs. They are mostly cluster developments, surrounded by conservation lands, although the concept of Florida Ranches appears to envision a return to the hunting plantation pattern that had dotted parts of northwest Florida.[117] More sprawling—and possibly an evolutionary step from Florida Ranches—is "FloridaWild," a development with properties of forty acres and more for outdoor enthusiasts, conservationists, or people who might want to create a "farm legacy".[118] Thus, the St. Joe Company has its own approach to rural land stewardship—sprawled across the face of the Florida Panhandle.

The St. Joe Company has also prepared a West Florida Lands Strategic Plan, which Joe Hedrick, of the Panhandle Citizens Coalition, calls "no less than an attack on an entire region's way of life."[119] He also believes the St. Joe Company "had to have been involved in the recent change of the Turnpike statute," as well as raising "the [residential units] threshold of Developments of Regional Impact from 300 to 500," noting that their SummerCamp project, near Carrabelle, in northwest Florida, is "exactly 499 houses".[120] To him, this is the mark of a "shadow government" at work, another term for a growth machine.

Rural Transportation Corridor Initiatives

Florida planning laws require coordination amongst state agencies, yet in 2006, and apparently with Governor Bush's urging, the Florida Department of Transportation (FDOT) independently embarked on a Future Transportation Corridors Initiative. A draft recommendation of the Century Commission for a Sustainable Florida recommends support of FDOT's corridor initiative, noting that, "No single project in existence today will have more of an impact on Florida's next 50 years than this effort."[121] True, but would the eventual impact on Florida be good or bad?

As Victoria Tschinkel, state director of the Nature Conservancy and former secretary of the Florida Department of Environmental Regulation, observed, "DOT is only trying to do what it should do—plan ahead," but, she went on to say this would put "DOT well ahead of the timeline of most state, regional and local planning processes."[122] In other words, if FDOT commits to the rural road corridors identified in the first draft of its plan they would be encouraging locations for future development that would be counter to existing plans. An effort is underway to make the remainder of the FDOT corridor planning initiative more participatory before it solidifies. This might help to place things in the order, Tom Lewis, former assistant secretary of the Florida FDOT and former secretary of DCA, once noted: "[T]ransportation is growth management and growth management is transportation, but it is growth management that should drive transportation."[123] It should not be the other way around. However, it appears that transportation—once again—may be the driving force behind rampant growth.

The nine currently proposed corridors may or may not reach construction stage,[124] but one of them, the 152-mile Heartland Parkway, stretching from Interstate 4 (between Orlando and Lakeland) to Alligator Alley (east of Naples) appears to be gathering political support. The rough alignment of the proposed parkway runs through or close to some of the RLSAs being proposed. The potentially sprawl-inducing rural lands stewardship program and the Heartland Parkway appear too timely and interdependent to be generated by unconnected interests. "Powerbrokers determined the footprints" of this highway and another "before the Turnpike authority [a unit of FDOT] ever ran its computer programs," said Cynthia Barnett, in an article titled, "Final Frontier".[125] Because state road-building funds are low, these corridors might be constructed through private-public partnerships, especially if the state leases toll roads to private enterprises, as current law allows. Such partnerships could also result in an increased number of billboards in a state already lax in regulating these roadside eyesores, as Citizens for a Scenic Florida would testify.

Governor Charles (Charlie) J. Crist, Jr., who took office in January 2007, has not jumped onto the prior administration's transportation corridor bandwagon, however. For example, he has yet to endorse the Heartland Parkway and he has said publicly that the state's transportation priorities should be where there are large populations of people.[126]

Not to be outdone by development interests in the peninsula, similar interests in "The Great Northwest" (a St. Joe Company term) received legislated authority in 2005 to create a Northwest Florida Transportation Corridor Authority (NwFTC) to improve U.S. Highway 98. This would include new routing between Pensacola and Wakulla County (south of Tallahassee). There may be no connection, but Highway 98 passes through or close to a number of St. Joe Company development projects. This action has drawn the ire of environmental groups, because the proposed roadway may run through major conservation areas.[127] Twelve organizations signed a letter to Governor Crist opposing the master plan adopted by the NwFTC; they believe "the Master Plan fails to fulfill in a responsible manner the Authority's purpose; was adopted without adequate public input; and would be highly detrimental to the ecosystems and wildlife of Northwest Florida."[128] Several of the projects, they write, "appear to serve only those private development interests that seek to open up currently undeveloped areas, encouraging an increased rate of urbanization/suburbanization."[129] Again, the mark of a growth coalition is evident.

Not a Pretty Picture

Loss of conservation and agricultural areas is one of the principal concerns of two studies recently sponsored by 1000 Friends of Florida. The first of the studies is called, *Florida 2060: A Population Distribution Scenario for the State of Florida.* The organization contracted with Paul D. Zwick and Margaret H. Carr, at the University of Florida's GeoPlan Center, to develop graphics depicting what land use might look like in Florida up to 2060. "Not a pretty picture," says 1000 Friends.[130] The projections indicate that about "7 million acres of additional land will be converted from rural to urban uses," and the counties expected to "undergo the most dramatic transformation, in rank order, will be Glades, Hardee, DeSoto, Hendry, Osceola, Baker, Flagler and Santa Rosa."[131] The Florida 2060 project "clearly shows that the State of Florida sits at the 'tipping point' related to land consumption for urban development."

For the second report, the organization used the Center for Quality Growth and Regional Development at the Georgia Institute of Technology to provide guidance to state leaders on how to deal with the projected growth in a proactive manner.[132] Combined, the two reports "provide a wake-up call for every Florida resident, business and elected official," said Charles Pattison.[133]

Hometown Democracy

Though Florida's intergovernmental development management system has been partially successful, it has been constantly softened by the political power of growth coalitions, the parochial perspective of localism, and political leaders who prefer to let the market system *alone* dictate the future of the state. Despite gradual erosion of the power of the system, it has refused to go away, thanks to the support of citizens who recognize the need to manage growth effectively. Still, growth problems continue to mount, and overly ambitious speculators in land development seem to find more and more ways to circumvent the system. This circumvention has generated a significant backlash movement called "Hometown Democracy".

Ross Burnaman, who along with Lesley Blackner leads the movement, says, "A valid criticism of Florida's planning efforts is the focus on accommodating short-term development interests, while poorly considering the long-term future uses of land, resources and public facilities such as schools and transportation systems."[134] Tiring of the continual onslaught of changes to local plans, they are campaigning to get a constitutional amendment on a statewide ballot—one that would require voters to approve changes to local comprehensive plans.

It has been said that Blackner's promotion of the Hometown Democracy proposal makes "veins throb in the foreheads of developers across Florida."[135] The throb has risen to a point where development interests have introduced a counter-ballot called Floridians for Smarter Growth, a counter-ballot sponsored by a builder-developer-Florida Chamber of Commerce coalition.[136]

In a discussion with the editorial board of the *St. Petersburg Times*, Tom Pelham agreed that, "Plan amendments should be rare, not willy-nilly,"[137] but he does not support the proposed Hometown Democracy amendment. What he advocates, say the editors of the *Times*, is a compromise solution "somewhere between the extremes of development-by-referendum and development-by-bureaucratic-wink-and-nod." The editors believe that Pelham is "on the right track as he recognizes the complaints without embracing the extreme response." They write that minimization of state oversight, arguably, has "helped stoke the Hometown Democracy movement." It remains to be seen whether the Hometown Democracy movement generates a sufficient number of signatures to get the amendment on the fall 2008 or 2010 ballots. If nothing else, the movement underscores the need for state leaders to improve Florida's intergovernmental development management system.

A Breadth of Fresh Air?

Governor Charlie Crist took office in January 2007. Among the early changes he made was to reappoint Tom Pelham as secretary of the Florida Department of Community Affairs (DCA). Pelham had previously served under Governor Bob Martinez during the early years of implementing the Local Government Comprehensive Planning and Land Development Regulation Act (see Chapter IX). Pelham was reported to say that he wants to "restore the Department of Community Affairs as an effective advocate and positive force for better planning for growth management in our state."[138]

Pelham's return renewed a sense of spirit at the DCA. His appointment seemed to promise a new attitude toward growth management. Maybe the department would get back to its earlier responsibilities of managing growth, with backing from the governor. However, backing from the legislature is another kind of maybe. That body passed the damaging 2007 "train wreck" growth management bill allowing little opportunity or time for discussion. There was a call for Governor Crist to veto the bill, but given last minute political maneuvering, he might not have been in a position to do so. The coming year will show whether the governor is truly a breath of fresh air and whether the legislature is of a mind to allow fresh air into their chambers. Hopefully this will happen, for as Pelham has pointed out, "We're trying to manage growth with an unmanageable statute."[139] An unmanageable statute equates to ineffectively managed growth; actually, all of Florida's growth management laws are in need regeneration.

Summary

Say hello to the threat of potentially over-zealous development of rural land stewardship areas—and goodbye to the quaint, rural Steinhatchees of today. Though urbanizing the rural countryside runs counter to policies of *compact* urban development (with emphasis on the *old* meaning of compact), rural development has become the new ambition of land speculators. Rural resources, especially agriculture and natural resources (like water recharge areas) are facing increased pressure from urban-type development. A selling point of developers is that rural land stewardship areas promise increased sustainability—but the promise will become reality only if the conservation easements which serve as their foundation are backed by the authority and *continuing resources* of state government in monitoring their use. Otherwise—localizing the words of President Eisenhower—Florida will continue to "live only for today, plundering ... the precious resources of tomorrow."

There was a significant shift in political philosophy toward growth management in 1999. Some specific and limited improvements were made over the following eight years but on the whole, amendments to planning laws increasingly made things easier for development interests. At the same time, the governor and legislature gradually dismantled the state's ability to intercede on poor decision-making by some local governments, thus reducing the effectiveness of growth management.

The Local Government Comprehensive Planning and Development Regulation Act of 1985 was enacted with the intent of retaining and improving the quality of life in Florida, but growth coalitions have found ways to mitigate that intent. Examples of good development have occurred in Florida, but over time and overall, many cuts have been made to that act and related acts, allowing questionable and costly-to-the-public development to occur. Thus, the historical driving force of excessive development for short-term profit continues to dominate the concept of decisions for the good of the general welfare.

Governor Charlie Crist took office in January 2007, and a hint of fresh air was felt. What remains to be seen is whether his administration will seize the opportunity for constructive change—for the sake of the people of Florida, especially the children. It is, after all, our children who will live with the legacy we leave them.

NOTES FOR CHAPTER XI

1   Seely, Sir J.E.B., from *The Growth of British Polity*, listed in *The Oxford Dictionary of Quotations*, Oxford, UK: Oxford University Press, 1979.

2   The Mel Tillis web page (www.meltillis.com/, February 28, 2007) reads much the same (February 28, 2007).

3   President Dwight D. Eisenhower, "Farewell Address to the American People," from *Public Papers of the Presidents of the United States*, Vol. 8, Washington, DC: GPO, 1960-61, pp. 1036-1039.

4   For a well-informed analysis of sprawl see Anthony Downs, "Some Realities about Sprawl and Urban Decline," *Housing Policy Debate* 10:4, Fannie Mae Foundation, 1999, p. 955.

5   The states in between are New Mexico, Arizona, Colorado, Utah, Nevada, Idaho, Oregon, and Washington.

6   Frank, James E., *The Cost of Alternative Development Patterns: A Review of the Literature*, Washington, DC: Urban Land Institute, 1989.

7   Greenwood, Daphne, "Assessing the Costs and Benefits of Local Growth," obtained from web.nccs.edu/ ccps/doc/ swea.rev.growth%20REDONE.doc on June 11, 2007.

8   Meek, Stuart, "Status of State Planning Reform," executive summary in "Planning Communities for the 21st Century," Chicago, IL: American Planning Association, 1999, p. 4.

9   U.S. Department of Housing and Urban Development, *The State of the Cities 1999*, third annual report, Washington, DC, June 1999, p. 21.

10 *The Economist (US)*, May 8, 1999, obtained from HighBeam Research, Inc., at www.highbeam.com, on July 10, 2007.

11 Ehrenhalt, Alan, "The Czar of Gridlock," *Governing*, May 1999, p. 20.

12 Ibid, p. 24.

13 Obtained by email from Richard A. Lehmann, on January 29, 2007.

14 Sightline Institute, "Two Years of Measure 37: Oregon's Property Wrongs," Seattle, Washington, 2007, p. 3.

15 Ibid, p. 2.

16 Ibid.

17 Ibid, p. 3.

18 Ibid, p. 16.

19 Obtained from 1000 Friends of Oregon, www.friends.org/issues/M37/index.html on July 18, 2007.

20 Urban Land Institute, "Building Florida's Future Through Regional Cooperation: ULI Florida Initiative's Symposium Looks at Next

Steps," March 2006, obtained from www.uli.org/AM/ Template.cfm?Section= Press_Releases1& ... on Jun 12, 2007.

21 Among the other members of the committee in 2005 were James W. Apthorp, Thaddeus Cohen, Sheri Coven, Carolyn A. Dekle, David H. Graham, Richard Grosso, Timothy T. Jackson, James F. Murley, James C. Nicholas, Charles G. Pattison, Richard Pettigrew, Robert M. Rhodes, Steve Seibert, and Nancy Stroud, some of whom are mentioned elsewhere in this book.

22 Urban Land Institute, *Building Florida's Future: State Strategies for Regional Cooperation*, a report from the ULI Florida Committee for Regional Cooperation, Washington, DC, 2005, pp. 20 and 21.

23 Ibid, p. 24.

24 Ibid, pp. 29 and 32, respectively.

25 Data derived from U.S. Census Bureau, "United States Summary: Population and Housing Unit Counts," p. 26 and Florida House of Representatives, "Policy and Budget Council, Meeting Packet," January 8, 2008, p. 6.

26 Obtained from FEMA website, www.fema.gov/news/ disasters_state.fema?id=12, on January 24, 2007.

27 *St. Petersburg Times*, "Nothing unscathed but patience," September 19, 2004, p. 4A; uninsured losses are not included in this figure.

28 Obtained from the FEMA website, www.fema.gov/news/ newsrelease.fema?id=29701, on January 24, 2007.

29 Herbers, John, *Governing* 3, August 1990, p. 9.

30 Evans, Thomas B., Jr., "Wise development is key to a national fund," *Tallahassee Democrat*, June 20, 2007, p. B1.

31 Ibid.

32 Evans, ibid.

33 Ibid. Not all of the first mentioned declarations might have been full-fledged wildfires.

34 Barnett, Cynthia, "The Carolina Connection," *Florida Trend* 50: 7, October 2007, p. 54.

35 Editorial, "Outward bound: Florida through the rear-view mirror," *Tallahassee Democrat*, January 12, 2007, p. 4E.

36 Dubard, Carolyn, presentation to the Florida Senate Education Pre-K-12 Appropriations Committee on January 25, 2007.

37 Obtained from http://realestate.msn.com/Buying/Article2.aspx?cp-documentid=51... on July 18, 2007. Having more than a 50 percent or 60 percent chance of lower home values by mid-2009 are the Florida market areas of West Palm Beach-Boca Raton-Boynton Beach (60.7 percent risk); Orlando-Kissimmee (56.3 percent); Fort Lauderdale-Pompano Beach-Deerfield Beach (54.2 percent); Miami-Miami

Beach-Kendall (52.4 percent); and Tampa-St. Petersburg-Clearwater (50.6 percent).

38   Seely, ibid.
39   As of 2003, the following boards, commissions, and departments fell under the cabinet system: Administration Commission, Board of Trustees of the Internal Improvement Trust Fund, Department of Highway Safety and Motor Vehicles, Department of Law Enforcement, Department of Revenue, Department of Veterans' Affairs, Division of Bond Finance, Electrical Power Plant and Transmission Line Siting Board, Florida Land and Water Adjudicatory Commission, State Board of Administration, State Board of Executive Clemency, and Financial Services Commission (which consists of the Office of Insurance Regulation and the Office of Financial Institutions and Securities Regulation).
40   Colburn, David R. and Lance deHaven-Smith, *Government in the Sunshine State: Florida Since Statehood,* Gainesville, FL: University Press of Florida, 1999, p. 116.
41   Dáte, S.V., *JEB, America's Next Bush: His Florida Years and What They Mean for the Nation*, New York, NY: Jeremy P. Tarcher/Penquin, 2007, p. 133.
42   Ibid.
43   Press release titled "Governor Bush Shares Vision for Florida," issued by the Office of the Governor, March 7, 2007.
44   Dáte, ibid, p. 161.
45   York, Marie, "What About the Public Interest?" *Planning* 69: 2, February 2003, p. 8.
46   Newman, Joe, "Bush talks tough on growth," *Orlando Sentinel*, March 30, 2005, pp. B1 and B7.
47   Florida Department of Community Affairs, "Planning Florida's Future," *Community Planning* 8: 4, Fall 1999, p. 1.
48   Seibert Steven M., "Growth Management in Review," *Florida Counties*, January/February 2000, p. 14.
49   Seibert, Steve, "Update on Growth Management," January 2000, obtained from www. 1000fof.usf.edu/GrowthAlert/ DCAsurveyUP.htm, on February 21, 2000.
50   Florida Department of Community Affairs, "Growth Management Survey Report," Tallahassee, FL, February 2000, p. 4.
51   Ibid, p. 7. Lance deHaven-Smith, a professor at Florida State University, prepared the survey.
52   Ibid, p. 4.

53 Seibert, Steven M., Secretary of the Department of Community Affairs, in the cover letter to the "Growth Management Survey Report," Tallahassee, FL, February 1999.

54 Florida Department of Community Affairs, "Summary of Florida's Regional Forums on Growth Management," www. dca/fl.us/fdcp/ DCP/Resources/publications/; Florida Office of the Governor, "Executive Order 2000-196," July 3, 2000.

55 1000 Friends of Florida, "Floridians' Attitudes Toward Proposed Changes to Florida's Growth Management Laws," Tallahassee, FL, April 26, 2000, p. 1.

56 Chapin, Tim and Charles Connerly, "Attitudes Towards Growth Management in Florida: Comparing Resident Support in 1985 and 2001," *Journal of the American Planning Association* 70: 4, 2004, pp. 443-452.

57 Florida Office of the Governor, "Executive Order 2000-196," July 3, 2000.

58 The other committee members were: J.D. Alexander, Patsy D. Blackshear, Paul R. Bradshaw, Judie S. Budnick, Mary Lisa Carlton, Thaddeus L. Cohen (later secretary of DCA), Chris Corr, Robert B. Crawford, J. Allison DeFoor, II, Paula M. DeLaney, Paula B. Dockery, Nancy M. Graham, James T. Hargrett, Jr., Alberta Hipps, Charles S. Lee, Frederick W. Leonhardt, John E. Manning, Susan E. Pareigis, Linda Pellegrini, Sergio Rodriguez, Barry B. Rutenberg, and Steven M. Seibert (then secretary of DCA). Ex-officio members were Thomas F. Barry, Jr., Allan Egbert, and David Struhs. Later the same year, Martinez was appointed as secretary of the U.S. Department of Housing and Urban Development.

59 Martinez, Mel, "Florida Growth Management Study Commission," *Florida Counties*, January/February 2001, p. 13.

60 Transcription of Governor Bush's presentation to the Growth Management Study Commission on August 28, 2000.

61 Martinez, Mel, chairman of the Growth Management Study Commission, "Statement Of Chairman Mel Martinez Regarding GMSC Efforts To Date," Tallahassee, FL, November 17, 2000.

62 Florida's Growth Management Study Commission, *A Livable Florida for Today and Tomorrow*, Tallahassee, February 2001; the needs are reordered to progress from state to regional to local to citizen concerns and involvement.

63 Lee, Charles, email to Governor Bush on February 13, 2001.

64 Bradshaw, Paul, email to Charles Lee on February 13, 2001.

65 Lee, Charles, email to Paul Bradshaw on February 15, 2001.

66   1000 Friends of Florida, "Growth Management Study Commission Issues its Final Report," *Foresight* 14: 1, Spring 2001, pp. 8-10; the statements are reordered to progress from state to regional to local level concerns.

67   §163.3247, *Florida Statutes*.

68   The other members are Mike Bennett, Laura Benson, Bob Bullard, Lula Butler, Chris Corr, Dennis Gilkey, John LaCapra, Charles Lee, Mary McCarty, Charles Pattison, Julio Robaina, Gary Schraut, Steve Uhlfelder, and Don Whyte.

69   Seibert, Steve, "Make this a place where our kids would live," *Tallahassee Democrat*, September 9, 2007, p. 6B.

70   Century Commission for a Sustainable Florida, first annual report to the governor and legislature, Tallahassee, January 16, 2007, p. 18.

71   Chapin, Tim and Heather Khan, *Assessing Florida Citizen Attitudes Towards Growth, Growth Management, and Quality of Life Issues: Final Report*, Department of Urban and Regional Planning, Florida State University, Tallahassee, 2006.

72   House Bill 0139.

73   House Bill 1617/1437.

74   1000 Friends of Florida, Growth Management Alert, April 29, 2001.

75   Hauserman, Julie, "State trims back growth reviews to 'big picture'," *St. Petersburg Times*, September 2, 2001. Hauserman obtained this information from two internal DCA memos.

76   Ibid.

77   Ibid.

78   *Pensacola News Journal*, "Growth speeds up, state's management slows down," May 16, 2002.

79   Senate Bill 1906.

80   Florida Department of Community Affairs, "2002 Legislative Highlights," *Community Planning* 11: 1, Spring 2002, p. 3.

81   Roth, Cari L. and Laura J. Feagin, "2002 Reforms to Growth Management," *The Florida Bar Journal* LXXVI: 7, 2002, pp. 57-61.

82   *Pinecrest Lakes, Inc. v. Karen Shidel*, 795 So. 2nd. 191 (Fla. 4th DCA 2001); at the Florida Supreme Court level it is identified as case # SC01-2429, May 31, 2002.

83   Pelham, Tom, "Respect for the Local Comprehensive Plan," *Florida Planning* XIII: 10, December 2001/2002, p. 1. Also see Terrell, Arline, "Citizen Enforcement of Comprehensive Plans Upheld, *Foresight*, 1000 Friends of Florida, Tallahassee, Winter 2001.

84   Grosso, Richard, "The Pinecrest Lakes Case: The Demolition Heard 'Round the State'," obtained from www.visulaw.nova.edu/faculty/documents/Pinecrest%Analysis.pdf, on August 3, 2007.

85   Ibid.

86   Ibid.

87   Florida Department of Community Affairs, "Governor Signs Laws to Overhaul Growth Management," news release, June 24, 2005.

88   Florida Department of Community Affairs, ibid.

89   Bush, Jeb, letter to Secretary of State Glenda E. Hood, dated June 24, 2005.

90   House Bill 1015/Senate Bill 716 and House Bill 2359.

91   1000 Friends of Florida, "2006 Legislative Wrap Up," updated May 17, 2006.

92   Wills, Marilynn, email message dated June 7, 2007.

93   1000 Friends of Florida, "Immediate Action Needed! – Growth Management," obtained from www. 1000friendsofflorida.org/reform/ 2007session.asp, on May 26, 2007.

94   1000 Friends of Florida, "Mixed Results from 2007 Session," obtained from www. 1000friendsofflorida. org/reform/ 2007%20session%20w…, on June 29, 2007.

95   Ibid.

96   The former secretaries who participated in the symposium and their terms in office were John M. DeGrove (Apr 1983-Jul 1985); Tom E. Lewis, Jr. (Jul 1985-Feb 1987); Linda Loomis Shelley (May 1992-Aug 1995); James F. Murley (Aug 1995-Jan 1999); Steven M. Seibert (Jan 1999-Jan 2003); and Colleen M. Castille (Jan 2003-Feb 2004). Information on the symposium may be obtained from the Florida Department of Community Affairs, 1000 Friends of Florida, or the Florida Chapter of the American Planning Association.

97   §163.3177(11)(d)1, *Florida Statutes*.

98   §163.3177(11)(d)2, *Florida Statutes*.

99   van Sickler, Michael, quoting Tom Pelham in "Towns crop up in plans along rural toll road," *St. Petersburg Times*, March 18, 2007, pgs. 1B and 5B.

100 Obtained from www.avemaria.com/residences/pulte.asp, on June 27, 2007.

101 Florida Department of Community Affairs, October 2007.

102 Florida Department of Community Affairs, "The Rural Land Stewardship Area Program: A Report to the Legislature," Tallahassee, January 2007.

103 Ibid.

104 Pelham, Tom, from an email message to RuBino on September 21, 2007.

105 Pulver, Dinah Voles, "Large-tract owners see stewardship as future," "In the News" 5: 5, May 3, 2007, obtained from *myregion.org* on July 14, 2007, p. 3.

106 From an interview with Charles Pattison, by RuBino, on December 8, 2006.

107 1000 Friends of Florida, Florida Wildlife Federation, and The Nature Conservancy, letter to The Honorable Tom Pelham, Secretary, Florida Department of Community Affairs, dated June 6, 2007.

108 Ibid.

109 Abberger, Lester, "2005 Legislative Overview," *Florida Planning* March 2005, p. 5.

110 Vantreese, Valerie L., Jerry R. Skees, and Craig L. Infanger, "Rural Land Preservation in Kentucky," University of Kentucky Cooperative Extension Service, College of Agriculture, Lexington, KY, 1998, p. 24.

111 American Farmland Trust, "Fact Sheet: Agricultural Conservation Easements, Farmland Information Center, Northampton, MA, 2004, obtained from www. farmlandinfo.org/documents/27762/ACE_1-04.pdf, on July 17, 2007.

112 Magers, Vince, "Savings Accounts: an update on conservation easements," *Planning* 72: 8, August/September, 2006, pp. 22-25. The quotation is from Jeff Podot, who wrote *Reinventing Conservation Easements: A Critical Examination and Ideas for Reform*, Cambridge, MA: Lincoln Institute of Land Policy, 2005.

113 §163.3177(11)(d)6,k, *Florida Statutes*. The Land Trust Alliance (LTA) reports that there are over 35 local, statewide, or national land trust members currently operating in Florida. These include the Apalachee Land Conservancy, the Conservation Trust for Florida, the Green Horizon Land Trust, the Nature Conservancy, and the Trust for Public Lands. An undetermined number of non-LTA member land trusts may also exist, with more on the immediate horizon. This information was obtained from the Land Trust Alliance at www. lta.org/resources/links/natl_sponsors.htm on July 27, 2007.

114 1000 Friends of Florida, *Florida 2060: A Population Distribution Scenario for the State of Florida*, Tallahassee, 2006. the quotation "a sea of urbanization" was taken from this publication.

115 Pittman, Craig, "Florida's Land Czar," *Planning* 69: 2, February 2003, pp. 4-9.

116 Obtained from www.1000friendsofflorida.org/Panhandle/New%20Ruralis..., on December 28, 2006.

117 "The St. Joe Company Outlines Vision for 'New Ruralism' ..., a report on a presentation made by Peter S. Rummell, chairman and CEO of the St. Joe Company, at the annual meeting of the National Association of Real Estate Editors, in Washington, DC, in June 2005; obtained from http:// findarticles.com/p/articles/ mi_m0EIN/ is_2005_June_4/ai_..., on August 2, 2007.

118 "The St. Joe Company Introduces 'FloridaWild' ...", obtained from http://findarticles.com/p/articles/mi_m0EIN/is_2006_March_3/ai_..., on August 2, 2007.

119 Hedrick, Joe, Panhandle Citizens Coalition, obtained from www.whoseflorida.com/panhandle_citizens2003.htm on September 22, 2007; listed on 1000 Friends of Florida website.

120 Ibid.

121 Century Commission for a Sustainable Florida, recommendation #10 in "Draft Recommendations," obtained from www.centurycommission.org/about.asp, on January 11, 2007.

122 Tschinkel, Vickie, "DOT could become planning agency by default," *Tallahassee Democrat*, December 9, 2006.

123 Lewis, Tom E., Jr., during the "Twenty-Year Retrospective of Growth Management in Florida," sponsored by the Florida Department of Community Affairs and held at the University of Florida, Gainesville, on February 10, 2005.

124 Roughly, the nine proposed corridors are (1) Pensacola to the Alabama line; (2) Panama City to the Alabama line; (3) West-central Florida (north of Tampa) to the Georgia line; (4) Tampa to Jacksonville, via Gainesville; (5) Orlando to Jacksonville; (6) Hernando County (near Brooksville) to Brevard County (near Melbourne); (7) Hernando County to Charlotte County; (8) Polk County to Collier County (the "Heartland"); and (9) Bradenton to north of Port St. Lucie.

125 Barnett, Cynthia, "Final Frontier," *Florida Trend*, July 2006, p. 49.

126 Pelham, Tom, secretary of the Florida Department of Community Affairs, in an email message to RuBino on September 21, 2007.

127 Ritchie, Bruce, "Proposed roads draw criticism," *Tallahassee Democrat*, June 21, 2007, p. E-1.

128 The Humane Society of the United States, 1000 Friends of Florida, Apalachicola River Keeper, Audubon of Florida, Clean Water Network of Florida, Defenders of Wildlife, Florida Institute for Conservation Science, Florida Wildlife Federation, , Natural Resources Defense Council, The Nature Conservancy, Nokuse Plantation, and the South Walton Community Council; these organizations co-signed a letter to Governor Charlie Crist opposing the adopted master plan for the U.S. 98 corridor on May 2, 2007.

129 Ibid.

130 1000 Friends of Florida, *Florida in 2060: Not a Pretty Picture?* an executive summary, December 2006.

131 Ibid.

132 1000 Friends of Florida, *A Time for Leadership: Growth Management and Florida 2060*, Tallahassee 2006.

133 Young, Vivian, "Projected to Double in 50 Years: Growth Leadership is Needed Now," *Florida Planning*, January 2007, p. 1.

134 Burnaman, Ross, "Statement of Ross Burnaman on Florida's Hometown Democracy Amendment," www.floridahometowndemocracy.com, obtained on January 21, 2007.

135 Vogel, Mike, "Who's Lesley Blackner?" *Florida Trend*, March 2007.

136 Ward, Kendric, "Florida Ballot Wars: The Empire Strikes Back," *TCPalm* (Treasure Coast and Palm Beaches), July 29, 2007; obtained from www.tcpalm.com/news/2007/jul/29/david-vs-goliath, on August 14, 2007.

137 *St. Petersburg Times*, "Developing A Middle Ground," a Times editorial, August 1, 2007; obtained from www. floridahometowndemocracy.com/Articles/Developing, on August 14, 2007.

138 Skene, Neil, "Act II: Calling growth management 'a mess,' new DCA Secretary Tom Pelham wants a rewrite," *Florida Trend*, August 2007, p. 94.

139 Ibid.

CHAPTER XII

CONCLUSION—AND LESSONS LEARNED?

> If men could learn from history, what lessons it
> might teach us! But passion and party blind our
> eyes, and the light which experience gives is a lan-
> tern on the stern, which shines only on the waves
> behind us![1] (Samuel Taylor Coleridge, 1835.)

The fate of Florida's intergovernmental development management system is in question. Nonetheless, prudent voices
caution, "… the progress we have made in Florida over the
last thirty years should not be overlooked or minimized."[2] "It
will be tempting," warns David Powell, a foremost land use
attorney, "to take out our frustrations with the current system
by tossing it onto the trash heap and starting over … the wiser
course would be to build on the successes we have had and
fix or replace the parts … that are outdated and broken, … ."[3]
His concern is echoed by growth management advocate Tom
Pelham, who wrote, "The solution [to the disappointments
and failures of the system] is not the elimination of the integrated planning process."[4] A place to start is to review lessons learned and lessons pending.

Before discussing lessons learned—or not learned—
let us remind ourselves of where planning has been and how
we got to where we are now. We have contemplated the history of planning in Florida through four hundred and fifty
years. Through these years, the forces that have influenced
development of Florida have remained strikingly similar.
These forces express themselves in the form of growth machines, politically powerful pro-growth coalitions capable of
influencing local and state land use decisions to their advantage. Speculative interests, coupled with political power have
shaped Florida into what it is today: a state with ever-boom-

ing population that is quickly racing beyond the ability to sustain itself.

The history of planning in Florida is a diverse story, laced with private schemes driven by speculation, public initiatives usually motivated by land reclamation and economic development, and a baseless hope that rising property values would support an ever-increasing need for additional public services and infrastructure. In addition, external political, economic, and environmental imperatives have affected planning choices and public policy during the unfolding of Florida's development history.

As the centuries passed, Europeans squabbled over possession of Florida. During the second Spanish period, however, Thomas Jefferson suggested to President George Washington that Americans should emigrate to Florida for the purpose of occupying and subverting the Spanish colony.[5] Many settlers moved into colonial Florida, seeking individual opportunity. The immigration continued into the territorial years and these new Floridians brought with them traditions of the American frontiersmen, traditions of unlimited and often rampant land speculation, localism, and a profound belief in limited governmental authority and minimal interference with private property rights.[6] These traditions continue to enliven and often frame the negotiation tables of local growth management debates today.

Though Florida's planning history traces back to villages housing pre-European aborigines and the detailed plans of Spanish settlements, the state did not experience its first modern era planned towns until St. Petersburg led the way in 1908, followed by a number of others in the 1920s. The latter were towns planned by visionary developers who designed places of special character, places such as Coral Gables, Kelsey City, Sarasota, and Venice. Sometimes a civic group, like the Garden Club of Palm Beach,[7] hired consultants to design attractive developments. Many of the towns planned in the early

1920s continue to reflect and represent Mediterranean architectural character and style, and the visual and spatial quality of Florida's early urban developments. However, these examples of early town planning were not the norm, most communities evolved from simple platted layouts to encourage lot sales without the benefit of foresight to community building.

During the 1930s, Florida and other states created state planning boards in response to a federal initiative designed to overcome a catastrophic national economic depression. Like other states across the nation, Florida created a State Planning Board that focused its attention on the physical environment. The data and plans the board developed led to public works projects funded by the U.S. Works Progress Administration, including civic improvement projects such as schools, armories, libraries, parks, and other public buildings. In 1935, Florida enacted its first intergovernmental planning law, which called for the preparation of a state master plan and permitted counties to form county planning councils. However, mobilization for World War II consigned planning to immediate wartime needs and quickly shunted aside most civic planning. The early part of the twentieth century, therefore, was a time of emergence and expansion for planning, followed by a waning of interest.

After the war, the national economy continued to ride an upsurge brought on by production during wartime. A tsunami of growth was beginning to show itself in Florida. Residential development began to spread across Broward and Miami-Dade counties, west and north of Fort Lauderdale and west and south of Miami and Coral Gables. A general absence of planning characterized a policy of benign neglect, reflecting an expectation that growth would bring an increase in tax dollars sufficient to provide needed water, sewer, schools, hospitals, and other public facilities and services. Private developers—not local governments—were expected to be responsible for providing minimum public facilities for the new developments. The expectation that new development would bring sufficient moneys to cover their infrastructure needs did not materialize, and the path to serious deficiencies in infrastructure and acute environmental degradation was established. The cost of growth began to raise its ugly head, but the heads of many public leaders remained in the sand.

There was little planning in Florida at that time, it was a time of quiescence. Local and state level planning had virtually disappeared as soon as federal aid ended. Later, the federal government stepped back into the picture by providing financial aid for infrastructure, urban renewal, and other public needs, including planning. During the late 1950s, the Florida Development Commission (FDC) assumed the role of state administrator of federal planning assistance funds, but the emphasis of the agency remained on economic development. Planning was not a function of their choosing, but the federal government required a state agency to administer the disposition of planning funds to interested local governments, and the FDC was it. Furthermore, the state legislature did not allow local governments to engage in planning without passing a special act for each local government that expressed a desire to prepare a plan. This was a major hurdle in trying to rejuvenate planning in Florida. Relatively few city and county governments were sufficiently motivated to overcome this legislatively imposed impediment to local planning.

The 1960s signaled a time for change: especially a time for state governments to reassume their partnership role in the federal system. Undoubtedly, the U.S. Supreme Court's 1962 decision in *Baker v. Carr*[8] was a milestone leading to this initiative. One of the significant outcomes of that decision was mandated reapportionment of state legislatures. In Florida, this federally ordered action, coupled with a growing awareness of environmental problems, social issues, and demand for governmental accountability led the way to governmental reform, including a rejuvenation of interest in planning. The Sunshine State began to awaken from decades of urban neglect, and interest in planning gradually re-emerged.

Meanwhile, Florida continued to experience platting of large housing developments across the state. Examples such as Cape Coral, Deltona, Lehigh Acres, Palm Coast, and Port Charlotte encompassed thousands of single-family lots. Though some of these were developed with paved streets, few included water treatment and distribution systems, and even fewer had sewage treatment and collection systems. Nonetheless, local governments welcomed these developments as a boon to local prosperity and growth. Little concern was attached to the future consequences of poorly planned large-scale developments.

Considerable change occurred in the structure of Florida state government in the late 1960s, as the result of a new state constitution in 1968 and a complete reorganization of the executive branch. Part of the reorganization saw state planning and budgeting transferred from the State Planning and Budget Commission (the Governor and Cabinet) to a new Department of Administration where it was housed in a Division of Planning and Budgeting.

In the early 1970s, the legislature and the governor united in fervent activism to set in place an environmental agenda that carried through the following three decades. When Governor Reubin Askew stepped into office in 1971, he found he had inherited a completely reorganized executive branch, at least as far as his direct responsibilities were concerned. (As always, the cabinet officers had their own agencies and others were under the joint jurisdiction of the Governor and Cabinet.) The stage was set for a statewide endeavor to manage the rampant growth in population. It became a time of new state planning and water management initiatives, like the Environmental Land and Water Management Act, which included the areas of critical state concern and developments of regional impact programs. This marked the dawning of an intergovernmental development management strategy. However, it was not until 1975 that the legislature enacted a mandatory local government comprehensive planning act.

The latter half of the 1970s was a time for implementing the components of the development management strategy. By 1976, a state comprehensive plan had been completed and forwarded to the legislature. Though adopted by resolution, the legislature expressed no strong desire to follow it, and the combined executive-legislative zeal for planning began to slip. The new legislative leadership apparently felt the most essential reforms already had been enacted, and there was little need to expand them. However, by 1980, regional planning was strengthened at the urging of Governor Bob Graham and the cooperation of a changed set of legislators. Combined executive-legislative zeal for planning returned, and together they tried to put the critical pieces of the intergovernmental development management system together—again. The result was a standard-setting set of changes to each level of Florida's intergovernmental development management system.

The late 1980s were devoted to refining the new changes and implementing them. Major improvements had been made to the state and regional planning law, but the most significant change was to the ineffective (though at the time thought to be promising) local planning act of 1975. Important among the changes to the latter was the oversight authority given to the Florida Department of Community Affairs (DCA) regarding the preparation, implementation, and maintenance of a new local growth management act. Inadequate oversight authority—compounded by a lack of funding support—had negated the intent of the earlier act. Another significant factor was that a state comprehensive plan was prepared and enacted into law in less than a year. Consistency with the state plan was mandated for state agency planning, regional planning, and local comprehensive planning. In part, the state plan was intended to serve as the point star for DCA decisions regarding the consistency of local plans with the state plan. As time passed, however, the state plan has been mostly ignored.

We should not pass this period without commenting on the Zwick Committee. This committee, in recognition of a projected $30 billion shortfall in transportation, water supply, and wastewater management needs, called for the creation of an infrastructure trust fund to support the needs of local governments.[9] A hesitant Governor Bob Martinez approved a state sales tax on services, the income from which was to go into an infrastructure trust fund. But within a year, he led a repeal of the tax. Thereafter, as John DeGrove put it, "The short fall was never met."[10] Thus, local governments have remained without needed state financial aid to cope effectively with their infrastructure burden.

As time swept toward the end of the twentieth century, Florida's intergovernmental development management system moved into maturity. Yet continued rapid growth and its negative effects stayed ahead of government's ability—and sometimes, desire—to manage growth effectively. In Florida, as well as nationally, new efforts for managing growth were emerging; among them were smart growth, strategic planning, visioning, new urbanism, and sustainable communities. Changes to managing growth were occurring, some of them making necessary adjustments learned from years of experience, others seemingly weakening parts of the system. The private property rights movement began to sweep the nation, and picked up Florida in the process. This put a restraint on land use regulation in the Sunshine State, but not to the extent hoped for by its proponents. Emerging differences in policy orientation between the executive and legislative branches, including the property rights legislation, moved growth management toward greater flexibility. The state's effort to manage growth was being pushed toward a slippery slope.

The degree of slippage became highly noticeable as the century ended and the new millennium began. The voters of the state put into office a development-oriented governor and legislators of the same ilk. Representatives of growth machines began to walk the halls of the state capitol with abandon. The attitude in the capitol was that the growth management program had failed, was not wanted, and was ripe for drastic change. Statewide surveys and workshops showed otherwise, but subtle dismantling succeeded in relaxing state government's ability to manage growth.

Having highly profited from the intense development along the coast and the fringes of urban areas, it did not take long for development interests to turn their attention to a new and vulnerable pasture: the state's remaining rural areas. Deceptively attractive sounding—yet potentially devastating—development concepts appeared, such as the rural land stewardship program and the proposed rural transportation corridors proposal. The quickening slide down the slope toward uncontrolled growth seemed unstoppable. Despite the efforts of a leading public interest group to portray the future of Florida as "not a pretty picture,"[11] the slide picked up speed. Another group, acting in frustration, is attempting to place a constitutional amendment on a statewide ballot that, in the eyes of the land conversion industry, "would stop development cold." If successful, the proposed constitutional amendment will allow voters to approve proposed amendments to their local comprehensive plan, a process somewhat similar to what is called "ballot-box zoning."[12]

A new governor took office in 2007, and it appears this might be the beginning of a weather change in Florida's effort to manage its unbridled pattern of growth. Whether the new administration brings a breath of fresh air or continues the slide toward undoing Florida's hard-won development management process remains for future historians to gauge.

Lessons Learned and Not Learned

Florida has made repeated attempts at setting up an effective intergovernmental development management system, with partial success.[13] Some lessons appear to have been learned in this process, but most of the lessons have been only partially learned or not learned at all. Building on our historical perspective, we present our view of what lessons fit into each of these categories.[14]

Lessons That Appear to Have Been Learned

Florida has gained from development in general, yet at the same time suffered from excessive development. Concerning the latter, it does not take much imagination to picture the even more dire condition the Sunshine State would be in today had not its new-age development laws been in place. Admittedly, more should have been done to manage growth effectively; nonetheless, Florida is still better off today than it might have been without its intergovernmental development management system in place.

Critics have been too quick to say that Florida's intergovernmental development management system—especially the local growth management component—has failed. We say differently: there have been numerous small and large examples of success. The progress made in Florida over the last thirty years should not be overlooked or minimized. As one observer noted, "The biggest successes [of the growth management laws] are the things you fail to see: Subdivisions that have half the number of houses than the developer originally proposed, parking lots that were redesigned to protect nearby lakes, shopping malls that weren't built because opponents successfully showed that the town already had enough unused retail space."[15] Local governments now have land use controls, based on an adopted and legally enforceable comprehensive plan, and tied to the state intergovernmental development management system. Development permits were much easier to obtain a few decades ago: "It was so simple then," a developer explained, "I just got some land outside the city limits, went down to the County building department, showed them the plans for my first building, and pulled a building permit. Then I started construction. That was it."[16] It is not so simple today, there are more regulations of substance, and though they have not slowed development (nor were they intended to), they have had a positive impact.

As the reader should realize, things have been learned or at least partly learned during the evolution of Florida's development management efforts. The list that follows may not be complete, but it does show that progress has been made. Be forewarned that these are subjective classifications, and they are not to be considered a measure of how *well* a lesson has been learned or its chance of being retained.

- Mandating planning: Planning, a function of management, should be an integral part of governance at all levels. Though some local governments will effectively merge planning with management voluntarily, and do it well, too many others tend to employ planning only in a limited way or not at all. Florida has learned—the hard way—that planning must be mandated. The majority of local governments will not make an effort to prepare and implement long-range plans or their effort may come too late to be effective. A community without long-range planning in its management toolbox may make costly decisions it otherwise could have foreseen.

- Oversight: To assure compliance with the law and efficient use of public dollars, a state agency (such as a Department of Community Affairs) should be assigned the responsibility for overseeing the preparation of local plans and development regulations and monitoring their progress. Furthermore, that agency needs to do more than just provide technical assistance to local governments. Though this is a lesson learned, the agency's oversight responsibilities were in jeopardy for a number of years.

- Sanctions: One of the reasons the 1975 local planning act was unsuccessful is that it carried no penalties for non-compliance with the law that mandated planning. This is like posting speed limits on a highway without being backed up by the highway patrol and fines. The 1985 local planning act rectified this fault. This also is a lesson learned.

- A plan as law: Even though a plan needs some degree of flexibility as conditions change, it also must be sustained as a whole and not allowed to be eroded by endless amendments. One way to mitigate erosion is to make a plan a legal document, as opposed to merely an advisory tool; in other words, make it a law. Limiting the number of times per annum a local government is allowed to amend its plan is also helpful. A lesson learned.

- Intergovernmental consistency: A lesson first recognized in the mid-1900s, but not seriously considered until the 1970s and 1980s, is that consistency in decision-making between state, regional, and local levels of government is necessary for planning and development management to be effective. For growth management purposes, vertical consistency is particularly imperative regarding linkages between land use, water, and transportation, three dynamics vital to any development. This is a lesson learned, but it needs close attention.

- Conflict resolution: Florida learned that planning can surface conflicts as participants in the planning process consider the potential impacts of development proposals. However, it is better to engage in such conflicts early, rather than later. One of the outcomes of this lesson resulted in the creation of conflict resolution options in the 1990s. Using conflict resolution may not always come to a sustainable resolution, but it is a path to consider before seeking a judicial remedy.

- A state plan need not take long to prepare: The process of preparing a state-level comprehensive plan can be made too long and drawn-out, as was learned in the 1970s when it took four to five years for the initial state plan to be completed. There were mitigating circumstances, however; there were no models or experience to guide its preparation, the completed plan was presented during a national recession that drew attention away from planning, and the interests of its initial supporters had drifted to other issues. Thus, the second (1985) state plan was completed within only a few months; giving little time for conditions to change during is preparation. A lesson learned.

- Land acquisition: The land acquisition programs of the 1970s and on through the 2000s have made valuable contributions to the management of growth and protection of environmentally, historically, and archeologically important lands. This is one of the better lessons learned, and land acquisition programs should continue to be aggressively pursued and broadened in scope as the years unfold.

- Initiating actions in land use control independent of waiting for a push (or aid) from the federal government: Florida's participation in planning in the 1930s, 1950s, and 1960s was largely the result of federal requirements, not because its state and local governments were especially interested in planning. This changed in the

1970s, when Florida began to put together its intergovernmental development management system, as well as in the 1980s when it strengthened that system. This is a lesson learned, at least about planning and development management.

The above list of lessons learned is probably not inclusive. Additional lessons might be added by other people who have had close contact with all or specific aspects of planning and growth management in Florida.

Lessons Partially Learned

Progress has been made with the following issues, but more needs to be accomplished.

- Consistency between a plan and tools for implementing a plan: Consistency between a plan and the land development regulations and other programs (e.g., the annual capital budget) that implement it was strengthened by making an adopted plan a law. However, state oversight, a factor in local plan preparation, was limited in regard to plan implementation, leaving oversight to the initiative of concerned citizens. However, implementation at the local level is at best spotty and inconsistent. This is a lesson without easy answers, but it needs attention.

- Consistency between units of local government: Mandating planning for local governments is meaningless unless all independent or semi-independent local government functions are required to prepare plans and that those plans are consistent with (supportive of) each other. This requirement includes general-purpose local governments (municipal and county), school boards, and special districts. This is a lesson still being learned.

- Citizen participation: Florida values the importance of citizen participation—to a limited degree. A local plan runs a risk of having little or no carrying power if only elected officials, the planning commission, and development interests are involved in the planning and plan implementation processes. Citizen participation has played an important role in contributing to the preparation of those plans. On the other hand, the implementation end of the process is the most difficult for citizens in terms of time and cost of monitoring and, if necessary, challenging unreasonable deviations to the plan through plan amendments. The cost to citizens for challenging a plan amendment needs attention.

- One size may soon fit all: The local growth management act started out by requiring every local government, no matter its size or makeup, to conform to the same plan preparation requirements. At the time, the framers realized it would be preferable to have a variable set of requirements, but lack of time and experience required that small, rural communities be held to the same requirements as urban areas. This caused understandable difficulties for rural areas, and it did receive later attention. However, with the recent emphasis on rural land stewardship area developments and rural transportation corridors, it appears a standard requirement for all may soon be appropriate.

- <u>Regionalism</u>: There are at least three significant development management related forms of regionalism in Florida: water management districts (WMDs), metropolitan (transportation) planning organizations (MPOs), and regional planning councils (RPCs).[17] Though the powers of these three regional organizations vary significantly, consistency between these regional entities must be assured. This places regionalism in the category of still more to be learned.

  o As agencies of the state, water management districts have become a decision making force in matters pertaining to regional water supply, consumptive use of water, aquifer recharge, surface water management, storm water management, flood protection, well construction, and other permitting responsibilities.

  o Like WMDs, metropolitan planning organizations have a func-

tional responsibility: transportation. But unlike the state
government created WMDs, they
are transportation policy-making
bodies[18] mandated by the federal
government.

o Unlike WMDs and MPOs,
regional planning councils have a
broad multipurpose responsibility.
The two regional bodies mentioned
above have policy making or
regulatory powers, powers the state
legislature has refused to extend to
RPCs. They remain advisory
bodies only, not allowed to act as
a permitting or regulatory entity.
They are required to attempt to
achieve consistency between plans
through a process of negotiation.
Hence, they have a relatively weak
role in intergovernmental affairs,
rendering them the least effective
of the three regional organizations
discussed here. Florida is without
a multipurpose regional entity that
can set regional policies independent of restrictions imposed in
defense of localism.

o Though some progress has been
made in multipurpose regionalism,
considerably more should be done.
But as has been said, "Mention
regional governance and the
drawbridge protecting the castle of

local democracy is immediately raised."[19] Thus, regionalism remains the weakest link in Florida's intergovernmental development management system. Planning author Melville Branch's caution of twenty years ago rings just as true today, "Cooperation between different governmental bodies necessary to effectuate regional planning is rarely achieved. Except in dire emergencies most individuals and institutions cooperate reluctantly and ineffectually."[20]

- Chief planner: Since the late 1960s, most of Florida's governors have recognized that they are the state's *chief* planner, a responsibility pointed out in the state constitution.[21] The governor is the person most responsible for—and should be most interested in—using planning as a management tool. However, in Florida's plural executive system, the governor must share portions of this management responsibility with the cabinet. This relegates the lesson to a category of only partially learned.

- Consistency between units of state government: Most large private corporations have learned from experience that they cannot afford to allow their sub-units to operate in an uncoordinated manner. This lesson should be as applicable to the public sphere as it is to private enterprise. At the state government level, state agency heads have an inclination to look only inward to the responsibilities of their own agencies. Too often state agencies tend to encourage their own special interest constituencies. This is understandable, but it can also be detrimental if their plans are not coordinated with other agencies, and it opens the possibility of disservice to the public interest (e.g., in 2007, the Florida Department of Transportation failed to properly coordinate with other relevant state agencies before releasing news about eight proposed rural transportation corridors). Progress definitely has been made, but, as just illustrated, it is still inconsistent.

- Need for balance: We recognize the need for *balance* between two maxims of the *Constitution of the United States*: protecting the public welfare (sometimes called the "public good" or the "common good") and protecting private property rights. The first appears in the preamble ("We the people ...") of the constitution and the second in the fifth amendment to the constitution. This issue needs to be under constant review to ensure that one right does not begin to covertly supplant the other. As a local government planning commission member said, "There is no constitutional right to pollute, or to build for private gain that leaves the public footing the bill."[22]

Many lessons have been learned or are still in the process of being learned, but the history of planning in Florida is ladened with lessons that failed to be learned or that have been purposefully ignored. The most apparent of these are discussed below.

- Conflicting objectives: Florida claims to support compact development while at the same time facilitating actions that contribute to sprawl. In addition, it claims to support agriculture[23] while simultaneously making it easier to place urban developments in rural areas. This makes it appear that Florida is well into the process of including "housing units" in their definition of agricultural products. Instead of a ping-pong match (being won by the sprawl side), Florida needs an approach that facilitates growth of compact and functionally well-planned urban areas while restraining sprawl. This is a lesson being almost totally disregarded.

- Financial responsibility: A state mandate for local and regional planning must be backed up with adequate state financial aid. The mandated local planning law of 1975 was passed with little, if any, financial support, and this and other omissions contributed to failure. Within ten years, it was necessary to replace that law with a new law that not only mandated planning, but also provided state financial aid for local governments to prepare their plans and land development regulations. This was a lesson learned. On the other hand, the need for *adequate* funding has not held up in the game of politics. For example, the concurrency requirement, which is directed only to current projects, was passed on the promise that the legislature would provide the funds necessary to eliminate the infrastructure backlog that local governments had built up over decades. This promise was not kept. Thus, though the concurrency requirement has been somewhat successful, it has not accomplished all that was intended, and it has been accused of discouraging higher densities (compact development) and contributing to urban sprawl, especially concerning roads. This is a lesson being ignored.

- Annexation: Competition among cities and counties is exacerbated by Florida's anachronistic annexation law that makes it difficult for cities to annex growing subdivisions, which are often created by aggressive public or investor-owned utilities or county commissions under pressure from growth coalitions. Municipalities should be freer to expand their jurisdictions as the area around them urbanizes and, with county governments and neighboring municipalities, set conclusive urban development and urban service boundaries. However, in the alternative, in counties with strong commitments to growth management, some cities have been induced by land owners to voluntary annexations to avoid county land development regulations. This topic needs attention, because the ability of cities to grow with voluntary annexations to avoid county land use regulations induces sprawl and loss of rural lands.

- The symbiotic relationship between monitoring and effectiveness: One of the greatest failings of Florida's planning process has been a *lack of follow-through*, a lack of adequate support for monitoring the progress of the process. The reality is that it costs money to do something right, and unsupported promises and words designed to put a spin on interpretation will not do it. This adage holds for special programs as well as plans; for example, Florida's rural land stewardship projects will need effective monitoring. Continuing financial support of programs is more efficient in the long-run than merely providing upfront authority with startup money only. Unfortunately, Florida earns a poor score on this matter.

- Opening rural areas to intensive development: In his memoir, *Mandate for Change*, President Eisenhower stated that the interstate highway system would open up the rural areas of the nation.[24] Today, the Florida rural transportation corridors proposal appears determined to do that very thing. The Eisenhower initiative brought considerable change to rural counties around large urban areas and, in Florida, its rural areas will likely experience irretrievable loss in agricultural, environmental, and scenic resources if the rural transportation corridor program moves forward. Florida has an opportunity to make this a lesson learned, but to this date, it is being ignored.

- <u>Keeping a buffer between hurricanes and intensive coastal development</u>: The issue may already be moot, but how many devastating hurricanes will it take before truly strong coastal land use controls or a coastal land purchase program is put in place? Property damage from hurricanes has been enormous. Intensive development has been allowed to locate in well-known high hazard areas, even when knowing the probable costs of potential hurricane strikes. Current policy puts the inevitable astronomical costs of damages on all the people of the state and, less directly, the nation. This is a lesson failed—miserably.

- <u>Water supply</u>: State government has done "relatively" well in managing its waters, but as the state approaches twenty million people (not counting the millions of tourists), its water sources need to be even more effectively and judiciously managed. Florida, once a water abundant state, is now faced with repeated crises in water supply. As Cynthia Barnett has boldly written, "We can continue to bend wetlands and growth laws, or we can demand their consistent enforcement."[25] Demanding—and supporting—consistent enforcement of wetlands and growth laws is likely to remain a lesson to which insufficient heed is given.

- <u>Wildfires</u>: As new town developments spread across rural areas, the potential of wildfire costs in life, personal property, and public expenditures is rising. Florida could rival California in wildfires if this threat is not taken more seriously. This is a lesson likely to be overlooked.

- <u>A state plan (or any plan) should provide direction for decision-making</u>:[26] It should not contain statements that are in conflict with each other and neutralize its direction-setting potential. The legislature inserted a statement into the legislative intent section of the 1985 State Comprehensive Plan that makes every goal and its objectives equal to any other goal and its objectives.[26] The State Comprehensive Plan, therefore, is virtually rudderless! This lesson continues to be ignored.

- <u>A state plan can be *too* comprehensive for effective management</u>: The State Comprehensive Plan is ignored. One of the reasons for this is that it is *too* comprehensive. It attempts to cover virtually every activity of state government. In addition, it contains numerous objectives that are in conflict with each other. The practice of state planning is still in its adolescence; therefore, it is better to restrict its focus on the most critical issues of a time. Limiting the comprehensiveness of the state plan can be accomplished by beginning with, but not being limited to the topics of urban development boundaries, conservation of agriculture and natural resource boundaries, hazardous areas, generalized land use, regional water supply, and regional multi-modal transportation systems. This would help the state plan to become the direction-setting document it is intended to be. This lesson is well recognized, but remains unattended.

Givens

Will rampant development continue in Florida in the manner and at the rate it has in recent decades? Our answer is the all too typical yes and no. Listed below is what we classify as *givens*, things that are likely to happen or remain the same.

- Florida will continue to experience population growth (albeit at decreasing percentage rates), and serious problems caused by inadequately managed development will continue to mount (e.g., in water supply, natural disaster damages, and public infrastructure and service needs). There is no turning back from this path, merely a hope of making the path less costly to the pocketbooks of the public and less damaging to the natural environment through better planning, plan monitoring, and plan implementation. (The last two processes are the weakest links in Florida's intergovernmental development management system.)

- The riding partners of land exploitation and localism, which are often manipulated by growth coalitions, will continue to exert influence over land use policies unless steps are taken to moderate these forces. This is unlikely. Our review of Florida planning history has shown that the appeal of land speculation for personal or corporate gain will continue to be more forceful than interest in long-term benefits for the public good (health, safety, and welfare). A reality of the planning world is that growth machines have historically exerted a far greater influence over land use decisions than have concerned citizens and well-trained public planners.

- Urban sprawl throughout Florida will continue to be driven by overly aggressive land speculators (despite occasional slowdowns in the housing market). Sprawl may not be the choice a local government *intentionally* takes, but it may be the unintended, cumulative impact manifested by some elected (and appointed) officials who are anxious to accommodate development interests that can financially support their continuance in public office. As a learned planner once said, "the political process, not rational choice, is the vehicle by which most planning proposals are adopted and implemented, a fact that planners forget at their peril."[28] In addition, the consequence of conflicting interests of cities within an urban county and the lack of effective urban-wide planning, also contribute to sprawl. Heightened citizen activism and local media interest have not been enough to stem the tide of sprawl.

- We have found that localism—that is, overly zealous, parochial localism—will prevail until regional (interlocal) problems worsen to a point where state government and/or the federal government are politically willing to step in and attempt (too late) to resolve the problems created. (Such intervention has already occurred in the form of Florida's water management districts and the federally required metropolitan planning organizations.) By then, the costs in terms of dollars and deprivation of quality of life will have become irretrievable.

- History also reveals that Florida is a self-inflicted revenue-deprived state that chooses to shift—not solve—today's problems onto what will be the already overburdened shoulders of future generations (our children, grandchildren, and newcomers). This could change, but it is unlikely.

- Continual generous approval of excessive, sometimes greed-motivated development is not going to generate the revenues to pay for needed infrastructure and services any more than it has in the past. The development industry may pay part of those costs through impact fees, but the unpaid balance is borne mostly by local taxpayers with the benefits accruing to the developers and newest homeowners. It is probably true that if the full cost of infrastructure improvements to support new development were to be borne by the developer then that cost would be transferred to the homebuyers or commercial customers. The flipside of this argument is that if the developer pays only a small share of the burden, then the remaining costs are transferred onto the shoulders of the people of the entire community through property taxes and other revenue generation techniques. Someone has to pay. Nonetheless, the citizens in a tax-resisting state like Florida will continually reject this need, leaving the state to face a questionable future.

- The forces contributing to rampant, almost uncontrolled development in other rapidly developing areas across the nation will likely be similar to those forces that have made effective management of growth so difficult to achieve in Florida. Thus, there may be lessons to be learned from Florida's experience by elected officials, planners, and interested citizens in rapidly changing areas like Asheville, North Carolina; Boise, Idaho; the Colorado front range; and Las Vegas-Henderson, Nevada.

- Concerning global warming, "Lloyd's [of London] has warned: 'The insurance industry must start actively adjusting in response to greenhouse gas trends if it is to survive.'"[29] If the insurance industry thinks global warming is this serious, then it really is serious. Global warming appears inevitable. Glaciers are melting at a startling pace, and if the degree of melt is maintained or increased, then the waters of the oceans will continue to rise. This portends a rise in sea level that will affect Florida's coastline and possibly even some inland subdivisions built on reclaimed wetlands and flood prone land. Given this prospect, steps should be taken to anticipate the problems of global warming that will create and act upon ways to resolve or moderate these problems. Governor Charlie Crist has taken at least one of these steps in naming a Governor's Action Team on Energy and Climate Change.[30] The problems of global warming will generate demands for response from the private sphere and all levels of public governance. All plans—local, regional, and state—need to address this matter—NOW. The citizens of Florida cannot afford to wait until *after* human and property damages occur, because the associated costs will be even greater then.

Concluding Thoughts

The concept of growth management has not failed; if anything, it is the support system to *implement* growth management that has failed. This can be blamed largely on a lack of sufficient state revenues to support local infrastructure development; the absence of a strong, well-coordinated regional presence; and a general lack of political will to manage growth *effectively*. To these factors must be added the political maneuvering of growth coalitions (growth machines) to adapt to the requirements of managed growth and successfully shift them to achieve their own development-oriented ends.

One of the advantages seized upon by a growth machine is that the membership of local and state leadership changes frequently. At the time a growth coalition forms, a different set of elected officials may be in office than when a plan was adopted. Consequently, some of the newer officials may not feel beholden to the standing plan (despite the fact that the plan is officially a law). Another self-advantage is that some developers, who become avaricious about selling and developing land, are powerful folks with deep pockets. As the history of planning in Florida shows, they can influence significant deviations from plans. They always have and —given Florida's history of sometimes heroic but mostly half-hearted efforts at *truly* managing growth—it appears they always will!

Public planning remains subject to the overpowering influence of rampant land speculation and the historical tendency for minimal government responsibility. Thus, growth management in Florida has too often been growth accommodating. This lesson may never be learned, but it is worthy of debate. On the other hand, let us not degrade the good planning accomplished over the course of the last three decades. Many competent local and regional planners, backed by committed public officials (both elected and appointed) and supported by dedicated citizens, have contributed to producing outstanding local and regional plans. These stalwart people are to be commended for their efforts to manage growth, oftentimes in political environments that resisted their efforts.

The future of Florida rests largely, but not solely, in the hands of the governor, the cabinet, and the legislature. But it depends also on the willingness of private corporations, small businesses, regional entities, local governments, and *every citizen* to become familiar with what has been happening, and to play a part in moving the state toward a less insatiable and more sustainable future. The state's quality of life can be preserved— and even enhanced—if everyone has a vision that allows moral and ethical decision-making to show the way—rather than a tendency to let self-interest lead.

NOTES FOR CHAPTER XII

1   Coleridge, Samuel Taylor, "Table Talk," 1835, in *The Oxford Dictionary of Quotations*, Oxford University Press, 2004.

2   Powell, David L., "Growth Management: Florida's Past as Prologue for the Future," *Florida State University Law Review* 28, 2001, p. 13.

3   Ibid.

4   Pelham, Thomas G., "Restructuring Florida's Growth Management System: Alternative Approaches to Plan Implementation and Concurrency," presented at the Richard E. Nelson Symposim on Florida's Growth Management Legislation, Gainesville, FL, October 13, 2000.

5   Rerick, Rowland R., *Memoirs of Florida*, Atlanta, GA: The Southern Historical Association, 1902, p. 101.

6   Gerckens, Laurence Conway, "Historical Development of American City Planning," in Frank S. So, et al., *The Practice of Local Government Planning*, Washington, DC: The International City Management Association, 1979, p. 24.

7   The Garden Club of Palm Beach, Florida, "The Plan of Palm Beach," prepared by Bennett, Parsons & Frost, Consulting Architects, Chicago, 1930.

8   369 U.S. 186, 1962.

9   Sipe, Neil G. and Earl M. Starnes, "Florida's Infrastructure Needs & Resources, 1982-2000: A Preliminary Analysis," in "Hard Choices, A Report on the Increasing Gap Between America's Infrastructure Needs and Our Ability to Pay for Them, Appendix 4, Florida," prepared for the Subcommittee on Economic Goals and Intergovernmental Policy of the Joint Economic Committee of the Congress of the United States, February 25, 1984, U.S. Government Printing Office, Washington: 1984, p. xv.

10 "Twenty Year Retrospective of Growth Management in Florida," a workshop featuring the current secretary and former secretaries of the Department of Community Affairs, held at the University of Florida, Gainesville, February 10, 2005; sponsored by the Florida Department of Community Affairs, Tallahassee. Information from notes taken by the authors.

11 1000 Friends of Florida, "Florida in 2060: Not a Pretty Picture?" executive summary, Tallahassee, Florida, December 2006.

12 California and Ohio allow ballot-box zoning; for analyses of its use, see Roger W. Caves, "Determining land use policy via the ballot box:

The growth initiative blitz in California," *Land Use Policy* 7, 1: 1990, pgs. 70-79 and Samuel R. Staley, "Ballot-Box Zoning, Transaction Costs, and Urban Growth," *American Planning Association Journal* 67, 1: 2001, pgs. 25-37.

13 For a brief review of lessons learned by Hawaii and Oregon, as well as Florida, see James C. Nicholas, "State and Regional Land Use Planning: The Evolving Role of the State," *St. John's Law Review*, 73, 4: 1999, pp. 1069-1089.

14 Other discussions on lessons learned or not learned include John DeGrove, "Growth Management in Florida: My Perspective on What Has and Hasn't Worked and Why," in "DCA Secretaries Share Their Views," 1000 Friends of Florida, obtained from www.1000Friendsofflorida.org/Growth_Manage_ Process_Rev...; Richard Grosso, section on "So How Is It Working?" in "Florida's Growth Management Act: How Far We Have Come, and How Far We Have to Go," *Nova Law Review* 20, 2: 591-659, 1996, see pp. 647-657 for referenced section; Thomas G. Pelham, "Restructuring Florida's Growth Management System: Alternative Approaches to Plan Implementation and Concurrency," presented at the Richard E. Nelson Symposium on Florida's Growth Management Legislation, Gainesville, FL, October 13, 2000; Robert M. Rhodes, "Florida Growth Management: Rights, Not Rights, and the Future," John M. DeGrove Distinguished Speaker Series, Center for Urban and Environmental Solutions, Florida Atlantic University, October 3, 2001; and Bob Rhodes, "Three Decades of Perfecting Growth Management," obtained from http:// sustainable.state.fl.us/fdi/fscc/news/state/9804/ cside98f.htm on January 29, 1999.

15 Hauserman, Julie, "Yes, we're growing, but into what?" *St. Petersburg Times*, as reported in "Florida Sustainable Communities Center State/Regional News," http://sustainable.state.fl.us/fdi/fscc/news/state/0003/spt-jh.htm, on October 6, 2005.

16 Powell, ibid., p. 1; this is shown as a quotation from an anonymous developer.

17 This definition of regionalism does not include consolidated governments (Jacksonville-Duval County), federated governments (Miami-Dade County), or other forms of cooperative regionalism, such as practiced in Broward and Pinellas counties.

18 Large MPOs, covering areas having a population of 200,000 or more, have "policy-making" power. Smaller MPOs are primarily advisory bodies.

19 American Planning Association, chapter on "Governance" by Arnold Cogan and Richard RuBino, in *Planning and Community Equity*, Chicago: APA Planners Press, 1994, p. 181.

20 Branch, Melville C., *Regional Planning*, New York: Praeger, 1988, p. ix. For similar remarks also see Scott A. Bollens, "Restructuring Land Use Governance," *Journal of Planning Literature* 7, 3: 211-226.

21 *Constitution of the State of Florida*, Article IV, § 1(a).

22 Parker, Daniel, "Sign and gain freedom from a squandered future," *Tallahassee Democrat*, December 13, 2007, p. 4B.

23 § 187.201(22), *Florida Statutes*.

24 Eisenhower, Dwight D., *Mandate for Change: The White House Years a Personal Account 1953-1956*, Garden City, NY: Doubleday 1963.

25 Barnett, Cynthia, *Mirage: Florida and the Vanishing Water of the Eastern U.S.*, Ann Arbor: University of Michigan Press, 2007, p. 191.

26 § 187.101(2), *Florida Statutes*.

27 § 187.101(3), *Florida Statutes*.

28 Alexander, Ernest R., "Approaches to Planning," in A.J. Catanese, *Planning and Local Politics: Impossible Dreams*, Beverly Hills, CA: Sage, 1974, p. 19.

29 Morrison, John and Alex Sink, "The Climate Change Peril that Insurers See," *Washington Post*, op-ed, September 27, 2007, p. A25. Morrison is state auditor of Montana and Sink is the chief financial officer of Florida.

30 The action team consists of twenty-one members, chaired by Michael W. Sole, who is secretary of the Florida Department of Environmental Protection, with Rick Baker, mayor of St. Petersburg, serving as vice-chair. Other members are Jeffrey Atwater, Thomas Boroughs, Camille Coley, Lisa Polak Edgar, James M. Fenton, Manley K. Fuller III, Dan Gelber, David Guest, Debbie Harrison, Lonnie Ingram, Mark Kaplan, Gerald Karnas, Al Lawson, Stan Mayfield, Jerry Montgomery, Armando Olivera, Charles Pattison, Kathleen Shanahan, and Jack Shreve.

SELECTED BIBLIOGRAPHY

This selected bibliography contains references considered to be useful for research into the history of planning in Florida, as well as for researchers who wish to compare this history with planning-related events across the nation. For additional information, see the endnotes to each chapter.

Abbott, Carl, *The New Urban America*, Chapel Hill, NC: The University of North Carolina Press, 1981.

Advisory Commission on Intergovernmental Relations, "The Federal Role in Regionalism," in K. Mathewson, ed., *The Regionalist Papers*, Detroit, MI: Metropolitan Fund, 1977.

Alexander, Ernest R., "Approaches to Planning," in A.J. Catanese, *Planning and Local Politics: Impossible Dreams*, Beverly Hills, CA: Sage, 1974.

Alexander, John F. and Earl M. Starnes, "Water Front Development and Change: Pensacola, Florida," in *Urban Waterfront Land*s, National Research Council, National Academy of Sciences, Washington, DC, 1980.

Alfred, Lloyd Firth, "Florida's Development of Regional Impact Process, Practice, and Procedure," *Journal of Land Use and Environmental Law* 1: 2, 1985.

Alinsky, Saul, *Rules for Radicals*, Vintage Books, New York, NY: Random House, Inc., 1972.

Altshuler, Alan. "Goals of Comprehensive Planning," *Journal of the American Institute of Planners* 31: 3, 1965.

_____, "The Intercity Freeway," in Donald A. Krueckeberg, ed., *Introduction to Planning History in the United States*, New Brunswick, NJ: Center for Urban Policy Research, Rutgers University, 1983.

American Law Institute, *A Model Land Development Code*, Tentative Draft No. 3, Philadelphia, PA: The American Law Institute, 1971.

American Planning Association, *Planning Communities for the 21st* Century, Chicago, IL: American Planning Association, 1994.

_____,, "The Evolution of City Planning," in Roger L. Kemp, ed., *Forms of Local Government: A Handbook on City, County and Regional Options*, Jefferson, NC: McFarland, 1999.

Anderson, Martin, *The Federal Bulldozer: A Critical Analysis of Urban Renewal 1949-62*, Cambridge, MA: The MIT Press, 1962.

Arnstein, Sherry R., "A Ladder of Citizen Participation," *Journal of the American Institute of Planners* 35: 4, 1969.

Ashford, Norman and Richard G. RuBino, "The Role of the State in Transportation," *Traffic Engineering* 42: 4, 1972.

Babcock, Richard F., *The Zoning Game*, Madison, WI: University of Wisconsin Press, 1966.

Babcock, Richard G. and Charles L. Siemon, *The Zoning Game Revisited*, Cambridge, MA: Lincoln Institute of Land Policy, 1990.

Bair, Frederick H., Jr. and Ernest P. Bartley, *The Text of a Model Zoning Ordinance*, Chicago: American Society of Zoning Officials, 1966.

Barbour, George M., *Florida for Tourists, Invalids, and Settlers*, publisher unknown, c. 1884; see Library of Congress catalogue.

Barnett, Cynthia, in Cynthia Barnett, "Saving Florida: A History of Growth Management in the Sunshine State," a thesis for the Master of Arts Degree, University of Florida, Gainesville, FL: December 2003.

_____, *Mirage: Florida and the Vanishing Water of the Eastern U.S.*, Ann Arbor, MI: University of Michigan Press, 2007.

Beckman, Norman, "Federal Long-Range Planning: The Heritage of the National Resources Planning Board," *Journal of the American Institute of Planners* XXVI: 2, 1960.

Binford, Henry C., *The First Suburbs: Residential Communities on the Boston Periphery 1815-1860*, Chicago, IL: University of Chicago Press, 1985.

Black, Russell Van Nest, *Planning and the Planning Profession: The Past Fifty Years 1917-1967*, Washington, DC: American Institute of Planners, 1967.

Bollens, Scott A., "State Growth Management: Intergovernmental Frameworks and Policy Objectives," *Journal of the American Planning Association* 58: 4, 1992.

Boorstin, Daniel J., *The Americans: The Democratic Experience*, New York, NY: Vintage Books, 1973.

Bosselman, Fred and David Callies, *The Quiet Revolution in Land Use Control,* Council on Environmental Quality, Washington, DC: USGPO, 1971.

_____, "A Role for State Planning," *Journal of Law and Public Policy* 12: 2, University of Florida, 2001.

Branch, Melville C., *Regional Planning*, New York, NY: Praeger, 1988.

Briffault, Richard, "Our Localism: Part I—The Structure of Local Government Law," *Columbia Law Review* 90: 1, 1990 and ibid, "Our Localism: Part II—Localism and Legal Theory," *Columbia Law Review* 90: 2, 1990

Brigham, Toby, P., "The Harris Act—will it be enough?" *Environmental and Urban Issues* 23: 1, 1995.

Brock, Hanson, "Primrose Paradise," Miami, FL: Strange Publishing Company, 1921.

Brooks, Michael P., "Four Critical Junctures in the History of the Urban Planning Profession: An Exercise in Hindsight," *Journal of the American Institute of Planners* 54, Spring 1988.

Brumback, Barbara C. and M.J. Marvin, eds., *"Implementation of the 1985 Growth Management Act: From Planning to Land Development Regulations*, Fort Lauderdale, FL: FAU/ FIU Joint Center for Environmental and Urban Problems, monograph #89-1, 1989.

Burby, Raymond J. and Peter J. May, *Making Governments Plan*, Baltimore, MD: Johns Hopkins University Press, 1997.

Burnett, Gene M., *Florida's Past: People & Events that Shaped the State,* Vol. 1, 1986; Vol. 2, 1988; and Vol. 3, 1991; Sarasota, FL: Pineapple Press, 1986.

Burr, Josephine G., *History of Winter Haven Florida*, Winter Haven, FL: The Larry Burr Printing Company, 1974.

Burt, Al, *The Tropic of Cracker*, Gainesville, FL: University Press of Florida, 1999.

Campbell, Alan K., ed., *The States and the Urban Crisis*, Englewood Cliffs, NJ: Prentice-Hall, Inc., 1970.

Carter, Luther J., *The Florida Experience: Land and Water Policy Experience in a Growth State*, Baltimore, MD: The Johns Hopkins University Press, 1974.

Caves, Roger W., "Determining land use policy vial the ballot box: The growth initiative blitz in California," *Land Use Policy* 7: 1, 1990.

Chapin, Tim and Charles Connerly, "Attitudes Towards Growth Management in Florida: Comparing Resident Support in 1985 and 2001," *Journal of the American Planning Association* 70: 4, 2004.

Christensen, Terry, "Land-Use Policy: The Politics of Growth," in *Local Politics: Governing at the Grassroots*, Belmont, CA: Wadsworth Publishing, 1995.

Clements, Patricia Lasche, *Legacy of Leadership: Florida Governors and Their Inaugural Speeches*, Tallahassee, FL: Sentry Press, 2004.

Cogan, Arnold and Richard RuBino, chapter on "Governance," in *Planning and Community Equity*, Chicago, IL: APA Planners Press, 1994.

Colburn, David R. and Lance deHaven-Smith, *Government in the Sunshine State: Florida Since Statehood*, Gainesville, FL: University Press of Florida, 1999.

Conant, James K., "In the Shadow of Wilson and Brownlow: Executive Branch Reorganization in the States, 1965-1987," *Public Administration Review* 48, 5: 1988.

Connors, Donald L., Anne Richard Jackowitz and Miriam A. Widmann, in Douglas R. Porter, *State and Regional Initiatives for Managing Development: Policies Issues and Practical Concerns*, Washington, DC: Urban Land Institute, 1992.

Corbett, John, "Proposed Revisions To Florida's Local Government Comprehensive Planning Act," *Florida Environmental and Urban Issues* IX: 2, 1982.

Council of State Governments, *State Responsibility in Urban and Regional Development* Chicago, IL: Council of State Governments, 1962.

Cox, Merlin G. and J. E. Dovell, *Florida from Secession to the Space Age*, St. Petersburg, FL: Great Outdoor Publishing Co., 1974.

Curry, Tilden, *An Evaluation of Its Relevance to Public Decision-Making and State Planning Methodology*, doctorial dissertation, Department of Urban and Regional Planning, Tallahassee, FL: Florida State University, 1978.

Dáte, S.V., *Quiet Passion: A Biography of Senator Bob Graham*, New York, NY: Most Tarcher/Penquin, 2004.

_____, *JEB, America's Next Bush: His Florida Years and What They Mean for the Nation*, New York, NY: Jeremy P. Tarcher/Penquin, 2007

Davidoff, Paul, "Advocacy and Pluralism in Planning," *A Reader in Planning Theory*, Andreas Faludi, ed., New York, NY: Pergamon Press, 1973.

Davis, T. Frederick, "The Disston Land Purchase," the *Florida Historical Quarterly* XVII, Gainesville, FL: 1939.

Deagon, Kathleen, "St. Augustine, First Urban Enclave in the United States," *North American Archeologist*, Vol. 3, Farmingdale, NY: Baywood Press, 1982.

de Camp, L. Sprague, *The Great Monkey Trial*, Garden City, NY: Doubleday & Company, Inc., 1968.

DeGrove, John M., "The Quiet Revolution 10 Years Laber," *Journal of the American Planning Association*, November 1983, p. 25.

_____, *Land Growth and Politics*, Chicago, IL: Planners Press, American Planning Association, 1984.

_____, "The Proposed Florida State Plan: Issues, Options and Process," *Florida Environmental and Urban Issues* XII: 3, April 1985.

_____, ed., "Florida: A Second Try at Managing Massive Growth Pressures," *Planning and Growth management in the States*, Cambridge, MA: Lincoln Institute of Land Policy, 1992.

_____, "The Emergence of State Planning and Growth Management Systems: An Overview," in Peter A. Buchsbaum and Larry J. Smith, eds., *State & Regional Comprehensive Planning: Implementing New Methods for Growth Management*, Chicago, IL: American Bar Association, 1993.

_____, "Florida's Growth Management Legislation: 1969 to 2000," paper presented at the Richard E. Nelson Symposium on

Florida's Growth Management Legislation, Gainesville, FL, October 13, 2000.

_____, *Planning Policy and Politics, Smart Growth and The States,* Cambridge, MA: Lincoln Institute of Land Policy, 2005.

DeGrove, John M. and Deborah A. Miness, *The New Frontier for Land Policy: Planning & Growth Management in the States*, Cambridge, MA: Lincoln Institute of Land Policy, 1992.

DeGrove, John M. and Nancy E. Stroud, "New Developments and Future Trends in Local Government Comprehensive Planning," *Stetson Law Review* XVII: 3, 1988.

deHaven-Smith, Westi Jo and Robert Paterson, "The 1986 Glitch Bill—Missing Links in Growth Management," *Florida Environmental and Urban Issues* XVI: 1, October 1986.

Doherty, Peter, "The Unending Story of Property Rights Abuses," *Journal of the James Madison Institute*, Spring 2002.

Douglas, Paul, *Regional Planning Councils in Florida*, Center for Practical Politics, Rollins College, Winter Park, FL, c. 1959.

Downie, Robert C., II., "Property rights: Will exceptions become the rule?" *Florida Bar Journal* 64: 10, 1995.

Downs, Anthony, "Some Realities about Sprawl and Urban Decline," *Housing Policy Debate* 10: 4, Fannie Mae Foundation, 1999.

Eagan, Dennis, the *Florida Settler*, a 160 page immigrants' guide, 1873.

Easton David, *A Systems View of Political Life*, New York, NY: John Wiley & Sons, Inc., 1965.

Ehrenhalt, Alan, "The Czar of Gridlock," *Governing* 12: 8, May 1999.

Eisenhower, Dwight D., "Farewell Address to the American People," from *Public Papers of the Presidents of the United States*, Vol. 8, Washington, DC: USGPO, 1960-61.

_____, *Mandate for Change: The White House Years a Personal Account 1953-1956*, Garden City, NY: Doubleday 1963.

Elazar, Daniel J., "The States and the Nation", in Herbert Jacob and Kenneth N. Vines, eds., *Politics in the American States,* Boston, MA: Little, Brown and Company, 1965.

Emerson, Kirk and Charles R. Wise, "Statutory approaches to regulatory takings: State property rights legislation issues and implications for public administration," *Public Administration Review* 57: 5, 1997.

Fagan, Brian, *The Long Summer: How Climate Changed Civilization*, New York, NY: Basic Books, Perseus Books Group, 2004.

Farr, James A. and O. Greg Brock, "Florida's Landmark Programs for Conservation and Recreation Land Acquisition," *Sustain* 14, 2006.

Feiss, Carl, "The Foundations of Federal Planning Assistance: A Personal Account of the 701 Program," *Journal of the American Institute of Planners* 51: 2, 1985.

Fernald, Edward A. and Donald J. Patton, eds., *Water Resources Atlas of Florida*, Tallahassee, FL: Institute of Science and Public Affairs, Florida State University, 1984.

Fernald, Edward A. and Elizabeth D. Purdum, *Water Resources Atlas of Florida*, Tallahassee, FL: Institute of Science and Public Affairs, Florida State University, 1998.

Florida Department of Public Instruction, *The WPA Guide to Florida: The Federal Writers' Project Guide to 1930s Florida*, New York, NY: Pantheon Books, 1939.

Florida Environmental Land Management Study Committee, "Final Report to the Governor and Legislature by the Environmental Land Management Study Committee," December 1973.

_____, *Final Report of the Environmental Land Management Study Committee*, Tallahassee, FL, February 1984.

Florida Growth Management Study Commission, *A Livable Florida for Today and Tomorrow*, Tallahassee, FL, February 2001.

Florida Office of the Governor, "Final Report to Governor Bob Graham of the Resource Management Task Force," January 1980.

Ford, Ann Suter, "Health Planning" in *The Practice of State and Regional Planning*, So, Frank S., Irving Hand, and Bruce McDowell, eds., Chicago: American Planning Association, 1985.

Frank, James E., *The Cost of Alternative Development Patterns: A Review of the Literature*, Washington, DC: Urban Land Institute, 1989.

Fuller, Walter P., *This Was Florida's Boom*, St. Petersburg, FL: Times Publishing Co., 1954.

Gallagher, Mary Lou, "Wise Use or Wise Marketing?" *Planning* 62: 1, 1996.

Gannon, Michael, *Florida: A Short History,*, Gainesville, FL: University Press of Florida, 1993.

_____, ed., *The New History of Florida*, Gainesville, FL: University Press of Florida, 1996.

Gans, Herbert, *The Urban Villagers*, Glencoe, NY: Free Press, 1962.

Gelfand, Mark I. *A Nation of Cities: The Federal Government and Urban America*, New York, NY: Oxford University Press, 1975.

Gerckens, Laurence Conway, "Historical Development of American City Planning," in Frank S. So, et al., eds., *The Practice of Local Government Planning*, Washington, DC: The International City Management Association, 1979, second edition 1988.

Goodman, I. Gordon, ed. and Eric C. Freund, assoc. ed., *Principles and Practice of Urban Planning*, Washington, DC: The International City Manager's Association, 1968.

Grad, Frank P., "The States' Capacity to Respond to Urban Problems," in Alan K. Campbell, ed., *The States and the Urban Crisis,* The American Assembly of Columbia University, Englewood Cliffs, NJ: Prentice-Hall, Inc.,1970.

Graham, Otis L., Jr., *Toward a Planned Society: From Roosevelt to Nixon*, New York, NY: Oxford University Press, 1976.

Grosso, Richard, "Florida's Growth Management Act: How Far We Have Come and How Far We Have Yet to Go," *Nova Law Review* 20: 2, 1996.

Healy, Robert G. and John S. Rosenberg, *Land Use and the States*, Baltimore, MD: Johns Hopkins University Press, 1979.

Henderson, Clay, "A dynamic opportunity to resolve land use disputes," *Environmental and Urban Issues* 23: 1, 1995.

Holbrook, Stewart H., *The Story of American Railroads*, New York, NY: American Legacy Press, 1981.

Howard, Ebenezer, *A Peaceful Path to Real Reform*, originally published in 1898 and republished in 1902 as *Garden Cities of Tomorrow*, Cambridge, MA: M.I.T. Press.

Howard, S. Kenneth, "Planning and Budgeting: Marriage Whose Style?" in Thad L. Beyle and George T. Lathrop, eds., *Planning and Politics: Uneasy Partnership*, New York, NY: Odyssey Press of Bobbs-Merrill, Inc., 1970.

Innes, Judith, *Implementing State Growth Management in the U.S.: Strategies for Coordination* 7, Institute for Urban and Regional Development Working Paper 542, Berkley, CA: University of California, 1991.

Jackson, Kenneth, *Crabgrass Frontier: The Suburbanization of the United States*, New York, NY: Oxford University Press, 1985.

Jacobs, Harvey, ed., *Who Owns America? Conflict Over Property Rights*, Madison, WI: University of Wisconsin Press, 1998.

Jacobs, Jane, *The Death and Life of Great American Cities*, New York: Random House, 1961.

Jahoda, Gloria, *Florida: A History*, New York, NY: W.W. Norton & Company, 1984.

Jonas, Andrew E.G. and David Wilson, eds., *The Urban Growth Machine: Critical Perspectives Two Decades Later*, Albany, NY: State University of New York Press, 1999.

Juergensmeyer, Julian Conrad, "Impact Fees after Florida's Growth Management Act," in John M. DeGrove and Jullian Conrad Juergensmeyer, eds., *Perspectives on Florida's Growth Management Act of 1985*, Monograph #86-5, Cambridge, MA: Lincoln Institute of Land Policy, 1986.

Kallina, Edmund F., Jr., *Claude Kirk and the Politics of Confrontation*, Gainesville: University Press of Florida, 1993.

Kayden, Jerold S.,"National Land-Use Planning in America: Something Whose Time Has Never Come," *Washington University Journal of Law and Policy* 3, 2000.

Knaap, Gerrit and Arthur C. Nelson, *The Regulated Landscape*, Cambridge, MA: Lincoln Institute of Land Policy, 1992.

Kreuckeberg, Donald A., ed., *Introduction to Planning History in the United States*, New Brunswick, NJ: The Center for Urban Policy Research, Rutgers University, 1983.

Lawson, Edward W., "The Discovering of Florida and Its Discoverer Juan Ponce de Leon," *The Hispanic American History Review* 27: 3, 1947.

Lepawsky, Albert, *State Planning and Economic Development in the South*, National Planning Association Committee of the South Report No. 4, Kingsport, TN: Kingsport Press, 1949.

Lincoln, Robert, "Implementing the Consistency Doctrine," in *Modernizing State Planning Statutes*, numbers 462-463, Chicago, IL: American Planning Association, Planning Advisory Service, 1996.

Logan, John R. and Harvey Molotch, "The City as a Growth Machine," *Urban Fortunes*, Berkeley, CA: University of California Press, 1988.

Logan, John R., Rachel Bridges Whaley and Kyle Crowder, "The Character and Consequences of Growth Regimes: An Assessment of 20 Years of Research," *Urban Affairs Review* 32: 5, 1997.

Lorenz, Amalia and Kirsten Shaw, "What do builders, politicians, farmers, and environmentalists have in common? Amazingly, they're all talking about smart growth … ,"*Planning* 56, 1990.

Lynch, Kevin, *A Theory of Good Urban Form*, Cambridge, MA: MIT Press, 1981.

Magers, Vince, "Savings Accounts: an update on conservation easements," *Planning* 72: 8, August/September, 2006.

Mahon, John K., *The History of the Second Seminole War 1835-1842*, revised edition, Gainesville, FL: University Press of Florida, 1992.

Maloney, Frank E., Sheldon J. Plager and Fletcher N. Baldwin, Jr., assisted by William Haddad, *Water Law and Administration, The Florida Experience*, Gainesville, FL: University of Florida Press, 1968.

Mandelker, Daniel R., ed., *Environmental and Land Use Controls Legislation*, New York, NY: Bobbs-Merrill Company, 1976.

Marlow, Kimberly A., "The Expanded Role of Resource Planning and Management Committees," *Florida Environmental and Urban Issues* XII: 1, October 1984.

May, James W., *Environmental Land and Water Management Act of 1972: Planning and the State Legislative Policy-Making Process*, research paper (thesis) prepared in fulfilling requirements for the degree of Master of Science in Planning, Department of Urban and Regional Planning, Florida State University, Tallahassee, FL., March 29, 1974.

_____, "Growth management: A 1984 Update," *Florida Environmental and Urban Issues* XII: 2, 1985.

McDougall, Walter A., *Freedom Just Around the Corner, A New American History,1585-1828*, New York, NY: Harper Collins Publishers, 2004.

Meador, Toni L., "Managing Growth on Florida's Gold Coast: Boca Raton and the Growth Cap," *Florida Environmental and Urban Issues* VI: 3, 1979.

Meek, Stuart, "Status of State Planning Reform," executive summary in "Planning Communities for the 21st Century," Chicago: American Planning Association, 1999.

Meier, George H., "Capital Facilities Planning and Budgeting: Is a State CIP Possible?" *Florida Environmental & Urban Issues* XII: 3, 1985.

Millward, Robert E., "PPBS: Problems of Implementation," *Journal of the American Institute of Planners* 34: 2, 1968.

Moguloff, Melvin B., *Saving the Coast: California's Experiment in Intergovernmental Land Use Control*, Lexington, MA: Lexington Books, 1975.

Mohl, Raymond A., "Ike and the Interstates: Creeping toward Comprehensive Planning," *Journal of Planning History* 2: 3, 2003.

Mollenkopf, John H., *The Contested City*, Princeton, NJ: Princeton University Press, 1983.

Molotch, Harvey, "The City as a Growth Machine: Toward a Political Economy of Place," *The American Journal of Sociology* 82: 2, 1976.

Molotch, Harvey, with John Logan, *Urban Fortunes: The Political Economy of Place*, Berkeley, CA: University of California Press, 1987.

Mormino, Gary R., *Land of Sunshine State of Dreams: A Social History of Modern Florida*, Gainesville, FL: University Press of Florida, 2005.

Morris, Allen, *Florida Place Names*, Coral Gables, FL: University of Miami Press, 1974

Morris, Allen and Joan Perry Morris, *The Florida Handbook 2005-2006*, Tallahassee, FL: The Peninsular Publishing Company, 2005.

Nicholas, James C. "State and Regional Land Use Planning: The Evolving Role of the State," *St. John's Law Review* 73: 4, 1999.

O'Connell, Daniel W., "Growth Management in Florida: Will State and Local Governments Get Their Acts Together?" *Florida Environmental and Urban Issues* XI: 3, 1984.

_____, "New Directions in State Legislation: The Florida Growth Management Act and State Comprehensive Plan," *Institute on Planning, Zoning, and Eminent Domain*, Dallas, TX: Southwestern Legal Foundation, 1986.

Olausen, Stephan A., *Sebring, A City on a Circle*, Southern Heritage Press, St. Augustine, FL, 1993.

Olmstead, Frederick L., Jr., "The Town-Planning Movement in America," *Housing and Town Planning, The Annals* 51, 1914.

1000 Friends of Florida, *Florida 2060: A Population Distribution Scenario for the State of Florida*, University of Florida Geoplan Center, Paul Zwick and Margaret Carr, p r i n - ciple Investigators, Tallahassee, FL. 2006.

Patric, Rembert W., *Florida Under Five Flags*, Gainesville, FL: University Press of Florida, 1967.

Pelham, Thomas G., *State Land Use Planning and Regulation: The Model Code and Beyond*, Washington, DC: Heath Co., 1979.

_____, "Adequate Public Facilities Requirements: Reflections on Florida's Concurrency System for Managing Growth," *Florida State University Law Review* 19, 1992.

_____, "The Florida Experience: Creating a Comprehensive Planning Process," in Buchsbaum, Peter A. and Larry J. Smith, eds., *State & Regional Comprehensive Planning: Implementing New Methods for Growth Management*, Washington, DC: American Bar Association, 1993.

_____, "Restructuring Florida's Growth Management System: Alternative Approaches to Plan Implementation and Concurrency," a presentation to the Richard E. Nelson Symposium on Florida's Growth Management Legislation, Gainesville, Florida, October 13, 2000.

Peterson, Jon A., *The Birth of City Planning in the United States, 1840-1917,* Baltimore, MD: The Johns Hopkins University Press, 2003.

Pittman, Craig, "Florida's Land Czar," *Planning* 69: 2, February 2003.

Popper, Frank J., *The Politics of Land-Use Reform*, Madison, WI: University of Wisconsin Press, 1981.

Porter, Douglas R., "San Diego's Brand of Growth Management: A for Effort, C for Accomplishment," *Urban Land* 48: 5, 1989.

_____, "Issues in State and Regional Growth Management," in Porter, ed., *State and Regional Initiatives for Managing Development: Policy Issues and Practical Concerns*, Washington, DC: The Urban Land Institute, 1992.

Powell, David L., "Managing Florida's Growth: The Next Generation," *Florida State University Law Review* 21: 2, 1993.

_____, "Growth Management: Florida's Past as Prologue for the Future," *Florida State Law Review* 28: 2, Spring 2001.

Powell, David L., Robert M. Rhodes and Dan R. Stengle, "A Measured Step to Protect Private Property Rights," *Florida State University Law Review* 23: 2, 1995.

Ransome, Coleman B., Jr., *The Office of the Governor in the South*, Tuscaloosa, AL: Bureau of Public Administration, University of Alabama, 1951.

Reed, Nathaniel P. "A New Citizens Watchdog for Sound Growth Management," *Florida Environmental and Urban Issues* XIV: 3, 1987.

Reilly, William K., ed., *The Use of Land: A Citizens' Policy Guide to Urban Growth*, New York, NY: Thomas Y. Croswell Company, 1973.

Reps, John W., *The Making of Urban America*, Princeton, NJ: Princeton University Press, 1965.

Rerick, Rowland R., *Memoirs of Florida*, Atlanta, GA: The Southern Historical Association, 1902.

Revels, Tracy Jean, "World War II-Era Florida: Change in the 1940s," in Mark I. Greenberg, William Warren Rogers, and Canter Brown, Jr., eds., *Florida's Heritage of Diversity*, Tallahassee, FL: Sentry Press, 1997.

Rhodes, Robert M., "Growth Management in Florida 1985 and Beyond," *Florida Environmental and Urban Issues* XIII, January 1986.

_____, "Concurrency: Problems, Practicalities, and Prospects, *Journal of Land Use and Environmental Law* 6: 2, 1991.

_____, "Florida Growth Management: Rights, Not Rights, and the Future," John M. DeGrove Distinguished Speaker Series, Center for Urban and Environmental Solutions, Florida Atlantic University, October 3, 2001.

Roberts, Diane, *Dream State*, Gainesville, FL: University Press of Florida, 2006.

Robinson, Charles Mulford, in John Nolen, ed., *City Planning: A Series of Papers Presenting the Essential Elements of a City Plan*, New York, NY: D. Appleton and Company, 1917.

Rocha, Elizabeth M., "A Ladder of Empowerment," *Journal of Planning Education and Research* 17, 1997.

Roth, Cari L. and Laura J. Feagin, "2002 Reforms to Growth Management," *The Florida Bar Journal* LXXVI: 7, 2002.

RuBino, Richard G., "An Evaluation: Florida's Land Use Law," *State Government* XLVI: 3, 1973.

_____, "States in Motion: Activity in State Land-Use Planning and Management," *Land-Use Planning and Economic Development*, Third Advanced Seminar in Economic Development, Lyndon B. Johnson School of Public Affairs, University of Texas at Austin, 20, 1974.

_____, "State Policy Management: A Question of the Will to Act," *Public Administration Review* 35, special issue, 1975.

_____, "Growth management Initiatives in Florida: From River Ranch to Saddlebrook," *Florida Environmental and Urban Issues* XI: 2, January 1984.

_____, "Can the Legacy of a Lack of Follow-through in Florida State Planning be Changed?" *Journal of Land Use & Environmental Law* 2: 1, 1986.

RuBino, Richard G. and William R. Wagner, *The States' Role in Land Resource Management*, Lexington, KY: Council of State Governments, 1972.

RuBino, Richard G. and Frank LaRosa, "Alternative Approaches to Intergovernmental Planning and Growth Management Systems," in Lance deHaven-Smith and Dena Hurst, eds., *Charting Florida's Future*, Tallahassee: Florida Institute of Government, 1999.

Salkin, Patricia E., "Smart Growth at Century's End: The State of the States," *Urban Lawyer* 31: 3, 601-648, 1999.

Sanford, Terry, *Storm Over the States*, New York, NY: McGraw-Hill Book Co., 1967.

Schnidman, Frank, "Resolving Platted Lands Problems: The Florida Experience," *Land Development and Assembly* 1, 1987.

Scott, Mel, *American City Planning Since 1890*, Berkeley, CA: University of California Press, 1969, p. 243

Seibert, Steven M., "The Countywide Planning Council: A Growth Management Alternative?" *Florida Environmental & Urban Issues* XII: 2, 1985.

_____, "Make this a place where our kids would live," *Tallahassee Democrat*, September 9, 2007.

Skene, Neil, "Act II: Calling growth management 'a mess,' new DCA Secretary Tom Pelham wants a rewrite," *Florida Trend* 50: 5, August 2007.

So, Frank S., Irving Hand, and Bruce D. McDowell, *The Practice of State and Regional Planning*, Chicago: American Planning Association and the International City Management Association, 1985.

Somers, Herman Miles, *Presidential Agency: The Office of War Mobilization and Reconversion,* Cambridge, MA: Harvard University Press, 1950.

Spagna, Neno J., "Transfer of Development Rights: The Collier County Experience," *Florida Environmental and Urban Issues* VI: 3, 1979.

Spohr, David, "Florida's takings law: a bark worse than its bite," *Virginia Environmental Law Journal* 16: 2, 1997.

Squires, Jeffrey F., "Growth Management Redux: Vermont's Act 250 and Act 200," in Douglas R. Porter, *State and Regional*

Initiative for Managing Development, Washington, DC: Urban Land Institute, 1992.

Staley, Samuel R., "Ballot-Box Zoning, Transaction Costs, and Urban Growth," *American Planning Association Journal* 67: 1, Winter 2001.

Starnes, Earl M., "Florida's Minimum Criteria Rule," in John M. DeGrove and Julian Conrad Juergensmeyer, eds., *Perspectives on Florida's Growth Management Act*, Cambridge, MA: Lincoln Institute of Land Policy, Monograph 85-5, 1985.

_____, "The Relationship of Architecture and Planning," in Joseph Wilkes, ed., *The Encyclopedia of Architecture*, Vol. 1, New York, NY: John Wiley, 1988.

_____, "Substate Frameworks for Growth Management," in *Growth Management, The Planning Challenge of the 1990's,* Jay M. Stein, ed. Newberry Park, CA: Sage Publications, 1993.

Starrett, L. Benjamin, "Concentrated Urban Growth: A Review of the Final Report of the Governor's Task Force on Urban Growth Patterns," *Environmental and Urban Issues*, Fall 1989.

Steiner, George A., "Problems in Implementing Program Budgeting," in David Novick, ed., *Program Budgeting: Program Analysis and the Federal Budget*, Cambridge, MA: Harvard University Press, 1965.

Stiftel, Bruce, "The Interpersonal/Organizational/Political View of Planning: Do Planners Believe It? Do Florida Schools Teach It?" *Florida Environmental and Urban Issues* XII: 3, 1985.

Stollman, Israel, "Ramapo: An Editorial & the Ordinance as Amended," in Randall W. Scott ed., *Management & Control of Growth*, Volume II, Washington, DC: The Urban Land Institute, 1975.

Stroud, Herbert B. and William M. Spikowski, "Planning in the Wake of Florida Land Scams," *Journal of Planning Education and Research* 19, 1999.

Stroud, Nancy E., "The Second Generation Legislation for Developments of Regional Impact," *Florida Environmental and Urban Issues* VIII: 1, October 1980.

_____, "Regional Planning Council Reform in Florida," in Gill C. Lim, ed., *Regional Planning: Evolution, Crises, and Prospects*, Totowa, NJ: Allensheld, Omman Publishers, 1983.

Teaford, Jon C., *City and Suburb: The Political Fragmentation of Metropolitan America, 1850-1970*, Baltimore, MD: Johns Hopkins University Press, 1979.

Tebeau. Charlton W., *A History of Florida*, Coral Gables, FL: University of Miami Press, 1971.

Turner, Robyne S., "Intergovernmental Growth Management: A Partnership Framework for State-Local Relations," *Publius: The Journal of Federalism* 20, Summer 1990.

Udall, Stewart L., *The Quiet Crisis*, New York, NY: Avon Books, 1963.

Urban Land Institute, *Building Florida's Future: State Strategies for Regional Cooperation*, a report from the ULI Florida Committee for Regional Cooperation, Washington, DC, 2005.

Van Doren, Mark, ed., *Travels of William Bartram*, New York, NY: Dover Publications, Inc., 1955.

von Hoffman, Alexander, "A Study in Contradictions: The Origins and Legacy of the Housing Act of 1949," *Housing Policy Debate* 11: 2, Fannie Mae Foundation, 2000.

Weingroff, Richard F., "Creating the Interstate System," *Public Roads* 60: 1, 1966.

Wilson, David E., *The National Planning Idea in U.S. Public Policy: Five Alternative Approaches* and *National Planning in the United States: An Annotated Bibliography*, Boulder, CO: Westview Press, 1980.

Wilson, William H., "Moles and Skylarks," in Donald A. Krueckeberg, ed., *Introduction to Planning History in the United States*, New Brunswick, NJ: The Center for Urban Policy Research, Rutgers University, 1983.

Wise, Harold F., *History of State Planning: An Interpretive Commentary*, State Planning Series 1, Washington, DC: Council of State Planning Agencies, an affiliate of the National Governors' Association, 1977.

Wise, Harold F. and Bertram Wakeley, "The Practice of State Planning and Policy Development," *State Government* 57: 3, 1984.

Wolfe, Peter, *Land in America: Its Value, Use and Control*, New York, NY: Pantheon Books, 1981.

Wulbern, Allan E., "Improvements Under Florida's Butler Act: Can We Have a Definition Please?" *Journal of Land Use & Environmental Law* 14: 2, 1999.

York, Marie, "What About the Public Interest?" *Planning* 69: 2, February 2003.

Ziewitz, Kathryn and June Wiaz, *Green Empire: The St. Joe Company and the Remaking of Florida's Panhandle*, Gainesville, FL: University Press of Florida, 2004.

Zwick, Charles J., Chair, State Comprehensive Plan Committee, in *Keys to Florida's Future: Winning in a Competitive World—The Final Report of the State Comprehensive Plan Committee to the State of Florida*, Tallahassee, FL. February 1987.

INDEX

Andrew (hurricane) 357
annexation 35, 43, 106, 332,
   455
anti-snob zoning law 146
Apalachee Bay 39
Apalachicola (city) 39, 233
Apalachicola Bay 42, 359
Apalachicola (river) 359
Apgar, Robert C. 272
Appalachian Regional Commis-
   sion 137
Approach to this Book 13
Apthorp, James 237
Areas of Critical State Concern
   (ACSC) 19, 200, 213, 214,
   231, 232, 247, 252, 269,
   272, 324, 361, 440
Areawide DRI program 280
Arizona 387, 390
Arline, Terrell K. 328
Army Air Force 117
Article III, section 19(h) 369
Arvida Corporation 8, 135
Asheville, North Carolina 462
Askew, Reubin O'Donovan vii,
   165, 203-205, 207, 208,
   210, 217, 218, 234, 237,
   239, 243, 250, 254, 259,
   266, 271, 390, 439
Association of Bay Area Govern-
   ments (ABAG) 153
Atlanta 105, 108, 303, 359,
   388
Atlantic Beach 154
Atlantic Missile Range 118
Atlantic Ocean 37, 45, 247,
   393
Atlantic Test Center 161
Auburndale 117
Audubon of Florida 402
Audubon Society 183
Ave Maria 353, 413, 414
Avon Park 7

B

Babcock 65
Babcock Ranch 353
Babcock, Richard F. 65
Baggs, Bill 203
Bahamas 1
Bair, Abernathy, and Associates
   122
Bair, Frederick H. 101, 109,
   121-23, 166
Baker 420
Baker, Rick 404
Baker v. Carr 17, 157, 168,
   180, 438
Baldwin 154
Baldwin, Fletcher N. 205
Balkus, Kosmos 240
Ball, Edward 8
Ballot Measure 49 389
ballot-box zoning 442
Banning, Walker vii
Barnett, Cynthia 289, 358, 394,
   419, 457
Barnstable County 305
Bartley, Ernest vii, 74, 121, 166,
   237, 245
Bartram, John 33
(Bartram), William 33
Battle Creek 265
Bay State assembly 305
Bayer, William W. 74
Belle Glade 124
Bennett, Parson & Frost 73
Berle, Milton 68
Bert J. Harris, Jr., Private Prop-
   erty Rights Protection Act
   21, 367
Bettman, Alfred 78, 79
Beverly Hills 186
Big Bend 185

C

Cabot (John) 30
Cadiz, Spain 2, 27
Caldwell, Millard Fillmore 159
California 67, 68, 153, 199,
    261, 304, 390, 391, 458
California Coastal Alliance 199
California Coastal Commission
    Act 199
Californicate 199
Callies, David 197
Calos Indians 1
Camp Blanding 117
Camp Gordon Johnston 117
Campbell, Alan K. 180
Campbell, Jack 144
Cape Canaveral 118
Cape Cod 200; Commission
    305, 388; Act 305
Cape Coral 439
Cape Fear 30
Cape Florida Light House 203
Cape Kennedy 161
Capital Facilities Planning and
    Budgeting Act 277
capital improvements program
    287, 315, 316
Capitol Region Council of
    Governments 304
Caribbean 2
CARL (Conservation and
    Recreational Lands program)
    317
Carlton, Doyle E. 75
Carolinas 30
Carr, Marjorie H. 183, 420
Carrabelle 117, 418
Carson, Rachel 140, 183
Carter, Luther J. 118
Cartoon Bank 28
Case-Shiller Home Price Index
    395

Cash, W. T. 53
Castille, Colleen 397
Castro 135
Catskill (watershed) 305
Cedar Key v, vi, 7, 39, 42, 43,
    91, 252
Celebration 351, 352
Celestial Railroad 50
Center for Practical Politics 154
Center for Quality Growth and
    Regional Development 420
Center for Urban & Environmen-
    tal Solutions 352
Century Commission for a
    Sustainable Florida 404,
    408, 418
Chapin, Tim 400, 404
Charles II 30
Charleston, South Carolina 30,
    62
Charley (hurricane) 392
Charlotte County 135, 179, 186,
    333
Charlotte Harbor 1
Chattahoochee (river) 359
Chesapeake Bay Commission
    263, 356
Chicago 14, 73, 141; Area
    Transportation Study 189;
    World's Fair 64
chief state planning officer 209
Childers, W.D. 245
Chiles, Lawton M. 323, 359,
    360, 362, 363, 365, 368, 370
Ch'lian-shu, Chung-shan 229
Christensen, Terry 202
Christian Indian survivors 31
Christianization 29, 30
Churchill, Winston 385
citizen activism 461
citizen participation 5, 10-12,
    20, 236, 254, 335, 336, 449

South Carolina 77, 134, 146
South Florida Everglades Area
    Planning Council 155
South Florida Jetport 203
South Florida Regional Planning
    Act 209
South Florida RPC 251
South Florida Water Management
    District (WMD) 186, 219,
    248, 322
South Miami 121
Southeast Banking Corporation
    307
Southeastern Regional Planning
    Commission 78
*Southern Burlington County
    NAACP v. Township of
    Mount Laurel* 264
Southern coastal management
    program 200
Southern Legal Council 337
Southwest Florida Regional
    Planning Council 251
Southwest Florida WMD
    219, 248
Soviet cities 196
Soviet Union 195
Spain 29, 32-36, 38
Spaniards vi
Spanish 9, 27, 29-32, 34, 35,
    56, 436; Caribbean 29;
    colonial tradition 29;
    colonists 28, 29; Crown
    2, 27, 35: explorer 56;
    Florida 29; Franciscan
    priests 30; King 35; land
    policy 34; settlement 2, 31
Special Treatment Overlay
    District 182
Spicer, Don 247
Spring Hill 186
St. Andrew Bay 42

St. Augustine 1, 5, 28-30, 33,
    37, 38, 50, 71, 121
St. Joe Company 8, 390, 417,
    419
St. Johns County 35, 42; Bluff
    27; River 27, 32, 33, 38,
    45, 53, 55, 317; Water
    Management District
    (WMD) 219, 248
St. Johns River basin 247
St. Louis 105
St. Lucie County 135, 251,
    412, 414; River 54
St. Marks 36, 37, 39, 42
St. Marks River 37; basin 248
St. Mary's 33; River 30, 35
St. Petersburg 64, 70, 71, 74,
    91, 142, 155, 280, 404,
    436; Beach 124; *Weekly
    Times* 71, 422
St. Petersburg-Clearwater 260
Standard & Poors 395
Standard City Planning Enabling
    Act 65, 210
Starke 117
Starnes, Dorothy Jean vi
Starnes, Earl M. i, ii, 117, 215,
    282, 303
Starrett, L. Benjamin 365
State and Regional Planning Act
    276, 314, 319
State Association of County
    Commissioners 284
State Capital Facilities Planning
    and Budgeting Process 275
State civil defense and prepared-
    ness plan 194
State Comprehensive Plan 169,
    241, 275, 282, 307, 310,
    312, 313, 315, 316 322,
    328, 333, 338, 369